VARIORUM COLLECTED STUDIES SERIES

The Practice of British Geology, 1750–1850

The time-honoured method of 'Boring the earth with the Lever' in search of minerals (as described in article I, pp. 3–8) from Blackie and Son's *Popular Encyclopaedia*, 1862, Article Mining, volume 7, Supplement, p. 710, plate CXLV, figure 1 (with grateful thanks to Anthony Bankes of Bankes Books, Bath).

Hugh Torrens

The Practice of British Geology, 1750–1850

Ashgate

VARIORUM

Published in the Variorum Collected Studies Series by

Ashgate Publishing Limited
Gower House, Croft Road,
Aldershot, Hampshire GU11 3HR
Great Britain

Ashgate Publishing Company
131 Main Street,
Burlington, Vermont 05401– 5600
USA

Ashgate website: http://www.ashgate.com

ISBN 0–86078–876–8

British Library Cataloguing-in-Publication Data
Torrens, H.S. (Hugh Simon), 1940–
    The Practice of British Geology, 1750–1850.
    (Variorum Collected Studies Series: CS736).
    1.Geology – History – 18th Century. 2. Geology – History – 19th Century.
    I. Title.
    551'.09033

US Library of Congress Cataloging-in-Publication Data
The Library of Congress Control Number was preassigned as: 2001046046.

The paper used in this publication meets the minimum requirements of the
    American National Standard for Information Sciences – Permanence of
    Paper for Printed Library Materials, ANSI Z39.48–1984. ∞ ™

Printed by St Edmundsbury Press, Bury St Edmunds, Suffolk

VARIORUM COLLECTED STUDIES SERIES CS736

CONTENTS

This volume contains xiv + 356 pages

PUBLISHER'S NOTE

The articles in this volume, as in all others in the Collected Studies Series, have not been given a new, continuous pagination. In order to avoid confusion, and to facilitate their use where these same studies have been referred to elsewhere, the original pagination has been maintained wherever possible.

Each article has been given a Roman numeral in order of appearance, as listed in the Contents. This number is repeated on each page and quoted in the index entries.

INTRODUCTION

Introductions to this series, at least those few to concern the history of geology, seem to require some reminiscence. I have been nostalgic at least twice recently (Torrens 2000; 2001a). Anyone who reads these articles will discover that I lack formal academic qualifications in history, the subject of this collection. This may cause some eyebrow-raising. But I have found the skills needed to investigate the histories of those who studied the earth little different from those needed to investigate rocks. The approach needed in investigating quarries is rather similar to what has to been done in archives, libraries and museums. The same problems of raw materials (whether sediment or records of human activity) occur. Both have suffered non-deposition and/or erosion. Gaps affect both rock and record.

In my geological thesis (1966) I had had to discover that many faunas, like that of the Morrisi Zone (Middle Bathonian, Jurassic), could often be distinguished only when fossils were collected from the rocks concerned to the nearest inch. Collecting to less discriminating levels meant, in such condensed and episodic rocks, that many faunas (and their separate records of the passage of time) would coalesce with others above and below. Because of this, I became a myopic stratigrapher. In my geological work I discovered that others before me had been equally interested in detail. William Smith (1769–1839) revealed his skills at detailed stratigraphy from 1800 onwards, by his recognition of the existence, and significance, of the thin Kellaways Stone (see IV 108). At the same time Smith noted that 'the Cornbrash, though but a thin rock, has not its organised fossils equally diffused, or promiscuously distributed. The upper beds of stone which compose the rock, contain fossils materially different from those in the under' (Smith 1819, 25–26). This fact was only rediscovered more than a century later (Douglas & Arkell 1932, 115). Since it was **practitioners** of geology, like Smith, who had so often made these detailed investigations of strata, I became interested in learning more of them.

As I turned to history, I duly became a mole-like historian, more interested in detail and the hidden, eroded aspects of the history of geology, than attempting to be any eagle-eyed surveyor of the past, like David Oldroyd who demonstrated these skills in his fine book of 1996 (Oldroyd 1996).

But his reviewers rightly complained that he had not sufficiently considered the practices of geology (*Metascience*, NS 11, 7–21, 1997). My first historical papers, in 1974, were concerned with the many abortive searches long ago made to find coal near Sherborne, in Dorset (see I 11–2). I had been amazed to discover, both that these attempts had been made at all (since it had long been known there was no conceivable coal to be found here), and that the main authority for these trials was still unidentified.

As a result, I was soon made to wonder how people could be sure that, during the British industrial revolution, 'the economic pressure of industry seems of itself not to have created a science of geology' (Porter 1973, 339). I saw the existing historiography of geology as too partial, especially, as Rupke has noted, because 'the economic aspect of geology was regarded as of little interest by the English school [of geology &] was thought not to merit academic rank' (Rupke 1983, 18 & 200). Jack Morrell seemed equally right to point out, of historical studies of English science in Victorian times, that 'the emphasis on gentlemanliness shows no sign of waning' (Morrell 1990, 988). I still wonder how Martin Rudwick can claim (in the same volume as that in which article IV was published) that 'around 1800 ... the practical use of fossils in stratigraphical correlation was less significant than their theoretical use as *archives of nature*' (Rudwick 1998, 119).

I believe we still know too little of the practice of geology, even in Britain, to be able accurately to arbitrate the relative contributions made by practitioners and theorists. The history of the practice of geology in the past has been too much neglected, like the vital activity shown in my Frontispiece; boring to investigate sub-surface strata in search of economically significant stratified materials like coal. Existing histories of geology have overwhelmingly considered past academic participants in geology and paid insufficient attention to those who merely practised it. A similar bias was noted by an American reviewer of the British National Motorcycle Museum in Birmingham in 1987. He noted this 'collection was heavily weighted in favor of large glamorous machines while small utilitarian cycles are seriously under represented... one looks in vain for any representative of the plethora of small motor cycles that for decades provided transportation for the masses' (Volti 1987, 97).

The thirteen papers collected here attempt to ponder such matters and to question, at least, some of the above claims. They investigate the careers of some once important figures in English, Welsh, Scottish, and Irish practical geology between 1750 and 1850. Some of them would have regarded themselves as more mining engineers or 'coal viewers', or 'mineral surveyors' (as mineral prospectors were first called – from 1808, see Torrens 2001b) or even as 'mere' inventors. Such men also travelled widely. Those included here went to Italy and both South (Peru) and North (Virginia and

Canada) America, making their historical trails more difficult to follow.

I must record the excitement behind some historical discoveries, such as finding that the first mining school in Britain was built by an unknown Irish mining engineer in the Breidden hills of Shropshire and/or Montgomeryshire (I 9; VIII 78), or the discovery in California of the remarkable, detailed, 1812 map showing one of the Royal Society's president Joseph Banks' estates, in Derbyshire (V 66, see also the cover of *Geology Today*, 17 (2), 2001). But such delights were offset by frustration with over-assessed academic life in Britain after the 1980s. Academic work, whether as geological historian or historical geologist (one was barred from being both!), was too easily thwarted by the senseless specialisation demanded by Research Assessment Exercises (see François Ellenberger quoted in Torrens 2000, 11–12).

Acknowledgements

I owe real thanks to my co-authors Bill Brice and Trevor Ford for allowing their papers to be reproduced. I am grateful to my friends John Fuller, Graham Hollister-Short, John Martin and the late John Thackray for their long support. I thank the Leverhulme Trust, the Royal Society and the 27 Foundation for funds and Tony Doré of Statoil, Mike Oates of British Gas, Peter Hill formerly of BP Exploration and others from Enterprise Oil for similar support and encouragement. As will be clear from the papers themselves, my debts to the many archivists, librarians and museum curators who have helped me are too great for individual acknowledgment.

H.S. TORRENS

Crewe, September 2001

References

Douglas J.A. & Arkell W.J., 1932, 'The Stratigraphical Distribution of the Cornbrash', *Quarterly Journal of the Geological Society of London*, 88, 112–170.

Morrell J.B., 1990, 'Professionalisation', pp. 980–989, in R.C. Olby et al. (eds.), *Companion to the History of Modern Science*, London: Routledge.

Oldroyd D., 1996, *Thinking about the Earth: A History of Ideas in Geology*, London: Athlone Press.

Porter R.S., 1973, 'The Industrial Revolution and the Rise of the Science of Geology', pp. 320–343 in M. Teich & R. Young (eds.), *Changing Perspectives in the History of Science*. London: Heinemann.

Rudwick M.J.S., 1998, 'Smith, Cuvier et Brongniart, et la reconstitution de la gohistoire', pp. 119–128, in G. Gohau (ed.), *De la Gologie son histoire*, Paris: CTHS.

Rupke N., 1983, *The Great Chain of History: William Buckland and the English School of Geology 1814–1849*. Oxford: Clarendon Press.

Smith W., 1819, *Strata Identified by Organised Fossils*, part 4, London: Arding.

Torrens H.S., 2000, 'Entering Geology's Third Century – What Have We Learnt?', *Open University Geological Society Journal*, 21 (2), 1–13.

Torrens H.S., 2001a, 'Interview with Richard Howarth', *INHIGEO Newsletter*, no. 33, 34–37.

Torrens H.S., 2001b 'The William Smith Lecture 2000: "Timeless Order: William Smith and the search for raw materials 1800–1820"' in Lewis, C.L.E. & Knell S.J. (eds.), *The Age of the Earth from 4004 BC to AD 2002*. Geological Society of London Special Publications, 190, 61–83 (in press).

Volti R., 1987, 'The National Motorcycle Museum, Birmingham, England', *Technology and Culture*, 28, 96–98.

ACKNOWLEDGEMENTS

Grateful acknowledgement is made to the following persons, editors, publishers and institutions for their kind permission to reproduce or reprint the articles included in this volume: the Open University Geological Society, Chandler's Ford (I); Ezio Vaccari on behalf of the Istituto Veneto di Scienze, Lettere & Arti, Venice (II); The British Society for the History of Science Ltd., Faringdon (III, IX); CTHS Press, Paris (IV); the Royal Botanic Gardens Kew (V); the Peak District Mines Historical Society Ltd., Matlock Bath (VI); The Sussex Archaeological Society, Lewes (VII); Institute of Irish Studies, Belfast (VIII); the Geological Society Publishing House, Bath (X); the Universidade Estadual, Campinas, Brazil (XI); *Geoscience Canada*, St John's (XII); Duke University Press, Durham, NC (XIII).

I

Some Thoughts on the Complex and Forgotten History of Mineral Exploration

INTRODUCTION

Marcia Greenwood, chancellor of the University of California, Santa Cruz, wrote in an editorial this year:

> The knowledge created by... scientists and those they have trained has been the basis for the creation of wealth, in very real ways, for this country [America] and the world. Some economists have estimated that 50% of the growth in the U.S. economy over the past few decades is a direct derivative of the federal investment in research.... Numerous documents and testimony recount the ways in which applications of the knowledge generated have led to products or processes that have transformed our world and created opportunities for the next generation. In short, many would argue that scientists, more than members of any other profession are creating the future.[1]

So my question is: Why is this such a tough time for so many scientists in Britain? What are we doing wrong? I think the above thoughts, about the application of knowledge and how science is transforming the world are very relevant to my subject – the history of mineral prospecting. To find oil in the North Sea, for example, involved an enormous amount of science and technology and was/is an enormous achievement. You cannot just wander out there with a bucket and collect North Sea Oil: somebody has to tell you where to find it, and then others have to extract it. It involves both science and technology and all these skills have to be taught...

HISTORY OF MINERAL PROSPECTING

The question of how minerals were found in the first place, prior to their being uncovered and mined, has been strangely neglected. In the National Coal Board's five volume History, the volume on the Industrial Revolution

---

[1]   'Desperately seeking Friends', *Science*, 272, p. 933 (17 May 1996).

Reproduced by kind permission from the Open University Geological Society.

1700–1830 is 491 pages long, all about where coal was mined and by whom, but only four are about how people went looking for it in the first place.[2] If you look at prospecting history on a world scale you find that prospecting was one skill much needed in newly colonised countries; when they arrived in Australia one of the first things they needed was coal.[3] So prospecting is an important activity. It seems strange that we have ignored it so much.[4]

By 1850, in Britain at least, geologists were so certain of what had been achieved by then that A.C. Ramsay (1814–1891), professor of geology at University College, London could then write with total confidence:

> 6 July 1849: As I rode home I found them busy on this side of Caernarvon sinking for coal. I hallooed to a man to hold my horse a moment while I ran into the field and talked with the sinkers, etc. They have gone down 70 yards or so,... [and] asked my opinion. I told them to let me know when they came to the coal, and I would come down and eat it.[5]

That may sound arrogant, but, as you will know by the end of this talk, the fact is that geologists and other scientists in Britain were by then able to tell where and how coal and other minerals were to be prospected for, although such knowledge was *not* always of interest to the mining community. What I want to do is to try and also discuss the importance and history of mining education to bring us back to the quotation with which I started.

The first point to note is the distinction between those minerals that occur in stratified form and those minerals that occur in veins. That the latter are much more difficult to prospect for, was already clear by the beginning of the eighteenth century. John Farey (1766–1826) wrote in 1811:

> Mineral treasures... arise from two very distinct causes: in the case of stratified or Stratigenous Minerals, or those which compose seams, beds, layers, measures or strata, as Coal, Iron-stone, Limestone.... [These can be traced] by its dip or inclination compared with the surface.... the others are, the Venigenous Minerals, which instead of forming Strata...

2   M.W. Flinn, *The History of the British Coal Industry*, volume 2 1700–1830, Oxford (1984).
3   T.G. Vallance, 'Sydney Earth and after: Mineralogy of colonial Australia 1788–1900', *Proceedings of the Linnean Society of New South Wales*, 108 (3), pp. 149–181 (1986).
4   See H.S. Torrens, 'The history of coal prospecting in Britain 1650–1900', in *Energie in der Geschichte*, papers presented to the 11th ICOHTEC (International History of Technology) Symposium, Dusseldorf, Germany, pp. 88–95 (1984).
5   A. Geikie, *Memoir of Sir Andrew Crombie Ramsay*, London, p. 148 (1895).

are applied as coats or linings to fissures and cracks or cavities, often nearly vertical, in certain rocky strata....[6]

I will concentrate here on 'the money-makers' in mineral prospecting history, coal and other stratiform minerals. This is for reasons I am sure you will understand. These were the materials of the Industrial Revolution. Some countries' mining traditions were very much longer than others. The German tradition is really supreme. A book first published in about 1500 *Das Bergbüchlein* gives a guide to German Mining Knowledge at that date.[7] We must remember, too, that much traditional British mining knowledge had come from Germany when Saxon miners came to Derbyshire and Scotland. But in Saxony, whence most of this German tradition came, they were hunting vein and ore minerals. These were very much harder to prospect for in an age before geochemistry.

In concentrating on coal and other stratified minerals we should realise that the fact that coal was a stratified mineral was already well known to a important mining Scotsman, George Sinclar, who died in 1696. He first taught philosophy at Glasgow University from 1654 then, (to prove nothing changes in British Universities) he was forced to resign and set up as an engineer and surveyor from 1666 to 1689. In 1691 he was rehired at Glasgow as Professor of Mathematics. In 1672 he produced his book *The Hydrostaticks or,... Fluid Bodies* while employed as a mineral engineer and surveyor. He had worked mainly in the Lothian coalfield and his Observation 24 is titled *A Short History of Coal*. In this he gives a good description of what was then known on coal and stratification. He devoted several pages to the means of prospecting for minerals and said there were three main ways to do this. The first, and the best, he called 'ranging over the metals' (metals in old Scots meant hard strata) and this is still basic mineral surveying, walking the country, making maps, and seeing what is sticking out of the ground. The other two methods were by sinking shafts and boring by 'instrument'.[8]

Such sunk shafts were wide enough for two people to stand in (see

6   J. Farey, *General View of the Agriculture and Minerals of Derbyshire*, volume 1, London, pp. 313–314 (1811).
7   W. Pieper, 'Ulrich Rülein von Calw und sein Bergbüchlein', *Freiberger Forschungshefte*, D 7, Berlin (1955).
8   G. S[inclar], *The Hydrostaticks or,... Fluid Bodies*, Edinburgh, pp. 258–302 (1672). On Sinclar see H. Briggs, 'Sinclar's Treatise of Coal-Mining 1672' *Transactions of the Institution of Mining Engineers*, 69, pp. 132–142, 177–178 (1925).

Fig. 1).[9] Boarding on the sides stopped the sides falling in. In this figure, after sinking about ten feet deep, the method used is Sinclar's third method of 'boring by instrument' using the range of bits and pieces on the right. The T-bar at the top (A) connects with boring rods, with male and female ends (D), and finally to a device called a nogger or chisel (E) to do the final cutting of 'normal' rocks. Another device (G) was used for the harder rocks. All these worked by being repeatedly, and percussively, dropped into such troublesome strata. A final device, the wimble, whimble or wumble (C), was then used for gathering the final paste produced by these operations. F & E were tools used to stop the whole rod string dropping down the borehole.

The first point to make is that the *quality* of data gathered by this device was low. The hole was only an inch or two in diameter. By percussing the rocks passed through, a paste (full of water) was created which was then collected with the wimble. In Sinclar's 1672 book he already recorded the fundamental problem of this device:

> *boaring...* with several rods of iron... is worse than [sinking]. It leaves the
> *Master* at an uncertainty (notwithstanding the *Coal* had been found) of
> its *goodness*, as to its *nature*, and as to its *thickness*. As to its *goodness*,
> because all that is found of the *Coal*, by this *boaring instrument*, is some
> small *dross*, which remains after the washing of the thing that's brought
> up in the *wumble*, by which none can judge of its *goodness* or *badness*.[10]

In other words you had so percussed the rocks penetrated, made them into such a paste, that this only brought up limited data to test. This was one of the major limitations on such early prospecting in Britain: it did not give good or reliable information.

The first English, as opposed to Scottish, Coal mining guide seems to have been published in 1708. It was entitled *The Compleat Collier: or, the whole Art of Sinking, Getting and Working Coal-Mines.*[11] The author of this, one J.C., is unknown, but he came from Newcastle-on-Tyne and his book covers prospecting for stratified minerals and 'discovering, by the SURFACE of the Earth, where COAL lies: and for preventing BORING where Coal is Not.' He was more enthusiastic about the technology used in boring:

---

⁹   Anon, 'On boring the Earth, for water or minerals', *Register of the Arts and Sciences* (3 April 1824).

¹⁰   Sinclar, *Hydrostaticks*, p. 295.

¹¹   Published by G. Conyers, London, 1708 and reprinted many times since.

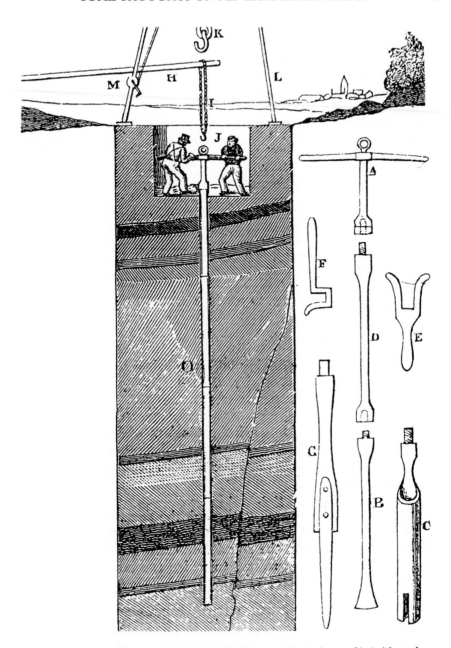

Fig. 1: 'Sinking a coal shaft and boring down through the base of it (with tools used and activities numbered A to O) from Anon. 1824'

> We have two labourers at a time, at the handle of the bore Rod, and
> they chop or pounce with their Hands up and down to cut the Stone or
> Mineral, going round, which of course grinds either of them small... and
> taking off the cutting Chisel, puts or screws on the Whimble or Scoop
> which then takes up the cut Stuff.

This technology had come from the Continent and was first used in
England by 1574 in Nottinghamshire[12] and it then spread rapidly to the
Northeast and, as we have seen, to Scotland. It was an extraordinarily
conservative technology and was in use for an enormous length of time. It
was still being used 378 years later! It was still unreliable, and could still
produce bad information. It is amazing to think that it was still being used
in Britain in 1952.[13] A writer in 1987 then claimed that this method was
highly 'cost-effective'. But even when only confirming the existence of
previously expected coal seams, history proves how bad and unreliable the
method could be even in known coal mining areas when people already
knew which seams they were about to bore into. For instance between 1804
and 1806 at Whitehaven, borers twice passed through 3 and 6 feet thick coal
seams completely unnoticed in what they drew up as they bored through it.
They were expecting coal to turn up in the boring dross, but the paste failed
to reveal it.[14] Fire damp held in the coal seams had blown water up the bore
hole to render what came up in the wumble useless.

However, despite such problems with retrieval, as John Farey wrote in
1811:

> In all mineral districts, there are Men who undertake boreing, and who,
> by constant practice, can tell with great certainty, by the fall of the noger
> [chisel] in jumping and turning round [as they pass through the rocks]...,
> all the changes and different known thin Measures.[15]

In other words the borers, skilled craftsmen, could tell by friction and
resistance where they were in a known sequence of coal and other seams. In
a *known* series of Coal Measures it was often quite reliable because you knew

¹² R.S. Smith, *Early Coal-Mining around Nottingham 1500–1650*, Nottingham University,
Dept. of Adult Education, p. 57 (1989).
¹³ F.G. Dimes, 'Correspondence', *Geology Today*, 2 (5), p. 138 (September October 1986)
& R.R. Lemon, 'Drilling by hand', *Geology Today*, 3 (4), p. 121 (July–August 1987).
¹⁴ H.S. Torrens, 'John Bateman Longmire (1785–1858): an English 'practical mineralogist' in Russia between 1817 and 1822', in progress.
¹⁵ Farey, *General View*, p. 321.

what you were looking for and you could prospect against a known sequence. The known sequence of Coal Seams in the South Wales Coalfield was already recorded by Edward Martin in 1806.[16]

But when hunting in areas in which coal was unknown, it was a hopelessly inefficient method as John Farey already pointed out in 1807, when discussing one of the most important of the attempts made to find coal *outside* the known coalfields of England. This was at Bexhill, Sussex between 1804 to 1809 and cost over £30,000. It was inspired by thoughts of reviving the once great charcoal-based iron industry of the Weald. The great expense led John Herschel (1792–1871) to cite this trial as a first example of the great value of a knowledge of 'the laws of nature to mankind' in 1831.[17] John Farey had visited the trial on 12 September 1806 and soon wrote an impassioned and highly informed rebuke to those involved.[18] He conjectured that perhaps their bore hole had passed through a piece of bituminous wood (the lignite common in Wealden deposits), if so 'something like the appearance of penetrating a coal-vein might be had in [such] borings'. He urged that 'the improved boring apparatus of Mr Ryan would have detected, and saved, perhaps, a most unparalleled waste of money in the measures [still] pursuing [at Bexhill]'.[19] The full story will be told in a paper for next year's International History of Science Congress at Liege in Belgium.[20]

There were two other vital problems with this old method of boring: if you did not like the idea of finding coal somewhere, and wanted to stop it (being a NIMBY – not-in-my-back-yard – sort of person) all you had to do was lob one of the boring rods or any iron bar down the bore hole and the whole thing simply jammed solid: one could not get it out, and one could not do much about retrieving it, so one had to abort the whole operation. That was negative. If you wanted to be positive and give those boring a hint they could not ignore, you simply crept out to the site at night and dropped a lump of real coal down the hole! The next morning the borers would turn up and, bingo, 'real coal' would soon be found. The whole operation

16   E. Martin, 'Description of the Mineral Bason...', *Philosophical Transactions of the Royal Society*, part 2, pp. 342–347 (1806).

17   J. Herschel, *Discourse on the Study of Natural Philosophy*, London, pp. 44–45 (1831).

18   J. Farey, 'On the finding of Coal in the South-Eastern Counties of England', *Agricultural Magazine*, [3] 2, pp. 22–31 (1808).

19   J. Farey, 'Article Colliery', in A. Rees (editor), *The Cyclopaedia*, volume 8, London (1807).

20   H.S.Torrens, 'Coal hunting at Bexhill 1805–1811: How the new science of stratigraphy was ignored', *Sussex Archaeological Collections*, 136, pp. 177–191 (1998).

became a wonderful opening for pranksters and, more important, for people who wanted to mislead.

NEW TECHNOLOGY

A new technological advance came via the completely forgotten Irishman, named above, James Ryan. I have had a very interesting last year or two trying to decide who to include as geologists in the new *Dictionary of National Biography*, being revised as part of some Millennial madness by the Government, the British Academy and Oxford University Press. One or two of the people I have been talking about will appear in this, because they were important but have been completely forgotten, because such technical people did not publish like academic figures in universities, and so history has forgotten them. One is this Irishman. He was born about 1770 and may have come from Donegal. He became 'mineral surveyor' to the Grand Canal Company of Ireland in 1800. They were building a canal west of Dublin, and on 28 February 1805 – an important date – Ryan patented his new invention, a cylindrical cutting device using a 'surgical trepanning' system, which will be familiar to all amateur brain surgeons reading this.

It consisted, as before, of a T-bar to which any number of boring rods could be strung together. It could, as before, go down some distance, but it now carried a hollow cylinder with four cutting edges on a crown saw of hardened steel, which was rotated mechanically to cut through the strata. It left a core of rock in the centre of the cylinder. One had now only to recover the cores (and they could be as long as the cylinder you recovered them in would allow, the diameter of which could be varied). Recovering the cores from the borehole was achieved by a pair of large inverse action Heath Robinson-type tongs. Ryan's invention now allowed cores to be recovered in sequence and oriented against a compass. It was really a quite remarkable device. It was demonstrated and approved by many scientists from the Board of Agriculture, the British Mineralogical Society, the Royal Society & the Geological Society, who all said what a novel device it was. James Ryan's advertising sheets and patent illustrate the device and how three such boreholes could reveal the stratigraphy of a complete hill, because they gave you cores, and revealed the dip and strike of the rocks of the whole hill.

Ryan's invention might have brought the start of an important technical break-through, allowing oriented cores to be recovered for the first time from boreholes. But the break-through failed to happen, as too many mining people simply regarded it as more expensive than the old method. The fact that it gave better quality data was not considered important. One terrible problem constantly shown by the history of technology in Britain is that if a device proves more expensive than the technology it replaced, people tended to take a short-term, and 'merely' economic, view of it. Instead of using a device invented in 1805 which gave newly *reliable* data, many carried on (some until 1952 over 147 years later) using antiquated technology which often gave useless information, comforting themselves that it was 'cost-effective'.

After Ryan's initial failure to interest people in his device, he instead developed it as a mine-ventilator. It could bore holes vertically and horizontally and so could be used to ventilate mines. Ryan, a very brave man, was revered in his lifetime by the South Staffordshire miners where he was long based. Many were rightly not persuaded that the Davy Lamp was the great safety device it was claimed to be. Anybody interested in statistics should look at the number of people who died in Coal Mining accidents, before and after the Davy Lamp was invented. This will show how the Davy lamp too often encouraged mining in areas which were really not at all safe. Ryan advocated better ventilation, not illumination, but was often ignored. In 1818 he went mining in Montgomeryshire on the English border, and here, somewhere in the beautiful Breidden hills, Ryan opened the first School of Mines in the British Isles. Unfortunately no records have yet been discovered to show whether this building survives or exactly where it was. It is humbling to point out that of all people a simple Irishman who died a pauper should have first tried to educate people about the value of geological science and the *value* of his 'new technology'. Too often they only knew the *price* of such advances. Ryan died in 1847 in Dudley in the West Midlands. The date of his patent, 28 February 1805, is significant.[21]

THE SCIENCE OF MINERAL PROSPECTING

We turn now to the 'science' of mineral exploration, with the same focus on stratiform minerals. We may start with John Aubrey (1626–1697), whose *Brief Lives* some of you may have read or seem dramatised on television? He wrote a manuscript *Chorographia* between 1662 and 1673, when our Royal Society was being founded. He was here concerned to make correlations

---

21   H.S.Torrens, 'James Ryan (c.1770–1847) and the problems of introducing Irish 'New Technology' to British Mines in the early Nineteenth Century', in P. Bowler and N. Whyte (editors), *Science and Society in Ireland*, Belfast (1997).

between geology and vegetation and hoped, for instance, to find that certain trees could be identified as indications of minerals, hoping to find thereby 'symptoms of subterranean treasure'. So the idea of botanical mineral prospecting is not new. Aubrey suspected that holly and oak went with coal, when he found they were abundant with coal around Newcastle and so felt the same symptoms might indicate coal in Wiltshire which, of course, they do not because the stratigraphy is different from Newcastle. But you can see a glimmer of an idea here.

The next person I want to talk about is the remarkable Thomas Robinson (died 1719), vicar of Ousby in Cumberland who wrote on 'How to Discover Minerals by the Adjacent Strata and Upper Cover', in other words how to try and use the strata as exposed or visible in streams or quarries to predict. His book of 1709 is particularly interesting because it emerges, from newly discovered material in the West Riding Record Office, that Robinson was highly involved in mineral prospecting there and was the leading mineral prospector in West Yorkshire. His account of prospecting carefully separates minerals in slats (what we would now call stratified) from minerals in veins. He correctly records that the dip of coal could help one to analyse what the covering rocks were, but he also said (wrongly) that coal was found in constant association with limestones, black shales and free-stones. These things are, of course, often found in true Coal Measures but they do not *indicate* Coal Measures. This was exactly the problem that soon emerged: when people found black shales they thought it was THE black shale found with Coal Measures and that they must soon be able to find Coal as well. It was very simple but completely wrong.

The emergence of geochemical prospecting can be seen in the work of that remarkable man, James Hutton (1726–1797) of Edinburgh, familiar to many as the father of modern geology. The bicentenary of his death will be celebrated in 1997. It was Hutton who first urged that alluvial materials should be searched in the way that geochemists now employ, looking in streams for ever enhancing proportions of minerals as you reach the source of that mineral. If you read Hutton you will find one of the things that interested him most was looking at the gravel in rivers, because it gave him a microcosm of what was going to be exposed in the region of the watershed. When he wanted to examine the contact between granite and schist he went to Glen Tilt and soon found blocks showing the contact in the stream. These told him that the contact was to be found in the region and could then be hunted for properly. It is a very basic geological prospecting tool and has been of great use in mineral exploration all over the world.

This indeed may been an original contribution by Hutton's; certainly when James Cook (1728–1779) set off on his first round-the-world expedition in 1768, Hutton's friend, and President of the Philosophical Society of Edinburgh James Douglas (1702–1768), advised Cook:

> Gravel and Sand found at the mouths of Rivers [Australian don't forget], help to give a notion of the Minerals and Fossils of the Countrys thro' which those Rivers take their course, such [information] therefore should be carefully collected and separately kept.[22]

People back home could then analyse such data and I think that this is probably one of the first manifestations of Huttonian research methods. We must not forget that at this period of the eighteenth century, the Americans were revolting, the Australians were being mostly locked up, and both were soon trying to set up colonies, which they had to manage. In California and Australia, people told me quite independently that the first materials of which they noted the lack, were not energy or coal – it was lime for cement in buildings. In Australia they had to send people to collect oyster shells to grind up to make lime. It was convicts who actually discovered coal deposits at the resultingly named Newcastle, north of Sydney. They were properly rewarded with their freedoms for such a useful discovery. So the point, obvious today, is that both energy and building materials were crucial for any such settlements and so mineral prospecting skills for such materials were also important.

There are several treatises in the eighteenth century. One, *A Treatise upon Coal Mining or an Attempt to Show Marks and Indications*, was by William Sharpe (1724–1783) who wrote it anonymously and published it himself in 1769. He was a Dorset schoolmaster and clergyman, born in Durham, who had been to Oxford University and was as well-informed about science as one could be at the time.[23] When he arrived in Dorset, he discovered to his horror that the local fuel was incredibly expensive by comparison with Durham and that the natives suffered 'agues' as a result of cold housing. So with a philanthropic motive all the proceeds of his book were to go to the poor of his Dorset parish. The book was largely a prospecting manual written by somebody who was both well educated and born in a mining community. Sharpe sent questionnaires to as many mine-owners as he

---

22   J.C. Beaglehole, *The Voyage of the* Endeavour *1768–1771*, Cambridge, p. 519 (1955).
23   H.S. Torrens, 'The Revd. William Sharpe', *University College Record*, 6, pp. 376–384 (1974).

could, asking them what information existed to try to find coal in Dorset in hopes of alleviating the problem of his parishioners.

His 'Strata Indicative of Coal' gave five 'indications' of coal present in a particular area. This represented both his and his correspondents' opinions. The five are: 1. Acidic streams – indicating Coal Measures nearby. 2. Ironstone – what he called gublin bat (we discover some wonderful words in these old writings) – was a constant associate of coal: if you found iron you found coal. This was theologically motivated, because of course the good Lord had sent one to be smelted by the other. Very simple but quite wrong. 3. Black shale or blue clay (Clunch) was a crucial 'indication'. He claimed there was a constant association between Coals and ordinary clay. This claimed association, common in what we today group as Coal Measures, became very misleading; other blue clays, like ironstones, did *not* indicate coal at all. 4. If there is coal at the surface this indicates the presence of coal in the area. This 'indication' alone has a germ of reliability. 5. The worst coal was always uppermost. So the slightest sign of bad 'coal' will improve as you work downwards. This created another problem, because this 'indication' encouraged people to be misled by the slightest 'indication'. The first find did not look very coal–like and was not very rich, but one only had to dig a little deeper to find something worthwhile etc. This last 'indication' was perhaps the most misleading of all.

Sharpe published an additional pamphlet in 1770, *An Appendix to a Treatise on Coal Mines........*, with a second edition reprinted in 1791. A unique copy of this survives in the Bodleian Library, thanks to a remarkable man called Richard Gough (1735–1809) who collected topographical literature from all over Britain. It gives a fascinating account of attempts to find coal near Sherborne, in north Dorset, where Sharpe was the schoolmaster and vicar. Sharpe was determined to record what coal mining failures had happened here – events which are not normally recorded, as with all failure. Round Sherborne, where there is no coal, Sharpe recorded a total of 8 attempts within a five mile radius, and at least six others attempts in Dorset are recorded.[24]

In Dorset, a non-industrialised county, only sources of domestic coal were needed. If Sherborne had been near Leeds or Dudley or an area where you wanted to develop industry, they would have been ever more furiously looking for such coal but similarly not realising that they would never find

---

[24] H.S.Torrens, 'Coal Exploration in Dorset', *Dorset County Magazine*, 44, pp. 31–39 (1975).

it, using such 'indications'. They might well have found it in these latter areas by accident, but had no scientific knowledge yet of how prospecting for coal was to be carried out. They had no knowledge yet of the stratigraphical column. Dorset attempts, as we all now know, were doomed to failure for stratigraphical reasons: here Jurassic, Cretaceous and Tertiary rocks all lie many hundreds of feet above any Coal-bearing rocks. The five geological horizons chosen for the known attempts in Dorset were all in 'misleading' black clays, in 1) Lias, 2) Forest Marble, 3) Oxford Clay, 4) Kimmeridge Clay and 5) Bagshot Beds; all black shales, all looking superficially like Coal Measures and misleading eighteenth-century coal hunters.

Trials in the Bagshot Beds in the south-east of Dorset, for instance, cost £15,000 in the 1770s. That was a lot of money and was completely wasted: they went right down through the Chalk, hoping that underneath would be a thick deposit of Coal. That was not the case, though you do, of course, find beds with lignite in the Lower Cretaceous or bituminous Kimmeridge Clay there to help mislead you. These Dorset descriptions were noticeable for three other features: first, the counter claims of likely prospects; nobody could agree on whether a particular trial was a good idea or not; there was absolutely no consensus. Second, nobody recorded what they found when they failed, so no one was able to learn by their mistakes. Third, and absolutely crucial, is the frequent record of sabotage and industrial action from Mendip miners. Mendip miners did not want coal found in Dorset because it might have put them out of work or have changed the basis for mining in the area. Sabotage, as we have seen, was easy, for negative results you just dropped an iron bar down the borehole. This blocked the whole thing off or if you wanted positive results you just dropped a piece of coal down which would be duly drawn up in the wumble to show them they were 'on to a certain winner'.

Such trials were apparently repeated in Europe – I have just produced a paper to be published in France about mineral prospecting and its history and discovered that such failed activities were also happening in France at the time of the French Revolution.[25]

---

[25]   H.S. Torrens, 'Le 'Nouvel Art de Prospection Minière' de William Smith et le 'Projet de Houillère de Brewham'': un essai malencontreux de recherche de charbon dans le sud-ouest de l'Angleterre, entre 1803 et 1810', in the *De la géologie à son histoire*, Paris (1998).

THE NEW SCIENCE OF MINERAL SURVEYING

All this was to change and might have changed faster. In 1790 a man called William Smith (1769–1839) saw an attempt for coal being made at a village in Hampshire in the New Forest. He wrote: 'I particularly noticed a boring for coal on the very different soils of the New Forest opposite the Shoe Alehouse at Plaitford'.[26] Smith was struck by the difference in soils here from the ones he was familiar with around Warwick and in the Midlands. He wondered what the rationale behind mineral surveying might be. In 1790 William Smith was 21. He trained at Stow-on-the-Wold as a land surveyor and is often called 'the father of English geology'. If such titles have any meaning, which is doubtful, I would rather see him called 'the father of mineral prospecting'. It was Smith who provided a basis for *scientific* prospecting by realising the importance of the stratigraphic column and by starting to unravel it. His stratigraphic column revealed that stratified mineral-bearing deposits were in a certain order. You could then use that order to prospect for minerals.

Smith's canal work in the 1790s had involved him in considerable excavation and showed him that rocks were ordered in sequence. Soon he discovered that fossils had considerable value in helping to understand where you were in that order. Smith made two major advances, one was to unravel the order of strata exposed in the quarries and canals he excavated in the Bath area. The other he expressed in his own words:

> Fossils have been long studied as great curiosities, collected with great pains, treasured with great care and at a great expense, and shown and admired with as much pleasure as a child's rattle or a hobby-horse is shown and admired... because it is pretty; and this has been done by *thousands who have never paid the least regard to that* wonderful order and regularity with which Nature has disposed of these singular productions, and assigned to each class [of fossils] its peculiar stratum.[27]

So you could identify strata against an ordered standard by the fossils found in them. Find a trilobite today and you know the age of the rock; find an ammonite and you know the age of another rock; you use such information to make stratigraphical statements. You have a canal excavation and a hillside exposure. By comparing the fossils at the top of the canal section

---

26   Smith MSS, Oxford University Museum.
27   J. Phillips, *Memoirs of William Smith*, London pp. 17–18 (1844).

with those at the bottom of the hillside section, you can complete the stratigraphical column in the area. Smith's was an absolutely fundamental discovery and his greatest achievement was to put it to use in mineral prospecting.

By 1799 Smith had elaborated the stratigraphical column in the area round Bath. It was remarkably accurate. Smith's Column shows a particular interest in the Coal. He was not interested in the now Palaeozoic rocks below, because these had no economic value to him; he was interested in finding Coal. His column started with the easily recognisable Chalk.[28] It then recorded, with remarkable accuracy, the stratigraphical order down to The Coal; the thicknesses of the strata involved; whether they bore springs; the fossils of each with other observations. The *Geological Map* Smith was at last able to published in 1815 was a remarkable achievement in mineral pro-specting. It now revealed the distribution of the myriad of similar blue clays exposed all over Britain and revealed the true order of what we today call Kimmeridge Clay (Oaktree Clay to Smith), Oxford Clay (Clunch Clay to Smith), the clays above the Chalk (today Tertiary), the Lias clays below, all the many clays that had so misled people previously. William Smith was now able to tell people that first, blue clays were a common and constantly recurring phenomenon in the British stratigraphical column and second, that there was only (at least in Britain) one major level at which Coal occurred, the Coal Measures. With this knowledge one could use the stratigraphical column to prospect for particular materials; whether lime-stone for smelting, or puddling clay for canals, or ironstone for foundries, if it was stratified you could find its position in the stratigraphical column and you could use that knowledge to prospect.

For me 24 March 1805 is another red-letter day in the history of geology. William Smith had heard of a trial being made to find coal at Brewham, near Bruton in Somerset. Miraculously the complete record of this attempt survives in the archives of Bruton School. Bruton was close to where Smith had been previously based in North Somerset. A prospectus for the trial in 1804 had again made the false claim that 'Brewham [on Smith's Clunch clay] by its striking similarity of soil, site and aspect with all [sic] countries abounding in collieries, is scientifically [sic] acknowledged to be the most eligible for a trial.'

Similarities of soil again: clays, Oxford Clay in this case, still misleading people into thinking they were Coal Measures. The trial here attempted to

---

28   Phillips, *William Smith*, 27, p. 30.

find a means of tendering one of the 'first necessities of life'. A Share Certificate even survives; a man in Wincanton was sent it as the bond for his subscription. Each first share was for £20 (a lot of money in 1804) and there were 148 subscribers, all investing money in a hole in search of a substance which was not there. On 24 March 1805 Smith visited the site, found fossils thrown out of the shaft from a depth of 120 feet, and on the first occasion that anyone had used fossils to identify the age of rocks at depth, identified the Kellaways Rock and proved instantly that this trial was much too high in the stratigraphic column to have any chance of reaching true Coal. Smith knew, with newly scientific certainty, that the people of Bruton were wasting their time. It is lucky that the great over confidence of the Brutonians had led them to sink a shaft, as a boring would have pulverised any fossils passed though into paste. Sadly Smith's advice was ignored because, of course, a very large investment of money had been made and people were not ready to believe it was all to be wasted.[29]

Smith's methods were taken up by a number of his pupils but soon a terrible rivalry developed between the gentlemen geologists of the newly formed Geological Society in London (1807) and the 'practical men' like Smith and Farey, who were barred from membership. John Farey, in particular, was a most remarkable man, one of the most polymathic people I have ever come across: a linguist, musician, pacifist, expert on technology, mathematician (Farey numbers are named after him) and a very fine geologist as well.[30] One of the most remarkable documents I have ever found was in the Sutro library, San Francisco. It is his coloured map dated 1812 of Ashover in Derbyshire, the area I first mapped as an Oxford undergraduate. It shows the eroded anticline, with the oldest rocks in the core. Overton Hall near the centre of the anticline was one of the several estates of Sir Joseph Banks (1743–1820), long President of the Royal Society, who commissioned Farey to make a map for him. The detail with which Farey has mapped the area is amazing. First, Farey had to make a topographical base map (Ordnance Survey maps not being available in 1812) then map all the geological detail. Above the core of toadstone [volcanic tuff] are 23 rocks in sequence, all separately mapped on a scale of one and a half inches to a mile, of Carboniferous Limestone and Coal Measures, with coal mines specifically

---

[29]   Torrens, 'Nouvel Art', gives the full history of this attempt and its lessons.

[30]   H.S. Torrens & T.D. Ford, 'John Farey (1766–1826): An unrecognised polymath (pp. 1–28) and John Farey Bibliography (pp. 29–44)' in J. Farey, *General View of the Agriculture and Minerals of Derbyshire*, Volume 1 (1811), Reprinted Peak District Mines Historical Society Ltd (1989).

marked.[31] Considering it was drawn in 1812, the detail is remarkable and as commentator has noted, from the detail 'one might easily suppose... the map was a late nineteenth century production'.[32] History has misled us into thinking there was no tradition of such detail then, simply because these maps were never published.

CONCLUSIONS

By 1805 there was a dual technological and scientific basis for scientific prospecting in Britain. Smith and his school had provided a key to the stratigraphic ordering of minerals and Ryan with his new technology had provided the key to properly exploring what actually lay below the surface. This information had been unavailable to people like Erasmus Darwin (Charles Darwin's grandfather), who made important contributions to geology, because it was he who first discussed the porosity and permeability of rocks and made us realise how oil and gas might migrate.[33] Darwin first published his supposed 'Section of the Earth' in 1791. He knew that rocks were often stratified but demonstrated how he and others then had no knowledge of how one mineral basin with sand, coal and clay, related to another basin with iron, coal and clay. He had no knowledge of what was above or below what; each basin was recorded as a separate entity.[34]

Smith and his fellow workers removed that ignorance and provided the rudiments of a stratigraphic column. We sometimes forget what a remarkably scientific achievement the creation of the stratigraphic column was. Smith was also aware of the complications and uncertainties that unconformities produced. He was not successful in exploring for Coal across the unconformity in Somerset at the base of the New Red Sandstone, but he was aware of the possibilities which such an unconformity had made possible. So it was properly scientific prospecting. One such attempt Smith supervised at Compton Dundon, near Glastonbury. I visited the village in 1976 to find if anybody knew about his coal trial, between 1813 and 1815, bored to a depth of 519 feet.[35] Somebody told me of an old man living there

---

31   H.S. Torrens, 'Patronage and Problems: Banks and the Earth Sciences', in R.E.R. Banks et al (editors), *Sir Joseph Banks: A Global Perspective (the Commemorative Volume for the 250th Anniversary of his birth)*, London pp. 49–75 (1994).

32   D. Oldroyd, *Thinking about the Earth: A History of Ideas in Geology*, London, p. 114 (1996).

33   *The Geological Society. The British Association lectures – 1993*, London, pp. 4–5 (1994).

34   E. Darwin, *The Botanic Garden*, London, Third edition, part 1 – additional notes, opp. p. 66 (1795).

35   The MSS section survives in the Geological Society of London archives.

who might know because he had been born there and was 90 years old. It took me hours to persuade him to come and have a drink at the pub to talk to me. He didn't feel like it, but as soon as he got to the pub, he cheered up and his memory started to be 'liberated'. He then took me to a field east of the village beside a lane (which I later found was marked 'Coal Pit Lane' on the six inch O.S. map!) and pointed out a slight depression at the top of the field, saying that was where the trial had been, 160 years before. He was very specific about it. A few years later I found William Smith's original map of the site, but in the Dorset Record Office. In 1976, the old man was recalling what had never been written down, but had been transmitted orally through at least three generations with absolute precision; he proved to have been about six feet out. I do not now sniff at people who tell me such things, but make a mental note to check such sources out, as I would any other source; oral history can indeed reveal a lot.

We are now nearly at the end of what I want to say. I want to tell you what happened to this new stratigraphic and technical knowledge and how badly and meanly it was at first received. We had had two British break-throughs, one in technology, one in stratigraphy, only one month apart and both made by people at the lower end of the social stratification so pervasive in British Society. The word stratification is an important one in British history. One of the things I notice in America is how easily people mix regardless of who their parents are or what they are supposed to be. Nobody cares if they are the daughter of a duke or the son of a cleaning lady, they just get on with being American. I think that is still often not the case in Britain, but whether these barriers can be broken down in the future remains to be seen. Anyhow, the point I think was crucial is that both these break-throughs were made by people of working-class origin which made the British Establishment (and its Geological Society) very suspicious that they could have made any such advances.

But in 1836, the Professor of Geology at Oxford, William Buckland (1784–1856), could reveal what a revolution Smith had brought to geological knowledge while Buckland had been there:

Before we had acquired by experiment some extensive knowledge of the contents of each series of formations which the Geologist can readily identify, there was no *a priori* reason to expect the presence of coal in any one Series of strata rather than another. Indiscriminate experiments in search of coal, in strata of every formation, were therefore desirable and proper [then], in an age when even the name of

Geology was unknown; but the continuance of such Experiments in districts which are now ascertained to be composed of the non-carboniferous strata of the Secondary and Tertiary series, can no longer be justified, since the accumulated experience of many years has proved, that it is only in... series... designated as the *Carboniferous Order* that productive Coal mines on a large scale have ever been discovered.[36]

Roderick Murchison, President of the Geological Society after Buckland, was more direct in 1839:

It is difficult to avoid expressing surprise, that in *this* part of England persons should be found so utterly ignorant of the geological succession of the strata, as to sink for coal beneath the Wenlock Shale... These mistakes occur simply through inattention to the inorganic remains [fossils], with which indeed few practical miners are acquainted. Hence the endless follies we now hear of, such as sinking for coal at Northampton through the inferior oolite, where it is demonstrable, that the unfortunate speculators can scarcely penetrate even the lias formation. Black, bituminous and pyritous shales, resembling beds of the coal formation, are quite enough to lead any common miner to believe that he 'smells' the Coal, and thus country gentlemen are duped by ignorant men.

These were strong words in the debate between practice against theory. The working-class miners, where practice was what mattered, soon got caught up in the social stratification of the academic improvers. The punchline in Murchison's writing read:

Whether the strata thus resembling coal measures, be a mile above or below the geological position of the carboniferous system, has never formed part of the education of these practical speculators.[37]

The gentlemen geologists of the Geological Society now determined to solve the ignorance of the 'practical men', through education. They thought they could solve it by opening a School of Mines, but in Jermyn Street, London in 1851. This 'stood forth as the first palace ever raised from the ground in Britain which is entirely devoted to the advance of science!'[38]

---

[36] W. Buckland, *Geology and Mineralogy considered with reference to Natural Theology*, volume 1, London, p. 524 (1837).

[37] R.I. Murchison, *The Silurian System*. London p. 488 (1839).

[38] Geikie, *Memoir*, p. 184.

Vital knowledge of this practical kind also finally reached universities. John Phillips, William Smith's nephew, lectured at Oxford in 1865 (exactly 100 years after the foundation of the Bergakademie in Freiberg, Saxony) on 'the discovery of coal and other valuable minerals in new situations'. Academics trying to get the message across were continually thwarted by attitudes in the mining community. The practical men did not want to know. The war between the two groups was a very real one and is absolutely fascinating. Of course London was a very stupid place to have erected any School of Mines. Why in London when the nearest mining activity was near Bristol or Gloucester? Did those who planned it really expect miners to walk to their Mining School in London to be informed about the scientific practice of mining? At the first session seven students turned up and none of them were from mining districts![39] War was now declared. One of the leading mining figures wrote:

> In many districts, those who have been intrusted with the management of mines, have often been scarcely removed in intelligence or acquirements from the rank of common workmen, their knowledge being frequently so limited, that the improvements made and the principles observed in one district are quite unknown in others.[40]

Attempts at education were rebuffed by these practical people. In 1851, just after the School of Mines was opened in London an old Cornish miner wrote of:

> what we are to expect from these so-called schools of mining-the production of vain bubbles at so much per head... We want local schools, where young men may be taught daily by practical teachers, as the majority of our miners,... can ill afford to leave their employment..., to get their heads filled with such visionary notions.... [Mining schools provide] a glaring proof of the injury done to the minds of young men by sending them to such schools.[41]

That I think is the point: why was London chosen? Even Evan Hopkins (1810–1867), a Fellow of the Geological Society, agreed that:

---

[39] G.W. Roderick & M.D. Stephens, *Scientific and Technical Education in Nineteenth-Century England*, Newton Abbot, p. 103 (1972).

[40] J.K. Blackwell, *Report on Ventilation of Mines*, London, p. 25 (1850).

[41] *Mining Journal*, 21, p. 483 (4 October 1851).

Unfortunately, the lectures of our theoretical geologists,... have hitherto rendered many a promising youth somewhat useless to our practical operations.... [They] thus strengthen the common opinion – viz: that *mining* schools appear to injure the mind, instead of doing any benefit... The *mine* is, as yet, the only school in which the practical sciences of geology and mining can be correctly and usefully acquired.[42]

This war between practice and theory is I think probably with us still today.

I have two further thoughts after 1850. Herbert Hoover (1874–1961), held very strong views on the value of education. He was a mining engineer and 31st President of the United States during the Depression. Can you imagine any mining engineer ever being Prime Minister of the United Kingdom? It is just not conceivable and this is part of our problem. In 1941 he wrote how 'British universities... refused to incorporate engineering into their curricula until much later than the Americans. In the meantime, the American engineers – especially the mining engineers – flooded the British Empire.'[43]

The second is more recent. Some of you may have read *English Culture and the Decline of the Industrial Spirit, 1850–1980* by Martin Wiener,[44] one of the most influential books ever written about Britain. Wiener is American but I am sure his book helped cause the onslaught on British universities which they still suffer today. But any claimed 'decline of industrial spirit' is a very complicated topic; it involves this battle between practice and theory which so occupies us today in Britain, as we destroy the whole philosophy on which the Polytechnics were based and which the history of mineral prospecting so reveals. The history of mineral prospecting is relevant because it reminds of one problem that we face today, the state of our universities. This returns us to the quotation I started with. Why in Britain is nobody interested in supporting universities or in thinking what is done in them important? We clearly have much to learn from our past.

---

[42]   *Mining Journal*, 21, p. 387 (9 August 1851).

[43]   T.T. Read, *The Development of Mineral Industry Education in the United States*, New York, Foreword p. xiii, (1941).

[44]   Cambridge (1981).

II

THE BRITISH «MINERAL ENGINEER» JOHN WILLIAMS (1732-1795), HIS WORK IN BRITAIN FROM 1749 TO 1793 AND AS A MINERAL SURVEYOR IN THE VENETO AND NORTH ITALY BETWEEN 1793 AND 1795.

I dedicate this paper to Virgilio Giormani
of Venice

Introduction

The history of the applications of geology to the «real» worlds of mineral exploration and prospection has been much less studied than the history of academic and other more theoretical aspects of geology (Torrens 1988). As a result the assumption is often made that the British, who largely failed to give any formal national training to their «mineral engineers» until about 1850, must have made rather little contribution to the establishment of mineral exploration skills, when compared for example with the Germans, who, in institutions like the Bergakademie in Freiberg, Saxony, had had formal State encouragement of mineral instruction nearly a century earlier (Porter 1973, p. 333).

On the other hand, we must remember that the century 1750-1850 was an Age of Revolutions. Germany's was Intellectual. That in France was Political (as John Williams was to discover!) whilst Britain's was Industrial. This last «Revolution» had been entirely fuelled by the native natural resources of the British Isles. As John Williams, the subject of this study, noted in 1787, «Britain receives more benefits from the bowels of the earth than perhaps any other nation» (Williams 1787). But such resources, however beneficial, had to have been located in the first place, however empirically. Since so many of the results of these experiments never reached paper (or at least paper which has survived), the historian can be easily misled and so is tempted to assume little such activity took place. The truth has to have been that there was much such activity.

To examine this problem, it is vital to uncover what «raw» archival or printed materials do survive of the careers of these, often unrecorded «mineral prospectors» (Torrens 1984) and especially those relating to men who were thought competent enough to be invited to work abroad in search of mineral deposits. Most often this was in search of coal, seen as *the* fuel which had allowed the British to gain such a long industrial lead, as in Russia (Torrens 1991) and other parts of Europe. But others later went much farther afield, like South America, in search of metals (Torrens 1995).

One of the earliest and most important of such men is the long forgotten Welsh-born John Williams (1732-1795), who went out to Italy to search for coal and other minerals in Dalmatia and the Veneto in 1793, but who died there in 1795, under rather tragic circum–stances. Williams' reward since his death has been a near-silence, like that shown by the entry in a standard work of 1971 (Challinor 1971, p. 208) that his «biography is unknown» except that he was «a director of mines».

When trying to investigate Williams' long-forgotten past, we face three major historiographic problems. The first is that he was a doer, not a thinker. Much of his 'practical' work will have suffered the normal 'papyrophobia' of such activities (Torrens 1994a, pp. 24-5). The second problem is that any Williams from Wales will have suffered the same historical fate as any English Smith or any North Italian Rossi or Bianchi. The sheer commonplaceness of his name in its original contexts means that there can be, and must remain, real confusion with others of this name.

The third problem is the most intractable. Williams spent different periods of his life in three different cultures; Welsh, Scottish and Italian. All were in part separated, at least potentially, by language and thus sadly separate history. The small amount of primary printed material uncovered about Williams has quite separate Welsh, Scottish, and Italian origins. From these it becomes clear how much better informed our single Welsh source was about Williams' origins and early years than any of the Scottish ones. Any Italian sources have remained ignorant of both.

The single Welsh source on Williams is due to his nephew, another John Williams of Kerry in Montgomeryshire, who informed Walter Davies (1761-1849) (Davies 1814, volume 2, pp. 323-5). Two of the Scottish sources, instead, rely on either Williams' son Mark Antony, a surgeon based in 1814 in Haddington, east of Edinburgh who informed Patrick Neill (1776-1851), then Secretary of the Wernerian Natural History Society in Edinburgh (Neill 1814a & 1814b) or on his maternal grandson William Anderson (1805-1866) (Anderson 1863, 1865). Anderson was a son of the marriage at Libberton, Midlothian on 29 August 1788 of Elizabeth Williams, one of John's daughters, to James Anderson. A third Scottish source, by James Millar (1762-1827) (Millar 1810, volume 1, pp. vii-viii), did not acknowledge any sources.

These four notices have very differing biasses and reliabilities. Gordon Herries Davies, who only knew of two (Millar 1810 & Neill 1814b), astutely noted (Davies 1969, p.138) how «sharply contradictory [they were] on many points».

Williams' Welsh origins

John Williams, according to the most reliable, Welsh, source was born in the parish of Ceri or Kerry, Montgomeryshire in «about 1732» (Davies 1814, volume 1, p. 324). Davies had been informed of this and other matters by Williams' nephew, yet another John Williams who still lived there. Scottish claims that Williams was the son of a Glamorgan clergyman (Neill 1814a, p. 255 & 1814b, p. 81) are incorrect. Kerry lay in a predominantly agricultural region of the Welsh borders. It is now a place famous for its sheep. Sadly, the prevalence of the name Williams means that 'our' John Williams can have been either the «son of Edward Williams [of] Gwernescob baptised 5 October 1731» or «ye son of John Williams of Weeg baptised 27 December 1732» (Anon. 1919, pp. 44 & 47). Since the Kerry parish registers give no names of the mothers of children (until the 1760's), no ages at death for people when buried there and fail to record any places of residence for those marrying, further genealogical exploration from this source is ruled out. Weeg and Gwernescob are neighbouring hamlets to the south west of the town of Kerry and the high probability is that both of the above families were already related.

Davies tells us only that Williams' «education went no higher than reading and writing a little English in the village school», but he was perhaps also bilingual in Welsh. Davies continues; «the operations of husbandry not being adapted to his innate genius, he quitted his native country before he was full grown, and was no more heard of there, until he had settled as a mineral surveyor in Scotland». This shows that he came from a farming family and had not been «bred a miner», as one Scottish source claimed (Millar 1810, volume 1, p. vii and has been repeated since by Cotterell 1985, p. 22).

But Williams clearly did spend some further time in Wales and as a miner. In his 1789 book *The Natural History of the Mineral Kingdom*, Williams refers to the following metal mines in Mid-Wales with which he was familiar.

1) Llangunog (Lead) (Williams 1810, volume 1, p. 228, 249; see Bick 1978, V, p. 25).

2) Darenfawr, Cardiganshire (Lead) (Williams 1810, volume 1, 230, pp. 350-1; see Bick 1978, III, pp. 10-15).

3) Cwmsymlog (Lead) (Williams 1810, volume 1, p. 349; see Bick 1978, III, p. 19).

4) Cwmystwyth (Lead) (Williams 1810, volume 1, p. 301, 349; see Bick 1978, I, p. 19).

From his further reference to the Duke of Powis' ownership of these mines and his note that «about forty years ago... I was pretty well informed of the mineral history» of Cardiganshire (Williams 1810, volume 1, p. 350), it is clear that Williams must have worked at all, or some, of these mines, for some period about 1749, when aged about 17 (Davies 1814, volume 2, pp. 509-18). Williams' first mining experiences were thus with veiniform minerals, not stratiform materials – like coal. No credence can be given to a much later, but Welsh, claim that «he is stated to have had a good deal of information from Iolo Morganwg [Edward Williams 1747-1826]» (Wilkins 1888, p. 335).

Williams next worked for some time in North Wales, where there were then large and important copper mines in Snowdonia and Anglesey, since his later Scottish patron, the 11th Earl of Buchan (David Stuart Erskine 1742-1829: see Lamb 1963), noted that Williams had «worked originally in Wales in the Copper Mines, and became an overseer there» (NLS MSS 996). This is confirmed by Neill (1814a, p. 255) who wrote that «while a boy he resided a good deal at the copper-mines of Anglesea». These mines were those visited by the geologist James Hutton (1726-1797) in 1774, a few years later (Jones et al. 1994-5). Davies (1814, volume 1, p. 324) also noted that Williams had «passed through Derbyshire» [another famous metal mining region] on his way into Scotland, but gave no other details.

Williams moves to Scotland

Williams' Scottish beginnings are badly recorded. One Scottish claim «that he was some time a soldier in the Dutch service» (Millar 1810, vii), simply cannot be confirmed. Printed records of the Scots Brigade in Holland (Ferguson 1899-1901) contain no reference to him and there seems little time available in which he could have so served in Holland.

The mystery surrounding Williams' earliest years in Scotland must be partly solved by the news (to which Charles Withers kindly drew my attention) that among the six surveyors and draughtsmen employed on the famous Military Survey of Scotland between 1747 and 1755 under General William Roy (1726-1790), "who have faded into obscurity", was a surveyor called John Williams (Whittington & Gibson 1986, p. 62). This seems certain to have been our John Williams.

As far as Williams' mining career in Scotland is concerned, James Millar stated, in a notice claimed by Williams' grandson as «incorrect in many respects and not sanctioned by his family» (Anderson 1863, volume 1, p. 133), that Williams «was engaged at [the famous lead mines at] Leadhills to superintend the process of extracting silver from lead» (Millar 1810). Some confirmation of this is given by Williams' own later references to these mines, which are near Wanlockhead in the South of Scotland (Williams 1810, volume 1, pp. 249-50 & 327). In addition Williams also noted his visits to a mine on the Isle of Islay (Williams 1810, volume 1, p. 344) and to the more famous mines at Strontian, in Ardnamurchan (Williams 1810, volume 1, pp. 227 & 249), which later yielded the element Strontium (Weeks 1948, pp. 302-5). Maybe all or some of these visits took place at this early stage in Williams' career?

Millar further claimed that Williams did not long remain at Leadhills, but that «soon after he came to Scotland, [he] was employed by some proprietors in the vicinity of Edinburgh to search for lead ore. He then became tacksman [a form of tenant in Scotland] of the coal of Carlops on the estate of Newhall [near Penicuik]..., unsuccessful in this undertaking, it was probably soon relinquished for an engagement with the Earl of Moray, to search for coal on his estate of Dunrobin, in the north of Scotland» (Millar 1810). These last estates belonged instead to the Earls of Sutherland (see below). This error must cast doubt on the reliability of the chronology given by Millar.

To add to the confusion with Williams' early years in Scotland, Neill (1814a, p. 256) instead placed Williams' time at the lead mines of Wanlockhead and at the silver mines of Silver Hills, West Linton (which are those noted above as 'in the vicinity of Edinburgh') *after* 1774. This was the same year to which Neill wrongly dated Williams' departure from Sutherland (see below)! So there must remain considerable doubt over the timing of Williams' early veiniform mining experiences in Scotland.

Williams' work for the Commissioners for the Forfeited Annexed Estates

This body, which Millar does not mention, became the main driving force behind Williams' next activities in Scotland. The Commissioners for the Forfeited Annexed Estates (hereafter CFAE) in Scotland were appointed in 1755 (Smith 1975). Their estates were those of the Jacobites, forfeited to the Crown after the political upheavals of the mid 18th century in Scotland, mainly in the Scottish Highlands (Wills 1973). Williams' first involvement with the CFAE came in 1763, when George Clerk-Maxwell (1715-1784), James Hutton's close friend and collaborator, sent Williams to Stobhall in Perthshire to search for coal and minerals there (SRO E 727/46/1, see Smith 1975, p. 53 & 1982, p. 32). Williams found an abundance of rock marle, lime and marble here (SRO E 777/138) and also made a trial for coal (SRO E 727/46/1). Williams was next sent by the Commissioners, who included Clerk-Maxwell, to look for coal in the North of Scotland, in Cromarty. Little was found, but by 16 June 1764 Williams had instead found coal in Sutherland (SRO E 727/45/6). He noted that «it was said there was plenty of coal on the Earl of Sutherland's estate» and, if the Earl did not intend to work this coal, proposed to ask the Earl for a lease and the Commissioners for an interest free loan of £1,000 for three years to help him work it (SRO E 727/45/6 & E 730/28). It was these early coal exercises at Dunrobin, in Sutherland, prospecting for and then working coals (now known to be of Jurassic age), which established Williams' career as a «mining surveyor» especially of coal and other stratified minerals.

His reports to the CFAE seem to have aroused Clerk-Maxwell's interest for he and James Hutton set off, in 1764, on an important fact-finding geological and mineralogical tour to the North of Scotland. This started from Edinburgh, and passed through the centre of Scotland via Loch Ness, to Inverness ending at Caithness. They returned south along the coast via Aberdeen back to Edinburgh (Playfair 1805, p. 45).

Williams and coal mining at Brora 1764-1769

Williams' hoped-for Sutherland coal mining lease was duly granted and as his grandson Anderson recorded, Williams now

«took the coal-mines of Brora, in the parish of Golspie, from the Earl of Sutherland, and a farm near them called Waterford. His daughter, Elizabeth,

[Anderson's mother] was born at Brora, 13th April 1765... The farm proved a bad speculation, as Mr Williams lost a large sum of money in improving it to no purpose». As for the coal mine, «after he had put up an engine at the coal mine, [it] took fire, by which he lost a considerable sum, indeed nearly all that he possessed» (Anderson 1863, p. 132).

Two surviving letters describe Williams' activities at Brora in 1765-1766 (EUL La.II 82/4 ff 362 & 365). They are to Mrs Cummyng, wife of the keeper of Lyon records and the first Secretary to the Society of Antiquaries of Scotland, James Cummyng (1732-1793). They are some of the earliest manuscripts by Williams to have survived. The first is dated 1 May 1765, just after Williams' return from Edinburgh. It noted their delightful situation close by the sea at Brora and that «we are now at the coal, and raise as much as serves my own house & have an excellent fire. I hope to be raising some little for sale in about three months». The second dated 25 March 1766, from Brora, discusses Williams' two families! Williams' also noted that a too sanguine friend of Mrs Cummyng had hoped to find a Gold mine «by no other symptom than hazle [hazel] bushes» growing on it. Williams then gives his own views of how Gold occurs in nature and what «marks and indications» of it he would accept. He was clearly already regarded as something of an expert in mineral prospecting. Other details of Williams' work at Brora, and that £80 was paid to him for subsistence, are given by Smith (1982, p. 32). The records of Williams' other work for the CFAE for the period 1765-1767 also survive (SRO E 728/42). Williams continued to work for the CFAE while involved in coal mining at Brora. In 1767 he submitted his report on the lime quarry at Englishtown in the parish of Kirkhall in Southern Scotland (SRO E769/132).

More personal details of Williams' time at Brora are given by a later geologist, John Farey (1766-1826), sent to Brora to report on the coal workings there early in the next century. He noted that Williams' activities here had started in about 1764 and ceased in 1769. Farey also observed the low quality of the coal seams there and «how little Williams then knew of collierying» (Farey 1815a, pp. 448-9 & 1815b, p. 9). Farey alone also recorded that Williams had been threatened by the Kirk Officers at Brora «on account of a natural [illegitimate] child who had been born to him» there (hence the two families above), whom Farey met in 1812, still living at Brora.

This threat, and his financial problems, caused Williams to give up his Brora coal lease in 1769 after five years. The crisis had arisen when Williams suffered two major financial failures at Brora. These were while «the earl and countess [of Sutherland] were at Bath, on account of the health of the earl who died there. The young countess, their daughter, on succeeding to the Sutherland title and estates, was an infant scarcely a year old. The Earl's factor [at Brora], a Mr Campbell Combie, was a very harsh and arbitrary person, and would not do anything for Mr Williams. He refused even to entertain his claim either for the loss he had sustained by the coal mines, or for the money he had expended in improvements on the farm» (Anderson 1863, p. 132).

The Earl, William Sutherland (1735-1766) and his wife both died at Bath in June 1766 and Elizabeth, their daughter who was born on 24 May 1765, had to succeed on 16 June 1766 (Gibbs 1953, volume 12, part 1, pp. 562-3) in a very disputed minority.

Farey noted that in 1769 Williams now supposedly «removed to East Lothian». This, if true, must have been the home base for the very itinerant lifestyle which Williams now adopted. William Anderson instead wrongly claimed that Williams only worked for the CFAE *after* the debacle at Brora and then only for only eighteen months (Anderson 1863, p. 132). Neill proves equally unreliable, wrongly stating that Williams was at Brora between 1770 & 1774 (Neill 1814a, p. 256)! In any case the Brora coal-works were abandoned, in 1777, not long after Williams' departure, amid the usual stories of their failure having been due to bribery (Adam 1972, pp. lxi & 222).

After 1769 Williams now became an itinerant mining surveyor for the CFAE all over Scotland. The historical trail of such people is often hard to follow but in this case good records survive of his work for the CFAE over the summers of 1769 to 1775 (Wills 1973, p. xiv & SRO E 730/27 and SRO E 730/46). These show that Williams was, by April 1769, back mineral prospecting for the CFAE at Elgin in the North of Scotland. Here he found a promising lime quarry (Adams 1979, pp. 147-8). His 1770 Report (SRO E730/27) is on a mineral survey of Stratherig and Delleathich. 1771 saw his mineral survey of Perth. 1772 and 1773 found him in Cromarty, Forres & Appin (SRO E 727/46/28 (1-3). In 1773 Williams discovered the slates at Ballachulish (SRO E 730/27), which were later to be much exploited. In 1774 Williams was busy in the Fort William area, and working on the excavation of vitrified forts he had discovered (see below). Williams' last survey for the CFAE, in 1775, was at Nairn (SRO E 730/27).

Williams' entire career with the CFAE in Scotland, deserves further study, to uncover his working methods as a surveyor & prospector (SRO E 727/41). Full summaries, over 1770-1775, together with

Clerk-Maxwell's responses to Williams' reports, still survive (SRO E 727/46/28-49). These contain the final recommendation by George Clerk-Maxwell, on 21 February 1776, that Williams' work on Scottish mineral trials be abandoned.

The Parallel Roads of Glenroy

During the first summer after Williams had departed from Brora, he had also been busy for the CFAE in the Highlands near Ben Nevis. A letter he wrote, in September 1769 (but not published until 1903), shows that he had been busy examining the later famous «Parallel Roads of Glen Roy», whose debated origins have since made them «one of the chief geological curiosities of the British isles». They are claimed to have been first described by the Scottish tourist, Thomas Pennant (1726-1798), in 1776 (Davies 1969, p. 279). Williams' description is earlier. It is in the form of a letter to the Earl of Findlater (James Ogilvy 1714-1770) who was to commit suicide the following year. Williams' letter recorded that were three such «roads» along Glen Roy, along each of which he had walked on their north sides. Williams, perhaps not surprisingly, thought these were old military roads built to oppose Norse invasions. But, baffled by why there should have been three of them, he imagined that some were for outgoing and some for ingoing troops etc (Cramond 1903). Williams concluded that they were «evidently more modern» than the forts and castles which he had also started to study in this region.

His discovery of the Vitrified Forts of northern Scotland

In March 1774 James Watt (1736-1819), the steam engineer, wrote a report on an intended canal between Fort William and Inverness (SRO CFAE MSS 1/53/1/4), in the north of Scotland. He too had been appointed by the CFAE, in August 1773, to survey this wild, rough country (Dickinson & Jenkins 1927, p. 38 & Bryden 1994). The route he chose was much the same as that later used when the Caledonian Canal was completed in 1822 (Cameron 1972). The route passed an ancient fort at Craig Patrick which Williams had also come across while working for the CFAE.

In a letter dated 18 June 1774 to George Clerk-Maxwell from Fort William, Williams described his detailed excavation of another fort at Knockfarril, Strathpeffar, Ross-shire.

«I wrote you from Inverness concerning the mineral appearances in the estate of Argaur & I then purposed writing to you again from Rosshire which I found I could not do to my satisfaction, till I had finished the sections of the old ruins; & when I had done, I made all possible haste to Appin to see the work there, from where I am just now returned. Upon the 20th ulto I began to dig into the old ruins on the top of Knockfarril, south side of Strathpeffar in Rosshire. The full name of the place, is... I began with 8 labourers to dig into the South Side of a high heap of ruins without the west end of the inclosed area, which seems to have been an outwork». He then describes the details of the excavation and the vitrification of the fort's fabric which he had discovered. «The rock it is built on, is a strongly coagulated beech, or what is commonly called, plumb pudding rock, in which is a considerable mixture of Lime, which would help to facilitate the vitrification. I hope to explain matters more fully, when I have the pleasure to wait upon you in winter, meantime, the favor of your commands will very much oblige Sir Your most obedt & most humble sert. John Williams» (SRO GD 18, Clerk of Penicuik MSS, vol 2, GD 18/5071).

George Clerk-Maxwell's response to this letter also survives. It noted that John Williams «seems to be the first man that noticed the stones [of these vitrified forts] being run together & apparently cemented by vitrification», which Williams thought had been man-made (SRO E 727/46/44). In 1777, when Williams no longer worked for the CFAE, he published his book on these forts (in two versions). The first, in quarto, was entitled *Letters from the Highlands of Scotland* (Williams 1777a), and was published in Edinburgh. According to Gough (1780, volume 2, p. 574), Williams thought Clerk-Maxwell, to whom the 13 letters he published had been addressed, «had taken too great liberties with his style». So Williams then issued another, now commoner, version in octavo, «with all its grammatical inaccuracies» as written. This (Williams 1777b) appeared by August (*Scots Magazine*, pp. 39, 442, August 1777). The work was even translated into Russian (Kulichin 1797). Both versions included letters, from James Watt to Clerk-Maxwell about Watt's visit to, and survey of, Craig Patrick fort, with Watt's sketch and section, and from Joseph Black (1728-1799), the Edinburgh chemist, to Williams about the «vitrification».

The first English observer of such forts, in 1769 Thomas Pennant, had only questioned whether the fort at Tor-down, near Fort Augustus (another of Williams' original «vitrified» sites) «was the antient site of some forge, or whether the stones which form this fortress had [instead] been collected from the strata of some *Vulcano*» (Pennant 1772, p. 185). Pennant hoped that «farther enquiry» would follow. This soon came, when reports from France that ancient volcanoes had been recognised there (Ellenberger 1979 & Torrens 1994b, pp. 50-3), reached England. Sir Joseph Banks' visits to Staffa and Iceland in 1772 were two of the most significant English reactions to this news from France.

One aspect of the fierce debate which now developed about these vitrified forts must have had a significant effect on Williams' later geological work. For some denied that such Scottish «vitrifications» could ever have been man-made. They thought instead that these forts must have been the sites of former volcanoes. This, at least, was the opinion of Thomas West (1720-1779), whose 1776 «account of a Volcanic Hill near Inverness» was published by the London Royal Society (West 1778). This hill was the same Craig Patrick fort that Williams had described the previous year. Another response to Williams' discoveries came from Dr James Anderson (1739-1808) who, in 1777, read a study of these fortifications, as a result of Williams' work (Anderson 1779). Anderson called them «the most remarkable of all the Scottish antiquities». He had heard about them direct from Williams, nearly three years before.

Williams' own response, by 1782, was to write an additional 14th letter which remains unpublished. A copy was donated to the Scottish Society of Antiquarians on 2 April 1782 (Smellie 1782, part 1, p. 95) but it now seems to be preserved only as a modern transcript (NLS MSS 996), bound in a copy of the octavo version of Williams' 1777 *Account*. In this 14th letter Williams hoped that his 1777 publications would have «prompted others to make such enquiries as would have thrown light upon the ancient history of... the Highlands». It confirmed Williams' failure to find any such vitrified forts south of the River Forth. But he had now found otherwise very similar, but *un*vitrified, forts at Duntarf in West Lothian and Dundonald in Ayrshire. He described these in this 14th letter, and emphatically concluded that no volcanic action could ever have been involved in the vitrification of such forts.

Williams' view that the vitrification was man-made, and never volcanic in origin, may have made him less inclined than many then to perceive volcanic evidence elsewhere in Scotland (see review by Kirwan 1799, pp. 263-280). By the time Williams came to Italy, the abate Tommaselli could note of him, in February 1794, «sento che Williams non riconosce per vulcanizzati gli Euganei. Gli ho fatto scrivere per la [signora] Treves a Udine una fortiss[im]a lettera, che l'obbligava ad esibirmi la prova, ma che siano prove e non parole. Costui venne a rovesciarci in capo l'idee» (Giormani 1996, footnote 99). Maybe Williams' later resistance to such volcanic ideas was one result of his experiences with these forts in Scotland?

The debate on vitrification proved both intense and country-wide, with Daines Barrington publishing a paper in London in 1782 (Barrington 1782). The debate was particularly strong in Scotland where those pillars of the Scottish Enlightenment, the economist Adam Smith (1723-1790) and the geologist James Hutton were also involved, in 1778 and 1786 (see Mossner & Ross 1977, p. 292, Eyles and Eyles 1951, p. 336 & Jones 1984, p. 231). Alexander Fraser Tytler (1747-1813), Professor of Civil History at Edinburgh University, read a detailed paper in 1783 (Tytler 1790) but not published until 1790. This concluded that the vitrification must have been both destructive and accidental, not constructive. But Robert Riddell (died 1794), friend of the Scottish poet Robert Burns, soon came down strongly in favour of their having been constructive and man-made in 1790 (Riddell 1792).

Williams' original book had discussed the origins of the forts which he had discovered in several parts of the Highlands (Piggott 1976, pp. 148-50 & 174). Williams seems to have been the first to have considered their origin and the first to have suggested that such vitrified walls had been purposefully, and constructively, «vitrified» by their creators. The intense debate on their origin is still not resolved. A first resolution had come in 1938 when V.G. Childe & W. Thorneycroft (Childe & Thorneycroft 1938) published a study showing how such effects could indeed be produced experimentally. They thought it was clear that «only rocks containing a suitable mixture of minerals in addition to silica» could be so fused. The mixed Old Red Sandstones which had been used at Finavon, Knock Farril and Craig Phaidrick (all forts originally recognised as «vitrified» by Williams in 1777) proved to be made of just the right materials for such vitrification (see reviews by Cotton 1955, pp. 94-101 and Cunliffe 1991, pp. 13 & 328). But a recent «experiment» for Yorkshire Television now at full scale produced only «limited localized vitrification» in 1980. This encouraged the old view that vitrification was originally a destructive act, one used to destroy such forts (Ralston 1986). It is little wonder that a historian of the Society of Antiquaries of Scotland (Stevenson 1981, p. 38) should have commented that vitrified forts are «a subject liable to excite controversy to this day»...

Williams and the Society of Antiquaries of Scotland (SAS)

The warmth of this Scottish debate on these forts, from 1777 onwards, must also have helped the highly political foundation of the Society of Antiquarians of Scotland in 1780 (Shapin 1974 & Emerson 1988). Its inaugural meeting was held on 14 November 1780 in Edinburgh, and was attended by 14 people, of the 37 whom the Earl of Buchan had invited to discuss the new Society. Among these 14 was Williams, a mineral surveyor elected to the Society that day, as «an associated artist» (a category of membership abolished in 1815; Smellie 1782, part 1, p. v & *Archaeologia Scotica*, 1831, 3, Appendix I, p. 75). He is noticed as an «early active member», by the Society's recent historian (Stevenson 1981, p. 38). The evidence that Buchan may have intended to inaugurate the Society in 1778 (Cant 1981, p. 27), suggests that Williams' 1777 *Vitrified Fort* publications were a greater stimulus to the Society's foundation than is obvious today.

Williams first surviving letter concerning the SAS was written to Buchan on 23 April 1781 (SAS letters in NMS). It discusses Williams' recent composition of «a few practical lectures upon the natural history of the mines, minerals and fossils of Scotland... and the utility of this branch of knowledge». This clearly relates to the early gestation of what later became Williams' published *magnum opus* (Williams 1789), but the proposed lectures seem never to have been delivered to the SAS. Williams next gave a geological specimen to the SAS on 2 October 1781 (Smellie 1782, part 1, p. 69) and his covering letter donating this «curiously marked stone», from his new home Gilmerton, also survives (SAS letters in the NMS).

Williams also read four papers to the SAS (Williams 1781, on Petrifications, 1782 on Marbles, 1783 on Volcanoes & 1792 on a Royal Forest) but only the last was ever published. Williams's second paper, on «marbles and ornamental stones» does at least survive in MSS, in NLS, where it is now headed

«for the Edinburgh Magazine – Notes concerning marbles and other fossils in Scotland communicated to the Earl of Buchan by the late Mr John Williams, mineral surveyor». The pages are numbered, in MSS, 180-183 and are probably survivals from the original copy books of the SAS, which must have passed back to Buchan. Williams' notes relate to:–

1. The Parian marble of Assint [Assynt] in the Highlands 2. A Limestone as white as snow north of Blair Gowrie

3. The «most beautiful Granites in the world» in the Base of Bineves and the hills to the east and on Jasper at Portsoy

4. Agate at Rothes of which the Countess of Finlater had had a snuff box made [Williams' earlier letter on the Parallel Roads of Glen Roy had been to her unfortunate husband]

5. On Porphyrie 3/4th of the way up the ascent of Bineves

6. A Flowered marble near Fort William

7. A Stratum of composite Granite up the shore opposite Kinedore in Moray

8. Another grey grained marble found on the north side of the ferry of Balaihylish [Ballachulish] with specks of lead ore

9. A Stratum of fine white clay on the shore of Sutherland of a «cleansing quality».

Williams ended this paper; «I have many times thought that if large and perfect specimens of these and many other curious and valuable stones found in the Highlands and North of Scotland were collected and made known they would have a tendency to the encouragement and improvement of the arts in Britain. In the course of time, the Highlands might be resorted to from all corners of the polite world for ornamental stones». This essay was apparently never published in the *Edinburgh Magazine*.

The topics of Williams' other two unpublished papers make one wish that they had survived, especially the first. We would then be able to discover what Williams thought of the significance of true fossils in the 1780's. This is a matter of real historical debate today, as far as the work of James Hutton in Scotland and, later, William Smith (1769-1839) in England are concerned. The papers on forests, and on marbles, both clearly relate to Williams' work for the CFAE, on which he had been active until 1776. Williams' view that forests had been too long neglected in the Highlands can be dated back to at least 1771 (Smith 1982, p. 98).

A second long letter to Buchan, dated 17 July 1783 (SAS letters in the NMS), was inspired by the news that «the noise of war will now cease», with the ending of the American War of Independence, but that it would instead bring the new necessity of «emigration from the Highlands». The letter gives Williams' ideas on «how the Highlanders may be kept at home». This was by improving the fishing industry on the west coasts of the area. This was the subject of the paper he later presented to the HAS, as we shall see, but which was only published in 1799 (Williams 1799a), after his death. Williams' other two papers to the SAS, on fossils and volcanoes, probably relate more to his new career as a mining surveyor and overseer, especially at Gilmerton Colliery near Edinburgh. This had started in about 1778 and to which we now turn.

Williams' work as a Scottish mineral surveyor 1776-1793

Williams' work for the CFAE had been abandoned on 21 February 1776. Anderson noted that Williams, after this, now took «a coal mine at West Calder», a town now in West Lothian, west of Edin-

burgh. Williams's later connection with Gilmerton Colliery then supposedly dated after this, from «about 1775» (Anderson 1863, p. 132).
Clearly both dates are too early. Further information comes from
some MSS writings of the Earl of Buchan. Buchan lived at Kirkhill,
near Broxburn from 1768 to 1788. Kirkhill was a place about which
Williams had submitted a report to the CFAE in 1767, on a lime
quarry there. Buchan noted that Williams

> «coming down into Scotland he there married and becoming attached to
> the country engaged himself in some coal projects in my neighbourhood at
> Kirkhill on the Coallieries of Sr W. Cuninghame of Livingstone. Finding
> him a well informed man I had him often with me & recommended him to
> Mr Erskine of Dux as overseer of Gilmerton Coallery where he was placed
> & did great credit to himself by his conduct» (NLS MSS 996), adding «I
> found him [Williams] employed in working a coal belonging to Sir William
> Cuninghame of Levingstone» (NLS MSS 1810 f 148). Livingstone lies to
> the south-west of Kirkhall.

The name of the first mine that Williams worked at, after his work
for the CFAE, is recorded by Neill (1814a, p. 256) who noted that Williams had first «superintended the coal-works at Blackburn near West
Calder». It seems that Williams must have been here over the years
1776-7, since Neill (probably more accurately than Anderson) wrote
that Williams next «became overseer and factor at Gilmerton Colliery,
belonging to Mr [Robert] Baird [died 1828] in 1778» and that he remained here «above thirteen years» i.e. until 1791 (Neill 1814a, p.
256). Since Baird was later the dedicatee of Williams' most important
publication, in 1790, it becomes clear that Williams' years at Gilmerton were the most significant of his Scottish coal-mining career.

Gilmerton is much nearer Edinburgh than Blackburn. Indeed it
was a colliery which supplied that city with coal. This proximity had
helped Williams develop the connections with the learned and antiquarian circles of Edinburgh that we have, and will again, note. Williams' appointment to Gilmerton in the first place had probably been
helped through his CFAE work, since we find that Williams' old
CFAE partner, the engineer James Watt, also shared a mutual connection. Watt's personal archive (now in Birmingham City Library) contains a sketch of the «Levels of Gilmerton Coal Mines» dated 1774.

But the main impetus for the Gilmerton appointment had clearly
come from his new patron, the Earl of Buchan, David Stuart Erskine,
who further recorded that

> «Mr John Williams, Mineral Surveyor, made himself known to me first
> at Kirkhill in W[est] Lothian where I resided from the year 1768 to 1788, I

found him employed in working a coal belonging to Sir Will[ia]m Cuninghame of Livingstone & as he seemed to me a worthy man and possessed of a great deal of practical knowledge in Geology tho' without much Science I invited him to reside some little time with me at Kirkhill & put such books into his hands as I thought might be usefull to him.–afterwards I recommended him thro' Mr Erskine of Dux, to the family of Baird of Newbyth by which he was appointed overseer on the Coal of Gilmerton where he resided many years & conducted himself with satisfaction to his employer. During this period of his employment at Gilmerton he came occasionally to Kirkhill where I encouraged him to commit his observations to paper and to make farther research in the Coal Country adjoining to Gilmerton» (NLS MSS 1810 f 148-149).

After Williams' varied work with the SAS he seems to have plunged more and more into the world of coal and mining, from his new base at Gilmerton. Here the limited patronage of the Earl of Buchan was to be crucial, as Buchan's own MSS confirm. With such encouragement, Williams was able to issue, late in 1780 and probably after his election to the SAS, his first printed *Proposals for executing by Subscription a TOPOGRAPHICAL ENGRAVED MAP of the coal country in Scotland*, at a scale of one inch to a mile, with a to-be-printed *Tract with Observations and a Journal of his intended Survey* (Williams 1780). These *Proposals* were presented to the Members of the SAS on 16 January 1781, not by Williams, «too modest to call the attention of the Society to the project», but by his old friend, the secretary James Cummyng. Cummyng noted how «remarkable [it was], that amidst all the attentions to natural history, since the days of Lord Bacon, in Britain beyond all other countries, nothing has been written on the subject of coal, except by a native of this country Mr Sinclair» [George Sinclar (died 1696)]. Despite Cummyng's patriotic call noting the importance of Williams' enquiries to Scotland (*Scots Magazine* 43, p. 51, January 1781), neither this map nor its *Tract* were ever published, through lack of sufficient subscribers. The one hundred needed, at 3 guineas each, never came forward.

Williams' next mining project was to have been different. It was to have an intended concentration on the technology of mining. This was the subject of an undated appeal to the Earl of Buchan (NLS MSS 1810 f 148), and must date from between 1781 and 1787. This appeal has been annotated by Buchan: –«Proposals by John Williams, Mineral Surveyor, for a Coal Progress thro' Scotland». It carries MSS numbers 394-396 and reads

«It gives me pleasure that you think the small treatise I have begun upon the Theory of Coal may be of use, when it is so far compleated as my poor abilities are cabable [sic]. When I began to write that paper, I proposed giving some hints about the practice but when I began to enter upon that branch, I found it was impossible for me to go any farther with matter of fact, than the few works I had seen or been concerned in, which I thought too confined for a matter of such importance[,] as circumstances required the practise to vary considerably in different places.

This reflection strongly suggested to me, that in order to [write] a generally useful treatise upon the Theory and practice of Colliery, a Tour or progress through all the coal works great and small in the South & North East and West of Scotland is neccessary – and a distinct account should be given of all the seams of coal in each work. Their quality and thickness &c their method of working and conveying the Coals to the Bank and the success of these methods. – To give a particular history of the interruptions or troubles in each work such as dykes, gashes, slips &c, and their method of getting the better of them. – The history of the roof and pavement of each seam, with other remarkable concomitant Strata, their method of securing the Roof if tender, and of guarding against the bad effects of a swelling pavement.

To give a compleat history of all the Machinary [sic] about each work, for drawing water and Coals, and their success. – Their method of conveying fresh Air and of guarding against the pernicious effects of damps or wild fire. – The price of the coal, noting the weight or measure and the quality of the comodity [sic] and every other circumstance relating to each work, useful or curious. The more I reflected upon this thought the more I was perswaded [sic] of the real utility of such a progress, and therefore I resolved to set about it, so soon as it is in my power. – but this would be attended with considerable expence, as it might be necessary to go down two or three days into some large and complicated works and would take some time to note down accuratly [sic] everything above ground. – I am convinced that such a Tour faithfully performed, and the history sensibly wrote would be of great use to Society, as every Coalmasters in any immergency [sic] could look into the book and see what is the practice or method used in other places in such a case. – And if the book was wrote with any spirit and taste it would not be void of entertainment, as it would when joined with the theoratical [sic] parts be a compleat history of that material branch of the mineral kingdom.

The first part would be an amusement and a guide to the Country Gentleman who wishes to know if there is Coal in his Estate, and your Lordship hath seen already that great care is taken that he is not amused by false appearances.

The second part will be more immediatly useful for Coalmasters and such as are going to open coalworks, as they can take a view of the practice in other works, compare it with their own in similar cases, and judge which is best – and it may be a pleasant amusement for some to have a compleat view of the internal wealth of the Country in this instance especially now when coal is become so great an article of commerce.

It may be proper in this progress to get the best history that can be procured of deserted works, which may be of singular use in future, when posterity would wish to know if such coals are worth opening and the circumstances which are for, or against it, and I cannot help thinking the Book in general would be of considerable utility in this respect; as there are but few Coalowners that keep a Journal or history and that book would be an universal printed history or record which may be examined at any time».

Williams' wish to then record details of «deserted coal works» for posterity addressed a real problem, and one by which British coal mines have been bedeviled ever since. It shows again how much of a pioneer in such matters Williams was. This seems to be the first such suggestion. But, as Williams' new *Prospectus* issued in 1787 noted, this second project had had to be abandoned by then as well, again through lack of patronage. Williams then wrote of his having

«once thought of a treatise of the practice of mining and coalery; but [that]... this would be a work of great labour which cannot be properly executed without an expensive progress to collate everything necessary»

But Williams was nothing if not persistent and at least his major *Treatise upon Coal*, noted as already in progress in 1780 and 1781, *was* finally published in 1790. It had been helped into print by another of the enlightened Societies which so characterised Scotland at this time, the Highland and Agricultural Society (HAS).

Williams & the Highland and Agricultural Society (HAS)

In 1785 the HAS, newly founded in 1784, offered its first premiums of 5 Gold Medals, one of which was to be for «supplying the want of coal» in the Highland region (Ramsay 1879, pp. 102-3). At least two entries were received in the competition for this medal (itself a significant fact), of which extracts or the complete essay were both eventually published. This may indicate that both were awarded Gold Medals, but the Society's records are defective. One of the gold medals was certainly awarded to Williams' «Essay on Coal», which seems likely to have been that presented to the HAS by Dr [Robert] Grant [whose Edinburgh University M.D. had been awarded in 1783], on 3 June 1785. This Essay was certainly awarded a HAS Premium on 2 December 1785 (Sederunt Book of the HAS). This «Essay» (Williams 1799b) was a foundation for Williams' much expanded two volume work, *The Natural History of the Mineral Kingdom*, dated 1789. But as his HAS prize essay of 1785 was not published until 1799, well after his death in 1795, it can have had hardly any influence, by comparison with his book (Williams 1789 [recte 1790]).

In a letter in Venetian archives (A.S.V. Inquisitori di Stato, b. 1248, fasc. III, c. 398, Alvise Zenobio a Lorenzo Marzari, 17 giugno 1794) his later Italian patron records that Williams had by then won «ripetuti premi che ebbe dalla Società delle Arti in Scozia» and so clearly more than the one for this «Essay on Coal». The Scottish Society of Arts here is clearly only an Italian confusion for the HAS. So Williams must have won a second Premium and/or Gold Medal for his other essay, which the HAS again only published in 1799 in the same volume of *Prize Essays* (Williams 1799a). This was his «Suggestions for promoting and improving the Fisheries upon the coasts of the Highlands». As we have seen, this had been the topic of a long letter to the Earl of Buchan in July 1783 (SAS letters in the NMS). So it is likely that this too had been read to the HAS in its early years. Jean Dunlop's history of such Scottish Fishery improvements hardly mentions Williams' pioneering part in their development (Dunlop 1978, p. 230).

Perhaps inspired by the fact that his HAS Coal Essay still remained unpublished, Williams issued, from Gilmerton, his new *Prospectus and Proposals for publishing an Essay towards a Natural History of the Mineral Kingdom in Two Parts* in January 1787 (Williams 1787). This was for the same *Treatise upon Coal*, which had been reported as in «great forwardness» in 1780 (Williams 1780). Apart from its new title, which gives further evidence that Williams was the author of the earlier HAS Prize Essay, this *Prospectus* listed the intended contents of his planned two volume work. It was then to be in only two parts, not the three later published in 1790. Part 2 of the latter, «on the natural history of mineral veins», was clearly a post-1787 addition. Part 1 was also then to have included a reprint of «Sinclair's *Treatise upon Coal*», supposedly published in 1762. The correct date is 1672, when George Sinclar who died in 1696, had published his book *The Hydrostaticks*. This included a short *History of Coal* among the *Miscellany Observations* (see Briggs 1925). The fact that Sinclair's work was already over a hundred years old in 1789, was perhaps the real reason it was not eventually reprinted by Williams. But its omission has since misled Briggs into thinking Williams had been unaware of Sinclar's work!

Williams's 1787 *Prospectus* noted that «Britain receives more benefits from the bowels of the earth than perhaps any other nation» and that he had «spent more of my time in the mines, and among rocks and mountains, glens and precipices, than perhaps any other mineral man on earth». His aims in publishing the book were

1) to help «gentleman of landed property... by guarding them against imposition from ignorance or craft» and

2) to improve the knowledge of the mineral kingdom, because «Britain is a great mineral country, and yet mineralogy is not taught in our universities, which I presume would be a very useful branch of learning».

Williams duly sent a copy of his 1787 *Prospectus* to the HAS, «requesting the aid and countenance of the Society in reference to a publication proposed by him related to Mines and Minerals». The Society's Board of Directors on 2 February 1787 only «resolved that presentation of this work shall be taken into consideration when published» (Sederunt Book of the HAS).

Williams' book The Natural History of the Mineral Kingdom *of 1790.*

The Earl of Buchan noted the partial genesis of this book:

«Williams had been formerly employed on a Coalliery in Sutherland [at Brora] and had made an extensive mineral survey in the Highlands of Scotland of which he had kept a Journal. From the whole mass of his Journals kept for 30 years Mr Williams drew up his history of the Mineral Kingdom which he published in the year 1789» (NLS MSS 1810 f 149).

This work was published in two volumes, and in 1789 according to its Title Pages. It is Williams' major and most geological work. It filled a real vacuum in English and European geological and mining literature. It was dedicated to Robert Baird (who died 1828) of Newbyth, East Lothian. But it actually appeared only in 1790. Williams' MSS letters in the NLS (MSS 996), separately presenting copies of volume 1 and 2 to Lord Buchan (one of his most important patrons), are dated 18 February and 19 March 1790. The first of February to the Earl notes: –

«the 1st volume of my natural history of the mineral kingdom is now printed & I have got a dozen copies put together one of which I beg leave to send to your Lordship herewith. The 2d vol is in the press and I expect will be soon ready».... The 1st is «sent now before the work is published». Williams notes that he is a «rustic philosopher» and asks Buchan to «recommend it to your very extensive acquaintance». A Post Script notes «I am anxious for yr Lord's opinion of my refutation of Dr Hutton's Theory of the Earth in my Preface».

In the second letter, of 19 March 1790 to the Earl, Williams again calls himself «a rustic philosopher» when sending volume 2 of *Natural History*, hoping it «deserves your approbation and patronage». Williams notes that «the inferences deduced from my observations, relating to the universal deluge are a little uncommon but I trust you will find they agree with the phenomena of nature». He concludes «I had your Lordship's promise long ago to aid me in the success of this work and I now entreat your countenance and patronage. I think it should be of utility to country gentlemen and you have a very extensive neighbourhood of them».

Williams' donation of his work to the SAS on 9 February 1790, must, from the above, relate only to the first volume (*Archaeologia Scotica*, 1831, 3, Appendix II, p. 30). Notices of the general availability of both volumes further afield, like that in the *Derby Mercury* of 8 July 1790, record it was only available «this day». But one gets the impression from its availability today that the book did achieve wide sales.

A short addition to the book had been made in 1788, just before publication, because of the first extended appearance of James Hutton's later famous *Theory of the Earth* (Hutton 1788), to which Williams took exception, largely on theological grounds. Williams, as we have seen, was an enthusiastic adherent of the Universal Deluge as a geological agent and cause of stratification. This new section of this book was in any event somewhat of a diversion, as Williams had rather little interest in such theoretical matters and was clearly more interested in his «observations». His attack against Hutton had been inspired because Williams was «more happy to live in a full persuasion... of admiring God in his works», than he thought Hutton was. To deny God, as he thought Hutton had done, brought his final outburst «let us turn our eyes from [this] horrid abyss»; the abyss of Hutton's imagination (Williams 1789, Preface). This outburst later earned Williams a small place in the battles between Huttonian and Neptunian geologists which took place early in the next century. The leading British mineral surveyor of the next generation, William Smith also criticised Williams' diluvial explanation of how strata had originated (Cox 1942, p. 89).

Williams' 1790 work deserves a fuller analysis elsewhere (a short summary is given by Cotterell 1985), but one modern historian has been less than enthusiastic, noting it only as «the one exception to the unhelpful empiricism of [British] mining guides... [but] which through sheer thoroughness almost bridges the gap between a mining treatise and a work of geology» (Porter 1973, p. 337). But Porter here revealed his own lack of historical awareness, when complaining that «Williams has no clear idea of the order of strata or general geology even of [Scotland]», when in 1789/1790 all such knowledge still remained to be uncovered! To demonstrate how very embryonic the state of knowledge of the stratigraphy of all the British Coal Measures then was, one has only to look at Richard Kirwan's almost contemporary paper «Observations on Coal Mines», read in 1789 (Kirwan 1790).

More recently Dennis Dean has correctly claimed that Williams misrepresented Hutton's theory. He also noted that, of the eleven pages that the *Monthly Review* had devoted to reviewing Williams' book (Chisholme and De Luc 1791), the first six concerned Williams' analysis of Hutton. This suggested to Dean that this «may have been the most influential portion of the [Williams] book» (Dean 1992, pp. 50-1 & 240). But, since one of the authors of the *Monthly's* review – Jean André De Luc (1727-1817) – was then involved in a bitter polemic with Hutton, he had his own reasons for giving, in this response, such an emphasis in a review of Williams' book.

Russian overtures to Williams

Williams, according to his grandson William Anderson, duly sent copies of *Mineral Kingdom* to

«George the Third [1738-1820], the unfortunate Louis the Sixteenth of France [1754-1793] and... the Empress Catherine of Russia [1729-1796]. The two former never acknowledged receipt. The Empress was the only one of these potentates who took any notice of the gift.., it is worthy of note that she patronized literary and scientific men, and invited them to her court. Mr Williams received a communication from St Petersburg, requesting him to proceed to Russia to survey minerals for that Empire» (Anderson 1863, p. 132).

The lack of response from English and French quarters is, however, very understandable! George III was busy recovering from his first illness of 1788-1789 (Macalpine & Hunter 1969) and Louis XVI was busy trying to save his head, which was duly removed, by the guillotine, on 21 January 1793 (Hardman 1993).

Williams' Welsh nephew adds that the Empress of Russia also «rewarded him with a gold medal of four ounces weight, with an appropriate inscription» in 1792 (Davies 1814, volume 1, p. 324). This arrived while Williams was in Italy, according to his new Italian patron, Alvise Zenobio,

«Credete ch'egli è uno dei più eminenti soggetti d'Inghilterra [sic!] in questa materia, in prova di che vi è il suo libro e i ripetuti premi che ebbe dalla Società delle Arti in Scozia, vi è una medaglia d'oro del valore di 60 zecchini [che] ricevè in questi giorni dall'Imperatrice di Russia...» (A.S.V. Inquisitori di stato, b. 1248, fasc. III, c. 398, Alvise Zenobio a Lorenzo Marzari, 17 giugno 1794).

This delayed receipt of Williams' prized Russian medal, while in Italy, must have helped to cause William Anderson's later confusion about Williams' true connection, or lack of one, with Russia. For Anderson incorrectly assumed, as another example of the ignorance that some members of the Williams family already had about their ancestor, that John Williams had taken up the invitation from the Empress to go to survey for minerals in Russia. Thus Anderson claimed that his grandfather had «accordingly left Scotland for that purpose [surveying in Russia] about the end of 1792, or early in 1793». But in order to equate this episode with other facts, as then known, Anderson was then forced to claim that Williams must have been on his way home to Scotland, after a supposed two and a half year stay in Russia, when he was «seized with a fever and died at Verona» in Italy in 1795 (Anderson 1863, p. 132 & 1865, p. 357)! Chronological evidence shows that Williams could never even have set off for Russia. The geographical evidence of his supposed return from Russia to Scotland via Italy-through a Europe seized with revolutionary fear – shows it as equally impossible. Williams had instead got trapped in a spider's-web world which then surrounded the Venetian Count Alvise Zenobio (1757-1817), in Britain.

Williams' departure from Scotland for Italy, via England

Williams, according to the slightly better informed Earl of Buchan, «having given displeasure to his employers or their agents [at Gilmerton]... was engaged by Count Zenobio to survey his lands in Italy where he died in the year 1791-2» (NLS MSS 996). The reasons for the «displeasure» here are as unclear as the date of Williams' death is wrong. But two possible causes for his departure can be revealed. One is that Williams might have absented himself from his work at Gilmerton without permission. We certainly find that in «1790 he visited his native parish in Wales» [after an absence of at least 40 years] bringing «with him his newly published *Mineral Kingdom*» (Davies 1814, volume 1, p. 324).

Another possible reason might be because «about the year 1791, he left Gilmerton and became engaged, along with the late Dr James

Anderson, in conducting *The Bee*, a periodical work then publishing at Edinburgh, and which acquired considerable reputation» (Neill 1814a, p. 257). The standard study of *The Bee*, a literary and scientific periodical published from December 1790 to 1794, makes no mention of Williams' part (Mullett, 1967), but we do know that Anderson and Williams had been in contact since at least 1774, when Anderson had learnt of Williams' discovery of the ancient Highland «vitrified» fortifications, on which Anderson read two papers to the SAS (Mullett 1968, p. 105). The *Prospectus* for *The Bee*, issued in Edinburgh in August 1790, is equally silent about any part Williams was intended to play (copy in BL).

Neill (1814a, p. 257) in his turn, claimed that Williams, after leaving Scotland, «spent nearly two years in travelling through England with Count Zenobia [sic], visiting all the great manufactures and mines of that country». The timing of this claim is impossible for we know that Williams was still working in Scotland for the Member of Parliament for Linlithgow, Sir William Augustus Cunynghame (1747-1828) Bart, well into 1793. This is the same man as one of Williams' earliest employers in Scotland, as noted above by the Earl of Buchan. We know of these final activities in Scotland from Williams' printed *Journal* of Cunynghame's commission which was published late in 1793 (Williams 1793). This gives daily details of Williams' activities on his Mineral Survey of Cunynghame's southern Scottish estates, from 18 March 1793 to 29 April 1793. Only when this had been finished, and written up, could Williams have been free to accompany Zenobio anywhere in England.

Our single Welsh source proves much more reliable on this stage of Williams' complex life. Davies noted that it only was for two *months*, «in July and August 1793, [that Williams] accompanied Count Zenobio, a Venetian, through the counties of Derby and York, inspecting manufactures, machineries, and especially mine works» (Davies 1814, volume 1, p. 324). The accuracy of these dates, which so exactly follow the end of Williams' 1793 work in Scotland, can be confirmed from other sources. For, in June 1793, a newly married couple from Dorset reported having recently met Count Zenobia [sic] at Matlock in Derbyshire (Anon 1903, p. 143). Then on 10 August 1793, Zenobio, now with Williams, called on the Derbyshire geologist White Watson (1760-1835) at Bakewell in Derbyshire. Watson's Common Place Book records that «Count Zenobio and Mr Williams, author on Mineralogy, called on W.W. and [they] stayed some time in the neighbourhood» (Watson MSS in private hands). Williams had clearly spent the months of July and August 1793 touring with his new Italian sponsor, Count Alvise Zenobio. It had been the *Mineral*

Kingdom, with Williams' prizes and medals, that had established Williams' credentials with Zenobio as such an «eminent» mineral surveyor.

Davies concludes that «under an engagement with [Zenobio], [Williams], perhaps inconsiderately, at this period of life [he was aged 61] undertook a journey in September, 1793, through Flanders, Germany and the Tyrolese, into the Venetian territory, to give his opinion of the mineral wealth of the Count's estates» (Davies 1814, volume 1, pp. 324-5). To this sad (mis)adventure we now turn.

Count Alvise Zenobio (1757-1817) and coal mining

The same Dorset couple who had noted Zenobio's visit to Matlock also recorded how Zenobio

«is so well known everywhere that you must have heard of him; he is continually writing and never receives less than a dozen letters in a day, he reads them only once and burns them all immediately... He is a Venetian nobleman and is banished Venice for having made himself too busy in political affairs. He is soon to be recalled to give an account of himself... He is a very pleasant, well informed man and has travelled all over the world» (Anon 1903, pp. 143-4).

Zenobio's destructive habit may have been because he was liable to be regarded as some sort of industrial spy at this time, which was «revolutionary» both in industrial and political terms, in a Britain highly sensitive to how much it was being spied on industrially. The scale of such «industrial espionage» from just the Venetian perspective is wonderfully revealed in Paolo Preto's new book (Preto 1994). Whatever the reason, the apparent lack of any Zenobio archive in England has certainly made this historian's task more difficult.

The history of attempts for coal in Italy deserves more attention than can be given here. Tuscany provided an early focus, as described by Mori (1976). Later the Tuscan Giovanni V. M. Fab[b]roni (1752-1822) became heavily involved in further attempts to find coal in the Tuscano from 1791 on, using English expertise and tools supplied through Sir Joseph Banks and the Wedgwood family of Staffordshire, whose archives yield new light on this episode (see Fabroni 1790). These earlier Tuscan activities coupled with British efforts to encourage proper Mineral Surveys of British Counties «ever since 1793» (Farey 1814, p. 335 & Kirwan 1811), the same year that Williams left for Italy, may have inspired both Zenobio's involvement in

Italian mineral surveying and his invitation to Williams to go out to Italy.

Count Alvise Zenobio was a nobleman of a famous Venetian family. He is a fascinating, if badly known, character. He is the «Carlo Zenobio» referred to by Giormani (1990, p. 221). Some short biographical details are given by Cicogna (1824-53, volume 3 (1830), pp. 274-5 & volume 4 (1834), pp. 633-4) and by Maggiolo (1983, p. 372). Virgilio Giormani and I hope to publish a longer study of his extraordinarily political Anglo-Italian career in due course, with special emphasis on his «revolutionary» activities, both in France and Britain. It was these which caused his eventual imprisonment by the British legislature and forced Williams' Italian mineral surveying commission to end in such disaster.

Zenobio had been based in, or was a frequent visitor to, England from at least 1783 (see Dawson 1958, pp. 214 & 843), so he had a long connection with that country. The revolutionary leanings for which he was expelled from Britain in 1795, did not stop him later publishing his work *Idea di una perfetta repubblica di David Hume* in 1798/9 in Milan (in addition to his other political tracts listed by Cicogna and in the North American *National Union Catalog*) or later returning to live in Britain once more. David Hume (1711-1776)'s *Idea of a Perfect Commonwealth* had been first published in 1752, as part of his *Political Discourses* (Hendel 1953, pp. 145-158). The original Venetian edition had been issued with a letter to Zenobio's mother's brother Alvise Emo (Venturi 1983, p. 352), so there were already family connections. John Williams was as much a product of the Scottish Enlightenment as Hume, and perhaps such early Italian-Scottish connections may even explain some of the later links between Zenobio and Williams?

Zenobio seems to have settled in England in 1782. In 1788, he was elected, as a resident of Pall Mall in London, a «perpetual member» of the Royal Society of Arts there (*teste* letter from Susan Bennett, RSA archivist, 27 March 1995). Zenobio was greatly interested in restoring the Venetian Empire and saw himself as allied politically with Britain against Napoleonic ambition, even if others did not. Zenobio was particularly interested in applying such «Useful Arts» as Williams possessed, to advance these Venetian aspirations.

We know of Zenobio's movements in Britain from a number of sources. Late in November 1791 he had returned to London from another visit to Paris (see B.M.C.V., Alvise Pisani a Giuseppe Albrizzi, 14 novembre 1791). By 1 April 1792 he was in «Judburg in Iscozia» [Jedburgh, Roxburghshire in the Scottish Borders] (A.S.V., Inquisitori di stato, b. 1248 fasc. III, c. 355, Zenobio a Lorenzo Marzari, 1 aprile 1792). On 10 July the Venetian resident in London, Orazio Lavezari, reported on «la absenza del predetto [Zenobio] da questa Capitale, il quale si ritrova da due settimane nella vasta e distante provincia del Yorkshire» (A.S.V., Inquisitori di stato, b. 444, Orazio Lavezari agli Inquisitori). By 24 July 1792 Lavezari could now report of him that «continuate le più diligenti ricerche, vengo di rilevare in oggi, che da alcuni giorni se n'era partito da quella provincia e se n'era andato in Iscozia fino ad Eidemburgo» (A.S.V., Inquisitori di stato, b. 444, dispacci, Orazio Lavezari agli Inquisitori).

By 26 July 1792 Zenobio had duly reached Edinburgh (A.S.V., Inquisitori di stato, b. 1248 fasc. III, c. 354, Zenobio a Lorenzo Marzari, 26 luglio 1792). By 31 July 1792 Zenobio had arrived at Taymouth, in Perthshire where he must have been staying with the new Earl of Breadalbane, John Campbell (1762-1834), at Taymouth Castle. That same day he wrote to Sir John Sinclair (1754-1835), the soon-to-be President of the British Board of Agriculture, about all the various agricultural improvements he wished to introduce into his Venetian territories. Sinclair rather ambiguously described Zenobio as «lively and good humoured and... impressed with such high ideas of the British character, as rendered him extremely unpopular in his own country» (Sinclair 1831, volume 2, pp. 395-7).

In an important letter of 8 August 1792, «dalla campagna in Inghilterra», Zenobio notes

«Ho terminato sollecitamente il mio giro nella Scozia;.... Ho pure ritrovato un superintendente di miniere tanto di carbon fossile come di metalli, ma siccome l'oggetto è sopratutto per publico benefizio e la spesa è grande, così attendo risposta da alcuni signori a cui ho scritto prima d'impiegarlo» (A.S.V., Inquisitori di stato, b. 1248 fasc. III, c. 357, Zenobio a Lorenzo Marzari, 8 agosto 1792).

The unusual qualifications of the «superintendente» here must refer to John Williams. This would mean that he had already been chosen for the Italian post Zenobio now had in mind. They must have met while Zenobio was in Edinburgh in the previous month. By 11 September 1792, Zenobio had returned to London (A.S.V., Inquisitori di stato, b. 156, lettera n. 220, Zenobio a Orazio Lavezari). On 18 September 1792 Pisani's letter to Giuseppe Albrizzi notes that «il nostro parente Zenobio è ritornato in campagna dove credo resterà qualche tempo, e non mi pare già tanto disposto al ritornare a Venezia» (B.M.C.V., ms. P.D., 261 b II, fasc. VIII, lettera n. 43, Alvise Pisani a Giuseppe Albrizzi, 18 settembre 1792).

On 2 October 1792 the owner of the Privilege for Searching and

Extracting Coal in the Venetian State, in a clear response to the letter that Zenobio must have written him on 8 August 1792 (as noted above), notified the Chiefs of the «Consiglio dei Dieci» that, in hopes of decreasing the cost of extracting coal from «the local mountains», he had sent letters both to England and to Germany, seeking a skilled person and that perhaps a person from England and another from Germany had set off for Italy already (A.S.V., Deputati alle miniere: suppliche e notifiche dal 1786 al 1796). From this it sounds as if Zenobio's activities had already resulted in a semi-official invitation being extended to John Williams? But it is equally clear that Williams would certainly not yet have been able to set out for Italy.

In April [1793] Zenobio informed Lorenzo Marzari

«Conduco meco una famosa persona per lavorare le miniere di carbone ed altre di metalli e intendo di farli visitare le montagne che si trovano nel Tirolo,... poi farle esaminare tutte le miniere dello Stato Veneto che siano in pessima condizione dall'ignoranza di chi le lavora ma il grande oggetto è quello del carbon fossile» (A.S.V., Inquisitori di stato, b. 1248 fasc. III, Zenobio a Lorenzo Marzari, 12 aprile [1793]. His letter continued «la ricchezza dell'Inghilterra viene sopratutto dalle immense miniere di questo carbone... Il carbon fossile quì in Inghilterra fa il più bel fuoco che imaginar si possa e va meno alla testa del fuoco delle nostre legne forti. Condurrò meco un giardiniere inglese...»

The end of 1792 and the beginning of 1793 had seen, in the wake of the now «revolutionary» activities taking place in France, the introduction of a new British «Act for establishing Regulations respecting Aliens arriving in this Kingdom or resident, in certain cases» (Goodwin, 1979, pp. 266-7 & *Gentleman's Magazine*, January 1793, pp. 83-5). The outbreak of the long war which was declared by France on Britain and Holland on 1 February 1793 found Zenobio still in London. By April/May 1793 Zenobio was again back touring «in the English country» (B.M.C.V., ms. P.D., 261 b II, fasc. IX, lettere n. 16, 17 & 22, Alvise Pisani a Giuseppe Albrizzi, 2 aprile a 14 maggio 1793).

By July and August 1793, as we have seen, Zenobio was touring in company with John Williams «through the counties of Derby and York, inspecting manufactures, machineries, and especially mine works». On 16 June 1793 Zenobio and Williams were together at Buxton in Derbyshire, and the former was writing

«Vi confermo che fra poche settimane certamente partirò per Venezia e prenderò la strada di Germania ed il Tirolo..» and that «questa macchina a fumo è una delle più belle invenzioni di mecanica in questo secolo... il mineralogista che viene con me [Williams] ne ha credo qualche cognizione. In quanto a questo mineralogista la spesa è grande, ma sono danari ben impiegati. È mia intenzione di andar seco a fare una visita di tutte le miniere nello Stato Veneto... In quanto alle montagne del Tirolo, non so persuadermi che non vi siano vari minerali e sopra tutto di carbone fossile, che sono... e nelle valli tra le montagne sopra tutto ove vi siano boschi; nel mio passagio dunque farà questo Mineralogista una visita» (A.S.V., Inquisitori di stato, b. 1248, fasc. III, c. 374, Zenobio a Lorenzo Marzari, 16 giugno 1793).

In this same latter Zenobio notes

«Condurrò... come vi dissi un giardiniere, ma desidero che questi sia pure agricoltore onde introdurre alcuni metodi di migliorare i terreni sopra tutto col mezzo di varie sorta di marne, che pur credo sinora poco conosciute in Italia.... [un] coltivatore inglese fece ultimamente un viaggio in Italia e in Francia per esaminarne lo stato dell'agricoltura e non potete credere quante sfavorevoli relazioni ne dice».

This last must be a reference to Arthur Young (1741-1820), the new Secretary of the Board of Agriculture in Britain, with whom Zenobio must also have been in touch. Young had started travelling in Italy in September 1789. The later publication of his *Travels* there provided a fascinating insight into the state of the country then, as viewed through English eyes (Young 1915 & Gazley 1973, pp. 246-255).

On 29 June 1793 Zenobio and Williams were now in Matlock, Derbyshire (A.S.V., Inquisitori di stato, b. 1248, fasc. III, Zenobio a Lorenzo Marzari, 29 giugno 1793). The next of Zenobio's letters is dated 1 August 1793 and is from Bakewell, also in Derbyshire, where as we have seen, he and Williams were visiting the English mineralogist White Watson. He notes

«In quanto alle mie intenzioni per il lavoro delle miniere, mi pare che vi trovate in un grosso inganno. Non è per cercar oro o altri preziosi metalli, che conduco meco a grossa spesa un professore inglese egli è per il carbon fossile che faccio... intrapresa, mentre questo materiale è il primo mobile delle manifatture che gl'inglesi devono la loro superiorità in ogni genere di lavori; che perisca in Inghilterra il carbon fossile e addio le loro manifatture, addio le loro ricchezze» (A.S.V., Inquisitori di stato, b. 1248, fasc. III, c. 378, Zenobio a Lorenzo Marzari, 1 agosto 1793)

On 19 September 1793 Pisani could report to Albrizzi that «il Zenobio è ora a Londra» (B.M.C.V., ms. P.D., 261 b II, fasc. IX, lettera n. 48, Alvise Pisani a Giuseppe Albrizzi, 19 settembre 1793). So Zenobio and John Williams must by then have travelled down to London from Derbyshire together. Later in that same month Williams set off, with only a coachman, through Flanders, Germany and the Tyrol to survey the Count's Italian estates, in expectation that his patron would follow him there shortly. Williams' departure from England would soon prove to have been most unfortunately timed.

A new letter from Zenobio dated 14 November 1793 now reveals that Zenobio was suffering problems in financing his many «schemes» (A.S.V., Inquisitori di stato, b. 1248, fasc. III, c. 383-384v, Zenobio a Lorenzo Marzari, 14 novembre 1793). Then on 23 November 1793 one of his fellow Venetian Procurators was the subject of an exciting letter from the temporary Consul in charge of British affairs in Venice, John Watson. The letter was to William Wyndham Grenville (1759-1834), who had introduced the Aliens Bill the year before and who was now the British Secretary of State for Foreign Affairs. It notes that Venetian Procurator Giorgio Pisani

«who was a very popular Man in this [Venetian] Government about 13 years ago, suspected together with several of his adherents, of entertaining principles of subverting this Government was with the others sent to separate places in this State in confinement, some are since dead». It continued that Pisani having been confined in Verona 10 years «was taken yesterday under military escort to the Castle of St Andrew awaiting transport to Cattaro... in perpetual banishment... all are suspected of having correspondence with the Jacobins of Paris» (PRO FO 81/9, p. 123). Giorgio's end was duly noted in a second letter from Worsley to Grenville from Venice, dated 18 September 1795: – «On Sunday last another Procurator Cavalier Giorgio Pisani died at his country house where he had been banished near two years... for taking too openly a part in favour of the French... Cavalier Pisani a relation of this one lately deceased has returned [here] from London. He has represented the present situation of Great Britain as alarming to a high degree & that a general discontent prevailed on account of the [Napoleonic] War» (PRO FO 81/10, p. 207).

This net of «discontent» next closed on Zenobio, still based in England and in January 1794 the «Zenobio Affair» duly exploded. He was, at first, asked to leave Britain. A description of this crisis (but which ignores any of the consequences for poor John Williams who had left for Italy months before) is available (Darmano 1872). Zenobio immediately he received the news of his expulsion, wrote to the «Resident de Venise» [Richard Worsley] on 28 January 1794, asking that the King's order demanding he leave Britain within days be revoked or rescinded (PRO FO 81/10 p. 13). Zenobio said he had now been established in Britain for 12 years, i.e. since 1782, and «if forced to leave suddenly it will nearly be his ruin». But, on 31 January 1794, Henry Dundas (1742-1811), the new British Home Secretary, wrote to Lord Grenville that the order for Zenobio to leave Britain before 3 February 1794 «could not be rescinded» (PRO FO 81/10, p. 9). The Venetian resident in London, Orazio Lavezari, also wrote to Grenville pleading on Zenobio's behalf but again without success (PRO FO 81/10, p. 15).

On 31 January 1794 Zenobio inserted the following notice in English newspapers

«Count Zenobio thinks it is his duty to inform his TRADESMEN and [etc]... that being suddenly ordered by government to quit the Kingdom in Five Days time, it is not in his power to settle in so short a period all his accounts...» (A.S.V., Inquisitori di stato, b. 1248, fasc. II, c. 86, ritaglio azzurro di giornale da Zenobio, Piccadilly, [London], 31 January 1794).

These financial problems now became the basis for a new charge against Zenobio. By 3 February 1794 he was imprisoned for debt to «i suoi creditori» (B.M.C.V., ms. P.D., 261 b II, fasc. X, lettera n. 6, Alvise Pisani a Giuseppe Albrizzi, 11 febbraio 1794 & B.M.C.V., ms. P.D., 261 b II, fasc. X, lettera n. 5, Giovani Valle [console veneto a Londra] ad Alvise Pisani, 3 febbraio 1794). This imprisonment «sospende la esecuzione dell'ordine della di lui partenza» (A.S.V., Inquisitori di stato, b. 1244, fasc. 230, c. 88, Orazio Lavezari agli Inquisitori, Londra, 28 febbraio 1794).

The British resident in Venice, Richard Worsley soon wrote to Grenville from Venice on 8 March 1794, to report that «a kind of apology of Count Zenobio's addressed to the people of Great Britain, has been handed about here, a more impudent attack upon the country I think is scarce possible. This Government [here in Venice] is so much irritated against Count Zenobio that I am strongly inclined to believe that they will strike him off the list of Patricians and confiscate his Estates which are considerable» (PRO FO 81/10, p. 19). This «Address» must be the manuscript «Protesta» noted by Cicogna (1834, p. 633).

Probably as a result of this news from Worsley, on 15 March 1794, «un messaggero del re si è portato alla casa di arresto del Conte Zenobio, intimando... di consegnarlo onde fosse trasportato a Dover per esser mandato fuori del Regno» but «il Ceriffo rispose che... non poteva farlo, essendo egli responsabile di tutto il debito del Conte Zenobio e garante presso i suoi debitori e che poteva soltanto consegnarlo in una prigione dello Stato». This was the infamous Newgate prison. But «è permesso ai prigioneri di dimandare altra prigione» (B.M.C.V., ms. P.D., 261 b II, fasc. X, lettera n. 12, Alvise Pisani a Giuseppe Albrizzi, 21 marzo 1794) «e ricercare quella di Kings Bench, carcere più dolce e meno soggetta ad infamia. Il diritto di scegliere questa prigione deve essere deciso dalli giudici della Contea di Middlesex, alli quali appartiene la giurisdizione civile e criminale di una parte della Città di Londra». But the judges being «nel presente nel Suffolkshire a Bury [St Edmonds], distante 60 miglia da Londra, colà adunque ha dovuto condursi il N[obil]. H[omo]. Zenobio accompagnato da guardie e da un Sceriffo» (A.S.V., Inquisitori di stato, b. 1244, fasc. 230, cc. 89v-90, Orazio Lavezari agli Inquisitori, 21 marzo 1794). According to a letter of Alvise Pisani (B.M.C.V., ms. P.D., 261 b II, fasc. X, lettera n. 13, Alvise Pisani a Giuseppe Albrizzi, 28 marzo 1794) on the «sabato passato [22 marzo 1794] egli è ritornato dal suo viaggio ed'ha ottenuto dal giudice d'essere collocato alla prigione di King['s] Bench, [London]».

These crises in the unsettled affairs of Zenobio (see also Giormani 1990, p. 221) was just as Williams was writing home from Italy of his being «embarrassed at the Count's conduct towards him, in not following him [out to Italy] according to his contract, nor supplying him with necessary means and instructions» (Davies 1814, volume 1, p. 325). Williams had now been over six months away in Italy. But dealing with Williams' complaints was quite impossible, as Zenobio was now still imprisoned in the King's Bench Prison in London! (B.M.C.V., ms. P.D., 261 b II, fasc. X, segue lettera n. 21, Alvise Zenobio a Alvise Pisani (copia), 28 maggio 1794).

Finally, to cut a very long story short here, on 13 March 1795 Zenobio, having now paid all his debts, was expelled, both from prison and from Britain, according to a letter from Alvise Pisani. This reads

«questa mattina è partito da Londra il signor conte Zenobio, condotto da un Messaggero del re, al porto di Jarmuth [Yarmouth] per essere imbarcato con altri cacciati dal Regno e tradotti al continente per un pachebote» (B.M.C.V., ms. P.D., 261 b II, fasc. X, lettera n. 72, Alvise Pisani a Giuseppe Albrizzi, 13 marzo 1795).

This expulsion was under the terms of the Aliens Act (see Giormani 1990, p. 221). By 8 May 1795 «Zenobio non ho nulla di più e so ch'è ancora ad'Hamburgo» as a political refugee in Germany (B.M.C.V., ms. P.D., 261 b II, fasc. X, lettera n. 79, Alvise Pisani a Giuseppe Albrizzi, 8 maggio 1795). It thus becomes finally and tragically clear that Zenobio, whose movements are now very uncertain, would have been unable to get back to Italy in any time to help Williams, who died alone at Zenobio's house in Verona late in that same month.

But Zenobio himself *was* eventually able to return to London, where he remained very active politically and where he died during the night of 31 December 1817 – 1 January 1818 (see *Gentleman's Magazine* January 1818, p. 88 & *Staffordshire Advertiser*, 10 January 1818). The former obituary noted, with some hostility, that «the political bias of the Count is well known. As a man of fashion and gallantry he took the lead at Versailles, when under the antient [sic] *regime*; at Baxters Club about the year 1790, he usually risked 5000£ every night». This was a gaming club then in St James Street, Piccadilly, London (Sheppard, 1960, volume 30, pp. 462-3).

Williams' final years in Italy 1793-1795

Williams had arrived in Italy in November 1793, after a journey through Germany and the Tyrol. Davies notes that Williams had at first «seemed to be in raptures of admiration at the stupenduousness, magnificent scenery, and stratification of rocks, in the Tyrolese Alps» as he passed through. He was also «in sanguine expectation of a plentiful harvest of mineral wealth in the states of Venice» (Davies 1814, volume 1, p. 325). He wrote a number of sadly now lost letters to his nephew in Wales but Davies directly quotes only from one; on the subject of the great durability of wood in underground mines there, a topic in which, as a mining engineer, Williams would have had a long interest. «It is the *Spanish Chestnut*, which I have found here in an old Roman mine, and the wood is now as sound as when first put in, about 2000 years ago».

The letter from Zenobio dated 14 November 1793, quoted above to reveal Zenobio's financial problems (A.S.V., Inquisitori di stato, b. 1248, fasc. III, c. 383-384v, Zenobio a Lorenzo Marzari, 14 novembre 1793), also gives news of Williams' activities in Italy.

«Non voglio decidere cosa alcuna prima del mio arrivo, mentre ho grande speranza che le scoperte del signor Williams e li piani che verranno suggeriti per l'organizzamento dei beni soggetti all'inondazioni dell'Adige [noi] possiamo molto aumentare il prezzo di quei beni. Mi scrive di già il signor Williams che vi sono traccie di carbone vicino a Egna e le terre sulle montagne sono ricche di ottima pietra a calce, la quale, oltre il suo valore essendo tanto utile come per fabbricare, come per fertilizzare i paesi incolti, è un sicuro indizio che vi sono miniere di piombo, rame, ferro, argento. Ho scritto sopra questo oggetto al signor Dalla Torre onde prendere le misure che se io fò dell'utile scoperte, ne deva pure avere parte nel vantaggio. Ma sopra questo importantissimo punto delle miniere di carbone e metalli il primo oggetto è quello nelli nostri Stati... infinito benefizio dunque potrebbe rendere la visita di un'uomo così esperto come il signor Williams... Intesi pure con piacere che in Istria vi sono gran miniere di carbone, mi metterò a farne la visita come pure in Dalmazia con il signor Williams, sono questi paesi inesplorati, dalla loro posizione molto promettenti. Vedete bene quanto motivi ho di affrettare il mio ritorno».

More news of Williams is then given in a letter of 17 December 1793 from Zenobio to Marzari (A.S.V., Inquisitori di stato, b. 1248, fasc. III, Zenobio a Lorenzo Marzari, 17 dicembre 1793). He notes

«mi riesce pure di sorpresa che non mi date alcuna nuova del signor Williams, avendo io già ricevuto 3 lettere da esso, una da Venezia e 2 dalli [Signor] Reck. Queste contengono le migliori notizie delle sue scoperte in Italia ed anche in parte del Tirolo. Le miniere di carbone in Arzignano sono abbondanti e di buona qualità, quelle di piombo nel Vicentino sono superiori alle più belle d'Inghilterra e basta ritrovar persone capaci di ben lavorarle, per renderle di gran profitto tanto publico come privato. Il signor Williams ha pur ritrovato delle miniere di Carbon fossile nel Veronese, superiori a quelle di Arzignano. Ho scritto al mio cognato e al cavalier [Giacomo] Nani onde ottenere dal Publico l'investitura e subito che sarò sicuro di questo, accorderò persone qui esperte per mettere in esecuzione i piani del signor Williams. Questo è una persona di eminente abilità e perfetta onestà e mi scrive che vede un vasto campo di publico e privato vantaggio nel lavoro delle miniere di carbon fossile e metalli nel nostro paese. Mi scrisse che nel Tirolo vi sono favorevoli apparenze ed essendo informato dal signor Dalla Torre che secondo le investiture, il Dinasta à un diritto a tutte le miniere...».

Further news of Williams' Italian activities, and Zenobio's intentions, comes in a letter of 31 December 1793 from Zenobio to Marzari (A.S.V., Inquisitori di stato, b. 1248, fasc. III, cc. 386-9, Zenobio a Lorenzo Marzari, 31 dicembre 1793). He announces that

«al principio della primavera o al finir dell'inverno partirò certamente per Venezia... [c. 389] Non vi posso dir niente intorno all'affare delli N.N.H.H. Gritti della loro miniera di carbone, mentre fino a che non ho le informazioni del signor Williams ed una mia visita personale, non posso decider niente sopra questo articolo. Intanto ricevo dal signor [Williams] le nuove più soddisfacenti delle sue scoperte ed ho ragione di lusingarmi che la visita di un uomo eminente nel suo terreno torni di gran vantaggio tanto publico che privato».

But in January 1794 the «Zenobio Affair» had suddenly exploded as we have seen, leaving John Williams in an impossible situation. We have already seen, from an Italian source, how the abate Giuseppe Tommaselli (1733-1818) had written on 16 February 1794, «sento che Williams non riconosce per vulcanizzati gli Euganei»

(Giormani 1996, footnote 99). These are the small hills just west of Padova, about whose origins there was then an intense debate (see Kirwan 1799, p. 273). Tommaselli continued «gli ho fatto scrivere per la [Signora] Treves a Udine una fortiss[im]a lettera, che l'obbligava ad esibirmi la prova, ma che siano prove e non parole. Costui venne a rovesciarci in capo l'idee». It would be nice to learn something of the Italian woman, Signora Treve or Treves, who so befriended Williams in Italy.

The last letter that John Williams wrote from Italy to his native Kerry was dated Easter Monday, [20 April] 1794. In this Williams now «seemed embarrassed at the Count's conduct towards him, in not following him [out to Italy] according to his contract, nor supplying him with necessary means and instructions» (Davies 1814, p. 325). These comments agree with the news of Williams given by Zenobio in a letter to Marzari of 27 April 1794 (A.S.V., Inquisitori di stato, b. 1248, Zenobio a Lorenzo Marzari, 27 aprile 1794), in which Zenobio says that

«ho ricevuto lo stesso venerdì [25 aprile] 3 lettere del signor Williams, due da Schio ed una da Venezia: tutte significano le più favorevoli viste, ma sì con varie spese indispensabili. Io gli rispondo che quantunque è ben giusto che le sue spese vengagli pagate, pure egli veda di andare con la possibile economia. Siccome trovo necessario di prolungare la dimora in Italia del signor Williams per sei mesi, così se sia a lui aggradevole, stipulerete una scrittura alle stesse condizioni di quella che scrisse in agosto».

Marzari's request to the Inquisitori to renew Williams' contract for a further six months was dated 21 May 1794 (A.S.V., Inquisitori di stato, b. 1248, supplica di Lorenzo Marzari agli Inquisitori, per conto di Alvise Zenobio, Venezia, 21 maggio 1794). It reveals that Williams' original contract had been at a salary of £300 a year with all travel and subsistence costs also paid. This request was for a new six-month contract to run from 1 August 1794 at the same rate. But the request is annotated «NON SI RINNOVI». Williams' problems in Italy were now to increase dramatically!

These are revealed by Zenobio in a letter to Marzari (A.S.V., Inquisitori di stato, b. 1248, Alvise Zenobio a Lorenzo Marzari, Londra, 6 giugno 1794)

«Ricevei ultimamente una lettera del signor Williams, il quale mi informa con molta mia sorpresa che avendovi ricercato di somministrargli il necessario per i suoi viaggi, gli avete scritto che non avevate da me tali ordini. Questo deve essere uno sbaglio, mentre chiaramente vi scrissi che i patti della nostra scrittura sono di pagargli servitù, alloggio e viaggi per le sue osservazioni ed un assegno di lire [sterline] 300 per un anno, con libertà dopo la espirazione del anno a ciascun parte di continuare a terminare l'accordo, cosa per... del signor Williams che desidero egli continui il suo impegno con me per altri sei mesi, in conseguenza del mio ritardo; e la stessa mia intenzione a voi comunico onde... p. ire l'accordo con esso».

Further problems are revealed in a letter of 17 July 1794 from Zenobio to Marzari (A.S.V., Inquisitori di stato, b. 1248, fasc. III, c. 398, Alvise Zenobio a Lorenzo Marzari, Londra, 17 giugno 1794)

«Mi riesce poi ancora inesprimibile mortificazione il divieto di continuare al signor Williams, tanto più quanto le ultime sue lettere, una delle quali vi accludo [this is now sadly missing!], mi dà le più giuste lusinghe di successo. Credete ch'egli è uno dei più eminenti soggetti d'Inghilterra in questa materia, in prova di che vi è il suo libro e i ripetuti premi che ebbe dalla Società delle Arti in Scozia [the HAS], vi è una medaglia d'oro del valore di 60 zecchini [che] ricevè in questi giorni dall'Imperatrice di Russia, vi è una pratica ch'ebbe di 40 anni nelle miniere di Scozia, vi è finalmente la più grande di tutte le prove: questa è che, dopo essersi impegnato con una persona venuta d'Irlanda per impegnarlo ad andare ad esplorare le miniere in quel paese, vedrete dalla sua lettera ch'egli intende lui stesso esborsar somme per lavorar le miniere e conta di costì stabilirsi; dunque non – bisogna siano tutte immaginazioni». The letter ends «Vi ripeto gli ordini che il signor Williams sia fornito del necessario siccome i termini della scrittura fra noi segnata l'esprimono; è pure tempo che riceva le tre cento sterline accordate».

Zenobio repeated these points in an application to the «Tribunale Supremo» of Venice (A.S.V., Inquisitori di stato, b. 1248, Supplica del Alvise Zenobio, Londra, 17 giugno 1794) and concluded

«che perciò tempo e la sua presenza sono necessari. Che in conseguenza se non viene permesso al supplicante che venga prolungato l'accordo col signor Williams per sei mesi (tempo nel quale si lusinga di essere rimpatriato) tutte le fatiche sono... inutili, tutto il denaro impiegato, di nessun uso, tutti i prospetti di Pubblico e privato benefizi interamente svaniti». The accounts for Zenobio's Venetian estate duly show that the sum of 1000 lire venete was paid to «signor Williams, mineralogista» during June and July 1794 from the estate (A.S.V., Inquisitori di stato, b. 1248, Carte avute da copiare nel Processo Zenobio).

Such contractual and financial problems must have put serious limitations on Williams' work in Italy. These are best revealed by the following, most poignant, description of Williams' problems in Italy (which all had a simple, if «revolutionary», explanation back in London) as given by Carlo De Rubeis in 1795. De Rubeis describes how

the zoologist, the abate Giuseppe Olivi (1769-1795) – for whom see
Gibin 1994 – just before his own death in the same year as Williams

> «Stava egli per raccogliere da moltissime lettere un *Saggio intorno allo
> stato mineralogico di tutte le Venete Provincie*: furono queste scritte in que-
> sti ultimi tempi da un Inglese Mineralogista, il Signor *Williams*, il quale da
> un ricco bizarro Patrizio Veneto [Zenobio] fu da Londra spedito e pagato
> generosamente, onde percorrendo la Dalmazia, e tutto lo Stato Veneto inse-
> gnasse a noi quali nascosti tesori per avventura possediamo. Era lo strano
> Inglese ignaro affatto della nostra lingua e della Francese; e quindi, come
> un muto, pellegrinò, osservò, e raccolse quanto di raro e di apprezzabile
> giudicava, mandando in deposito i vari saggi mineralogici appresso al Con-
> sole di sua Nazione a Veneto» (De Rubeis [1795], pp. 17-8).

This Consul was the same Sir Richard Worsley, Baronet (1751-
1805), British resident there from 29 November 1793 until the Revolution on 15 May 1797 (Bindoff 1934, 193), who had been so busy
informing the British authorities of Zenobio's activities in Venice!
De Rubeis then continued

> «Fatal avvenimento! Morì quasi all'improvviso il Mineralogista a Vero-
> na pochi mesi sono, e per' secolui il risultato delle sue cognizioni, e l'inten-
> to del suo mecenate. L'unica persona, che dallo straniere fu fatta consape-
> vole di quanto andava scoprendo, era una gentil Giudea, onor del suo sesso
> che ama e conosce il sistema Botanico di Mr. *Lamarque* [Lamarck], ed a cui
> è famigliare la lingua Inglese. Non poteva codesta colta donna, amante del-
> la Storia Naturale, ignorare il nome dell'*Olivi*, e non coltivare la di lui ami-
> cizia. Per la qual cosa affidò a lui le moltiplici Lettere dell'Inglese Minera-
> logista, delle quali l'*Olivi* era in procinto di donarne un *Saggio*».

At least the name of the «Giudea», Signora Treve or Treves, has
been revealed by Giormani (1996). But sadly neither Williams' letters nor Olivi's *Saggio* seem to have survived the 200 years since
both died in Italy (Giormani 1996, note 99 & Gibin 1994). This was
within three months of each other as Olivi died on 24 August 1795.

Williams' death in Verona and its aftermath

Davies recorded that «soon after the date of this last letter [April
1794, Williams] was supposed to have died in Venice». Neill (1814a,
p. 258) instead stated that he had died at the end of the year 1797 and
was aged 67! In fact Williams had died in Verona on 29 May 1795,
not at the Count's house in Venice as his Welsh relatives supposed

(Davies 1814, volume 1, p. 325), and must have been at most 64 years old. Scottish newspapers, like the *Edinburgh Advertiser* (July 14 to 17 1795 p. 38) and the *Edinburgh Evening Courant* (Saturday July 18 1795, p. 3), first reported that

«letters from Verona in Italy, mention the death, on 29th May last, of Mr John Williams, Mineral Surveyor, author of the History of the Mineral Kingdom, 2 vols, 8vo, and of several essays: It is reported that he has discovered coal in Italy after a very minute search».

Other obituary notices appeared, but only copying the above, as the *Derby Mercury* (30 July 1795), p. 1); the *Scottish Register* (1795, vol. 6, p. 358); the *Gentleman's Magazine* (vol. 65 (2), July 1795, p. 614, and the *Scots Magazine* (vol. 57, August 1795, p. 545).

Neill (1814a, pp. 257-8) stated that Williams, while in Italy, had «set on foot the working of limestone, coal and ironstone on some of the Count's estates near Verona and was going on well with these improvements, when he was unfortunately seized with a typhoid fever, which proved fatal». This records at least a cause of death (Neill 1814a, p. 258), and reveals a little of what Williams had achieved before his premature death so far from home, although we must note that Neill had been two years out in dating Williams' death, and may once again not be wholly reliable.

At least we can now reveal that Williams's financial affairs were put into some sort of order after his death. An agreement of December 1795 records

«Ogni e qualunque differenza insorta o che insorger potesse per occasione dei conteggi e pretese spiegate dalla signora Margherita Williams erede, testamentaria del quondam Gio[vanni] Williams suo padre a motivo dell'accordo stabilito tra il N.H. ser conte Alvise Zenobio da una ed il detto fu signor Gio: Williams dall'altra, cogl'articoli d'accordo stabiliti in Londra 23 luglio 1793 e ratificato per altri sei mesi colla susseguente sua lettera 27 aprile 1794, scritta dal detto N.H. da Londra al detto fu signor Williams, resta con la rispettabile mediazione del nobile signor Giovanni Watson...».

The agreement further noted

«A saldo e totale compimento d'ogni e qualsisia pretesa di detta signora Margherita erede ut supra, nessuna eccettuata, s'obbliga il signor Lorenzo Marzari come procurator di detto N.H. ser conte Alvise Zenobio d'esborsare nel termine di sei mesi computabili dal giorno presente al suddetto nobile signor console Britannico, come procuratore della detta signora Margherita la somma di zecchini novecento veneti, sono piccole lire diecinove mille ottocento, da cui dovrà essere rilasciata la corrispondente ricevuta a saldo e compito pagamento d'ogni pretesa di detta erede» (A.S.V., Inquisitori di Stato, b. 1248, copia della convenzione (di... Giuseppe Camerata, sopraintendente alla Facoltà Zenobio, agli Inquisitori, 31 dicembre 1795) tra il console d'Inghilterra e Lorenzo Marzari... 15 dicembre 1795).

A later note of the same date adds

«Fu poi trovato e definito coll'unita [no. 5] convenzione 15 cadente col signor Console d'Inghilterra, come procuratore dell'erede di certo Villiams mineralogista, ch'era stato accordato dal N.H. Zenobio colla qual Carta fu concluso di pagarsi entro 6 mesi zecchini 900, ribassando di molto le pretese intavolate dall'erede suddetta, ch'erano di zecchini 1200 circa...» (A.S.V., Inquisitori di Stato, b. 1248, relazione per il trimestre di agosto, settembre e ottobre agli Inquisitori, di Giuseppe Camerata, fedel ragionato (e destinato sopraintendente della Facoltà Zenobio), 31 dicembre 1795.

If this matter was finally settled, it has not proved possible to locate the will that Williams must have made. Nor has it proved possible to locate Williams' burial record in Verona, or any grave. Another serious loss is that of Williams' portrait, recorded by Anderson (1863, p. 132) as then in the «Scotch Antiquarian Society Institution in Edinburgh». This institution's collections have had a very chequered career (Bell 1981) and the portrait is now unknown to the SAS, the National Museums or to the National Portrait Gallery in Edinburgh. The founder of the SAS, the Earl of Buchan, had commissioned an early series of portraits of members of the SAS. To these were added, on 2 April 1782 an additional series of six more portraits, «in black lead as large as life». All had been done by the Scottish artist John Brown (1749-1787), corresponding member of the SAS (Smellie 1782, part 1, p. 91).

Sadly today, of these additional six portraits, only that of Williams cannot be identified. One's frustration is heightened by the fact that the Scottish National Portrait Gallery does still possess nine unidentified John Brown portraits from this SAS series, of which one is of a woman (Smailes 1990, pp. 351-2 & 388). Of the remaining eight, Williams seems most likely to be that today numbered PGL 58, in terms of his dress and likely age in 1782 etc. One must hope some further documentation may come to light.

Williams post-mortem reputation

Two years after his death a mysterious Russian translation of Williams' book on the Vitrified Forts of Scotland, made by V. Kulichkin, was published in St. Petersburg, Russia (copy in BL – 867 i 30). Princess Dashkova (1743-1810), the close confidante of the Empress Catherine of Russia, had been living in Scotland in 1777 and travelling through the Highlands (Hyde 1935, pp. 140-7 & Cross 1980, pp. 131-3 & 238), just as Williams' results were published. She may well have been the inspiration for its eventual translation. Princess Dashkova had been, as another result, party to one of the finest, and earliest, expositions of the new Huttonian Theory of the Earth in 1787 (Craig 1978, pp. 3-5). But published claims that the Empress Catherine II (1729-1796) of Russia herself visited Britain in 1776 prove as unfounded (Tomkeieff 1950) as the claim that Williams had journeyed to Russia!

Part one of the first edition of Williams' *Mineral Kingdom* was translated into German by Adolph A. F. W. Danckelman and published at Dresden in 1798. A copy of this rarity is at the University of Illinois library (Ward & Carozzi 1984, p. 527). Danckelman, who attended the Freiberg Bergakademie in 1795 (Gottschalk 1867, p. 237), also added many notes to Williams' original text. That even part of this work was chosen for translation indicates the value then placed on the work by those involved in teaching coal mining in Saxony. By 1809, «nearly the whole work has [now] been translated into the German at the request of [Abraham] Werner, and is accompanied by many valuable notes by the [new] translator Heinrich Meuder, [another] pupil of Werner» (Anderson 1809, pp. 243-4). Meuder, who had earlier translated Jameson's *Mineralogische Reisen durch Schottland* in 1802 (Meuder 1802) had also attended Werner's Bergakademie in 1798. Meuder rose to become a Bergamtassessor in Freiberg, but he died in 1811 (Gottschalk 1867, p. 239) and so this project to publish a new complete translation of Williams' book was abandoned. But again it demonstrates the value placed on Williams' work in Saxony twenty years after its publication.

In England the next commentator on Williams' book was the English mineralogist John Mawe (1766-1829) (Torrens 1990). Mawe's 1802 book *The Mineralogy of Derbyshire* contained a critical «account of Mr. Williams's Book, called the Mineral Kingdom» (Mawe 1802, pp. 176-199). Mawe called the book «prolix and confused» but still considered it to have sufficient value for the detailed analysis he gave of it to be of value.

A wish for a new English edition was also expressed in 1805, when Gilbert Laing reported to John Pinkerton (1758-1826) that

«friends of Williams... have offered Longman [the London publisher] a new and enlarged edition from the author's manuscripts. It is a pity that this book should not fall into the hands of some good editor, who had travelled through Scotland, and has mineralogical knowledge enough to enlarge the book with personal observations, Dr [John] Murray [1778-1828] of this place [Edinburgh] would be well qualified» (Pinkerton 1830, volume 1, p. 325).

This note helps to date one of the MSS notes by the Earl of Buchan in the NLS (MSS 1810 f 149), since this had noted that «a second edition of [Williams *Mineral Kingdom*] has been prepared by Mr Murray, Lecturer in Chemistry with additional matter and re-marks» and so must date from 1805 or just after. But, in the end, it was not John Murray, who had written the 1802 response *A compar-ative view of the Huttonian and Neptunian Systems of Geology* to John Playfair's *Illustrations of the Huttonian Theory of the Earth* (1802), who undertook the second edition of Williams' book which was to appear in 1810.

In 1808 the leader of the Scottish Wernerians, Robert Jameson (1774-1854), commented that «Williams was an excellent observer who made many useful observations on the independent coal forma-tion» but he now wrongly claimed Williams as «our country-man» (Jameson 1808, p. 41). Another Edinburgh Wernerian geologist, Dr Charles Anderson (1793-1855) noted in 1809 that Williams' book was «by a miner of great sagacity and skill» (Anderson 1809, p. 245).

When Williams' book appeared in its second edition in English in 1810, it was with Williams' original anti-Huttonian preface removed and instead a long supplement by its new editor, Dr. James Millar (1762-1827), added. The removal of the preface which had attacked Hutton was highly geo-political, within the strained politics of the warfare between Huttonians and Neptunians then so rife in Edin-burgh (Wawn 1982 & Dean 1992, pp. 144-162). The suppressed preface of 1810, was however soon reprinted, through the agency of John Farey in 1817 (Williams 1817). Farey had just visited Edin-burgh to report on a new water supply for the city and had discovered the value of Williams' book. Farey first published an anonymous note, by «A Correspondent» or «An Engineer», in 1817 about the suppression of Williams' Preface in 1810 ([Farey] 1817), before ar-ranging for its reprinting in London. But Farey must have had his own geo-political reasons for wishing to reveal the value of Wil-liams' work and its anti-Huttonian preface. This seems to have been because of the amount of stratigraphic data he found in Williams' book. Farey wished such data to be highlighted, as part of his crusade to improve stratigraphic knowledge and attention to it at this time, and to lessen attention to the sort of theorizing that Hutton had in-dulged in.

The section of Williams' original book (Williams 1810, volume 1, pp. 133-155) «of the Indications of Coal, and Methods of searching for it» was reprinted in North America in 1814 (Bruce 1814, pp. 167-182). But perhaps the most interesting comment on Williams' book is that it was still being recommended as a text by both practical (i.e. Thomas Tredgold 1788-1829) and academic geologists (i.e. William Buckland (1784-1856), as late as 1817 and 1822, over thirty years after its first publication (see Tredgold 1817, p. 127 & Melmore 1942, p. 323).

Later writers, by now historians, commented on Williams' book. Charles Lyell in 1830 noted that «it was a work of great merit for that day [1790] and of practical utility, as containing the best account of the coal measures» (Lyell 1830, p. 67). Rev. John Fleming also noted that this book had «greatly advanced the study of practical geology, not only in Edinburgh, but throughout Scotland» (Fleming 1859, p. 9). The German historian of geology Karl Zittel called the book «remarkably complete» (Zittel 1901, p. 109). E.B. Bailey & D. Tait of the Geological Survey of Scotland (Bailey & Tait 1921, p. 83) called it «an exceptionally full account of the Coal Formation». More modern appraisals of the book by historians of geology are given by Davies 1969, Challinor 1971, pp. 65, 70-2 & 76-83, Porter 1977 pp. 136, 153-4 & 178, Huggett 1989, pp. 65-7 & Huggett 1990, p. 68). The literature on the history of Scottish coal mining, on the other hand, strangely ignores it (Duckham 1970). It remains the best memorial of an enthusiastic, energetic, and remarkably competent man, who was clearly regarded as the best mineral surveyor of his generation in Britain but whom history has otherwise since sadly forgotten.

The Earl of Buchan well summed up John Williams

«in the 2d volume of Williams' book are many things worthy of deep attention for tho the worthy Man was deficient in learning commonly so called he was by no means so in what related to the subject of his discussions» and «considering poor Williams as an illiterate miner his work is wonderful & it certainly does contain a vast variety of useful matter drawn from actual observation in the course of more than 40 years experience» (NLS MSS 996)

Abbreviations

ASV   Archivio di Stato, Venezia
BL   British Library, London
BMCV   Biblioteca del Museo Correr, Venezia
CFAE   Commissioners for the Forfeited Annexed Estates

II

EUL   Edinburgh University Library
HAS   Highland and Agricultural Society, Edinburgh
NLS   National Library of Scotland, Edinburgh
NMS   National Museums of Scotland, Edinburgh
PRO   Public Record Office, Kew & London
SAS   Society of Antiquaries of Scotland
SRO   Scottish Record Office, Edinburgh

Acknowledgements

These are due first to the *Istituto Veneto* for making this first attempt to appraise the work of John Williams possible. Many have helped me, like Fionna Ashmore (Edinburgh), Jan Ballard (Philadephia), Susan Bennett (London), David Bick (Newent), Roy Boud (Leeds), Norman Butcher (Edinburgh), Luca Ciancio (Rovereto), Pat Crichton (Hopetoun), Roger Emerson (London, Ontario), Roger Flindall (Nottingham), Jane Hill (Edinburgh), Jean Jones (Edinburgh), Dorothy Laing (Edinburgh), Rosalind Marshall (Edinburgh), Rosalind Mitchison (Ormiston), Renato Pasta (Firenze), Martin Phillips (Keele), Paolo Preto (Padova), Marion Ramsay (Edinburgh), Raffaello Vergani (Padova) & Charles Withers (Edinburgh). But above all I thank Ezio Vaccari (Verona) for his constant encouragement in these stupid times for scholars like us when all research expenses have had to be met from my own pocket.

To Virgilio Giormani (Venezia), whom I had never met, I owe an enormous debt for showing how generously the spirit of the enquiring mind still exists in Italy. Without his wonderful assistance in ransacking Venetian archives for information for me, I would have known very little about what had actually happened to Williams in Italy and would have remained in real ignorance of the English causes of his problems there. I dedicate this paper to him with real thanks and my best wishes for his happy and active retirement from academic life.

BIBLIOGRAPHY

R.J. ADAM, *Papers on Sutherland Estate Management 1802-1816*, Scottish History Society, series 4, volumes 8 & 9. Edinburgh, 1972.
I.H. ADAMS, *Papers on Peter May – Land Surveyor 1749-1793*. Edinburgh, 1979.
C. ANDERSON, (translator), *Abraham Werner's New Theory of the Formations of Veins*. Edinburgh, 1809.
J. ANDERSON, *An account of ancient Monuments and Fortifications in the Highlands of Scotland*, «Archaeologia», 5, pp. 241-266, 1779.

W. ANDERSON, *The Scottish Nation.* Volume 1. Edinburgh, 1863.

W. ANDERSON, *Genealogy and Surnames.* Edinburgh, 1865.

ANON., *The Diaries & Correspondence of Anna Catherina Bower.* London, 1903.

ANON., *The Registers of Kerry, part 3 [1708-1760]* in *Collections historical & Archaeological relating to Montgomeryshire and its borders.* Volume 39. Welshpool, 1919.

E.B. BAILEY & D. TAIT, *Geology* pp. 63-99 in *Edinburgh's Place in Scientific Progress.* Edinburgh, 1921.

D. BARRINGTON, *Observations on the vitrified walls in Scotland,* «Archaeologia», 6, 1782, pp. 100-103.

A.S. BELL, *The Scottish Antiquarian Tradition.* Edinburgh, 1981.

D.E. BICK, *The Old Metal Mines of Mid Wales.* Parts 1-5, Newent, 1978.

S.T. BINDOFF, *British Diplomatic Representatives 1789-1852.* (Publications of the Camden Society, series 3, volume 50). London, 1934.

H. BRIGGS, *Sinclar's Treatise of Coal Mines 1672,* «Transactions of the Institution of Mining Engineers», 69, 1925, pp. 132-14.

D.J. BRYDEN, *James Watt, merchant: the Glasgow years 1754-1774* in D. SMITH (editor), *Perceptions of Great Engineers: Fact and Fantasy.* London, 1994, pp. 9-22.

A. BRUCE, *Publications Coal,* «American Mineralogical Journal», 1, 1814, pp. 166-182.

A.D. CAMERON, *The Caledonian Canal.* Lavenham, 1972.

R.G. CANT, *David Steuart Erskine, 11th Earl of Buchan, Founder of the Society of Antiquaries of Scotland,* in A.S. BELL, 1981, (q.v.), pp. 1-30.

J. CHALLINOR, *The History of British Geology: A Bibliographical Study.* Newton Abbot, 1971.

V.G. CHILDE & W. THORNEYCROFT, *The Experimental Production of the Phenomena distinctive of Vitrified Forts,* «Proceedings of the Society of Antiquarians of Scotland», 72, 1938, pp. 44-55.

A. CHISHOLME & J.A. DE LUC, *Review of «The Natural History of the Mineral Kingdom»,* «The Monthly Review», 6, 1791, pp. 121-131.

E.A. CICOGNA, *Delle Iscrizioni Veneziane.* Volumes 1-6. Venezia, 1824-1853.

M. COTTERELL, *The Natural History of the Mineral Kingdom»,* «The Edinburgh Geologist», no 18, 1985, pp. 21-25.

M.A. COTTON, *British Camps with Timber-laced Ramparts,* «Archaeological Journal», 111, 1955, pp. 26-105.

L.R. COX., *New Light on William Smith and his Work,* «Proceedings of the Yorkshire Geological Society», 25, 1942, pp. 1-99.

G.Y. CRAIG, (editor) *James Hutton's Theory of the Earth: The Lost Drawings.* Edinburgh, 1978.

W. CRAMOND, *The parallel roads in Glenroy,* «Transactions of the Banffshire Field Club», 1902/3, pp. 18-22.

A.G. CROSS, *«By the Banks of the Thames»: Russians in Eighteenth Century Britain.* Newtonville, 1980.

B. CUNLIFFE, *Iron Age Communities in Britain.* Third edition. London and New York, 1991.

D. DARMANO, *Inediti documenti sulle vicende di Alvise Zenobio,* «Archivio Veneto», 3, 1872, pp. 278-300.

G.L. DAVIES, *The Earth in Decay.* London, 1969.

W. DAVIES, *General View of the Agriculture & Domestic Economy of South Wales.* Two volumes. London, 1814.

W.R. DAWSON, *The Banks Letters.* London, 1958.

D.R. Dean, *James Hutton and the History of Geology*. Ithaca, 1992.

C. De Rubeis, *Elogio amichevole dell'abate Giuseppe Olivi*. Padua, [1795], [also in «Nuovo Giornale d'Italia», 7, no 25 (10 ottobre 1795), pp. 193-9].

H.W. Dickinson & R. Jenkins, *James Watt and the Steam Engine*. London, 1927.

B.F. Duckham, *A History of the Scottish Coal Industry*, Volume 1 1700-1815. Newton Abbot, 1970.

J. Dunlop, *The British Fisheries Society 1786-1893*. Edinburgh, 1978.

F. Ellenberger, *Précisions nouvelles sur la découverte des volcans de France*, «Histoire et Nature», 12/13, 1979, pp. 3-42.

R. Emerson, *The Scottish Enlightenment and the End of the Philosophical Society of Edinburgh*, «British Journal for the History of Science», 21, 1988, pp. 33-66.

V.A. Eyles & J.M. Eyles, *Some Geological Correspondence of James Hutton*, «Annals of Science», 7, 1951, pp. 316-339.

G.V.M. Fabroni, *Dell' Antracite o Carbone di cava detto volgarmente Carbone Fossile, compilazione fatta per ordine del Governo*. Firenze, 1790.

J. Farey, *Notes and Observations on part of the Eleventh and the Twelfth Chapters of Mr Robert Bakewell's "Introduction to Geology..."*, «Philosophical Magazine», 43, 1814, pp. 325-41.

J. Farey, *On certain accidents to which Coal-works are liable...*, «Philosophical Magazine», 45, 1815a, pp. 436-52.

J. Farey, *On the coal works in Sutherland*, «Monthly Magazine», 40 (2), 1815b, pp. 9-11.

J. Farey, *On the causes of injustice which authors sometimes suffer from other writers... particularly the late Mr Williams...*, «Philosophical Magazine», 50, 1817, pp. 116-121.

J. Ferguson, (editor), *Papers illustrating the History of the Scots Brigade in the Service of the United Netherlands*. (Publications of the Scottish History Society nos 32, 35 & 38). Edinburgh, 1899-1901.

J. Fleming, *The Lithology of Edinburgh*. Edinburgh, 1859.

J.G. Gazley, *The Life of Arthur Young 1741-1820*. Philadelphia, 1973.

V. Gibbs, and others (editors), *The Complete Peerage*. 13 volumes. London, 1910-1959.

C. Gibin, *La Geometria della Natura*. Padova, 1994.

V. Giormani, *La mancata introduzione della Macchina a Vapore nelle bonifiche dello Stato veneto nell'ultimo Decennio del '700*, «Studi Veneziani», 17, 1990, pp. 157-224.

V. Giormani, *1793-1795: La breve stagione concorsuale di Giuseppe Olivi tra Padova e Venezia*, «Studi Veneziani», 30, 1996, pp. 269-318.

A. Goodwin, *The Friends of Liberty*. London, 1979.

C.G. Gottschalk, *Verzeichniss Derer, welche seit Eröffnung der Bergakademie und bis Schluss des ersten Saculum's auf ihr studirt haben*, in Band 2, *Festschrift zum hundertjährigen jubiläum der Königl. sächs. bergakademie zu Freiberg am 30 juli 1866*. Dresden, pp. 221-95, 1867.

R. Gough, *British Topography*. Two volumes. London, 1780.

J. Hardman, *Louis XVI*. New Haven & London, 1993.

C.W. Hendel, *David Hume's Political Essays*. Indianapolis & New York, 1953.

R.J. Huggett, *Cataclysms and Earth history*. Oxford, 1989.

R.J. Huggett, *Catastrophism: systems of earth history*. London, 1990.

J. Hutton, *Theory of the Earth...*, «Transactions of the Royal Society of Edinburgh», 1, 1788, pp. 209-304.

H.M. Hyde, *The Empress Catherine and Princess Dashkov*, London, 1935.

R. JAMESON, *System of Mineralogy*. Volume 3. Edinburgh, 1808.

J. JONES, *The Geological Collection of James Hutton*, «Annals of Science», 41, 1984, pp. 223-244.

J. JONES, H.S. TORRENS & E. ROBINSON, *The Correspondence between James Hutton (1726-1797) and James Watt (1736-1819), with two letters from Hutton to George Clerk-Maxwell (1715-1784)*, «Annals of Science», 51, 1994 & 1995, pp. 637-653 (part one) & 52, pp. 357-382 (part two).

R. KIRWAN, *Observations on Coal-mines*, «Transactions of the Royal Irish Academy», 2, 1790, pp. 157-70.

R. KIRWAN, *Geological Essays*. London, 1799.

R. KIRWAN, *Proposed Mineral Surveys of the British Counties [in 1793]*, «Tilloch's Philosophical Magazine», 37, 1811, pp. 8-10.

V. KULICHIN, (translator) of John Williams' book on the Vitrified Forts of Scotland, published in St Petersburg, 1797, (copy in British Library – press mark 867 i 30).

J.G. LAMB, *David Steuart Erskine, 11th Earl of Buchan: A study of his Life and Correspondence*. Ph.D. thesis, St Andrews University.

C. LYELL, *Principles of Geology*. Volume 1. London, 1830.

I. MACALPINE & R. HUNTER, *George III and the Mad-Business*. London, 1969.

A. MAGGIOLO, *I Soci dell'Accademia Patavina dalla sua fondazione (1599)*. Padova, 1983.

J. MAWE, *The Mineralogy of Derbyshire*. London, 1802.

S. MELMORE, *Letters in the Possession of the Yorkshire Philosophical Society*, «North Western Naturalist», 17, 1942, pp. 317-332.

H.W. MEUDER, (translator) *Herrn R. J[ameson]'s mineralogische Reisen durch Schottland*. Leipzig, 1802.

J. MILLAR, *Biographical notes on Mr Williams*, in J. WILLIAMS, 1810 (q.v.), Volume one, Preface, pp. vii-viii.

G. MORI, *L'estrazione dei minerali nel Granducato di Toscana durante il periodo di riforme (1737-1790)*, «Studi di storia dell'industria», Roma, 1976, pp. 83-141.

E.C. MOSSNER & I.S. ROSS, *Correspondence of Adam Smith*. Oxford, 1977.

C.F. MULLETT, *The «Bee» (1790-1794): a tour of Crotchet Castle*, «South Atlantic Quarterly», 66, 1967, pp. 70-86.

C.F. MULLETT, *A Village Aristotle and the Harmony of Interests: James Anderson (1739-1808) of Monks Hill*, «Journal of British Studies», 8, 1968, pp. 94-118.

P. NEILL, (translator of J.F. D'Aubuisson's) *An Account of the Basalts of Saxony*, Edinburgh, 1814a. (Williams *the mineralogist* on pp. 255-258).

P. NEILL, *Biographical Account of Mr Williams, the Mineralogist*, «Annals of Philosophy», 4, 1814b, pp. 81-3.

T. PENNANT, *A Tour in Scotland 1769*. Second edition. London, 1772.

S. PIGGOTT, *Ruins in a Landscape*. Edinburgh, 1976.

J. PINKERTON, *The Literary Correspondence of....* Two volumes. London, 1830.

J. PLAYFAIR, *Biographical Account of the late Dr James Hutton*, «Transactions of the Royal Society of Edinburgh», 5, 1805, pp. 39-99.

R. PORTER, *The Industrial Revolution and the Rise of the Science of Geology*, in M. TEICH & R. YOUNG (editors) *Changing Perspectives in the History of Science*, London, 1973, pp. 320-43.

R. PORTER, *The making of geology: Earth science in England, 1660-1815*. Cambridge, 1977.

P. PRETO, *I Servizi Segreti di Venezia*. Milano, 1994.

I. RALSTON, *The Yorkshire Television vitrified wall experiment at East Tullos, City of Aberdeen District*, «Proceedings of the Society of Antiquarians of Scotland», 116, 1986, pp. 27-40.

A. Ramsay, *The History of the Highland and Agricultural Society of Scotland.* Edinburgh, 1879.

R. Riddell, *Observations on Vitrified Fortifications in Galloway,* «Archaeologia», 10, 1792, pp. 147-150.

S. Shapin, *Property, Patronage, and the Politics of Science: The Founding of the Royal Society of Edinburgh,* «British Journal for the History of Science», 7, 1974, pp. 1-41.

F.H.W. Sheppard, (editor) *Survey of London,* volume 30, *The Parish of St. James, Westminster.* London, 1960.

J. Sinclair, *The Correspondence of the Right Honourable Sir John Sinclair.* Two volumes. London, 1831.

H. Smailes, *The Concise Catalogue of the Scottish National Portrait Gallery.* Edinburgh, 1990.

W. Smellie, *An historical account of the Society of Antiquaries of Scotland,* «Archaeologia Scotica», part 1 (1782), part 2 (1784).

A.M. Smith, *The Forfeited Estate papers: a study of the work of the Commissioners for the Forfeited Annexed Estates 1755-1784.* Ph.D. thesis, St Andrews University, 1975.

A.M. Smith, *The Jacobite Estates of the Forty-Five.* Edinburgh, 1982.

R.B.K. Stevenson, *The Museum, its Beginnings and its Development,* in A.S. Bell, 1981, (q.v.), pp. 31-85.

S.I. Tomkeieff, *The Empress Catherine and Matthew Boulton* «The Times Literary Supplement», 22 December 1950, p. 815.

H.S. Torrens, *The history of coal prospecting in Britain 1650-1900,* in *Energie in der Geschichte* (Proceedings of the 11th Symposium of ICOHTEC (International History of Technology) Symposium), Dusseldorf, Germany, 1984, pp. 88-95.

H.S. Torrens, *Hawking History,* «Modern Geology», 13, 1988, pp. 83-93.

H.S. Torrens, *Under Royal Patronage: the early work of John Mawe (1766-1829) in geology and the background of his travel in Brazil in 1807-10,* in M. Lopes & S. Figueiroa (editors), *O Conhecimento Geologico na America Latina.* Campinas, Brazil, 1990, pp. 103-113.

H.S. Torrens, *J.B. Longmire (1785-1858), a Lakeland Geologist and his work as a Coal Prospector in Russia 1817-1822,* «Proceedings of the Westmorland Geological Society», 5, 1991, pp. 12-14.

H.S. Torrens, *Jonathan Hornblower (1753-1815) and the steam engine: A historiographic analysis,* in D. Smith, (editor) *Perceptions of Great Engineers: Fact and Fantasy.* London, 1994a, pp. 23-34 & pls 1-3.

H.S. Torrens, *Patronage and problems: Banks and the Earth Sciences,* in R.E.R. Banks, and others (editors) *Sir Joseph Banks: a global perspective.* Kew, 1994b, pp. 49-75.

H.S. Torrens, *Joseph Harrison Fryer (1777-1855): geologist and mining engineer, in England 1803-1825 and South America 1826-1828. A Study in Failure,* in S. Figueiroa and M. Lopes, (editors) *Geological Sciences in Latin America: Scientific Relations and Exchanges.* Campinas, Brazil, 1995, pp. 29-46.

T. Tredgold, *On the advantages that may be expected to result, from the study of the principles of Stratification,* «Philosophical Magazine», 50, 1817, pp. 124-7.

A.F. Tytler, *An Account of some Extraordinary Structures on the Tops of Hills in the Highlands...,* «Transactions of the Royal Society of Edinburgh», 2, 1790, pp. 3-32.

F. Venturi, *Scottish echoes in eighteenth-century Italy,* in I. Hont & M. Ignatieff, (editors) *Wealth and Virtue.* Cambridge, 1983, pp. 345-362.

D.C. Ward & A.V. Carozzi, *Geology Emerging.* Urbana, 1984.

A. WAWN, *«Gunnlaugs saga ormstungu» and the Theatre Royal Edinburgh: melodrama, mineralogy and Sir George Mackenzie*, «Scandinavica», 21, 1982, pp. 139-151.

M.E. WEEKS, *Discovery of the Elements*. Easton, Pennsylvania, 1948.

T. WEST, *An Account of a Volcanic Hill near Inverness*, «Philosophical Transactions of the Royal Society of London», 67 (2), 1778, pp. 385-7.

G. WHITTINGTON & A.J.S. GIBSON, *The Military Survey of Scotland 1747-1755: A Critique*, «Historical Geography Research Series» no. 18, (1986) pp. 1-66.

C. WILKINS, *The South Wales Coal Trade*. Cardiff, 1888.

J. WILLIAMS, *Letters from the Highlands of Scotland addressed to G.C.M. Esq.* Edinburgh (copies in NLS & Bodleian library, Oxford), 1777a.

J. WILLIAMS, *An Account of some remarkable Ancient Ruins lately discovered in the Highlands... of Scotland*. Edinburgh, 1777b.

J. WILLIAMS, *Proposals for executing by subscription a topographic engraved map of the coal country*, 1780. Copies in NLS and Bodleian Library, Oxford (the latter among the MSS additions for the third edition of Gough 1780 – volume 4 – f. 383).

J. WILLIAMS, *On petrifactions; with an Account of the Fossil Oak found in the Coalpits at Gilmerton near Edinburgh*, read to the SAS on May 1 1781 (see List of Communications in «Archaeologia Scotica», 1831, 3, p. 150), but never published.

J. WILLIAMS, *Discourse concerning Marbles and other Stones in Scotland, useful for the purposes of Sculpture and Ornamental Architecture*, read to the SAS on June 12 1782 (see List of Communications in *Archaeologia Scotica*, 1831, 3, p. 152), but never published. Williams' original MSS survives in NLS (MSS 996).

J. WILLIAMS, *Hints respecting Volcanoes*, read to the SAS on June 12 1783 (see List of Communications in «Archaeologia Scotica» 1831, 3, p. 154), but never published.

J. WILLIAMS, *Prospectus and Proposals for publishing an Essay towards a Natural History of the Mineral Kingdom*. Edinburgh, 1787 (copies in NLS & Princeton University Library, USA).

J. WILLIAMS, [recte 1790] *The Natural History of the Mineral Kingdom*. Two volumes. Edinburgh, 1789.

J. WILLIAMS, *Plan for a Royal Forest of Oak in the Highlands of Scotland*, read to the SAS on June 19 1781 (see List of Communications in «Archaeologia Scotica», 1831, 3, p. 150), published in 1792 in «Archaeologica Scotica», 1, 1792, pp. 28-38.

J. WILLIAMS, *Journal of a Mineral Survey upon the Estates of Sir W.A. Cunynghame Bart from Mid Calder to Polkemmet*. Edinburgh 1793 (copies in the Hopetown Papers, ref NRA (S) 2717 bundle 147, and NLS – LC 1282 (18)).

J. WILLIAMS, *Suggestions for promoting & improving the Fisheries upon the coasts of Highlands and isles*, «Prize Essays and Transactions of the Highland and Agricultural Society», 1, 1799a, pp. 250-274.

J. WILLIAMS, *Excerpts from «An Essay on the Means of supplying the want of Coals, and of providing Fuel upon a Highland Estate with the smallest loss of time and trouble»*, «Prize Essays and Transactions of the Highland and Agricultural Society», 1, 1799b, pp. 313-323.

J. WILLIAMS, *The Natural History of the Mineral Kingdom*. Second edition, edited by James Millar. Two volumes. Edinburgh, 1810.

J. WILLIAMS, *Preface to «the Natural History of the Mineral Kingdom by John Williams, Mineral Surveyor, F.S.S.A»*, «Philosophical Magazine», 50, 1817, pp. 189-200 & 274-287.

V. WILLS, *Reports on the Annexed Estates 1755-1769*. Edinburgh, 1973.

A. YOUNG, *Travels in France and Italy during the years 1787, 1788 & 1789*, London, 1915.

K. ZITTEL, *History of Geology and Palaeontology*. London, 1901.

III

Geological communication in the Bath area in the last half of the eighteenth century

I am as delirious as ever, still preferring a coal-pit or stone quarry to the Bath Assembly, or a Court Ball.[1]

[E. M. da Costa to Ralph Schomberg of Bath, 1761]

Introduction

Records of geological activity in the Bath area in the last half of the eighteenth century are certainly relatively sparse.[2] There are two main reasons for

In collecting material for a study of this nature one quickly incurs numerous debts to the many librarians and archivists who so courteously look after and aid access to the collections in their care. My debts to these people are so many that I cannot name them here but must single out the three institutions in Bath itself without which this paper could not have been written and thank especially John Kite and all the staff of the Bath Reference Library, Bob Bryant of the Bath Record Office and Philip Bryant of Bath University Library, as well as my own University Library and archivist (Ian Fraser) for similarly valued help. Joan Cliff did wonders in typing my illegible manuscript.

For stimulating discussion and help on specific points I also thank Victor Adams, Robin Atthill, Jim Bennett, David Bick, Gavin Bridson, Warren Derry, Desmond Donovan, Joan Eyles, D. G. Hickley, Hal Moggridge, Roy Porter, Ian Rolfe, R. E. Schofield, John Thackray, Anthony Turner, and Michael Walcot.

[1] J. Nichols, *Illustrations of the literary history of the eighteenth century*, vol. iv, London, 1822, p. 769.

[2] At the conference in 1977 out of which this volume arose, Alex Keller discussed the carefully preserved multi-volume correspondence of the naturalist and fossilologist, E. M. da Costa (1717–1791). He rightly claimed this allowed, because of its complete nature, a study of those interested in fossils at this time as a group, and not just as individuals. This paper has the same aims for much of the same period but is framed instead round one place, Bath in Somerset (now Avon). Any study of this type is fraught with pitfalls, because of the incomplete nature of the material on which it is based, which was always dispersed and much of it since lost (or unknown to me), unlike the da Costa archive, which has survived intact as one accumulation. However, it would be wrong to assume even the da Costa archive was an entirely complete record of fossilology of the period. Josiah Wedgwood senior wrote of da Costa in 1774 to Thomas Bentley thus: 'Doctor [Thomas] Percival has sent me the famous naturalist Da Costa with injunctions to be very civil to him—I gain'd a little relief by sending him 2 miles to see a Flintmill but that is over, and now I am oblig'd to be rude to him whilst I write' (Wedgwood to Bentley, 7 August 1774, Wedgwood Archives Keele University 18551-25); and again ten days later: 'I do not know what character da Costa has . . . However he is

[218]

this. Firstly, much of the activity would have been devoted to collecting geological specimens and especially fossils; such collections, however much treasured by their makers, have long since been dispersed and records of this activity are likely only in references in letters. Secondly, even the records of the organised geological activities of the first two Bath Philosophical Societies, which both flourished in the late eighteenth century, have similarly been dispersed and scattered to the winds. Despite such massive erosion of the basic source material, a study of the Bath area still seems well worth attempting for two reasons. First, the special place Bath occupied in the last half of the eighteenth century 'as the most fashionable place for idling and the most famous watering place in Britain',[3] where one would imagine the collecting of facts and specimens of geological significance would naturally take its place along with the other multifarious activities of the numerous visitors. Second, the special place Bath has occupied since 1827 as the so-called 'cradle of English geology' from the work of William Smith (1769–1839) in this area from 1791 to about 1805.[4]

The special nature of Bath society in the eighteenth century

Despite the massive amount of secondary literature Bath has engendered, there is still 'no professional economic or social history of Bath' in the eighteenth century.[5] There is, however, massive documentation of the popularity of Bath as a resort for medical aid or leisure activity. The most eloquent surviving testimonies to the former are the monumental inscriptions to the many visitors who also died in Bath, which to this day line the walls of Bath Abbey.[6]

> These walls adorned with monument and bust
> Show how Bath Waters serve to lay the dust
>
> Henry Harington (1727–1816)

gone. I left him on Tuesday, and he left the country on Wednesday. Dr P——l is very high in his incomiums of da C. as a very sensible man of the most extensive knowledge and equally extensive correspondence with the literati all over Europe, amongst whom the Doctor says he is very much esteem'd. I thought him the most disagreeable mortal who bore the name of Philosopher that I had ever known—Or I should not have left him so soon' (Ibid., [16 August 1774], 18552-25). One should not be surprised after this to find, as we do, only letters from Percival to da Costa and not from Wedgwood (who was of course deeply interested in geological matters) indexed in the da Costa archive.

³ A. J. Turner, *Science and music in eighteenth-century Bath*, Bath, 1977, p. 15.

⁴ Thus baptised by J. Hunter, *The connection of Bath with the literature and science of England*, Bath, 1827, p. 14.

⁵ J. H. Plumb, *The commercialisation of leisure in eighteenth-century England*, Reading, 1973, p. 20.

⁶ J. Britton, *The history and antiquities of Bath Abbey Church*, London, 1825, pp. 148–51.

The leisure life of Bath was described thus at its zenith in about 1791: 'No place in Europe, in a full season, affords so brilliant a circle of polite company as Bath. The young, the old, the grave, the gay, the infirm and the healthy all resort to this vortex of amusement. Ceremony, beyond the usual rules of politeness, is totally exploded.'[7] Barbeau[8] has described the range of social and literary activities available in Bath; music,[9] the theatre,[10] and bookselling[11] all thrived. The surviving editions of guides, directories, and newspapers produced for the visitors to Bath give a further indication of the size of the leisure industry, and there is a considerable if disseminated literature available on some of its different aspects.

The scientific activity has however been largely ignored. Barbeau stated of Bath inhabitants in the eighteenth century that 'there was little desire for literary or scientific knowledge',[12] but this is certainly not true of a nucleus of Bath residents and visitors who took an active interest in a wide range of aspects of literature and natural philosophy.[13]

Many people from Warner[14] onwards have also claimed that Bath lacked a solid trading and manufacturing base[15] at this time and that industry—that vital catalyst—was absent from Bath. While this may be true of heavy industry, it is certainly not true if, with J. H. Plumb,[16] one considers the tourist trade as an industry. As R. S. Neale has shown 'it was a city where a multitude of skills were in high demand to build, maintain, furnish, feed, clothe and entertain its wealthy residents and visitors. The city was a paradise for the consumer industries',[17] and Warner's claim that Bath in 1801 had no manufactures and little trade can be easily discounted for this single reason. The activities of one closely knit group of tradesmen who settled in

---

[7] *The universal British directory of trade, commerce and manufacture*, Vol. ii, London, 1793, p. 89. (Compiled *c*.1791.)

[8] A. Barbeau, *Une ville d'eaux anglaise au XVIIIe siècle. La société élégante et littéraire à Bath sous la reine Anne et sous les Georges*, Paris, 1904. (English edn.,1904.)

[9] I. Woodfield, *The celebrated quarrel between Thomas Linley (senior) and William Herschel: an episode in the musical life of 18th century Bath*, Bath, 1977; Turner, op. cit. (3).

[10] A. Hare *Theatre Royal, Bath: the Orchard Street calendar 1750–1805*, Bath, 1977.

[11] H. R. Plomer et al., *A dictionary of printers and booksellers who were at work in England from 1726–1775*, Oxford, 1932; lists twenty-seven booksellers active in this period in Bath. G. Pollard, *The earliest directory of the book trade by John Pendred 1785*, London, 1955; adds several more active at this date. For surviving records of some of the circulating libraries run by these men see P. Kaufman, 'The community library: a chapter in English social history', *Trans. Amer. Phil. Soc.*, 1967, n.s. lvii, part 7, pp. 20–21, 62.

[12] Barbeau, op. cit. (8), p. 114.   [13] Turner, op. cit. (3), pp. 81–95.

[14] R. Warner, *The history of Bath*, Bath, 1801, p. 344.

[15] R. Porter, 'Metropolis, enlightenment and provincial culture: the social setting of Herschel's work', unpublished transcript, lecture given in Bath 1977.

[16] Plumb, op. cit. (5), p. 3.

[17] R. S. Neale, 'The industries of the city of Bath in the first half of the nineteenth century', *Proc. Somerset Archaeol. Natur. Hist. Soc.*, 1964, cviii, 132–44; see also R. A. Buchanan, *The industrial archaeology of Bath*, Bath, 1969.

III

Bath in this period from many different places has been briefly documented;[18] they included ironmongers, wine merchants, corn factors, brewers, coachbuilders, and pleasure garden proprietors—all representative of the very important service industries so well developed at this time in Bath.

There were indeed two major service industries which were both vital to the expansion of Bath *and* the level of geological activity in the city. These were the building industry[19] and the stone quarrying industry,[20] both of which would have had profound geological significance and afforded 'much speculation for the naturalist and virtuoso' as Stebbing Shaw noted[21] of the fossils and materials thrown out of the foundations for the Lansdown Crescent built from 1789 to 1793.

Geological activity

Bath enjoyed a major boom in the mid-eighteenth century when new building on a large and beautifully planned scale produced one of the most fashionable resorts in Europe. Bath had been popular before this on account of the mineral waters and the hot and cold baths. John Woodward (1665–1728) had been a medical visitor there in August 1722[22] and was a friend or at least acquaintance[23] of the Bath physician Thomas Guidott (1638–1705) who practised here for nearly forty years[24] and wrote much on the Bath waters, and others nearby. Another important scientific figure with early Bath connections is John Theophilus Desaguliers (1683–1744),[25] early itinerant science lecturer and curator of experiments to the Royal Society from 1716 to 1743. He was a frequent lecturer at Bath and resided here at intervals, being a constant visitor to the Royal Cumberland Lodge of Masons established at Bath in 1733.[26] In the following year, he published a detailed description of the Bath quarry tramroad built in 1731 by Ralph Allen (1694–1764) to run from his Combe Down quarries down to the River Avon.[27]

[18] H. S. Torrens, *The evolution of a family firm: Stothert & Pitt of Bath*, Bath, 1978.

[19] W. Ison, *The Georgian buildings of Bath from 1700 to 1830*, London, 1948.

[20] J. J. Cartwright (ed.), 'The travels through England of Dr Richard Pococke . . . during 1750, 1751, and later years', *Publ. Camden Soc.*, 1888, n.s. xlii, 154–8; K. Hudson, *The fashionable stone*, Bath, 1971.

[21] S. Shaw, *A tour to the West of England in 1788*, London, 1789, p. 294.

[22] M. E. Jahn, 'John Woodward, Hans Sloane and Johann Gaspar Scheuchzer: a re-examination', *J. Soc. Bibliogr. Natur. Hist.*, 1974, vii, 23–4.

[23] J. Woodward, *An attempt towards a natural history of the fossils of England*, Part 1, London, 1729, pp. 154–5.

[24] *Monthly mag.*, 1807, xxiii, 24; J. Britton, op. cit. (6), pp. 88–91.

[25] M. E. Rowbottom, 'John Theophilus Desaguliers (1683–1744)', *Proc. Huguenot Soc.*, 1968, xxi, 196–218.

[26] R. E. M. Peach, *Historic houses in Bath and their associations*, 2nd series, London and Bath, 1884, p. 26.

[27] A. Elton, 'The prehistory of railways', *Proc. Somerset Archaeol. Natur. Hist. Soc.*, 1963, cvii, 31–59.

This expansion in quarrying the local Bath Stone was to meet the demand created by the activities of John Wood the elder. Desaguliers provided the first detailed description of any railway system in English,[28] and he also gave details of the cranes then in use in the quarries.

All this activity in expanding the town of Bath would have encouraged the study of the embryonic science of 'geology', in that it would at least have greatly facilitated the direct observation of rocks and their obvious stratification in the many excavations needed, as well as the collecting of fossils. Alexander Pope (1688–1744) was one person who was considerably encouraged in his collecting; he stayed some months in 1739 with Ralph Allen at Widcombe near Bath. Pope had some years before, in 1725, finished his grotto at his Twickenham house, which fancifully used shells, flints, iron ore, mirrors, or whatever came to hand to create a place of surprise. After his visit to Bath, Pope resolved to improve it and add some Bath curiosities provided by Allen such as Bristol diamonds, alabaster, spars, and snakestones (ammonites), which were all duly incorporated.[29]

More scientific study of the rocks of the area came from John Wood, father and son. John Wood the elder (1704–1754) was the architect and builder who changed Bath 'from a mean looking town to the most beautiful in England' and it is no surprise in view of his vocation to find him devoting chapters on the 'Situation of Bath; of its vales and of its hills' and on the 'Soil of Bath and the fossils peculiar to it' in his *Description of Bath*, which we can take as a summary of Bath geological knowledge and interest at the midpoint of the century.[30] It contains geographical and geomorphological material of no particular note and details of the Bath springs, which were the major attraction to so many visitors. Wood has been criticised for his absurd credulity as to past history, but he was not being more credulous than many others of his time in writing 'in the formation of the Hills that surround the hot springs, Nature seems to have had a spiral Motion so as to form a kind of Volute', an idea found in the writings of many others before and after. Wood connected with this 'the spiral figures [ammonites] which I shall hereafter show to be peculiar to the soil of Bath and perhaps no where else to be met with in such great abundance and in such infinite variety'.[31] The chapter on the soil and fossils is of more interest as it gives rudimentary stratigraphic information and quotes and criticises the late John Strachey (1671–1743) on the local coal mines. Wood observes that the soil near Bath abounded with fossils 'mostly with such as are of a Spiral Figure and such as our Naturalists believe to have been formed in Nautili Shells', and also 'multitudes of

[28] M. J. T. Lewis, *Early wooden railways*, London, 1970, pp. 251–77.

[29] B. Boyce, 'Mr Pope in Bath, improves the design of his grotto', in C. Camden (ed.), *Restoration and 18th century literature*, Chicago, 1963, pp. 143–53.

[30] J. Wood, *Description of Bath*, (1st edn., 1749) 2nd edn., 2 vols., London, 1765, i, chapters VI, VII (facsimile reprint, Bath, 1969).   [31] Ibid., i, 55.

conical stones with elliptical bases found in almost all the stratas of clay and marl within Bath' (i.e., belemnites).[32] He notes also the beds of gravel abounding with different round fossils (i.e., flint echinoids) and concludes 'many other little miracles of nature abound in the soil of Bath to excite a Man's Curiosity to examine into them; and an Age may be spent in a Pursuit of this kind so abundant are the Fossils wherever the Ground is penetrated . . .'.[33]

Wood mentions no contemporary collectors other than himself, but another writer, Charles Lucas (1713–1771), in his 1756 *Essay on waters*, paid tribute to one of the most active of the Bathonian geological virtuosi of this time, Thomas Haviland.[34] He was an apothecary born circa 1706 probably in Bath, and first heard of in 1740 as a subscriber to Thomas Short's *Essay on mineral waters*. By 1753, he had started an extensive correspondence with E. M. da Costa which continued until 1762;[35] he was also a friend and correspondent of traveller and naturalist Thomas Pennant (1726–1798) to whom he gave fossil bivalves 'found in a stoney bank near Bath',[36] and of naturalist John Ellis (c.1705–1776) with whom he corresponded on botany as well as geology in 1755.[37] In 1756, Lucas described Haviland as an excellent apothecary and an accurate botanist with an extensive collection of local Bath fossils as well as others from further afield. His fossil collections seem to have been his main interest, to judge by the Gainsborough portrait of him painted about 1762 which shows two Lower Lias molluscs prominently on his bookshelf and a 1761 edition of Lewis's *Materia medica* in his hand.[38] There is sufficient evidence to show that Haviland, who died in 1770, was both an active and diligent collector and classifier of fossils.[39]

Almost contemporary with Haviland in Bath was the physician Ralph Schomberg (1714–1792) who settled in Bath in the 1750s. He was another of da Costa's correspondents and also a friend of Haviland.[40] He had previously been in medical practice in Yarmouth, being resident there in 1752 when he was elected a Fellow of the Society of Antiquaries in London. Da Costa specifically sought his help from Bath in augmenting his collec-

---

[32] Ibid., i, 61. [33] Ibid., i, 63.

[34] C. Lucas, *An essay on waters*, 3 parts, London, 1756, iii, 235–8.

[35] British Library Add. MSS. 28538, ff. 45–65, dated 1753–62.

[36] Thomas Pennant, 'Reliquiae diluvianae or a catalogue of such bodies as were deposited in the earth by the deluge', British Museum (Natur. Hist.) Palaeontology Library MSS., vol. iii, 339.

[37] S. Savage, *Catalogue of the manuscripts in the library of the Linnean Society of London, Part IV: Calendar of the Ellis manuscripts*, London, 1948, p. 13.

[38] Original portrait in the National Museum, Stockholm; see W. D. I. Rolfe, in J. M. Chalmers-Hunt (ed.), *Natural history auctions 1700–1972: a register of sales in the British Isles*, London, 1976, p. 33.

[39] Bath *Chronicle*, 20 December 1770. [40] Nichols, op. cit. (1), pp. 762–9.

tions as Schomberg 'was in a place—the quarries of which abound in figured fossils'.[41]

It was also Schomberg who recommended John Walcott the elder (died 1776) to Fellowship of the Society of Antiquaries in 1766—his certificate stating he was well versed in history, the *belles lettres* and antiquity.[42] He came from Ireland, owning estates at Croagh near Limerick, a city of which he was made a Freeman in 1750.[43] In 1753 he married a Cork merchant's daughter and his second son named Edmund was born there in 1756.[44] Sadly, the relevant parish records have been destroyed so we are unable to confirm the place and exact date of his eldest son John's birth—who has been claimed as the first Bath geologist [this is now revealed by a pedigree at the College of Arms as 8 August 1754 at Cork—H.T.]. John Walcott senior brought his family to Bath some time between 1756 and 1766 while living off the rents from his Irish estates. Under these conditions his eldest son John fostered an eager interest in all branches of natural history. In a deed of 1759 he is described as about four years old which would suggest he was born in 1754/5[45] and agree with his next youngest brother's known birth in 1756. Their father died in 1776[46] and left evidence of wide scholarship in his library sale catalogue[47] which amounted to 1,675 lots and contained most of the standard works on natural history and geology of the time. His nonconformist attitude was reflected in his burial entry in the registers of Weston near Bath.[48] This trait reappeared strongly in the eldest son, John Walcott junior.

It must have been largely due to the father's influence that John junior took up the study of natural history. He published his first work in 1778–9 in fourteen monthly parts; this was a never completed British Flora which had the laudable intention of providing accurate engravings of the common British plants at a price within the pocket of all but the poorest.[49] Despite encouragement from Erasmus Darwin, it was discontinued in 1779, presumably for lack of subscribers.[50] John Walcott's next book appeared in July or August 1779 at two shillings and six pence, when he was still only twenty-four years old.[51] It was entitled *Descriptions and figures of petrifications*

[41] Ibid., p. 766.   [42] Archives of Society of Antiquaries of London.

[43] *North Munster Antiq. J.*, 1945, iv, 124.

[44] British Library Add. MSS. 29743, ff. 64 and 66.

[45] Public Record Office. Dublin. D 18681, 1 March 1759.

[46] *Notes and Queries*, 1896, 8th series, ix, 383.

[47] British Library press-mark 824.b. 17 (6).   [48] Transcript in Bath Reference Library.

[49] Each part was one shilling; an original wrapper of part 13 is preserved in University College (Natural Sciences Library), London.

[50] Letter from Darwin to Walcott, 3 January 1780, transcribed on front end paper of a copy of Walcott's *Flora Britannica*, in the E. Green Collection, Bristol City Reference Library.

[51] *London Mag.*, 1779, xlviii, 374.

[224]

found in the quarries, gravel-pits, etc. near Bath, and deserves careful attention as it was acknowledged and used by Bath's most famous later geologist, William Smith.[52] It is prefixed by a quotation from Benjamin Stillingfleet's *Miscellaneous tracts relating to natural history,* a work which had been in his father's library:[53]

> Nor are those innumerable petrifactions, so various in species, and structure, to be looked upon as vain curiosities. We find in our mountains, and even in the middle of stones, as it were embalmed, animals, shells, corals, which are not to be found alive in any part of Europe. These alone, were there no other reason, might put us upon looking back into antiquity, and considering the primitive form of the earth, its increase, and metamorphosis.[54]

This book contains descriptions and excellent figures drawn by Walcott himself of the many fossils 'found lodged in stone in almost every part of the environs of Bath'.[55] It ascribes all these to a former universal deluge and displays an impressive grasp of the literature. It classifies these fossils into several groups, such as (i) internal moulds of bivalves of which Walcott observed, 'shells are never filled with stone different from that in which they are lodged', or (ii) ammonites, which 'as far as I have observed the flats of these [*Coroniceras*] lay parallel and conformable to the surface of the stratum in which they are enclosed'.[56]

Localities are, however, rarely given and then never with the accuracy we would hope for; no stratigraphic information is given. He refers merely to freestone [equivalent to the Great Oolite limestone] or limestone [equivalent to the Lias] or simply gives localities as on 'the Ploughed Fields'. He is at his best when seeking affinities with living shells, some of which he figures side by side with the fossils.[57] He also confesses himself defeated by the affinities of some fossils now known to be extinct.

Although in no way breaking new ground, it was and is a remarkable achievement for a twenty-four-year-old, especially for the accuracy of the drawings, which allows the greater proportion of the forms figured to be identified to specific level today. This accuracy of observation and illustration is nowhere better shown than in his *Spiriferina Walcotti* (a Lias brachiopod named in his honour by James Sowerby in 1822)[58] in which the calcified internal spiralia are beautifully shown.

---

[52] W. Smith, *Stratigraphical system of organized fossils*, London, 1817, p. v.

[53] See note (47), lot 894.

[54] Walcott quoted from Stillingfleet (2nd edn., London, 1762, p. 175), who himself was quoting from C. Gedner, *Of the use of curiosity.*

[55] Walcott, *Descriptions and figures of petrifactions . . .* , Bath, 1779, p. iii.

[56] Ibid., pp. 13, 30–31. [57] Ibid., figs. 46–7.

[58] *Mineral Conchology*, 7 vols., London, 1812–46, iv, 106, plate 377, fig. 2.

Although it cannot be proven, Walcott's personal contacts with other scientists outside Bath seem to have been very limited. References to him in manuscript collections are very few and uninformative and he is remarkably badly known for a man who produced four natural history books. One of the most likely influences on his early work in botany and geology was Edward Jacob's (1710?–1788) botanical book published in 1777. Jacob was a surgeon from Faversham, Kent,[59] who began collecting London clay fossils in the 1740s and published on them in the *Philosophical Transactions* in 1754. Like John Walcott senior, he was a Fellow of the Society of Antiquaries.[60] The main influence on Walcott junior seems to have been Jacob's *Plantae Favershamienses* (1777) rather than any personal contact; this last book shows a similar style of presentation to Walcott's more impressive productions, even down to an identical biblical quotation on the two botanical title pages. *Plantae Favershamienses* has a short 'Appendix exhibiting a short view of the fossil bodies of Sheppey' and this too seems likely to have influenced Walcott's book on Bath petrifications two years later.[61]

In November 1779, a few months after Walcott's book had been published, Caleb Hillier Parry (1755–1822) settled as a physician in Bath, where he soon built up one of the most prosperous practices.[62] This, sadly, is the reason no more is heard of Parry's intended work on the fossils of Gloucestershire. He issued printed *Proposals for a history of the fossils of Gloucestershire* in 1781 — no copy of which appears to survive [Parry's 1782 *Prospectus* does survive: British Library, 1881.b 6 vol. 2 — H.T.]. But both John Britton,[63] the topographer and later friend of William Smith, and Parry's son, Charles Henry Parry[64] referred to it, mentioning work Parry had devoted to it before first his extensive practice and then other scientific and agricultural interests caused him to set it aside. It was intended to include all that was known on the subject of organic remains and the discovery of the original manuscripts that were in existence in 1830 would be of major importance.[65]

Parry built up extensive collections of fossils which were later augmented

---

[59] A. Percival, 'Biographical note on Edward Jacob', in E. Jacob, *History of Faversham*, reprint ed. J. Whyman, Sheerness, 1974, pp. 55–61.

[60] John Walcott senior also possessed a copy of Jacob, *History of Faversham*; see note (47), lot 716.

[61] *Plantae Favershamienses [or] a catalogue of the more perfect plants growing spontaneously about Faversham in the County of Kent, etc.*, London, 1777.

[62] H. Rolleston, 'Caleb Hillier Parry', *Ann. Med. Hist.*, 1925, vii, 205–15.

[63] Britton, op. cit. (6), p. 131.

[64] C. H. Parry, 'Parry', in W. Macmichael (ed.), *Lives of British physicians*, London, 1830, pp. 275–304 (300).

[65] An appeal in 1890 for information about them yielded nothing, nor has a recent appeal been successful; 'Gloucestrensis', 'Dr Parry's proposed history of Gloucestershire fossils', *Gloucestershire Notes and Queries*, 1890, iv, 507–8.

[226]

by his purchase of those of William Cunnington (1754–1810) of Heytesbury, Wiltshire in 1810.[66] We can only assume that Parry's birthplace (Cirencester), his scientific training at Warrington Academy and Edinburgh
University, and the publication of Walcott's book so soon before his arrival
in Bath, all aroused his interest in fossils. Parry certainly possessed a copy of
Walcott's book which contains the later signatures of his son and S. P. Pratt,
two further generations of Bath geologists.[67] In 1820, his son Charles Henry
Parry (1799–1860) recorded in his manuscript autobiography a visit to Tog-
hill near Bath, 'once famous for its quarries and specimens — recorded by my
Father in his MSS. notes to Walcott's Petrifications',[68] confirming that Walcott's book was indeed a major influence on Parry's work in geology.

In December 1779, a letter from Thomas Curtis (c.1739–1784) to Edmund
Rack (1735–1787), both then living in Bath, led to the formation late in that
year of the first Bath Philosophical Society.[69] John Walcott junior was
a founder member while Caleb Parry had been elected a member by March
1783.[70] This Society has been strangely ignored, but it certainly predates that
at Manchester, founded 1781, and often wrongly claimed as the oldest of the
provincial philosophical societies.[71] Little is known about Thomas Curtis,
a gentleman of means and well applied leisure whose idea the Society was;
but it bore instant though short lived fruit under the enthusiastic secretaryship of the Quaker Edmund Rack. Rack had moved to Bath in 1775 better to
enjoy the literary life there, and he was soon energetically channelling the
indigenous and immigrant talent of the place into an Agricultural Society
which celebrated its bicentenary in 1977.[72] The Philosophical Society[73]
was a private society of never more than twenty-five ordinary members.[74]
Among these for a short while were men of the calibre of Joseph Priestley
(1733–1804)[75] and William Herschel (1738–1822), and it is the latter's mem-

---

[66] R. Cleeveley, 'The Sowerbys, the Mineral Conchology and their fossil collection', *J. Soc.
Bibliogr. Natur. Hist.*, 1974, vi, 421; J. Britton (ed.), *Beauties of England and Wales*, vol. xv,
London, 1814, p. 314.   [67] In possession of the writer.
[68] Charles Henry Parry autobiographical memoirs, Bodleian Library, Oxford, MSS. Eng.
Mis. d. 613, p. 204.
[69] E. Rack, 'A dissultory journal of events, etc. at Bath Dec. 22 1779 to March 22 1780', Bath
Reference Library MSS. 1111.
[70] T. Curtis to C. Blagden, Royal Society MSS. Blagden letters C. 135 (28 March 1783) and
C.142 (no date, but soon after the last).
[71] E.g. by J. M. Edmonds, 'The geological lecture-courses given in Yorkshire by William
Smith and John Phillips 1824–1825', *Proc. Yorkshire Geol. Soc.*, 1975, xl, 373.
[72] K. Hudson, *The Bath and West — a bicentenary history*, Bradford-on-Avon, 1976.
[73] A preliminary study with a list of members and the printed rules of the Society are to be
found in Turner, op. cit. (3). Two more members can now be added to the twenty-seven listed
there.   [74] Turner, op. cit. (3), p. 88.
[75] Priestley's previously unknown connection with the Society is given by Rack, op. cit.
(69). He had also already been in contact with Joseph Townsend (1739–1816), later William

bership until 1782 which provides much of the information we have about the Society. The thirty-two papers Herschel submitted to the Society on physics, metaphysics, and astronomy have largely been published[76] and give the quite false impression that the Society was not at all concerned with studies of natural history. New material shows this to be wrong, as it equally shows that technological discussion at the Society was minimal, unlike the contemporary Lunar Society, which Priestley later joined on moving from Calne in Wiltshire to Birmingham in 1780.[77]

Members with an active interest in natural history included William Watson junior (1744–1824), MD Cambridge 1771, FRS 1767, who was related by marriage to Samuel Galton junior (1753–1832) of the Lunar Society and who supported Galton's certificate for Fellowship of the Royal Society in 1785. Watson published on zoology[78] and was keenly interested in botany and geology.[79] Caleb Hillier Parry (1755–1822), MD Edinburgh 1778, who has already been mentioned, as has John Walcott (1754–1831), were also members, along with John Walcott's friend Matthew Martin (1748–1838), who published several works on both botany and entomology and who contributed natural history papers to the Society.[80] Martin was a friend and correspondent of William Withering, one of the major naturalists of the Lunar Society.[81] John Coakley Lettsom (1744–1815), MD Leyden 1769, FRS 1773, and Matthew Dobson (died 1784), MD Edinburgh 1756, FRS 1778,[82] were two members of the Society who were active in geology. A full study of the membership and activities of this and later Bath Philosophical Societies is in progress by the author, but preliminary evidence already shows that fossils and their origins were discussed at Society meetings following an initial paper by Thomas Parsons (1744–1813), who was a Baptist minister in Bath and also, like his better known father Robert (1718–1790), a stone mason and carver.[83] This latter activity, which Thomas continued up to 1791 at least, would explain a knowledge of, and interest in fossils.[84]

Smith's friend; J. Priestley, *Experiments and observations relating to various branches of natural philosophy*, vol. i, London, 1779, p. 208.

[76] J. L. E. Dreyer (ed.), *The scientific papers of Sir William Herschel*, 2 vols, London, 1912, i, pp. lxv–cvi.

[77] R. E. Schofield, *The Lunar Society of Birmingham*, Oxford, 1963, p. 189.

[78] *Phil. Trans.*, 1778, lxviii, 789–90,

[79] C. C. Hankin, *Life of Mary Anne Schimmelpenninck*, London, 1860, pp. 89–91.

[80] A. A. Lisney, *A bibliography of British Lepidoptera 1608–1799*, London, 1960, pp. 222–3.

[81] Catherine Wright to William Withering, letters 1784–1787, Royal Society of Medicine Library, London.

[82] Dobson's membership of the Bath Society is given by his obituary notice in the *Bath Chronicle*, 29 July 1784, probably written by Edmund Rack. I owe this reference to the kindness of Warren Derry.

[83] R. Gunnis, *Dictionary of British sculptors 1660–1851*, London, 1968, pp. 292–3.

[84] He is perhaps the P.T. who signs a letter to the *Gentleman's Mag.*, 1788, lviii, 793, about

[228]

Edmund Rack also seems to have spent a good deal of what little free time was left over from acting as Secretary to both the Philosophical and Agricultural Societies thinking about, discussing and collecting in natural history and geology. In May 1779, on a journey to Sidmouth in Devon collecting subscriptions for the Agricultural Society in Bath, he collected some living corals at the coast. In August 1779, he wrote about these to the *Gentleman's Magazine*,[85] and on 13 January 1780 they formed the subject of the second paper submitted to the Bath Society, while they were further discussed in William Herschel's first papers to the Society.[86] Rack submitted his mature reflections on these animals to the Royal Society in 1782.[87]

After the subject of fossils had first been presented by Thomas Parsons, as the fifth paper to the Bath Society on 21 January 1780, Rack himself seems to have devoted much attention to the subject. Perhaps the best demonstration of this is in the Bath Agricultural Society Accounts from 1780 onwards, which include the following entries:[88]

1780 June 28
Expences of Journey into Dorsetshire to collect Subscriptions to the Agricultural Society *and* Natural Curiosities.
10 days   £4-15-0

1780 Sept. 10
To Fossils   1-3

1780 Sept. 14
A Box for Fossils   1-6

1780 Sept. 24
Carriage of a Box of Fossils from Norfolk   2-2

1780 Oct. 24
Carriage of Sea Shells and Fossils—Weymouth   2-6

1780 Nov. 10
Carriage of Basket Fossils from Charmouth   2-9

1780 Nov. 16
Carriage of Basket from Charmouth   1-7

1780 Dec. 9
Carriage of Fossils and Petrefactions from Portland   4-4

After this entries become less specific and we find instead:

the 'thousands of petrifications of once living animals' to be found in the excavations then in progress on the slopes of Lansdown.

[85] *Gentleman's Mag.*, 1779, xlix, 432–3.   [86] Dreyer, op. cit. (76), pp. lxvi–lxvii.
[87] Royal Society of London MSS. Letters and Papers VIII, no. 8, 12 p.
[88] Bath Agricultural Society archives, vol. 10, accounts for 1777 to 1796, Bath Record Office.

1781   May 26
    Journey into Dorsetshire collecting subscriptions   £1-9-9
    carriage of a Box   2-6

This journey is again closely followed by the carriage of a box which we may assume again contained minerals (fossils to Rack) or fossils (petrifactions to Rack) as before, and that subscriptions were not the only thing Rack was collecting in Dorset!

In 1781, Rack and the Rev. John Collinson (1757–1793) issued the first proposals for their intended *History of the County of Somerset*.[89] Further proposals seeking subscriptions were issued in 1784 and 1785.[90] Rack's part in this work was to survey the topography and natural history of each Somerset parish, which he did assiduously from 1781 to 1786. Rack died before the work was published in three volumes in 1791 by Collinson and 'so has almost lost the credit due for his work'.[91] The recent discovery of Rack's original manuscript for this work[92] shows what a great deal he had accomplished and allows his major share of this work to be correctly assessed. His travels over Somerset for this project gave him opportunities to travel widely in the south-western counties and to meet fellow fossilologists. One such was the Rev. John Wickham (1730–1783) of Horsington in South Somerset. He had graduated BA at Oxford University in 1749, where he had attended James Bradley's lectures on natural philosophy[93] and made the acquaintance of William Huddesford (1732–1772), curator of the Ashmolean Museum,[94] to whom he sent fossils from the Dorset coast in 1760. Wickham was also in contact with the naturalist Gustave Brander (1720–1787) (as was John Walcott),[95] and William Curtis (1746–1799), the Quaker botanist.[96] Wickham was a most enthusiastic collector of fossils, as both Smart Lethieullier (1701–1760), who in 1760 described him as 'as fairly catch'd in the fossil trap as any one I have ever met with',[97] and his monumental inscription in Horsington church testify. Wickham seems to have been the rediscoverer of the celebrated Liassic ammonite marble of Marston Magna, Somerset, specimens of which he presented in 1782 to the Woodwardian museum in Cambridge. Information about his discovery of this marble was transmitted in 1784 by his friend Rack to both John Hunter[98]

[89] 'Anecdotes of Mr Edmund Rack', *Europ. Mag.*, 1782, i, 361.

[90] E. Green, *Bibliotheca Somersetensis*, 3 vols., Taunton, 1902, ii, 317.   [91] Ibid., i, 429.

[92] Smyth of Long Ashton MSS. (uncatalogued), Bristol Record Office.

[93] R. T. Gunther, *Early science in Oxford*, vol. xi, Oxford, 1937, p. 370.

[94] Bodleian Library. Ashmolean MSS. 1822, f. 87.

[95] *History of the collections contained in the Natural History Departments of the British Museum*, 2 vols., London, 1904, i, 269–70.

[96] W. H. Curtis, *Life of William Curtis*, Winchester, 1941, pp. 16–17.

[97] R. T. Gunther, *Early science in Oxford*, vol. iii, Oxford, 1925, p. 224; a reference I owe to the kindness of Joan Eyles.

[98] J. Hunter, *Observations and reflections on geology*, London, 1859, pp. xliii–xliv.

[230]

and to the Society for Promoting Natural History, in London, founded in 1782.[99]

Another member of the Bath Philosophical Society with an interest in fossils was John Arden (1720–1791), an important example of that particularly eighteenth-century phenomenon, the itinerant lecturer in science.[100] After an active career lecturing and teaching throughout England, he settled in Bath in 1777 for about six years. At this time he was already the friend of many well known scientists such as Priestley (a fellow Philosophical Society associate)[101] and Josiah Wedgwood.[102] He had previously lectured in Bath at least twice in 1769 and 1770,[103] and he must have found audiences and life here congenial for we find him as a founder member of the Agricultural Society, soon after his arrival in Bath, to which he soon offered the use of his 'very complete Apparatus of Philosophical Instruments',[104] and two years later in 1779 of the Philosophical Society. In 1777 we also find his eldest son, James (1752–1842), corresponding a little acrimoniously with E. M. da Costa about the purchase of a 'fossil' collection of over 700 specimens both 'native and extraneous', which arrived from da Costa in August.[105] It seems at least possible that John Arden may have used these in his Bath lecture courses which Edmund Rack attended, although no mention of such lectures appears in his printed synopses. He also may have delivered special lectures on fossils and minerals as da Costa was doing at the same time in London.[106]

In 1782 the Society for Promoting Natural History was founded in London. 'Mr John Hamlyn—Miniature painter at Bath' was admitted an honorary member at the second meeting. He was merely interested in geological specimens as curiosities, to judge by the flint from his collection figured in 1781.[107] Other members of this society with strong Bath connections were Edmund Rack (honorary member 1783), John Walsh of London (ordinary member 1785), John Coakley Lettsom of London (ordinary member 1786); both Walsh and Lettsom were already members of the Bath Philosophical Society. Another honorary member (1784) was James Stephens of Camerton near Bath, who was one of William Smith's earliest patrons and one of the

---

[99] A. T. Gage, *A history of the Linnean Society of London*, London, 1938, p. 5. (The original MSS. of Rack's papers survive in the Society's archives.)

[100] Turner, op. cit. (3), pp. 83–6.

[101] J. Priestley, *Experiments and observations relating to various branches of natural philosophy*, vol. ii, Birmingham, 1781, pp. 379–82.

[102] Arden to Wedgwood, letters dated 1763–64, Wedgwood Archives, Keele University (1616/9, 1-30225/6). [103] *Bath Chronicle*, 29 December 1768, 1 March 1770.

[104] T. F. Plowman, 'Edmund Rack', *J. Bath West England Agr. Soc.*, 1914, 5th series, viii, (p. 21 of offprint). [105] British Library Add. MSS. 28534, ff. 118–21.

[106] V. A. Eyles, 'The extent of geological knowledge in the eighteenth century', in C. J. Schneer (ed.), *Toward a history of geology*, Cambridge, Mass., 1969, pp. 159–83 (175–9).

[107] *Gentleman's Mag.*, 1781, li, 617 and fig. 1.

chief instigators of the Somerset Coal Canal, which was of such significance in Smith's career. Rack contributed at least two papers to this Society on fossils and their origins, which must also have been read to the Bath Society. The London society was 'much interested in exploring fossil bodies'.[108] Among the bodies they explored were the jaw of an unknown animal with many teeth from the Dorset coast (perhaps an Ichthyosaur) exhibited by Hamlyn and fossil plants sent by Stephens from Camerton, which had been found in sinking one of his collieries, later to be served by the Coal Canal. Dr Henry Menish (died 1809) of Chelmsford, who was elected an honorary member of the London society in 1785 also appears in contact with Rack before this time; the Bath Agricultural Society accounts record, in Rack's hand, their payment of the postage on a 'Packet from Dr Menish' on 24 July 1784, no doubt again containing fossils for the use of Rack and the members of the Bath Philosophical Society.[109]

For the period from 1777, with the foundation of the Bath Agricultural Society, through 1779, with the foundation of the Philosophical Society, Rack appears as the focal point of scientific activity in Bath, and especially in its dissemination outside the area, until his death in 1787. Apart from the Society for Promoting Natural History, he was in contact with other Agricultural Societies, as well as the Society of Arts, the Royal Society in London, and the Literary and Philosophical Society, founded in 1781 in Manchester. After 1779 the German, Georg Lichtenberg (1742–1799), would surely never have written to Herschel himself in early 1783 of his earlier visit to Bath, 'Good Heavens! had I but known, when I spent some days in Bath in October 1775 that such a man [i.e. Herschel] was living there'.[110]

Not only did the Bath Philosophical Society bring Herschel forward, it also effectively improved scientific communication to and from Bath between the inhabitants and numerous visitors to Bath,[111] through its indefatigable secretary Edmund Rack. With his illness in 1786 and death in early 1787 this channel of communication ceased and the Society was dissolved.[112]

Several areas of geological communication have not yet been touched on. We have little record of the role of museums in the area. Certainly by this time travelling displays of natural curiosities—like Rev. Robert Ferryman's primarily zoological collection in April 1789[113]—would have been visiting

---

[108] The Society archives are preserved in the Linnean Society Library, London.

[109] See note (88).

[110] M. L. Mare and W. H. Quarrell, *Lichtenberg's visits to England*, reprint, New York, 1969, p. 95.

[111] For an estimate of some of the numbers of visitors to Bath in this period, see S. McIntyre, 'Towns as health and pleasure resorts—Bath, Scarborough and Weymouth 1700–1815', University of Oxford D.Phil. thesis, 1973, p. 463.   [112] Turner, op. cit. (3), p. 95.

[113] D. Lysons, *Collectanea*, 5 vols., no place, n.d., (British Library press-mark 1889 c5).

[232]

Bath, but of these we have till now little evidence. A museum was set up in Bristol in 1784 at the Baptist Academy there [114] and certainly contained fossils and other geological material by 1799, but the first reference to such a collection on public display in Bath is not found until 1809 when the largely Natural History Museum at 21 Union Street was open.[115] Similarly little is known about the sale of geological specimens in Bath at this time. Rack's Journal mentions private collections of fossils and minerals apparently for sale in Bath and of these details can sometimes be found in the advertisement columns of the local press (see Figure 9).[116] The first dealer as such to be located is James Lintern, listed as 'Music and Petrefaction Warehouse, Abbey Yard' in the 1787 Bath Directory. He died in February 1817 and was, with his brother Walter (who died in 1806), a well known publisher of music and a musical instrument maker.[117]

Casual visitors to Bath, of which there were multitudes at this time, may also have widened the circles of geological communication, both in the area and outside. Details of visitors are sparse and we know no more of James Hutton's (1726–1797) visit here than that it took place in September 1774.[118] Jean André de Luc (1727–1817) was a frequent visitor from 1773,[119] his first year in England, and in 1785 he married a Bath widow at St James's church in Bath.[120] In 1787 he too noted the regular stratification and abundant fossils,[121] temporarily exposed in the feverish building activity on the slopes of Lansdown, north of Bath, which were commented on by several other writers.[122] Others resident in Bath for short periods could be mentioned, such as David Erskine, eleventh Earl of Buchan (1742–1829), who lived in Bath until the death of his father there in 1767, and who was a friend of

[114] Gentleman's Mag., 1784, liv, 485–6.

[115] Wood & Cunningham (publishers), The improved Bath guide; or picture of Bath and its environs, Bath, [1809], pp. 78–9. For Rack, see note (69). William Smith's offices in Bath at 2 Trim Bridge (Torrens, op. cit. (18), pp. 20, 22) from 1802 to 1805 contained his fossil collections on display but not, apparently, to the public; L. R. Cox, Proc. Geol. Ass., 1941, lii, 16.

[116] E.g. 'Medals, coins, fossils, etc. to be sold . . .', Bath Chronicle, 2 January 1783; 'All the pictures, prints, drawings, medals, coins, fossils and shells, the property of Mr Hamlyn (who is going abroad)', Bath Chronicle, 8 May 1783.
Reproduced as Figure 9. Mr Hamlyn is the miniature painter John Hamlyn mentioned above.

[117] James is claimed as the original ascriber of the title 'The harmonious blacksmith' to Handel's well known composition which he supposedly published with this title. No copy survives to prove this, but a James Lintern, blacksmith, appears in the 1837 Bath directory as further evidence of a strangely triangular family business. E. Blom (ed.), Grove's dictionary of music and musicians, 5th edn., London, 1954, v, 250.

[118] E. Robinson, 'The Lunar Society: its membership and organisation', Trans. Newcomen Soc., 1964, xxxv, 153–77 (163)

[119] J. A. de Luc, Geological travels in some parts of France, Switzerland and Germany, 2 vols., London, 1813, ii, 368.   [120] Bath Chronicle, 10 February 1785.

[121] J. A. de Luc, Geological Travels, 3 vols., London, 1810–11, ii, 206–13.

[122] See notes (21) and (84).

BATH, MAY 1, 1783

TO be SOLD by AUCTION,
By WILLIAM CROSS,
On Wednefday the 14th inftant, and following days,
At the Exhibition-Room in Bond-ftreet,
All the PICTURES, PRINTS, DRAWINGS, MEDALS,
COINS, FOSSILS, and SHELLS, the property of
Mr. HAMLYN, (who is going Abroad.)
Among them are the Works of the following Ancient and Mo-
dern Mafters, viz.

Della Bella	Vandeift	Guercino
Polydore	Cuyp	P. Veronefe
Antonio	Teniers	Hemfkirk
Callott	Grimm	Titian
Pouffin	Gainfborough	Carlo Maratti
Brueghel	Weft	Vandvke
Spagnoletto	Worlidge	Carracci
Parmegiano	Raphael	L. Da Vinci, &c.

A capital picture of Mofes and the Children of Ifrael at the
foot of Mount Horeb, by Parmegiano., beautiful Drawings ele-
gantly framed and glazed.

The Medals, Coins, &c. are near 3000 Greek, Roman; large,
middle, and fmall Brafs, and Denarii, in feries; a fuperb collection of Englifh Silver in fine prefervation; feveral hundred
Town-pieces and Tokens, Medallions in Silver and Brafs of ex-
qoifite workmanfhip, by Daffier, Hammerani, &c.

The Foffils comprehend native and extraneous petrifactions,
chryftals, marqnifetts, fpars, filver, copper, tin, lead, and iron
ores; fome fpecimens of porphyries, granates, &c. Shells for
the cabinet or grotto; a repofitory or book-cafe, handfome ma-
hogany medal cabinets, nefts of drawers; a large iron cheft, &c.

The whole 'tis prefumed forms a Collection fuperior to any
of the kind ever offered for fale in Bath.

To be viewed on Monday and Tuefday preceding the fale,
which will begin each morning at eleven o'clock.

Catalogues to be had at the place of fale, and of W. Crofs,
uphoïder and undertaker, in Milfom-ftreet; and of Meffrs. Oliver
and Ridout, the corner of High-ftreet, Briftol.   [2888

FIG. 9. 'All the pictures, prints, drawings, medals, coins, fossils and shells,
the property of Mr. Hamlyn', Advertisement, *Bath Chronicle*,
8 May 1783

[234]

Alexander Catcott (1725–1779) of Bristol and the dedicatee of the second edition of Catcott's *Treatise on the deluge* (1768). He sent Catcott word in 1766 of the discovery of a forty foot 'Young Whale' in the Lias of Weston, near Bath.[123] Another short-stay resident of Bath was the physician, Dr John Berkenhout (1730–1791), MD Leyden 1765,[124] who lived and practised here between 1781 and 1782, meeting William Herschel with whom he corresponded in 1788.[125] Berkenhout had published an influential three volume *Outlines of the natural history of Great Britain* (1769–71) with good coverage of geological material, and a revised edition came out after his Bath period in 1788.

Practical geology

One field of geological communication was certainly germane to the development of the science in the area—the field of economic geology as we would call it today, i.e., the activities of the so-called 'practical men'. Such men had a long association with three geological facets of the area: the Bath stone industry, the associated Bath building industry, and the nearby Somerset coalfield centred on Radstock to the south of Bath, whence came the coal used in the Bath market.[126]

Prospecting for Bath stone or for coal in the Somerset coalfield did not present great problems in this period. In the Somerset coalfield there was already a considerable tradition of surveying skills which could be called on,[127] as William Smith did soon after his arrival in the Somerset coalfield.[128] But practical men were *also* active in areas far outside the coalfields in the search for further deposits of coal needed to fuel the growing industrialisation of the country. Records of the many attempts made to find coal outside the coalfields are not likely to be usually available for the simple reason that people would not chronicle futile attempts after their expensive failure had become known. John Farey wrote in 1807[129] of hundreds of instances, known to himself or William Smith, of such futile attempts to find coal in the southern and eastern counties of England where none was to be found. I shall describe one such case for the light it sheds on the work of such coal

[123] Lord Cardross to Catcott, 17 October 1766, Catcott MSS., Bristol City Reference Library. [124] *Dictionary of national biography*.
[125] Berkenhout to Herschel, 1 February 1788, Herschel MSS. W13 B 60, Royal Astronomical Society Library, London.
[126] J. A. Bulley, 'To Mendip for coal—a study of the Somerset Coalfield before 1830', *Proc. Somerset Archaeol. Natur. Hist. Soc.*, 1953, xcvii, 46–78. [127] Ibid., pp. 63–5.
[128] J. G. C. M. Fuller, 'The industrial basis of stratigraphy: John Strachey (1671–1743) and William Smith (1769–1839)', *Amer. Ass. Petrol. Geol. Bull.*, 1969, liii, 2272–3.
[129] J. Farey, 'Coal', in A. Rees (ed.), *The cyclopaedia or universal dictionary of arts, sciences and literature*, vol.viii, London, 1807.

hunters and 'practical men' in the days before scientific prospecting methods were developed.[130]

Attempts to find coal near Bath in the eighteenth century were very few because the supply from the nearby coalfield was able to meet the demand. Farther inland in South Somerset and Dorset, coal was much more expensive because of the added and considerable cost of carriage from the mines and it was here that attempts were frequent. The best documented attempt known to me was at Shaftesbury in Dorset, twenty miles south of the coalfield, in 1791, the year of William Smith's arrival in Somerset.[131] Shaftesbury was then a thriving county town with a population of over two thousand. It had long felt the need for cheaper coal; the first recorded attempts to find it were in about 1690 when specimens of the Upper Kimmeridgian shale, in which the attempt was made, yielding diagnostic ammonites and a large pliosaur vertebra, were found and passed into John Woodward's collection where they are still preserved today in Cambridge.[132] The attempt was made to the south of the town, which is built on Upper Greensand unconformably overlying the Kimmeridge clay which superficially resembles, and was many times mistaken for, the Coal Measures. Attempts were made in this Kimmeridge clay again in 1791; we first hear of this adventure in a Salisbury newspaper notice of December 1790[133] which reported 'so great an appearance [of coal] as to afford well-founded hopes of success' and that other attempts had also been made about sixty years previously.

The 1791 adventurers were inspired especially by two events. Firstly by other attempts in 1790 farther afield; one at Chard in Somerset on the Lower Lias shales, which inevitably came to nothing but which did not stop further attempts in the very same place in 1826, the other in Hampshire under the management of a Mr Jeffery of Salisbury, thought to have been Henry Jeffrey (c. 1767–1819) a chemist there. The site of this attempt is not known but seems likely to have been the trial, personally observed by William Smith in the spring of this same year opposite the 'Shoe Ale-House' at Plaitford[134] only eleven miles south-east of Salisbury, in the much more recent Bagshot Beds of the Tertiary, and was equally unsuccessful.

The Shaftesbury attempt was also inspired by the advice of a famous,

[130] A preliminary account has appeared in H. S. Torrens, 'Coal exploration in Dorset', *Dorset Mag.*, 1975, no.44, 31–9.

[131] Documented: (a) 'MSS. Shaftesbury occurrences — topography, miscellaneous 1820–1830 collected by John Rutter' at Shaftesbury Museum. This contains a collection of the original minutes, bills and printed ephemera relating to the 1791 trial.

(b) MSS. draft c. 1827 of 'An historical and descriptive account of the town of Shaftesbury', by John Rutter, which was never published; Dorset Record Office D/50/1.

[132] J. Woodward, *An attempt towards a natural history of the fossils of England*, London, 1728, tome ii, 52, 99.   [133] *Salisbury and Winchester Journal*, 20 December 1790.

[134] J. Phillips, *Memoirs of William Smith Ll.D.*, London, 1844, p. 5.

[236]

though now little known, itinerant science lecturer, John Warltire (c. 1739–1810),[135] who lectured much at Bath [136] and in the West Country, specifically at Salisbury in 1775 and 1786.[137] Indeed, one of his 1786 lectures dealt with the formation of minerals and petrifactions (see Figure 10). He gave his opinion in 1786, according to two of the 1791 adventurers who must have attended his lectures, that there was 'one continuous bed of coal from Henstridge Ash [in Somerset] to Sherborne [in Dorset]', eight miles apart.[138] He was probably referring to the arcuate and faulted outcrop of Forest Marble of Middle Jurassic age, between these places, which many people before and after were also to confuse with true Coal Measures. John Warltire was of Greek descent and had settled in England by 1762. He quickly became a sought after and popular itinerant lecturer in natural philosophy and his help was acknowledged by Joseph Priestley in isolating oxygen in 1774. Erasmus Darwin (1731–1802) invited his help about the same time and Warltire instructed both Darwin's and Josiah Wedgwood's children in science. He was elected an early honorary member of the Manchester Literary and Philosophical Society in 1782, and by the time of his visit to Salisbury he was at the height of his reputation. White Watson (1760–1835), mineral dealer of Bakewell, attended his lectures there in 1781 when he specifically lectured on mineralogy, and Watson also obtained chemical analyses of rocks from him.[139] William Gregor (1761–1817) was inspired with a taste for mineralogy from his lectures in Bristol [140] and John Farey (1766–1826), the geologist, also refers to him with approval.[141] He can be regarded with Arden as representing the best in eighteenth-century itinerant science lecturers.

We can see then that there were good grounds from a contemporary viewpoint for another attempt for coal near Shaftesbury. The 1791 attempt was made by a group limited to twenty local gentlemen and tradesmen who all initially agreed to subscribe £20 each to finance the attempt. In the available manuscript sources their names are merely listed, but it has proved possible to identify the majority of the adventurers.[142] The secretary was

[135] D. McKie, 'Mr Warltire, a good chymist', *Endeavour*, 1951, x, 46–9; N. G. Coley, 'John Warltire 1738/9–1810 itinerant lecturer and chemist', *West Midlands Stud.*, 1969, iii, 31–44.

[136] *Bath Chronicle*, 21 September 1776, 21 March 1788.

[137] *Salisbury and Winchester Journal*, 13 November 1775, 13 November 1786. For these references and note (133) I am greatly indebted to Victor Adams.

[138] Richard Pew to John Rutter, 12 February 1819, Shaftesbury Museum, see note (131); Rev. W. Blandford to Miss C. Bower, 6 February 1791, Dorset Record Office KW8.

[139] W. Watson MSS. 1303, Derbyshire Record Office 589, Z.Z.6; W. Watson, 'On Entrochal Marble', Bakewell, 1826, single sheet.

[140] L. Trengrove, 'William Gregor (1761–1817) discoverer of titanium', *Ann. Sci.*, 1972, xxix, 362.

[141] J. Farey, 'Cursory geological observations lately made . . .', *Phil. Mag.*, 1813, xlii, 58.

[142] Drawing on a variety of sources but especially 1783, 1784 and 1791 *Directory* lists and the fine collection of Shaftesbury deeds preserved in the Dorset Record Office.

MR. WARLTIRE prefents his compliments to the Ladies and Gentlemen of the City, Clofe, and Neighbourhood of SALISBURY, informs them that he intends opening his Courfe of Twelve Lectures, at the Parade Coffee-Houfe, on Monday the 13th of November, at half after fix in the evening, on the following fubjects:

The Properties and Ufes of the COMMON Air.

The Nature of the PRESSURE of Fluids, conftruction of various Machines for raifing, and advantageoufly applying Water, &c.

The Doctrine of MECHANICS, and the application of that Branch of Science to the raifing and moving heavy Bodies, &c.

The Science of OPTICS, or the application of different Glaffes to form the various kinds of Microfcopes, Telefcopes, &c.

The conftruction of the Natural Eye, illuftrated by Diffection.

The Difcovery, Progrefs, prefent State, Power, Ufes, &c. of ELECTRICITY.

GEOGRAPHY and ASTRONOMY.—Many new Ideas applied to explain Branches of that Science hitherto not underftood.

The Method of procuring and applying to ufeful Purpofes MANY KINDS of Air—being new Difcoveries.

The Theory of the Earth, applied to account for the Formation, Change in Appearance, Alteration of the Properties, &c. of MINERALS and PETRIFACTIONS.

The Nature and Effects of HEAT, LIGHT, PHLOGISTON, &c.

The Utility of Mechanical and Chemical Philofophy to Mankind in general explained.

Mr. Warltire affures the Ladies, that NATURAL Philofophy, as now taught, is at once inftructive and enterta'ning; every opinion being illuftrated by experiment—which he is enabled to do, having in his poffeffion a very extenfive and elegant Apparatus, confifting of an ORRERY of a very complete kind,—GLOBES much improved,—AIR-PUMPS with the lateft improvements,—MODELS of MECHANICAL and HYDRAULIC Machines,—a complete collection of OPTICAL INSTRUMENTS,—an extenfive ELECTRICAL APPARATUS,—every thing neceffary for the Chemical Part,—a curious Philofophical Collection of MINERALS, &c. &c.

SUBSCRIPTION ONE GUINEA.

For the accommodation of Ladies and Gentlemen from the country, and fuch as cannot make it convenient to attend in the Evening, a Morning Courfe as above will commence on Thurfday the 16th inft. at 12 o'clock at Noon. [769

FIG. 10. Announcement of lectures on natural philosophy by John Warltire, *Salisbury and Winchester Journal*, 13 November 1786

[238]

Charles Bowles (1766–1837), a Shaftesbury solicitor and brother of fellow adventurer, Rev. William Lisle Bowles (1762–1850), cleric and poet, the best known of the twenty and the only one to achieve an entry in the *Dictionary of national biography*. The Treasurer was the local Shaftesbury banker, Edmund Ogden (c. 1748–1812), who is two years later found on the Dorset and Somerset Canal Committee. Apart from these, we find two described as gentlemen, including the Mayor, two clergymen apart from W. L. Bowles (all three were Oxford trained), one tailor-cum-publican, one other solicitor, one other publican, two grocers, two tanners, one edge-tool maker who supplied ironmongery and expertise for the attempt, one brewer, one surgeon, one post-horse supplier, and one who is difficult to categorise called Lawson Hudleston (c. 1745–1811), who, after Oxford University, had entered the Indian Civil Service and was highly regarded as an inventor and patentee. The chairman and the man largely responsible was another local surgeon called Richard Pew (1752–1834), MD St Andrews 1804. He is in many ways the most interesting of the group, having been trained at Edinburgh University (1775–7), where he became a Fellow of the Royal Medical Society and a friend of Joseph Black (1728–1799), who (by his lectures) interested Pew in chemistry and geology and with whom Pew later corresponded.[143] Pew published a chemical pamphlet in 1796 acknowledging his debt to Black. Pew had travelled on the continent as physician to the Bristol merchant James Ireland (c. 1725–1814) before settling at Shaftesbury. This explains Pew's connections with Bristol and Bath circles and his election as an honorary member of the Bath Agricultural Society in 1792.

Another subscriber with Edinburgh connections was the surgeon and Mayor in 1790, John White (died 1793), on whose estate the main attempt was made. His son, John White junior (1767–c. 1808), was in 1789 a medical student at Edinburgh University where he attended John Walker's (1731–1808) course on natural history.[144] We can see from Scott's edition of Walker's lecture notes dating from circa 1788 what White would have been introduced to on the subject of strata and geology.[145]

Another of the adventurers, whose education is also likely to have encompassed some geology, was the treasurer, Edmund Ogden. He was born in Liverpool about 1748 and in 1764, at the age of sixteen, entered the well known Dissenters' Academy at Warrington.[146] He would have been taught natural philosophy by John Holt (died 1772) and if he remained a student until 1767 he would have had the opportunity of attending John Reinhold

---

[143] Pew to Black, 12 October 1784, Black MSS. ii, 228–9, Edinburgh University Library.

[144] MS. list of students, at the class of natural history in the University of Edinburgh, 8 May 1789, Edinburgh University Library. I owe this information to the kindness of Joan Eyles.

[145] H. W. Scott (ed.), *Lectures on geology by John Walker*, Chicago, 1966.

[146] J. F. Fulton, 'The Warrington Academy (1757–1786) and its influence upon medicine and science', *Bull. Inst. Hist. Med.*, 1933, i, 50–80.

Forster's (1729–1798) lectures on natural history and mineralogy given from 1767 to 1769.[147] Ogden had moved to Shaftesbury by 1772. Ogden also recorded receiving help with the attempt to find coal from a 'Mr Bright of Bristol' in April 1791, when he also asked Bright to send two men from Bristol to supervise the boring operation. They duly arrived. Mr Bright must be Richard Bright senior of Bristol (1754–1840), fellow banker and fellow Warrington Academy student (entered 1769). Bright and Ogden were related by both families having married into the Heywood family—a Liverpool banking family which included the treasurer of the Warrington Academy from its foundation. Bright was an early devotee of both geology and mineralogy,[148] and in 1780 he was elected an honorary member of the Chapter House Philosophical Society in London,[149] whose members included Richard Kirwan (1733–1812), John Whitehurst (1713–1788), and many other eminent scientists,[150] such as James Watt, Josiah Wedgwood senior and Joseph Priestley, all with an active interest in geology and mining operations.

Backed by all this range of contemporary skills, advice and experience, the team of twenty was convinced that Coal Measures were to be found on the outcrop of the Kimmeridge clay near Shaftesbury, and they made three different attempts to find them. The first went down to a depth of 405 feet using the same boring irons as the Hampshire attempt of 1790, before being abandoned. Surveyors and miners from Salisbury, Wells and Bristol were all involved. But the search proved quite futile and was abandoned in 1792. Another similar venture started in 1804, this time in the hope that the Oxford clay at Brewham near Bruton, a few miles north in Somerset, would yield coal. This venture cost a good deal more—£2750—and reached 652 feet depth.[151] It is an identical story of misapplication with some of the same names, like Pew and Richard Messiter (1759–1830), a Wincanton solicitor, involved in this as in the Shaftesbury trials. The numerous attempts to find coal in the Jurassic and higher parts of the stratigraphic column in England in the last part of the eighteenth and early parts of the nineteenth century necessitate rejection of Rachel Laudan's claim that the ability to identify strata was 'commonplace' at this time.[152]

[147] M. E. Hoare, 'Johann Reinhold Forster (1729–1798): problems and sources of biography', *J. Soc. Bibliogr. Natur. Hist.*, 1971, vi, 4.

[148] Buckland, obituary notice of Bright, in address to Geological Society, 1841, *Proc. Geol. Soc. Lond.*, 1841, iii, 520–2.   [149] Wedgwood archives, Keele University.

[150] R. W. Corlass, 'A Philosophical Society of a century ago', *Reliquary*, 1878, xviii, 209–11.

[151] G. Sale, *Four hundred years a school: a short history of King's School, Bruton*, Bruton, n.d., unpaginated.

[152] R. Laudan, 'William Smith. Stratigraphy without palaeontology', *Centaurus*, 1976, xx, 210–26 (225).

III

Summary: The nature of late eighteenth-century geological activity in Bath

In a notably hostile review of R. E. Schofield's book on the Lunar Society of Birmingham, D. W. F. Hardie made the valid point that 'in democratic societies at least to assert guilt by association is generally considered bad law; finding significance by association and association alone, is equally bad historical procedure'.[153] Similar problems of association are raised on another front by Paul Kaufman who, writing of eighteenth-century reading and book-borrowing habits, noted that 'we cannot ever assume how much the library borrower anywhere did actually read—if he read—without some evidence'.[154] In short, even if a man borrowed or bought a particular book, we cannot from this be sure he read it! While in the case of C. H. Parry's ownership of John Walcott's 1779 book on Bath fossils we *can* prove Parry was directly influenced by it,[155] we are much less able to *prove* the significance of the association of different men who worked at the geology of Bath in the late eighteenth century. However, if we were to take D. W. F. Hardie too seriously, we would never attempt even to demonstrate the facts of such associations at all. This is all that has been attempted here. Peter Medawar has said that 'the factual burden of a science varies inversely with its degree of maturity' and this is also true of the history of science, which is still at a very immature stage in its development.[156] This paper is purely a preliminary attempt to document some of the basic factual data in the development of eighteenth-century geology, as it applies to a particular but significant English city.

In general it can surely be shown that there *was* a considerable amount of geological activity in this period in Bath, and that this activity has previously been almost entirely ignored by writers, like Barbeau, who have concentrated on the social and literary activity.[157] One can also demonstrate that, via such people as Edmund Rack and his fellow members of the first Bath Philosophical Society, there was considerable communication of that activity to the regions outside Bath both during the life of the Society and after. It is worth at least noting the wide social composition of the membership of the Philosophical Society, ranging in religious persuasion from Quaker, lapsed Catholic, Presbyterian, Methodist (both Wesleyan and Huntingtonian) to Church of England; and ranging in background from tradesmen (stone carver, optician, soap boiler, coal merchant, and so on) to clergy, itinerant lecturers, gentlemen, and physicians and surgeons. Medical men

---

[153] D. W. F. Hardie, [review of R. E. Schofield, *The Lunar Society of Birmingham*], *Business history*, 1966, viii, 73–4. See also M. Berman, [review of A. E. Musson and E. Robinson, *Science and technology in the Industrial Revolution*], *J. Social Hist.*, 1972, v, where the same point is made. [154] P. Kaufman, *Libraries and their users*, London, 1969, pp. 34, 88. [155] See note (68). [156] P. B. Medawar, *The art of the soluble*, London, 1967, p. 114. [157] See note (8).

comprise ten out of the twenty-nine known members, and physicians with medical degrees eight out of the twenty-seven identified members. Of these eight, six were at least partly educated at Edinburgh, with medical training at Leyden, Oxford, Cambridge and Glasgow also apparent. The contribution of the medical men was a significant one. Also of significance is the fact that of the twenty-nine, fourteen are mentioned in the *Dictionary of national biography*, twelve were elected Fellows of the Royal Society, and of the remainder some, like John Walcott, at least deserved—but never got—notice in the *DNB*. One very important point about the nature of eighteenth-century Bath society in general has already been well made by Roy Porter.[158] This is the lack of an indigenous culture there. The many visitors were attracted to Bath for particular reasons and the tradesmen, physicians and others who settled there, often for short periods, were all drawn to Bath from elsewhere for related reasons. This is shown by the fact that only two of the twenty-nine Bath Philosophical Society members (and one not positively identified) can claim to have been born in Bath. All the others whose places of birth are known were born elsewhere. This essentially peripatetic Bath culture was thus one singularly lacking in roots.

William Smith's contribution

One of the reasons this paper was undertaken was to examine Smith's debts to previous workers on Bath geology. To extend the analogy, if Bath *was* the cradle of modern English geology, was Smith the father or merely the midwife to previously conceived ideas?

William Smith (1769–1839) arrived in High Littleton, seven to eight miles from Bath, in 1791. By 1817 we have his acknowledgement of one obvious and direct connection with this previous activity in his use of John Walcott's book of 1779, but it is not known when Smith first encountered this book.[159] The man Smith himself mentions[160] as the first interested in his geological activities was Thomas Davis (c. 1749–1807) of Horningsham, Wiltshire, agent and land steward of the Marquis of Bath's estates at Longleat where he served from about 1763 to 1807.[161] Davis was also in direct contact by 1800[162] with the one man who might have directly stimulated Smith's interest in fossils, James Stephens (c. 1748–1816), squire of Camerton near Bath, chairman and one of the major promoters of the Somerset Coal Canal, a major colliery owner and the man 'on whose estates [in 1796] Smith first

---

[158] Porter, op. cit. (15), p. 11.   [159] See note (52).
[160] Wm. Smith MSS. 1831, Department of Geology, Oxford University.
[161] Monumental inscription in Horningsham church by Henry Westmacott.
[162] L. Blomefield, 'Copy of a letter from Mr Stephens of Camerton near Bath to Mr Davis of Longleat on the subject of diseases of wheat dated August 22 1800', *Proc. Bath Antiq. Field Club*, 1877, iii, 12–16.

put in practice his ideas of draining derived from a knowledge of the strata',[163] while he was still employed by the Canal Company. As we have seen, Stephens was a keen naturalist, a collector and student of fossils, and he had been elected an honorary member of the Society for Promoting Natural History in London in 1784. How, and if, Stephens did influence Smith's geology is not yet known.

Smith was elected a member of the Bath Agricultural Society on 13 December 1796,[164] probably supported by the next of his early contacts, the Rev. Benjamin Richardson (c. 1758–1832), with whom Smith was seemingly in contact by 1797[165] having been introduced to him by Davis. Even before his election to this Society, Smith's influence on Bath geological communication may have been felt. In April 1796 a letter appeared in the *Monthly Magazine* dated 17 March and written by John Hodder Moggridge (1771–1834) of Stokehouse, Bradford-on-Avon near Bath, describing a 'Wonderful Phenomenon in Mineralogy'.[166] This was an illustrated description of the massive current bedding found in the Bathonian Combe Down Oolite at Bath of which the writer sought an explanation.[167] One could be forgiven for regarding this as evidence of an interest in the local geology quite independent of Smith. John Moggridge senior (1731–1803) was a clothier from Bradford-on-Avon and from 1794 Lord of the Manor of Dymock, Gloucestershire,[168] and he was also much involved with his son, from the end of 1797 at least, in coal mining operations, in the Newent coalfield, with Richard Perkins and his son of Oakhill, Somerset, who had been involved in this coalfield since October 1795.[169] Richard Perkins junior (c. 1773–1850) was the son of another Richard Perkins (?1753–1821) who was a surgeon in Oakhill. Perkins senior had accompanied Samborne Palmer (1758–1814) of Timsbury, another colliery owner, and William Smith on their famous fact-finding mission for the Somerset Coal Company management committee to the North of England, Shropshire and Wales in August and September 1794.[170] Since, in November 1794, just after their return, Richard Perkins junior had married John Hodder Moggridge's sister Elisabeth at Dymock,[171] we can see that the independence of John Moggridge's geological interests from those of William Smith now needs to be proved rather than assumed,

[163] W. Smith, *Observations on the utility, form and management of water meadows*, Norwich, 1806, p. 54; see Phillips, op. cit. (134), p. 16.

[164] Archives of Bath Agricultural Society, v, 182, Bath Record Office.

[165] J. A. Douglas and L. R. Cox, 'An early list of strata by William Smith', *Geol. Mag.*, 1949, lxxxvi, 180–88 (182).

[166] *Monthly Mag.*, 1796, i, 205.   [167] Turner, op. cit. (3), pp. 13–14.

[168] J. E. Gethyn-Jones, *Dymock down the ages*, privately published, 1951, p. 30.

[169] D. E. Bick, 'The Newent Coalfield', *Gloucestershire Hist. Stud.*, 1971, v, 75–80; D. E. Bick, 'The Oxenhall branch of the Herefordshire and Gloucestershire Canal', *J. Railway Canal Hist. Soc.*, 1972, xviii, 71–5.

[170] Phillips, op. cit. (134), pp. 6–14.   [171] *Gentleman's Mag.*, 1794, lxiv, 1054.

for it seems quite likely Smith was the catalyst for the twenty-five-year-old Moggridge junior's interest in Bath geology.[172]

In June 1799 Smith was introduced to the Rev. Joseph Townsend (1739–1816), Rector of Pewsey, whose association with Smith is well known. One aspect of this association has however not been previously reported and may well have had a considerable influence on the early diffusion of Smith's ideas both in and around Bath. In late 1798 the second Bath Literary and Philosophical Society was instituted.[173] Records of this Society are even fewer than those of the first, but it has so far proved possible to identify ten members of it, including three who had belonged to the first Society. Sir William Watson, who had been such an important member of the old Society, was one of them and he seems to have played a leading role in the new Society. The member, however, with major geological interests was Joseph Townsend, who was certainly a member by late 1804.[174]

About the same time as Smith met Townsend, he also came into contact with William Cunnington of Heytesbury near Warminster (1754–1810), and in the next year Smith presented his geological results to the Bath Agricultural Society which voted him public thanks at the General Meeting on 10 June 1800, at which he was present, 'for his communication and observations relating to some new Improvements in Agriculture and Mining at the same time requests him to favor the Society with his further remarks on the subject'.[175] Two days later the newly elected secretary of the Society, Nehemiah Bartley, wrote on behalf of the Society to Smith 'thanking him for his observations on the various strata and to request further communications'.[176] A further connection with Bartley is that his third son, Thomas (1780–1819), previously a canal agent with the Kennet and Avon Canal, became for a short time clerk to Smith about 1800.[177]

It seems clear that Smith's total isolation from scientific contact was hardly a reality after his election to the Bath Agricultural Society. Just as Herschel was greatly helped by the activities of the Bath Philosophical Society, three of its members supporting his election as Fellow of the Royal Society, so it seems that Smith was similarly aided by the activities of the Bath Agricultural Society a few years later. Edmund Rack's two creations had certainly justified themselves.

[172] For valued help with genealogical information on the Moggridge and Perkins families, I gladly thank Hal Moggridge, Robin Atthill and the Gwent County Archivist.

[173] F. Shum, *A catalogue of Bath books*, Bath, 1913, p. 20; J. Britton, 'Bath', in A. Rees (ed.), *The cyclopaedia or universal dictionary of arts, sciences and literature*, vol.iii, London, 1803.

[174] James Currie to William Roscoe, 7 February 1805, Roscoe MSS. 1108, Liverpool Reference Library.

[175] Archives of Bath Agricultural Society, v, 10 June 1800, Bath Record Office.

[176] Ibid., iii, 12 June 1800.

[177] B. Richardson to W. Smith, 31 December 1804, Wm. Smith MSS., Department of Geology, Oxford University.

[244]

Of the innovative nature of Smith's geological work there is very clear testimony. Using Walcott's 1779 book and Rack's manuscript notes on the 'Natural history of Somerset' of about 1785,[178] as barometers of the state of Bath geology just before Smith arrived in Somerset, we can see how clearly original and rapid his advances were. Both Walcott and Rack were mainly interested in fossils and minerals as collectors, of whom there were then a large number in the Bath area,[179] no doubt a direct result of the abundantly fossiliferous nature of the area; but neither paid any significant attention to the vital recording of localities of specimens or to the stratification of rocks.

The most eloquent testimony to the nature of Smith's achievement comes from those with whom he came into contact before the close of the century, such as William Cunnington, who wrote to Sir Richard Colt Hoare in 1809 in a letter describing the distribution of rocks and fossils along the Swindon to Chipping Norton road that 'the longer I live the more I am convinced of the importance of Smith's system [of identifying strata] and more heartily do I wish him to lay it before the public for examination'.[180] Similar comments came from Joseph Townsend, as quoted by Richardson:

> We [i.e., Townsend and Richardson about 1800] were soon much more astonished by proofs of [Smith's] own collecting that whatever stratum was found in any part of England the same remains would be found in it and no other. Mr Townsend *who had pursued the subject 40 or 50 years* and had travelled over the greater part of civilised Europe declared it perfectly unknown to all his acquaintance.[181]

The coal hunters also bear passive but eloquent testimony to this originality. The attempt for coal in the Oxford clay at Brewham, near Bruton, was one which Smith personally warned against in 1805, and his originality in mineral surveying and prospecting using his knowledge of the strata cannot be challenged. Dr Richard Pew, who, as already described, was involved in both the 1791 Shaftesbury attempt and the 1804 Bruton attempt, was to write in 1819, nearly thirty years after his first involvement in coal hunting, that

> Mr [Robert] Bakewell's Elements [*sic*] of Geology [1813] or Mr Smith's Maps of the strata [1815] I think will throw a doubt upon the courage

---

[178] This consists of a separate notebook in Rack's hand listing clays, marls, ochres, tripelas, fossils (i.e. minerals), spars, crystals, stones, geodes, and fossil shells found in Somerset with an 'Account of the coal mines near Stowey and Faringdon and Chew Magna' which is almost entirely derived from John Strachey's pioneer work. These notes intended for and partly used in John Collinson's *History of Somersetshire* give no clue that Rack was aware that Somersetshire strata could be identified or tabulated in any way; MSS. at Bristol Record Office.

[179] Phillips, op. cit. (134), pp. 17, 28.

[180] R. H. Cunnington, *From antiquary to archaeologist*, Aylesbury, 1975, p. 141.

[181] B. Richardson, letter of 10 February 1831, in A. Sedgwick, address on announcing the first award of the Wollaston prize, *Proc. Geol. Soc. Lond.*, 1831, i, 270–9; emphasis added.

and expectation of finding coals here about [Shaftesbury], nevertheless from the strong *seeming* indications of coal between the bottom of East Stour Rill [Corallian Beds] and Toomer Rill [Forest Marble], Lord Digby, the Marquis of Anglesey and Sir Rich^d. Hoare did at my suggestion about [1816] employ a Mr Bailey a miner from Staffordshire to make a survey.[182]

Despite Smith, Pew was still not finally aware of the reliability of prospecting techniques, for this part of the geological column, of which he had been totally ignorant before 1805.[183]

We may leave the final word on Smith to one man well able to judge, the Quaker William Matthews (1747–1816), who settled in Bath in 1777 as a brewer and coal merchant.[184] He was a founder member of both the first Bath Philosophical Society and the Agricultural Society of which he was *also the second and highly successful secretary from 1787 to 1800, taking* over from Edmund Rack.[185] He was thus in a well positioned vantage point for judging Smith's contribution to the development of geology in Bath. Early in 1800 he too called attention to Smith's novel discoveries, in a work published in Bath, writing thus:

> Then, hail, ye patriots, who can prize renown
> On peaceful plains, where sylvan honours crown!
> Let morning air invigorate your pow'rs,
> And plans of increase mark your passing hours.
> Waste long-neglected acres be your care,
> And barren wilds with fruitful fields compare.
> The depth and kind of surface-soil explore,
> How mark'd with fatness, or how tinged-with ore;*

---

* Mr SMITH, an ingenious land-surveyor, of Midford,

[182] See note (138).

[183] There is a serious need for research into the evolution of coal prospecting techniques both inside and outside the known coalfields. If the experience from Somerset is typical, practical men can be demonstrated as often particularly bad at identifying strata. For the Bruton attempt of 1804–10, already twice noted, the sinker in charge of a notably abortive trial was Gregory Stock, mining agent of Ashwick, Somerset, who later appears as a source of stratigraphic information for the southern part of the Somerset coalfield supplied to W. Buckland and W. D. Conybeare, 'Observations on the South-Western coal district of England', *Trans. Geol. Soc.*, 1831, 2nd series, i, 210–316 (270–1). The lunatic waste of money spent searching a second time for coal on Chard Common, Somerset,in 1826, went on employing Samuel Barton of Nottingham to bore at a point he chose himself on the Lower Lias shales where as he said 'the local Coal Measures appeared to be the most laid bare'! He bored a 7½ inch diameter hole 379 feet deep which failed to leave the Lias. (Somerset Record Office, DD/CN box 28, bundle 21.) Barton, a coal agent, was one of the men who helped John Farey with his survey of Derbyshire. See his *General view of the agriculture and minerals of Derbyshire*, London, 1811, p. xvii; he might thus have known better.

[184] Turner, op. cit. (3), p. 90.   [185] See note (72).

> near Bath, has studied with success this subject, and the
> publick, it is hoped, will ere long be benefited by a publi-
> cation of his important discoveries respecting the general
> laws of nature in the arrangement and external signs of
> under-strata, inclusive of fossils and minerals.[186]

This is a clear acknowledgement of the originality of Smith's skill at identifying the strata of Bath.

[186] W. Matthews, *A dissertation on rural improvements*, Bath, 1800, 65.

IV

LE « *NOUVEL ART DE PROSPECTION MINIÈRE* » DE WILLIAM SMITH ET LE « *PROJET DE HOUILLÈRE DE BREWHAM* » : UN ESSAI MALENCONTREUX DE RECHERCHE DE CHARBON DANS LE SUD-OUEST DE L'ANGLETERRE, ENTRE 1803 ET 1810

Résumé. – À la fin de l'année 1803, un groupe d'entrepreneurs vivant dans – ou aux environs – de la ville anglaise de Bruton, dans le Somerset (sud-ouest de l'Angleterre), décidèrent d'essayer de trouver du charbon dans cette région. Ils lancèrent bientôt une souscription locale pour réaliser cette recherche. Lorsqu'elle fut émise, au début de 1804, leur dessein était de réunir la somme – alors énorme – de deux mille livres (en actions de vingt livres chacune). Cette somme devait permettre de réaliser les explorations nécessitées par la recherche de charbon qu'ils pensaient devoir exister dans cette région. Leur concession notait que, «*Brewham* [aujourd'hui deux petits villages juste au nord-est de Bruton], *par la frappante similitude de son sol, de son site et de son aspect avec tous* [sic] *les pays où les houillères abondent, est scientifiquement* [sic] *reconnu pour être le plus digne d'être choisi pour un essai*». Cette souscription permit de réunir l'argent nécessaire et la plus grande partie des explorations commença bientôt. La tentative fut seulement abandonnée en 1810 quand le puits eut atteint une profondeur supérieure à 650 pieds (200 mètres), sans rien trouver excepté de l'eau.

Abstract. – Late in 1803 a group of English entrepreneurs living in, or near, the English town of Bruton in Somerset, decided to try to find coal in the area. They soon set up a local subscription to achieve this. Their proposals, when issued early in 1804, were to raise the – then enormous – sum of £2,000 (in shares of £20 each). This was to enable proper explorations to be made for the coals which they thought must occur in that area. Their claim noted that «*Brewham* [two small villages just north-east of Bruton] *by its striking similarity of soil, site and aspect with all* [sic] *countries abounding in collieries, is scientifically* [sic] *acknowledged to be the most eligible for* (such) *a trial* ». This subscription raised the money needed and major explorations were soon started. The whole attempt was only wound up in 1810 when their shaft had reached a depth of over 650 feet (200 m), but found nothing except water.

INTRODUCTION

« *Die englische Nation hat darin einen grossen Vorzug vor andern, dass ihre wissenschaftlichen Männer das ins Ganze Versammelte, sowie das einzeln Gefundene baldmöglichst in Tätigkeit zu bringen suchen ; am sichersten kann dies geschehen durch allgemeine Verbreitung des Gewussten. Hiezu verschmähen sie kein Mittel...* » (Goethe 1824 in Schmid, Goethe, Schriften, 1949, p. 332).

Hugh Miller (1802-1856) écrivait également en 1841, avec un authentique pragmatisme écossais que « *la géologie, d'une manière particulière, fournit à l'intellect un exercice de* [...] *caractère annoblissant. Mais cela a également un prix. Le temps et l'argent gaspillés en Grande Bretagne uniquement pour la recherche de charbon dans des régions où des géologues bien informés auraient immédiatement proclamé la recherche sans espoir, aurait fait beaucoup plus que couvrir les frais entraînés par la poursuite de la recherche géologique à travers le monde* » (Miller, Old Red Sandstone, 1861, p. 196). J'espère que cet article constituera une contribution à ce domaine méconnu de l'histoire et de la signification de la prospection des ressources minérales, qui est une partie si vitale de la géologie moderne et des perspectives d'emploi de mes étudiants d'aujourd'hui. L'histoire qui est racontée ici montre que le caractère désespéré de cette tentative anglaise de recherche de charbon, qui débuta en 1803, avait été démontré dès 1805 par

William Smith (1769-1839), un pionnier dans l'interprétation de l'«*ordre naturel*» des couches d'Angleterre.

À la fin du dix-huitième siècle, un groupe d'entrepreneurs anglais vivant dans, ou aux environs de la ville de Bruton, dans le Somerset (sud-ouest de l'Angleterre) décida d'essayer de trouver du charbon dans cette région. Leur premier contrat pour y affermer des terres remonte à 1798 (Bruton School Archives – ci-après BSA – B V 15), ce qui suggère que la «*fièvre du charbon*» des années 1790 (Torrens, 1979, p. 228-232) avait déjà atteint Bruton. Mais ce contrat avait seulement pour but d'exploiter du charbon quelque part dans le domaine *(«Manor»)* de Bruton. Cette vague tentative qui ne commença jamais, devait être liée au projet de canal du Dorset et du Somerset, qui devait relier la Manche au Canal de Bristol, conçu pendant une autre fièvre – cette fois de construction de canaux! – qui fit l'objet d'une promotion active dans les années 1790. Le tracé proposé pour ce canal devait traverser tout droit la région dans laquelle on prévoyait de faire des essais de recherche de charbon (Clew, 1971, p. 29).

Quand ce canal fut projeté pour la première fois, en 1793, le charbon était le premier et l'«*article de commerce* [le plus] *certain* [qui] *puisse suffire à lui seul à couvrir les frais*» de construction (*Bath Chronicle*, 17 & 31 janvier 1793, p. 2). En 1796 ses promoteurs incluaient Henry Sampson Michell (qui souscrivit 500 £), Isaiah Maggs (300 £), George Prince (200 £), John Sharrer Ward (500 £) et Stephen White (100 £). Tous furent bientôt activement impliqués dans le «*projet de houillère*» de Brewham. En outre, Richard Messiter (1759-1830), le chef du bureau chargé des travaux du canal était aussi l'un de ses banquiers.

Il est cependant remarquable que sur les sommes importantes – entre 146 000 et 200 000 £ –, estimées nécessaires entre 1795 et 1796 par William Bennet, l'ingénieur géographe du canal, pour construire le canal qui ne fut jamais terminé, «*pas plus de 70 000 £ furent souscrites et [...] seulement environ 58 000 £ furent réellement reçues par la compagnie*». Ce fut à cause de *l'état dégradé du pays, de l'influence de la Révolution française, des sommes importantes levées par des emprunts gouvernementaux, et des prix élevés qui accompagnaient ces événements*» (Anonyme, 1825, p. 2).

L'ESSAI DE RECHERCHE DE CHARBON DE BREWHAM ENTRE 1803 ET 1805

À la fin de 1803, les entrepreneurs de Bruton mirent sur pied une nouvelle tentative de décou-

verte de charbon et lancèrent une souscription locale pour aider à payer les frais d'exploration. Ils avaient alors déjà choisi le site de Cook's Farm dans le petit village de North Brewham, à l'est de Bruton. Celui-ci était encore plus proche du tracé projeté du «*D & S Canal*». Des «*Propositions* [imprimées] *de participation au projet engagé pour la découverte de charbon à Brewham, Somerset*», datées du 24 novembre 1803, furent bientôt mises en circulation (BSA B V 7). Elles ont été reproduites par Torrens (1975, p. 35). Cette nouvelle tentative était peut-être encore plus directement liée aux infortunes déjà en cours du «*D & S Canal*»? À la fin de 1803, celui-ci avait été abandonné, «*tant il était difficile de se procurer de l'argent à 5% d'intérêt, pendant la reprise de la guerre*» (Anonyme, 1825, p. 4). Mais il était certainement encore envisagé aussi tard que 1811, que «*lorsque le Dorset & Somerset Canal sera prolongé* [jusqu'à la côte méridionale de l'Angleterre], *toute la côte méridionale du comté de Dorset sera accessible au même commerce* [charbon, blé et fer]» (Anonyme, 1811, p. 24). Les entrepreneurs de Brewham ont bien pu penser en 1803 qu'investir plus directement dans ce «*charbon*» serait un investissement plus «*sûr*». Le prix du charbon du nord du Somerset avait été opportunément augmenté peu de temps auparavant (*Bath Journal*, 3 janvier 1803, p. 3). L'accès à un tel charbon leur aurait alors permis de profiter du canal à terme, quelle que soit la date à laquelle il ouvrirait. Ils avaient encore à découvrir combien ils se trompaient!

Les entrepreneurs de Brewham cherchaient initialement à lever la somme respectable de 2 000 £, divisée en cent actions de 20 £. Cela afin de permettre le démarrage des explorations proprement dites de recherche du charbon. Dès que cette somme aurait été levée, une Assemblée générale se tiendrait pour nommer un Comité de douze souscripteurs chargé de diriger l'entreprise. Un trésorier serait aussi nommé et il faudrait se procurer une «*parcelle de terrain et des ouvriers pour faire un essai sérieux*». Le secrétaire était à cette époque un certain James James, de Cole, un village proche de Bruton.

L'avis imprimé suivant (BSA B V 8 & WRO 383/906) était plus instructif. Daté du 21 février 1804, il était intitulé «*Un essai pour la découverte de charbon à Brewham près de Bruton, Somerset*». Son préambule remarquait fort justement que le charbon était l'une des «*premières nécessités de la vie*» et affirmait que «*dans un pays* [le Somerset] *si généralement connu pour abonder en mines, l'essai que l'on projette maintenant de faire, ne peut être qualifié avec justice ou raison de spéculation vaine* [original en italique]

Un essai malencontreux de recherche de charbon

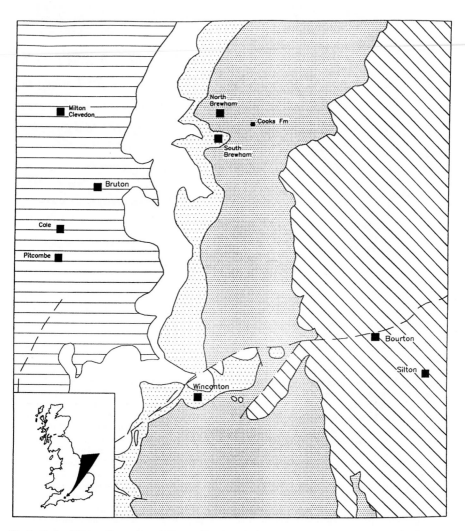

Fig. 1 : Carte géologique des environs de Bruton, Somerset, Angleterre. Les couches les plus anciennes affleurent
à l'ouest. Deux failles sont figurées en tiretés.
On distingue d'ouest en est : le Fullers Earth et les couches sous-jacentes (hachures horizontales), le
Forest Marble (blanc), le Cornbrash (pointillés), le Kellaways Clay and Rock (environ 3 mètres, à la base)
surmonté par l'Oxford Clay (grisé) et un ensemble de couches s'étageant du Corallien au Crétacé
(hachures obliques).
(Document original)

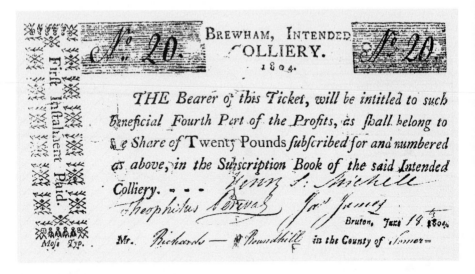

Fig. 2 : Billet d'action délivré en juin 1804 à M. Thomas Richards, de Roundhill, Somerset. (Reproduit avec l'aimable autorisation de Miss G. Richards, de Wincanton)

même par l'homme le plus intéressé ». Cela faisait partiellement référence au bassin houiller du nord du Somerset (Down et Warrington, 1971), qui exploitait ce que nous savons aujourd'hui être du charbon d'âge carbonifère. Mais les entrepreneurs de Brewham justifiaient leur essai par d'autres motifs qu'ils prétendaient plus scientifiques puisque *« Brewham, par la frappante similitude de son sol, de son site et de son aspect avec tous* [sic] *les pays où les houillères abondent, est scientifiquement* [sic] *reconnu pour être le plus digne d'être choisi pour un essai ».* Autrement dit, le choix de Brewham devait être fondé sur les similitudes superficielles qu'on pouvait y observer en surface.

1000 £ avaient alors été souscrites et, *« de manière à fonder son exécution sur un plan systématique, le Comité provisoire élu par les souscripteurs actuels, offre au public les clauses suivantes ».* Premièrement, qu'un ingénieur compétent devrait être consulté *« sur l'emplacement et les meilleurs moyens »* et que, sur sa décision, des ouvriers et un contremaître compétent devraient se mettre au travail. Deuxièmement, que les salaires devraient être payés par le contremaître et que des comptes détaillés de tous les frais payés seraient imprimés. Enfin, qu'*« étant donné qu'il est dans l'intention du*

présent Comité de fonder cette entreprise sur la base la plus désintéressée, enthousiaste et libérale, ils offrent d'agir bénévolement et gratuitement, aucun frais ne devant être encouru excepté ceux qui concernent directement l'essai ».

Le nom du très important ingénieur n'a pas été conservé, pas plus que la raison pour laquelle le site choisi fut celui de North Brewham, à moins que ce fût simplement en raison de sa connexion aisée avec le canal projeté. On pourrait supposer que les comptes finaux de 1810 (BSA B V 14) mentionnaient le nom de l'ingénieur. Le 1er janvier 1807 quelques cordages furent vendus *« par M. William Bennett »* et ensuite, après l'abandon de l'essai, le 17 septembre 1807 figure une entrée, *« Encaisser par la vente de tous les matériels par William Bennett ».* Un homme portant ce nom travaillait alors comme ingénieur, à la fois pour les compagnies du Somerset Coal et du Dorset and Somerset Canal, et était bien connu de William Smith (1769-1839), le géologue et ancien géomètre expert de la Coal Canal Company. Bennett avait survécu à la crise subie par cette compagnie en 1799, à la différence de Smith, qui avait été renvoyé. C'est pourquoi il serait facile de penser que ce William Bennett est aussi devenu l'ingénieur des entrepreneurs du charbon de Brewham. Mais il est beaucoup plus probable que ces indications concernent le commissaire-priseur et expert du même nom qui exerçait alors à Bruton (*Bath Chronicle*, 7 janvier 1808, p. 3).

Des copies du prospectus de février 1804 furent alors expédiées. Deux se trouvent dans les archives (WRO 383/906) de l'antiquaire, historien local et propriétaire foncier Sir Richard Colt Hoare (1758-1838), membre de la Royal Society depuis 1792 et membre de la Society of Antiquaries depuis la même année (cf. Woodbridge, 1970). Une lettre datée du 25 février 1804, que lui avait adressée Theophilus Perceval de Bruton, qui était alors le secrétaire de ce qui n'était encore que le « *Comité provisoire* », accompagnait le prospectus ; elle subsiste également (WRO 383/906). La lettre de Perceval proclamait que « *le risque* [de souscrire] *une action comparé à la probabilité d'une découverte* [de charbon] *est hors de proportion et je me flatte que vous ayant convaincu* [...] *que le projet n'est pas* [...] *une entreprise commerciale inconsidérée et vaine, vous m'autoriserez à honorer de votre nom la liste des souscripteurs* » puisque Perceval « *était d'opinion que 2000 ou 3000 £ au plus permettront de mener l'essai à son terme : ainsi, si l'on doit trouver le charbon, ce que je crois fermement devoir être le cas, la moitié de l'argent judicieusement dépensé nous amènera jusqu'aux veines* [de charbon] ». Hoare possédait de vastes terres dans les environs immédiats, sa famille ayant acheté Bruton Abbey en 1778 (Couzens, 1972, p. 49) mais il ne souscrivit jamais à ce « *projet de houillère de Brewham* ». Il existe une raison manifeste à cela : son contact avec William Smith (voir plus loin).

Précision non dénuée d'intérêt, Perceval avait été « *autrefois de Paris* ». Il avait dû venir en Grande-Bretagne pour des raisons en rapport avec la Révolution française, mais on ne connaît ni l'exacte raison ni la date précise de sa venue. Tout ce que l'on sait est qu'il avait reçu les « *Lettres* » lui accordant la semi-naturalisation en tant que « *fileur de soie, présentement de Bruton* », sous sceau privé de la Couronne (« *by British Privy Seal* »), le 31 mai 1811 (PRO H. O. 4), selon une copie certifiée datée du 8 juin 1811 qui se trouve actuellement dans la collection Brian Shingler (Shingler, 1995). Il serait particulièrement intéressant de découvrir ce que Perceval connaissait éventuellement des méthodes de prospection du charbon alors utilisées en France, avant son implication à Bruton.

Un nouveau document conservé par BSA (B V 9), daté du 14 avril 1804 et signé par les cinq membres du Comité provisoire traite du bail à prendre sur la terre de Cook's Farm qui avait alors

été choisie pour l'essai. Le bail était consenti par les administrateurs (Governors) de l'école privée (Free School) de Bruton qui possédait la terre (Sale, 1950). Cette école venait de traverser une période particulièrement difficile occasionnée par une guerre ouverte entre le directeur, le Révérend Edward Michell (1737-1799), nommé en 1769 et les administrateurs de l'école. La mort de Michell en 1799 (Sale, 1950) a dû être considérée par les administrateurs comme un soulagement. Elle encouragea aussi clairement les aptitudes d'entrepreneurs de certains d'entre eux puisque ceux-ci autorisèrent alors l'affermage, en vue de l'essai, de terres appartenant à l'école. L'un des administrateurs était le fils de l'ancien directeur, l'avoué (« *attorney* ») local Edward Michell ; lui et H. S. Michell qui lui était clairement apparenté firent également bientôt partie du Comité pour l'essai de recherche de charbon. L'affermage de Cook's Farm devait durer 21 ans. Les eaux de la rivière Brue, qui traverse la ferme, devaient être utilisées par les entrepreneurs comme force motrice. L'acte d'affermage de 21 pages est daté du 2 mai 1804 (BSA B V 11, avec diverses corrections sur B V 15) et devait courir à partir du 31 mai 1804. Une quote-part du 1/20e de tout le charbon produit devait être payée à l'école pendant les trois premières années, s'élevant ensuite à 1/13e pour les deux années suivantes et à 1/10e pour les années restantes du bail.

Theophilus Perceval fit bientôt insérer une annonce en vue d'« *un homme respectable* [...] *pour entreprendre comme contremaître le fonçage de puits de mine* [sic] *à Brewham* » (*Bath Chronicle*, 17 mai 1804, p. 2). Le fonçage du puits de mine commença précisément le 11 juin 1804 (BSA V 4). Cela suppose que le Comité était ici déjà particulièrement confiant, car fréquemment la prospection de charbon plus hypothétique était alors faite uniquement par sondage (Torrens, 1984, p. 90-91).

Un avis signala bientôt dans le *Bath Chronicle* du 29 novembre 1804 (p. 3, col. 3) que « *d'après certains indices, on peut espérer que la recherche de charbon de Brewham sera couronnée de succès* ». En janvier 1805, un rapport d'avancement imprimé, signé par le secrétaire, désormais officiellement désigné, Theophilus Perceval fut publié, « *avec le plus agréable empressement* » sur la « *Situation et l'avancement du* [...] *projet de houillère de Brewham* » [BSA B V 13], pour demander aux souscripteurs le paiement de leur troisième versement de 500 £.

Ce rapport d'avancement est remarquable par sa franchise :

« Peu habitués aux diverses branches de l'entreprise comme les membres du Comité l'étaient eux-mêmes, ils eurent à demander des informations. Les études théoriques leur apportèrent une autorité insuffisante. Avec un zèle égal à leur désintéressement, ils consacrèrent volontiers une grande part de leur temps à des demandes pratiques faites aux patrons de houillères réputées. Ils reçurent d'eux une information claire et judicieuse dont les effets subséquents nous donnent des espoirs très proches du succès absolu. La partie mécanique de nos travaux, désormais presque terminée, est telle qu'elle donnera satisfaction à tout témoin ayant des connaissances scientifiques ».

L'état précis des dépenses du second versement de 500 £ était également détaillé. Jusqu'alors, les dépenses les plus importantes avaient été pour les *« salaires des puisatiers 111 £ »* et pour *« des outils, du fer et 150 yards de palplanches* [destinées à garnir les côtés du puits] *141 £ »*.

La note donnait une vue très précise de leurs espérances *« géologiques »* :

« les couches déjà traversées sont par leur aspect et leur nature exactement les mêmes sous lesquelles, dans beaucoup de Comtés, on exploite le charbon. Plusieurs mines – à quelques miles de la route de Newcastle à Durham ; à l'ouest de Dudley, dans le Staffordshire ; et la plupart des mines du Shropshire – montrent à peu près les mêmes principaux morts-terrains comme l'argile, la marne et les roches que nous avons dans les puits de Brewham. De nombreux échantillons de ces couches ont été envoyés et transportés dans ces différents Comtés et montrés à de vieux mineurs expérimentés qui pensent de manière unanime que le charbon doit être incontestablement trouvé à Brewham, à une profondeur plus ou moins grande. Une similitude FRAPPANTE est également visible à Batheaston, à deux miles et demi de Bath, près de la route de Londres : – Une centaine de souscripteurs, à raison de 50 £ par action, ont creusé deux puits ; leur profondeur est d'environ 33 brasses (= 61 m) ; leurs argile, marne et roche sont si semblables qu'elles ne peuvent pas être distinguées de celles de Brewham ; et ils considèrent ainsi ces couches comme le critère des veines de charbon existant au-dessous, que, pour leur souscription de 5000 £ on leur en a offert récemment 5000 £ de plus, pour l'achèvement total de l'entreprise ».

Cette prétention au sujet de la *« similitude du sol »* concerne seulement la *« Clunch Clay »* locale (comme l'appelait William Smith ; on l'appelle aujourd'hui *« Oxford Clay »*). Le site de la mine de Brewham et toutes les couches qui y avaient jusqu'alors été traversées montraient en vérité un *« sol »* d'argile sombre qui **était** superficiellement très similaire à celui des autres travaux miniers cités. Cela fournit la preuve que de telles *« similitudes superficielles »* étaient le seul critère utilisé par le comité de Brewham pour guider leur *« entreprise »*.

En outre, la prétention spécifique concernant la *« similitude du sol »* de Brewham avec celui rencontré dans les travaux miniers entre Newcastle et Durham, à l'ouest de Dudley et dans le Shropshire, que l'on sait aujourd'hui être tous d'âge carbonifère, prenait sa source dans un livre publié en 1769 (Sharpe, 1769, p. 44, 45 et 50), qui fut écrit anonymement par un pasteur du Dorset, le Révérend William Sharpe (1724-1783) (Torrens, 1974). Ce livre était en vérité la source probable de cette prétention, quoique la force de la tradition orale dans des matières telles que l'exploitation des mines de charbon ne peut en aucun cas être sous-estimée. Mais Sharpe lui-même les citait d'après le livre récemment publié l'année précédente par l'auteur français J.-F.-C. Morand (1726-1784) : *L'Art d'exploiter les mines de charbon de terre*. Celui-ci avait à son tour distillé l'information de publications ou traditions anglaises encore plus anciennes ! Nous y voyons la preuve de la relative pauvreté des sources imprimées relatives à une activité *« pratique »* comme l'exploitation minière du charbon.

L'ESSAI DE BATHEASTON (1804-1813)

L'essai de recherche de charbon, à l'est de Bath, au nord de Bruton, mentionné ci-dessus comme semblable, appartenait cependant à une catégorie totalement différente et c'est de façon erronée qu'il a été comparé à leur essai par les entrepreneurs de Brewham. Dans le nord du Somerset, les couches nommées *« Red Ground »* par William Smith étaient bien connues pour recouvrir en discordance les couches productives de charbon. Ce fait était bien connu de William Smith depuis ses premières explorations dans le bassin houiller du Nord Somerset. Il était naturel et tout à fait scientifique de prospecter **dans cette région** en utilisant les possibilités offertes par les propriétés liées aux discordances espérées pour chercher le charbon au-dessous de celle-ci (Farey, 1811, p. 116). Qualifier ultérieurement d'*« incroyable »* cette recherche faite à Batheaston, comme l'ont fait récemment deux experts (Buchanan, 1980, p. 31) est faire tout simplement preuve d'ignorance.

L'essai de Batheaston avait débuté peu après celui de Brewham. Il fut mentionné pour la première fois à la mi-avril 1804, quand on remarqua que « *les opinions les plus favorables* [sur ses résultats] *sont données par les minéralogistes les plus compétents* » (*Bath Journal*, 16 avril 1804, p. 2). On notera que William Smith ne faisait pas partie de ces minéralogistes car il n'avait pas encore été consulté. Un premier appel à souscription parut le même mois, quand à nouveau « *les meilleurs avis sont entièrement favorables* » (*Bath Journal*, 23 avril 1804, p. 2). Smith devint impliqué seulement après cela, comme le montre en juillet 1804 un nouvel avis selon lequel « *une tentative* [devait] *être faite par M. William Smith pour montrer l'existence et la succession des couches associées au charbon* » (*Bath Journal*, 16 juillet 1804, p. 3). Comme à Brewham, tout l'essai jusqu'à une profondeur de 101 mètres fut fait par fonçage, mais finalement deux puits furent foncés. On recourut ici au forage seulement après qu'une profondeur de 101 mètres fut atteinte et on le poursuivit jusqu'à 208 mètres.

Pour raccourcir cette longue histoire, le travail se poursuivit jusqu'en 1813 dans cet essai de Batheaston, lorsqu'il fut abandonné sans succès. L'histoire de cet autre essai mériterait également d'être racontée en détail. À une profondeur de 130 mètres, l'essai de Batheaston atteignit comme prévu la discordance espérée mais il pénétra ensuite directement dans des couches stériles qu'on pense actuellement être les « *Upper Cromhall Sandstones* », connus dans cette région pour être situés juste au-dessous des couches productives de charbon (Kellaway, 1991, p. 26-30). Mais en dépit de son insuccès, il s'était agi là, à la différence de Brewham, d'une prospection entièrement **scientifique**.

L'IMPLICATION DE WILLIAM SMITH À BREWHAM

Peu de temps avant 1803, quand débuta l'essai de Brewham, William Smith avait commencé ses efforts de défrichage, à la fois pour enregistrer l'ordre des couches présentes en Angleterre et pour démontrer l'importante signification de cette connaissance en guidant et contrôlant l'inspection minière dont l'Angleterre avait tant besoin. En 1799, Smith était sans travail et espérait que sa connaissance stratigraphique si nouvellement acquise démontrerait sa valeur pour bâtir une seconde carrière (Eyles, 1969 ; Torrens, 1994). Les années 1799-1803 l'avaient vu occupé d'un bout à l'autre de l'Angleterre à conseiller pour le drainage des terres, les travaux de défense contre la mer et le « *nouvel art d'inspection minière* », comme il appelait maintenant – ainsi que son élève le plus connu, John Farey (1766-1826) – ses nouvelles compétences et sa connaissance stratigraphique, lorsqu'il conseillait pour ou contre des prospections minérales particulières. En 1803, l'Angleterre était une nouvelle fois engagée dans une guerre longue et coûteuse avec la France. Cela stimula en Angleterre une industrialisation plus complète et rapide.

À la fin de mars 1805, environ neuf mois après que l'essai de Brewham eût sérieusement commencé, Smith était dans l'ouest de l'Angleterre. Son journal indique pour le 21 mars 1805 « *installation à Yeovil* » et la même semaine, sur la page opposée de son journal, on lit : « *affaires de Tuson et Moody à Ilchester et Kingham – Bruham Pit* ». L'« *installation à Yeovil* » était chez Mrs Maria Goodford (1757-1848), l'un des premiers employeurs de Smith et la veuve de John Old Goodford (décédé en 1787, mais qui apparaît encore de manière très posthume en 1815 comme souscripteur de la carte géologique de Smith !). Ici, le travail de Smith était à Mudford, dans le sud du Somerset. Sa visite avait pour but de conclure des arrangements financiers pour son travail de drainage et d'amélioration des biens de Mrs Goodford. D'après son journal, pendant son voyage retour à Bath, Smith demanda, presque certainement le 24 mars 1805, à voir le projet du « *projet de houillère de Bruham* », quand il « *revint de l'ouest à Broadfield Farm* » pour rentrer à sa base près de Bath (MS Smith OUM). Les souvenirs autobiographiques plus tardifs (MS Smith OUM) confirment qu'il avait

« voyagé à Bath en 1805 tôt dans l'année dans l'espoir de conclure mes affaires non réglées avec la [Somerset] Coal Canal Company [qui l'avait congédié en 1799] mais la même perversité que j'avais expérimentée a prévalu. Pendant mon séjour dans l'ouest j'ai revisité beaucoup de mes anciens travaux de drainage et la machinerie que j'avais installée dans une grange à Mudford près de Yeovil, Somerset pour battre et moudre le blé. On forait alors le puits de Brewham ».

Dès qu'il retourna à Broadfield Farm, ravi que les fossiles trouvés en profondeur dans des fonçages comme celui de Brewham, puissent aussi être utilisés pour conseiller les prospections là où aucune autre information de surface n'était disponible (contrairement à ce que prétend Laudan, 1976), Smith écrivit de Bath la lettre suivante

IV

datée du 26 mars 1805 à son ami de longue date et premier soutien, le Révérend Benjamin Richardson (1758-1832)

« Je suis désolé de n'avoir pu trouver moyen de vous rendre visite à mon retour de l'ouest dimanche soir [le 24]. Les gens de Brewham ont creusé un puits profond de 40 yards [37 m] pour remonter de beaux échantillons de Callaways Rock. J'ai deux exemplaires d'huître lobée que je serais heureux de vous montrer et quelques autres informations et échantillons recueillis pendant mon voyage » [MS Smith, OUM].

Smith savait que ces fossiles, nommés aujourd'hui *Gryphaea (Bilobissa) dilobotes* Duff, étaient très caractéristiques de la pierre de Kellaways, une unité lithologique par ailleurs très peu caractéristique (Torrens, 1989, p. 59-60), dont il savait bien qu'elle est située à des centaines de mètres au-dessus de toute couche de charbon que l'on pouvait espérer dans la région de Bruton. John Phillips, le neveu de Smith, attesta ultérieurement que : « *aux environs de Wincanton, à une époque où il [Smith] était employé professionnellement dans cette région, un projet ridicule de cette sorte [un autre essai pour un charbon impossible] était en cours de réalisation à Bruham ; et, en dépit des remontrances de M. Smith et de ses intelligents amis, les spéculateurs procédaient à de ruineuses dépenses à travers le clunch [appelé aujourd'hui Oxford Clay], la roche de Kellaway, avec "la petite huître lobée"* [...], *jusqu'à ce qu'ils pénétrassent dans la série oolitique* » [Phillips, 1844, p. 66]. Il est clair que Smith réalisa immédiatement qu'il était impossible de trouver du charbon à Brewham car ce site était situé trop haut dans l'échelle stratigraphique qu'il avait établie. Il est également clair que lui, et d'autres, dirent cela aux entrepreneurs, soit alors, soit peu après. Mais ceux-ci ne furent pas impressionnés. La longue tradition d'utiliser les similitudes « *simplement* » superficielles que le sol de Brewham possédait avec celui de régions connues pour produire du charbon, qui **était** véritablement semblable, demeurait toute puissante.

LE « *PROJET DE HOUILLÈRE DE BREWHAM* » DE 1805 A 1810

La première preuve de la poursuite de la « *houillère* » provient du nouvel avis publié dans le *Bath Chronicle* du 18 avril 1805 que « *les travaux du projet de HOUILLÈRE de BREWHAM étant*

dans un état de progrès, et la machinerie pour l'épuisement de l'eau [une roue à eau] *du puits étant complète, les propriétaires sont prêts à traiter pour la poursuite du travail avec toute personne qui puisse être disposée à l'entreprendre. – Le puits a actuellement une profondeur de 40 yards* [exactement comme lors de la visite de Smith], *et les propriétaires proposent de le foncer jusqu'à 80 yards de profondeur et de forer ensuite 80 yards* ». Theophilus Perceval était encore le Secrétaire. Dans le même temps, pour manifester la confiance persistante, ou plutôt l'optimisme un peu « *fou* » des entrepreneurs de Brewham, leur puits se poursuivit uniquement en creusant. Ils abandonnèrent bientôt toute phase finale de forage, proposée par cet avis, pour un puits entièrement foncé. À Batheaston, où un résultat heureux était toujours beaucoup plus probable, ils avaient montré une prudence opposée et continuèrent sous la direction de William Smith en pratiquant un forage.

Le 6 janvier 1806 fut reçu le dernier versement de la souscription originelle de 2000 £. Un appel supplémentaire de 5 £ fut ensuite reçu de chacun des soixante souscripteurs le 1er janvier 1807 et un versement final de 5 £ des cent souscripteurs originaux fut payé le 1er juillet 1807. Cela faisait un total de 2800 £ censées avoir été souscrites par 148 personnes, bien que, pour montrer que certains commençaient maintenant à douter du résultat, on identifia ultérieurement cinq défaillants (qui devaient en tout 25 £) lors du paiement final !

Déjà en mai 1807, le puits réalisé à l'aide d'une roue à eau de neuf mètres de diamètre, atteignait une profondeur de 588 pieds (181 m) (*Sherborne and Yeovil Mercury*, 25 mai 1807). Le creusement du puits de Brewham se poursuivit jusqu'à Noël 1807, lorsque « *les eaux firent irruption sans qu'il fût possible de s'y opposer manuellement* » à une profondeur de 652 pieds (201 m) (BSA B V 14). Le Comité fit alors face à de nouveaux problèmes. Un nouvel avis du 28 décembre 1807 est ainsi libellé :

« par suite d'un message **spécial** du directeur Mr Stock, une réunion extraordinaire du Comité a été convoquée et s'est tenue aujourd'hui au puits. De l'exposé des faits présenté à la fois par le directeur et par le contremaître des puisatiers et de l'enquête du Comité, tous éprouvèrent la nécessité la plus impérieuse de solliciter la présence des souscripteurs le lundi 11 janvier 1808 à 11 heures du matin à l'Auberge de la Boule bleue de Bruton pour recevoir un rapport qui concerne très matériellement l'intérêt de chaque souscripteur. Un repas sera préparé et servi à 3 heures précises » (*Salisbury and Winchester Journal*, 4 janvier 1808 ; voir également *The Castle Cary Visitor*, 5, n° 110, février 1905, p. 111, et *Bath Chronicle*, 7 janvier 1808).

Cet avis et les comptes finaux (BSA B V 14) qui relatent que les salaires des puisatiers avaient été payés entre décembre 1806 et janvier 1808 par un certain M. Gregory Stock, nous donne au moins le nom du directeur de l'entreprise. Gregory Stock (actif entre 1806 et 1824) était venu des houillères du nord du Somerset où on le trouve à nouveau comme *« agent des mines »*, basé à Ashwick, North Somerset. Il peut avoir été le Gregory Stock qui fut baptisé dans la chapelle presbytérienne de Shepton Mallet, Somerset, le 3 août 1780. Il fut ultérieurement l'un de ceux qui aidèrent les géologues William Buckland (1784-1856) et William Conybeare (1787-1857) dans leurs *Observations on the South-Western coal district of England*, publiées en 1824.

La réunion de Bruton qui se tint début janvier 1808 dut adopter la seule décision possible. Le Secrétaire fit paraître comme il se doit un nouvel avis daté de Bruton, 25 janvier 1808, pour annoncer :

« Enchères publiques
Projet de Houillère de Brewham. »

« Par suite d'une résolution adoptée à l'Assemblée générale des souscripteurs, le lundi 11 janvier, le Comité DONNE [...] UN AVIS PUBLIC, que le lundi 15 février seront VENDUS AUX ENCHÈRES, à l'Auberge de la Boule bleue de Bruton, à 11 heures du matin, le BAIL des LOCAUX, une ROUE À EAU, et tous les autres MATÉRIELS utilisés dans le projet de houillère... Des renseignements complémentaires peuvent être obtenus par demande adressée soit à M. F. (*recte* E.) Michell, avocat à Bruton, soit au Secrétaire » (*Bath Chronicle*, 4 février 1808).

Évidemment, cependant, beaucoup de souscripteurs devaient être mécontents de cette capitulation devant la puissance de la nature, et les enchères furent ajournées. Si bien qu'*« au printemps 1808, plusieurs essais furent* [alors] *faits pour intéresser le public et lever les sommes nécessaires pour une machine à vapeur. Ces essais se révélèrent stériles ».* Alors seulement *« fut ordonnée la vente des matériels, mais la vente ne fut finalement pas décidée et le compte ne fut pas clôturé par le secrétaire avant le 17 septembre 1808 ».* La somme de 101 £ resta entre les mains du secrétaire et fut également divisée entre tous les

souscripteurs originels. Chacun reçut seulement 13 shillings et 7 pence sur leurs investissements de 20, 25 ou 30 £ [BSA B V 14]. Un avis daté du 28 juillet 1810, de la liquidation de toute l'entreprise par le Comité de gestion parut dans le *Bath Chronicle* du 2 août 1810. Il annonçait que la remise en état du domaine satisfaisait enfin les administrateurs (*« governors »*) de l'école de Bruton. On demanda aux souscripteurs encore en arrérage de payer les sommes qu'ils devaient et de faire toutes les autres demandes qu'ils avaient concernant le *« projet de houillère »* avant que les comptes ne fussent clôturés. Une réunion finale eut lieu le 13 août 1810. Le rapport final du Comité qui en résulta, daté du 14 août 1810, notait que *« la remise en état du terrain* [avait] *commencé* [septembre 1808] ; *l'hiver arrivant, les ouvriers ne progressèrent que lentement et ils ne terminèrent pas leur travail avant juin 1809, à la satisfaction de MM. Harding et Michell, deux gentilshommes du Comité de gestion qui consacrèrent beaucoup de leur temps et de leur attention à l'affaire. Des demandes furent faites, et répétées personnellement et par lettres, aux administrateurs pour une levée* [de leur bail] : *cela, le Comité de gestion ne l'obtint pas avant le 28 juillet 1810 ! ! ! »* (BSA B V 14). Il n'y aurait donc pas de *« projet de houillère de Brewham »* !

Theophilus Perceval, leur secrétaire originaire de France, fut bientôt impliqué dans une autre affaire ennuyeuse. On découvrit à la fin de 1812 que ses moulins à soie de Bruton avaient utilisé une quantité de *« soie crue de Valence »* qui avait été dérobée à Londres. Au jugement qui suivit, Perceval témoigna et déclara qu'*« il avait été fileur de soie pendant 17 ans »* (*Times*, 1ᵉʳ octobre, p. 3 et 2 novembre 1812, p. 3). Cela s'accorde avec sa carrière commencée en 1795 à Sherborne dans le Dorset (voir ci-dessous). Il a dû se demander alors si sa venue en Angleterre avait été une si bonne idée... !

LA COMPOSITION DU COMITÉ
D'ENTREPRENEURS

Les membres du Comité d'entrepreneurs et les dates auxquelles ils sont connus pour avoir été actifs dans cet essai de recherche de charbon (indiquées entre crochets) sont mentionnés dans l'Annexe 1. Ils ont été identifiés d'après les registres paroissiaux, les testaments, des annuaires – en particulier la rubrique *« Bruton »* de l'*Universal British Directory* (Anonyme, 1793) – et de nombreuses autres sources pour tenter d'analyser les raisons de leur participation.

Deux d'entre eux, Richard Messiter et David Payne, souscrivirent ultérieurement à la *Geological Map* de William Smith publiée en 1815, mais en raison de la banqueroute du premier survenue en 1815, il est peu probable qu'il ait payé ou même reçu son exemplaire. Dans cette liste, le grand nombre de banqueroutes (cinq) est remarquable, comme l'est la grande difficulté de retracer la suite de la carrière de ces gens ! La plupart des membres du Comité ont dû être, comme la grande majorité des 148 autres *« entrepreneurs »* impliqués dans l'essai de Brewham, simplement dans l'espoir d'un profit financier. Cinq, cependant : I) James James, taillandier, propriétaire d'un moulin à eau et d'une usine à Cole ; II) Daniel Maggs, fabricant de toile à matelas et fondeur de fonte à Bourton, Dorset, qui était impliqué ici avec son frère Isaiah Maggs (1748-1827) de Hookhill House, Silton, Dorset, un fabricant de toile de lin ; III) Henry S. Michell, propriétaire de moulins ; IV) Theophilus Perceval, un fileur de soie de Bruton et précédemment de Paris, et V) John Sharrer Ward, un autre fileur de soie de Bruton, espéraient clairement obtenir une énergie meilleur marché pour leurs usines et moulins. Les frères Maggs, en particulier, avaient débuté une dynastie d'importantes entreprises locales. La postérité, avec son habituel dédain un peu snob pour les gens aux mains calleuses, a trop longtemps ignoré leur travail. Ils méritent quelque recherche concernant leur origine et leurs réalisations.

LES CONSÉQUENCES À LONDRES DE L'ESSAI DE BREWHAM

Smith rédigea quelques notes au sujet de l'essai de Bruton, telle celle-ci datée du 1ᵉʳ mars 1807, selon laquelle il n'avait *« jamais [été] certain de déterminer le tracé de cette roche* [la pierre de Kellaways] *vers l'ouest jusqu'au fonçage du puits de recherche de charbon à Brewham, lorsqu'elle fut découverte à la profondeur de 40 yards sous l'argile schisteuse (« shale »)* (cf. *Journal to the West*, MS Smith, boîte 30, dossier 4, OUM). On lit également dans une autre note datée du 9 novembre 1810 que le *« Clunch Clay était très profond dans le puits foncé pour une recherche de charbon à Brewham »* (MS Smith, boîte 30, dossier 1, OUM). Mais il semble n'avoir rien fait de plus à ce moment. Cependant, son élève John Farey avait déjà pu signaler en février 1806 (juste au moment où l'essai de Brewham faisait l'objet des poursuites les plus enthousiastes) :

« En enquêtant dans le voisinage, nous trouvons que presque toutes les terres en friche, les marais, les landes, ou les parcelles de mauvaise terre, ont, à un moment ou à un autre, été mentionnés par des chercheurs de charbon ignorants comme contenant du charbon. Nos enquêtes ont mis en lumière des centaines d'exemples où des sondages et fonçages pour trouver du charbon ont été entrepris dans des situations semblables, et sur des avis similaires, dans les parties méridionale et orientale de l'Angleterre, exécutés au prix de lourdes dépenses, parfois presque ruineuses pour les intéressés, bien que constituant une source de profit pour les prétendus chercheurs de charbon » (Farey, 1806).

Cela montre clairement combien d'autres essais mal informés (et aujourd'hui oubliés) pour un tel charbon ont été faits avant 1806. Mais aussi certains que Smith, Farey et d'autres aient pu alors l'être quant à la fiabilité de leur compétence stratigraphique nouvellement acquise pour modérer de telles prospections minérales, d'autres n'étaient clairement pas encore si certains. Pendant le mois de mars 1808, Smith écrivit à nouveau à Richardson, qui vivait à Bath :

« Je regrette de ne pas avoir eu la possibilité d'obtenir un compte rendu du fonçage du puits de Brewham qui me permettrait de dessiner une coupe précise des couches traversées – on ne doit pas perdre de temps pour obtenir ces renseignements et également des spécimens de chaque couche, comme les plus fortes confirmations auxquelles nous pouvons faire appel pour prouver la vérité de notre système. Cela et l'expérience de Road Common ont fait beaucoup pour la science géologique. Grâce à eux et aussi grâce au puits de Batheaston, la faisabilité de prédire ce qu'on peut trouver est clairement établie. Je n'ai pas eu la possibilité de vous dire, avant de quitter Bath, combien j'ai été amusé de voir chez M. Denny de beaux échantillons de l'oolite supérieure (la Grande Oolite) *du puits de Bruham, qui lui a été envoyé comme Millstone. Cela vaudrait la peine que vous demandiez à les voir pour vous rendre compte des abus grossiers des chercheurs de charbon »* (MS Smith OUM).

Rien d'autre ne semble avoir été fait par Richardson, autant qu'on puisse s'en assurer d'après les manuscrits disponibles. Pas plus qu'on ne peut apporter plus de lumière sur l'autre essai de recherche de charbon, celui de Road Common dans le Wiltshire, excepté que clairement, à nou-

Un essai malencontreux de recherche de charbon

veau, Smith l'avait déconseillé avant 1808 et à nouveau pour des motifs stratigraphiques. Tout ce qu'on en connaît par ailleurs est ce qu'a écrit Joseph Townsend (1739-1816), un autre des partisans précoces de Smith : «*d'une manière semblable, quelques gens ignorants se laissèrent persuader, à grands frais, d'essayer de trouver du charbon à Road Common, à environ dix miles au sud de Bath, où l'on trouve le Cornbrash*» (Townsend, 1813, p. 427). Ceci est un niveau juste au-dessous de celui dans lequel eut lieu l'essai de Brewham et à nouveau excessivement élevé dans la série stratigraphique.

La lettre de Smith à Richardson avait été inspirée par une série de visites que des membres de la Geological Society of London, nouvellement formée, avaient faites pour voir la collection de fossiles de Smith dans sa maison de Londres. Il y a eu beaucoup de discussions sur l'objet de ces visites. Rudwick (1963, p. 339) a prétendu qu'il y eut seulement une unique visite et que son but principal fut «*non d'examiner ses collections mais de rechercher son concours*», mais que Smith avait refusé. Les détails précis ont été rendus confus par le fait que le journal de Smith pour 1808 n'a pas été retrouvé.

Dix ans plus tard, Smith lui-même écrivit qu'«*au début de 1808, M. Greenough et Sir James Hall vinrent à Buckingham Street et virent la collection, et* [que] *le 8 mars* [ils] *répétèrent leur visite*» (Sheppard, 1920, p. 216), tandis que John Phillips (1844, p. 71) parla de **visites** en mars 1808. La première lettre relative à cette question dans les archives de Smith est une lettre de John Farey à Sir James Hall (1761-1832), datée du «*lundi soir 7 mars 08*». On y lit : «*M. Farey... l'informe que M. Smith vint en ville la nuit dernière et repart dans un jour ou deux : sur quoi M. F. souhaite que Sir J. puisse rencontrer M. Greenough et lui-même chez M. S., au bas de Buckingham Street, Strand, à gauche, à 10 heures et 1/2 demain matin*». Farey, Greenough et Hall virent alors précisément la collection mais il ne fut pas possible à Smith d'être présent.

Dans une lettre à son frère John, Smith écrivit le 15 mars 1808, «*hier* [en réalité le jour précédent parce qu'il manqua la poste] *avais avec moi le président et les membres de la Geological Society qui a été fondée pour l'examen des couches, cela la nuit dernière à Sir Joseph Banks' Levee*». Smith confirma cela dans une lettre qu'il écrivit de Londres le 17 mars 1808 à Thomas Walters (1757-1847), l'instigateur de l'essai de Batheaston. Elle est intitulée «*Batheaston*». On y lit :

«*Je suis heureux d'entendre que le fonçage (de votre puits de Batheaston) ait fait autant de progrès – L'apparition du Red Ground dans votre terril («pit bank») sera, je l'espère, suffisante pour convaincre tout le monde que le charbon y apparaîtra aussi certainement à son tour...*»

Après avoir discuté d'autres détails de ce fonçage, la lettre de Smith concluait :

«*P.S. La question de la stratification régulière (que votre puits a beaucoup contribué à prouver) est maintenant en cours d'examen par une Geological Society fondée dans ce but. Dimanche dernier, G. B. Greenough, M[ember of] P[arliament], et de nombreux autres membres examinèrent la disposition de mes fossiles [distribués en suivant l'ordre stratigraphique dans la maison londonienne de Smith depuis 1804]*».

Ces lettres démontrent qu'une seconde (ou peut-être même encore une autre) visite, à laquelle Smith **était présent**, avait eu lieu le dimanche précédent, le 13 mars 1808, quoique l'historien W. H. Fitton essaya ultérieurement de conclure que de telles visites s'étaient seulement produites **avant** la fondation de la Geological Society en 1807 (Fitton, 1833, p. 43). Le 20 mars 1808 une autre lettre de Smith à Benjamin Richardson confirma cette visite ultérieure et constata :

«*Je me flatte que la question des strates soit bientôt bien étudiée par la nouvelle Geological Society créée dans ce but – Je crains que vous n'ayez vu quelques-uns de leurs papiers imprimés car dans la liste des membres honoraires de votre voisinage, j'ai observé les noms de MM. [Joseph] Townsend et [Thomas] Meade [tous deux élus en 1807 ; Richardson fut seulement élu plus tard en 1808]. M. Greenough M. P., le Président, et plusieurs des membres passèrent quelques heures dans ma maison dimanche dernier [le 13] à examiner ma collection et le soir je les ai rencontrés chez Sir Jos[ep]h Banks [à l'une des réunions régulières du dimanche soir de Sir Joseph]*».

Smith écrivit une autre lettre le 23 mars 1808 à William Cunnington (1754-1810) de Heytesbury dans le Wiltshire, également converti précocement, dès 1797, à la fiabilité des conceptions de Smith sur la régularité de la stratification. Sir Richard Colt Hoare, le propriétaire terrien de Bruton, avait accepté en 1804 de financer les futures fouilles archéologiques de Cunnington. Cette relation peut également expliquer pourquoi

IV

Colt Hoare ne souscrivit jamais pour l'essai de Brewham car Cunnington lui avait sûrement parlé de son caractère stupide. La lettre se poursuit ainsi :

« Si Brewham est dans le périmètre de vos sorties, vous m'obligeriez beaucoup en obtenant des précisions sur chacune des couches qu'ils ont traversées dans leur récente tentative pour trouver du charbon.

Veuillez, s'il vous plaît, les consigner dans l'ordre où elles ont été traversées et [en indiquant] l'épaisseur de chacune avec une indication des restes organiques [fossiles vrais] qu'elles renferment et – les parties du puits où l'eau fit irruption et toute autre précision que vous pouvez obtenir.

J'espère que vous m'excuserez de vous déranger [en vous demandant] d'être si minutieux lorsque vous saurez que la nouvelle Geological Society fondée spécialement pour constater la véritable stratification des îles Britanniques peut être beaucoup mieux convaincue de la véracité de mon système si le compte rendu des fonçages [cités] ci-dessus provient d'une tierce personne ».

Il devient maintenant clair que la véritable raison de ces visites faites à Smith en 1808 – qu'elles aient été deux, trois ou davantage jusqu'à cette date – était de régler la principale question pendante entre les parties. C'était de savoir si le « *Système* » de Smith et son modèle stratigraphique était aussi sûr et universel que Smith et son cercle le prétendaient. On sait à quel point G. B. Greenough, le premier président de la Société resta longtemps sceptique à ce sujet (Greenough, 1819). Les réunions ne peuvent clairement avoir eu pour but de discuter pour savoir si Smith accepterait de collaborer avec la Geological Society puisque celle-ci ne croyait pas alors à ses découvertes. Malheureusement, aucun journal de Greenough pour 1808 ne semble avoir subsisté pour aider à confirmer cette interprétation.

Le cercle d'amis de Smith resta loyal vis-à-vis de la qualité et de la finalité de son travail. Townsend écrivit en 1813 à quel point « *à Bruham* [sic], *près des collines de **craie** de Bradly Nole, un puits a été très irrationnellement foncé pour* [chercher] *du **charbon** à travers la plupart des couches précédentes* [Forest Marble], *jusqu'à une profondeur de six cents pieds et la base du puits est dans les lits supérieurs de la grande oolite* » (Townsend, 1813, p. 128). En août 1817, lorsque fut publiée la troisième partie des *Strata identified by Organized Fossils*, de Smith, le fossile du « *puits de*

Bruham » fut dûment consigné comme *Gryphaea incurva*, avec la remarque que « *bien que cette pierre* [de Kellaways] *apparaisse rarement à l'affleurement, les récentes fouilles* [faites] *pour* [chercher] *du charbon à Bruham prouvèrent qu'elle est parfaite en profondeur et qu'elle y contient l'huître lobée ou Gryphus (échantillon b au British Museum) et les autres fossiles organiques par lesquels elle est le plus distinctement caractérisée* » (Smith, 1817a, p. 23-24). Le mois suivant, quand Smith publia son *Stratigraphical System* dans lequel il énumérait sa collection alors vendue au British Museum, après une étude additionnelle il rapportait désormais cette forme à « *la variété Gryphaea dilatata. Huître lobée. Côté gauche très fortement lobé, valve inférieure profonde* » (Smith, 1817b, p. 61). John Farey, dans un article oublié, put montrer combien ces Gryphées lobées pouvaient alors créer des confusions à la fois en raison du manque de noms disponibles permettant de les distinguer (Farey, 1819, p. 124-125) et de leur extension géologique encore incertaine.

Le « *Système* » de Smith était scientifiquement sain et extrêmement fiable mais la réception de ce jugement ne fut pas facilitée par la résistance initiale exercée par certains membres de la Geological Society of London. Le message pénétra seulement assez lentement dans la conscience du grand public et des communautés de mineurs. Nous en voyons confirmation lorsque le Comité de Brewham publia ses comptes finaux en 1810, avec une liste de 148 entrepreneurs désappointés. Ses mots de conclusion étaient encore très agressifs :

« Il nous reste à exprimer le regret que nous éprouvons de n'avoir pas rencontré le succès que nous avions toujours espéré, et quoique les veines de charbon qui *existent* [original en italique] au Sud des Lime Rocks [le Mountain Limestone des Mendips] aient échappé à nos recherches, nous ne doutons pas qu'un jour futur, des entrepreneurs plus audacieux et plus persévérants placeront notre assertion hors de portée des contradictions » (BSA B V 14).

Deux des souscripteurs de Brewham avaient précédemment été impliqués dans un autre essai semblable, également situé trop haut dans la série stratigraphique, à Shaftesbury en 1791, à une vingtaine de kilomètres au sud-est. Celui-ci devait également avoir été connu de Smith et de son cercle dès 1805 comme ayant été semblablement mal inspiré. C'étaient Richard Messiter et Richard Pew, M.D. (1752-1834), le président de la tentative faite en 1791 à Shaftesbury. Pew

Un essai malencontreux de recherche de charbon

écrivit le 12 février 1819 à John Rutter, l'historien de Shaftesbury, au sujet de cette tentative de 1791 :

« Nous dépensâmes autant que je peux m'en souvenir 400 £ mais, comme je l'ai dit précédemment nous n'arrivâmes pas aux couches de charbon [...] ni à rien de semblable et si vous regardez les Elements of Geology de M. Bakewell (*cf.* Bakewell, 1815) ou dans les cartes des couches de M. Smith, je pense que cela jette un doute sur le « Courage » et l'espérance de trouver du charbon par ici [Shaftesbury] ». (MS conservé au Shaftesbury Museum).

Néanmoins, même Pew n'était pas encore complètement convaincu de la futilité de telles tentatives (Torrens, 1979, p. 228-232).

CONCLUSION

En 1819 la confiance de Smith en lui-même était suffisante pour qu'il écrivît simplement sur une coupe géologique dessinée à travers le Somerset que « *cette partie de la Clay series n'a pas été épargnée par les essais* [de recherche] *de charbon* » (Smith, 1819). Dès 1841, cette idée de la futilité de tels essais était entièrement considérée comme admise, comme le démontrent les commentaires de Hugh Miller cités au début. John Phillips le confirma en 1871 :

« [La géologie] a en vérité déjà interrompu de nombreux essais insensés de [recherche de] charbon dans lesquels on ne pouvait s'attendre à aucun bon résultat [...]. On peut croire que les jours ne sont plus (nous perdons certainement rapidement leur souvenir) où les forages ou « puits de mine » de Bruham (et de nombreux autres endroits), excitaient [...], tournaient en ridicule [...] et occasionnaient de lourdes dépenses à des propriétaires terriens innocents » (Phillips, 1871, p. 494).

Les gens avaient réalisé depuis longtemps que Smith avait été parfaitement correct de mettre en garde contre l'essai de Brewham en 1805 et que Townsend avait eu entièrement raison de qualifier d'« *absurde* » dès 1813 la tentative de Brewham. Il avait alors été déjà abondamment prouvé que l'ordre stratigraphique que Smith avait défini, au moins dans la majeure partie du sud et de l'est de l'Angleterre, était généralement fiable.

POURQUOI L'ESSAI DE BRUTON FUT-IL SI MALENCONTREUX ?

Les entrepreneurs de Brewham avaient « *simplement* » confondu les argiles appelées par Smith « *Clunch* » [= Oxford Clay et au-dessus son Kellaway Rock] et les argiles des « *Coal Measures* », situées beaucoup plus bas. Comme beaucoup d'autres avant et après eux, dans de très nombreux autres endroits de Grande-Bretagne, ils s'étaient fourvoyés dans leurs coûteuses explorations à cause de simples « *similitudes lithologiques* ». En 1805, les spécimens fossiles avaient permis à Smith d'identifier immédiatement le « *Kellaway Rock* ». Cela lui avait également immédiatement permis de dire à ceux qui fonçaient le puits de Brewham qu'ils perdaient leur temps en cherchant si haut dans la succession des strates. La preuve la plus évidente, un spécimen de *Gryphaea* du puits de Brewham, subsiste encore comme témoignage éloquent dans la belle – bien que jamais étudiée – collection de Smith au Natural History Museum de Londres [NHM L 1529].

Cette histoire – et ce spécimen – fournit une bonne preuve pour soutenir la revendication de Smith, en 1818, d'avoir été responsable de l'introduction du « *nouvel art de prospection minière* » (Sheppard, 1920, p. 219). Le jour où ce fossile fut récolté semble avoir été la première occasion, au moins en Angleterre, d'utiliser correctement les connaissances biostratigraphiques pour diriger une prospection minière. Cela fut probablement la première fois qu'on réalisa ce que nous considérons aujourd'hui comme admis dans le monde entier – à savoir l'identification correcte d'une strate donnée d'après ses fossiles, même lorsqu'ils ont été récoltés en profondeur dans un puits (ou aujourd'hui dans un sondage). La confiance de la première opinion de Smith est tout à fait remarquable. Comme il l'a dit à Richardson en mars 1808 dans une lettre citée ci-dessus : – « [L'essai de Brewham] *et l'expérience de Road Common ont beaucoup fait pour la science géologique. Grâce à eux et aussi au puits de Batheaston la* [possibilité] ***pratique de prédire ce qu'on peut trouver*** (souligné par l'auteur du présent article) *est clairement établie* ».

Le fait que les entrepreneurs de Brewham et quelques membres de la Geological Society de Londres mirent si longtemps à être convaincus prouve combien l'avance prise par Smith était grande, au moins en Angleterre. Cependant parce qu'il était alors tellement en avance sur les connaissances antérieures, l'avis de Smith fut ignoré. Mais ce fut la première occasion, au moins en Grande-Bretagne, où un avis stratigraphique compétent fut disponible pour aider à interrompre une prospection coûteuse de substances minérales stratifiées.

Les progrès que la **science** géologique avait faits, dès 1805, en permettant une prospection scientifique de substances minérales stratifiées, soutenue par un étalon stratigraphique connu et approprié, allaient être utilisés ultérieurement comme un argument remarquable en faveur de l'**utilité** de la science en général, au cours de la première moitié du dix-neuvième siècle. La citation de Hugh Miller (1841) donnée au début de cet article démontre la force que cet argument avait déjà acquise alors.

Un bon exemple montrant combien cette utilité était grande est donné en 1831 par John Herschel qui souligne comment la science peut *« nous montrer comment éviter d'entreprendre des choses impossibles »* (Herschel, 1831, p. 45). C'était dans un livre décrit par Robert Chambers (1802-1871) comme *« un traité* [qui était] *l'un des plus philosophiques jamais produit dans notre pays »* [Secord, 1995, p. 177]. Herschel citait, comme premier exemple de la manière dont une telle impossibilité avait été révélée par la science, un essai avorté, exactement similaire, de recherche d'un *« impossible »* charbon, entrepris à Bexhill dans le Sussex. C'était un essai fait entre 1804 et 1809 et déconseillé — exactement comme Smith avait déconseillé celui de Brewham — par John Farey, l'élève de Smith, à partir de 1807 (Farey, 1808). Il était également clairement impossible que des quantités ou des qualités exploitables de charbon puissent être trouvées dans le Sussex, en dépit, à nouveau, des *« similitudes* [superficielles] *de sol »*. Ici, un tel avis fut une fois de plus ignoré et des dépenses beaucoup plus importantes engagées (*The Standard*, 20 avril 1889, p. 3).

ÉPILOGUE

Tout cela peut passer pour une histoire très provinciale alors qu'il s'agit d'honorer François Ellenberger, un historien des sciences d'envergure internationale. Aux yeux d'un Français, cette histoire pourrait même être jugée comme une contribution typiquement insulaire propre à un habitant d'une île qui est encore si psychologiquement *« au large »* de l'Europe continentale. Mais je crois cependant que ce point de vue serait erroné car l'essai de recherche de charbon de Bruton pose à mon avis des questions d'intérêt véritablement international.

En premier lieu, il faut savoir quelle est à cette époque l'histoire des essais comparables de recherche de charbon et d'autres substances minérales stratifiées dans le reste de l'Europe. La connaissance stratigraphique rudimentaire qui existait alors, par exemple en France, y était-elle mise au service de telles prospections ? Par exemple, Sir Joseph Banks, le président de la Royal Society, semble avoir imaginé qu'il n'apportait pas simplement de l'eau à la rivière quand il écrivit à Barthélémy Faujas de Saint-Fond (1741-1819) à Paris, en septembre 1811, pour lui annoncer la nouvelle compétence de William Smith et de ses élèves en tant que *« prospecteurs miniers »* (Torrens, 1994, p. 68).

Gérard Bignot (1989, 1996) a publié une fascinante étude des tentatives faites, juste après le début de la Révolution française, pour trouver du charbon en Haute-Normandie, de manière à remplacer celui qui était alors importé à grands frais de Cardiff, au Pays de Galles. Ces essais **ne furent pas** faits avec les méthodes anglaises de *« laisser-faire »*, comme à Brewham, mais sous le contrôle d'un *« Conseil des Mines »* mis en place en juin 1794 par le *« Comité de Salut public »* dans le but de coordonner les recherches. Mais le même optimisme enthousiaste, bien que malencontreux, concernant le résultat éventuel, est remarquable dans les deux pays.

En 1795, Guillaume Castiau, minéralogiste et ingénieur, fut autorisé à entreprendre des recherches à ses frais. Il était stimulé par la conviction que les veines de charbon connues dans le Hainaut et les Flandres sont situées sur le même axe que celles connues au sud-ouest de Littry et de Plessis en Normandie. Il soutint qu'une recherche entreprise sur cet axe, juste au sud de Dieppe, montrerait ces mêmes veines en profondeur. Dès juillet 1806, alors que l'essai de Bruton était en pleine activité, ils avaient atteint une profondeur de 332 mètres mais n'étaient également pas descendus plus profondément que des couches connues **actuellement** pour être d'âge kimmeridgien. Ces prospections du Nord de la France n'utilisaient clairement aucune connaissance stratigraphique en tant que telle, mais seulement des rudiments d'une *« géologie structurale »* prématurée. Il n'est donc pas surprenant que ces essais faits à Saint-Nicolas d'Aliermont furent aussi infructueux que ceux de Brewham.

Une autre question est de savoir si la nouvelle connaissance stratigraphique mieux documentée acquise par Werner en Saxe avait déjà permis de guider une telle prospection minière en Allemagne, avant la date de l'essai de Bruton. Le fait que j'aie été incapable de répondre à cette question est peut-être une conséquence de mon insularité. Mais je pense que ces questions révèlent une

Un essai malencontreux de recherche de charbon

défaillance plus sérieuse des historiens dans le domaine de l'exploration de l'histoire des applications de cette science – si hautement susceptible d'applications – qu'est la géologie.

ANNEXE I – LE COMITÉ D'AVENTURIERS DE BRUTON
[les dates de participation à l'essai sont indiquées entre crochets]

1) Thomas ANDREWS (actif entre 1790 et 1804) venait d'Upton Lovell, Wiltshire. Sur un projet de bail pour Brewham Lodge, il est qualifié en 1800 de petit propriétaire (« yeoman »). Il loua temporairement cette maison à son propriétaire Thomas Southcote à l'époque de la recherche de charbon avoisinante. La nièce de Southcote épousa en 1783 un autre membre du Comité, H.S. Michell. En 1812, quand Andrews (encore de Brewham Lodge) fut déclaré en faillite, il fut décrit comme « fermier, négociant et colporteur (« chapman ») (London Gazette, 30 juin 1812) [1804 : l'initiale du prénom d'Andrews fut indiquée par erreur comme étant J.].

2) James HARDING (env. 1735-1816), fermier et gentilhomme de Wincanton en 1794, mais de Hengrove, Milton Clevedon lorsqu'il s'impliqua dans l'essai de recherche de charbon [1808-1810].

3) Son fils, James HARDING Junior (env. 1765-1836), fermier et gentilhomme de Milton Clevedon. [1810].

4) Robert Griffin HOLE (env. 1765-1836), petit propriétaire (« yeoman ») de Bruton. [1810].

5) James JAMES (1770-1842), taillandier, propriétaire d'un moulin et d'une usine, de Cole House, Pitcombe. [Secrétaire : 1803-1804]. Il fit faillite vers la fin de 1810 (Staffordshire Advertiser, 5 janvier 1811) et ses propriétés furent vendues aux enchères (Sherborne and Yeovil Mercury, 15 avril 1811).

6) Daniel MAGGS (1756-1825), fabricant de toile à matelas et inventeur d'une batteuse en 1811 puis, ultérieurement, fondeur à Bourton, Dorset. Il fut le fondateur d'une importante entreprise d'ingénierie connue par la suite comme Maggs & Hindley. [1804-1810 ; ses initiales sont indiquées par erreur en 1804 comme M. D. Maggs].

7) Richard MESSITER (1759-1830), banquier de Wincanton et des entrepreneurs de Brewham. Il fit faillite en 1815 (Staffordshire Advertiser, 16 septembre 1815) et s'enfuit aux États-Unis où il mourut près de New York en 1830 (Sweetman, 1903, p. 215-217). [1805].

8) Edward MICHELL (env. 1771-1829), avoué (« attorney ») à Bruton et notaire (« solicitor ») du projet de houillère. [1808-1810].

9) Henry Sampson MICHELL (env. 1758-1831), chirurgien et apothicaire, propriétaire de terres et de moulins à Whaddon (Waddam) House, Bruton. [1804-1810].

10) David Beaumont PAYNE (actif entre 1800 et 1831), de Wincanton, banquier de l'essai de recherche de charbon et ultérieurement banquier à Bath et à Wells. Fit faillite en 1831 (Staffordshire Advertiser, 2 juillet 1831). [1805].

11) Theophilous PERCEVAL (actif entre 1795 et 1829), venait originellement de Paris (France) et a dû arriver en Angleterre à l'époque de la Révolution française. On le trouve d'abord à Sherborne, Dorset lorsqu'il se maria à Bruton. Il fut fileur de soie à Bruton de 1800 à 1829, date à laquelle il fit également faillite (Staffordshire Advertiser, 8 août 1829). Il a dû alors retourner en France. [1804 et secrétaire du Comité de 1805 à 1810].

12) George PRINCE (1749-1831), épicier, mercier et banquier de Bruton. [1804-1810].

13) Richard RING (1782-1838), avoué (« attorney ») de Wincanton. Son père, John RING (décédé en 1794), également avoué (« attorney ») avait été propriétaire d'une partie du domaine (« Manor ») de Nord- et Sud-Brewham en 1791. [1804].

14) John Sharrer WARD (env. 1771-1857), de Bruton de 1798 à 1838 ; en 1834 également de Sherborne, Dorset. Fileur de soie de Bruton et possesseur d'un brevet pour une machine à filer la soie (1805). Aussi tard qu'en 1831, Ward employait 230 personnes dans ses moulins à soie de Bruton. Il était l'un des industriels les plus importants de Bruton où il mourut le 20 avril 1857, à l'âge de 86 ans (Bath and Cheltenham Gazette, 29 avril 1857). [1810].

15) Stephen WHITE (décédé en 1824), fermier et gentilhomme de Sheephouse Farm, Bruton. [1810].

ANNEXE II – LE SITE DU PROJET DE HOUILLÈRE DE BREWHAM.

Le site exact de Brewham demeure incertain. Les archives de l'essai indiquent que les terres devaient être remises en état aux frais des entrepreneurs après la fin de l'essai. L'une des pierres d'achoppement pour tout règlement définitif avec les administrateurs (« Governors ») de l'école était cette complète remise en état des terres pour une utilisation agricole. Ainsi, les chances que subsiste encore une preuve topographique importante sont ici très réduites. Il existe néanmoins quelques indices. Tout d'abord, on peut rejeter l'affirmation que le site était « quelque part près de Yarnfield

Gate» (Couzens, 1972, p. 57). Cela est géologiquement impossible car Yarnfield Gate (GR 768377) est situé sur l'Upper Greensand (Crétacé).

En 1974, D. G. HICKLEY, alors économe de l'école de Bruton, me montra un site qui présentait une profonde dépression et, derrière, un tas de déblais nettement visible à Cook's Farm (GR 737367), dans l'angle nord-ouest du petit bois (Copse), aujourd'hui couvert d'une abondante végétation. Tricia Stainton, l'actuelle propriétaire de la ferme, m'a montré plus récemment un autre terrain nettement remanié, à environ 500 yards (450 mètres) plus au sud. J'ai tendance à penser que le premier est le véritable site. Cela pour deux raisons. La première est que la roue à eau fournissait la force motrice principale pour le fonçage du puits, pour remonter les matériaux extraits par les puisatiers et pour épuiser l'eau qu'ils rencontraient. D'autre part, William Smith a indiqué que l'essai était situé « sur la rive de la rivière Brue près de Brewham Lodge » (MS Smith OUM). Ces deux indices sont déterminants pour affirmer que le premier site, qui est situé à côté de la rivière, est bien le site réel.

ABRÉVIATIONS

BSA : Bruton School Archives, Bruton, Somerset.
DRO : Dorset Record Office, Dorchester, Dorset.
NHM : Natural History Museum, Londres.
OUM : Oxford University Museum, Parks Road, Oxford.
PRO : Public Record Office, Londres.

SRO : Somerset Record Office, Taunton, Somerset.
WRO : Wiltshire Record Office, Trowbridge, Wiltshire.

REMERCIEMENTS

BP Exploration Co. Ltd a, de façon très appropriée, en raison du thème de cet article, aimablement fourni une aide financière qui a rendu possible les recherches nécessitées par sa préparation. Les administrateurs (« Governors ») de l'école de Bruton ont eu la courtoisie de m'autoriser à consulter et citer les importantes archives dont ils ont la charge. Les archivistes des DRO, SRO et WRO m'ont apporté toute l'assistance possible. Une aide spécifique m'a été apportée par Ben Bather (Londres), Martin Bodman (Londres), Stella Brecknell (Oxford), Puffy Bowden (Wincanton), David Bromwich (Taunton), Jean Gaudant (Paris), D.G. Hickley (Bruton), Derrick Hunt (Bath), Michael McGarvie (Frome), comme toujours, Stella Pierce (Bath), Hugh Prudden (Montacute), Miss G. Richards (Wincanton), Brian Shingler (Bruton), Tricia Stainton (Brewham), Caroline Thorne (Bourton) et Angela Ward (Silton). Dennis Dean (Evanston, USA), Jean Jones (Edimbourg), Cliff Nelson (Washington, DC), David Oldroyd (Sydney), Jim Secord (Cambridge) et Ken Taylor (Norman, USA) ont aimablement lu et commenté une première version de cet article dont Jean Gaudant (Paris) et François Forney (Nancy) ont assuré la traduction.

RÉFÉRENCES

Anonyme (1793). Universal British Directory (entry for Bruton), vol. 2, London, British Directory Office, p. 390-391.

Anonyme (1811). An Authentic Description of the Kennet & Avon Canal, London, Richardson, 30 p.

Anonyme (1825). The Dorset and Somerset Canal Navigation, London, Livermore, 15p. (copy in DRO).

BAKEWELL, R. (1815). An Introduction to Geology, second edition. London, Harding, 492 p.

BIGNOT, G. (1989). Une conséquence de la pénurie énergétique en France durant la Révolution : la recherche (vaine) de charbon de terre en Haute-Normandie. Minéraux et Fossiles, n° 165, (juillet-août 1989), p. 27-33.

BIGNOT, G. (1996). Une recherche infructueuse de charbon de terre aux environs de Dieppe (Haute-Normandie) à la fin du dix-huitième siècle. Obstacles conceptuels et technologiques. Trav. Comité fr. Hist. géol., (3), 10, p. 37-54.

BUCHANAN, C. A. & R. A. (1980). The Batsford Guide to the Industrial Archaeology of Central Southern England. London, Batsford, 208 p.

BUCKLAND, W. & CONYBEARE, W. D. (1824). Observations on the South-western Coal District of England. Trans. Geol. Soc. London, (2), 1, p. 210-316.

CLEW, K. (1971). The Dorset and Somerset Canal. Newton Abbot, David & Charles, 116 p.

Un essai malencontreux de recherche de charbon

COUZENS, P. (1972). *Bruton in Selwood*. Sherborne, Abbey Press, 118 p.

DOWN, C. G. & WARRINGTON, A. J. (1971). *The History of the Somerset Coalfield*.Newton Abbot, David & Charles, 283 p.

EYLES, J. M. (1969). William Smith : Some Aspects of his Life and Work. *In* : SCHNEER, C. J. (ed.), *Toward a History of Geology*. Cambridge (Mass.), MIT Press, p. 142-158.

FAREY, J. (1806). Canal. *In* : REES, A. (ed.), *The Cyclopaedia*, vol. 6, London, Longman, (unpaginated - 142 p.).

FAREY, J. (1808). On the finding of Coal in the South-Eastern Counties of England. *Agric. Mag. (Dickson's)*, (3), 2, p. 22-31.

FAREY, J. (1811). *General View of the Agriculture and Minerals of Derbyshire*, vol. 1, London, McMillan, 532 p.

FAREY, J. (1819). On the Importance of knowing and accurately discriminating FOSSIL-SHELLS... *Phil. Mag.*, 53, p. 112-132.

FITTON, W. H. (1833). *Notes on the Progress of Geology in England.*, London, Taylor, 48 p.

GREENOUGH, G. B. (1819). *A critical examination of the first principles of Geology*. London, Longman, 336 p.

HERSCHEL, J. F. W. (1831). *A preliminary discourse on the Study of Natural Philosophy*. London, Longman, Rees etc., 372 p.

KELLAWAY, G. A. (1991). The Work of William Smith at Bath. *In* : KELLAWAY, G. A. (ed.), *The hot Springs of Bath*, Bath, City Council,p. 25-54.

LAUDAN, R. (1976). William Smith. Stratigraphy without Palaeontology. *Centaurus*, 20, p. 210-226.

MILLER, H. (1869). *The Old Red Sandstone* ; *or, new walks in an old field*. Edinburgh, Adam and Charles Black, 385 p.

MORAND, J.-F.-C. (1768-1774). *L'Art d'exploiter les mines de charbon de terre*, vol. 1. Paris, Saillant and Nyon, 725 p.

PHILLIPS, J. (1844). *Memoirs of William Smith*. London, Murray, 150 p.

PHILLIPS, J. (1871). *Geology of Oxford*. Oxford, Clarendon Press, 523 p.

RUDWICK, M. J. S. (1963). The Foundation of the Geological Society of London. *Brit. J. Hist. Sci.*, 1, p. 325-355.

SALE, G. (1950). *Four hundred Years a School.*, Dorchester, Abbey Press, unpaginated.

SCHMID, G. (ed.) (1949). *Goethe (J.W. von)*. *Die Schriften zur Naturwissenschaft* : *Schriften zur Geologie und Mineralogie, Zweiter band, 1812-1832*. Weimar, Hermann Böhlaus Nachfolger, 438 p.

SECORD, J. (ed.) (1994). *Vestiges of the Natural History of Creation and other evolutionary writings by Robert Chambers*. Chicago and London, University of Chicago Press, 2 vol., 390 et 254 p.

[SHARPE, W.] (1769). *A Treatise upon Coal-Mines*. London, For the Author, 105 p.

SHEPPARD, T. (1920). *William Smith* : *His maps and memoirs*. Hull, Brown, 253 p.

SHINGLER, B. (1995). Letter. *Bull. Somerset Industr. Archaeol. Soc.*, 69, p. 18-19.

SMITH, W. (1817a). *Strata Identified by Organised Fossils*, Part 3. London, Arding, p. 17-24.

SMITH, W. (1817b). *Stratigraphical System of Organised Fossils... in the British Museum*, Part 1. London, Williams, 118 p.

SMITH, W. (1819). *Geological View and Section through Dorsetshire and Somersetshire*. London, Cary.

SWEETMAN, G. (1903). *The History of Wincanton*. London, Williams and Wincanton, Sweetman, 296 p.

TORRENS, H. S. (1974). The Revd. William Sharpe (1724-1783). *University College Oxford Rec.*, 6, p. 376-384.

TORRENS, H. S. (1975). Coal Exploration in Dorset. *Dorset County Mag.*, n° 44, p. 31-39.

TORRENS, H. S. (1979). Geological communication in the Bath area in the last half of the eighteenth century. *In* : JORDANOVA, L.J. and PORTER, R. (eds). *Images of the Earth*, Chalfont St Giles, British Society for the History of Science, p. 215-247.

TORRENS, H. S. (1984) The history of coal prospecting in Britain 1650-1900. *In* : *Energie in der Geschichte (papers for the 11th Symposium of ICOHTEC)*, Düsseldorf, Verein Deutscher Ingenieure, p. 88-95.

TORRENS, H. S. (1989). In commemoration of the 150th anniversary of the death of William Smith (1769-1839). *Trav. Comité fr. Hist. Géol.*, (3), 3, p. 57-63.

TORRENS, H. S. (1994). Patronage and problems : Banks and the Earth Sciences. *In* : BANKS,

IV

R.E.R. *et al.* (eds.), *Sir Joseph Banks : a global perspective,* Kew, Royal Botanic Gardens, p. 49-75.

TOWNSEND, J. (1813). *The Character of Moses established for veracity as an historian,* vol. 1. London, Gye, Bath and Longman, 448 p.

WOODBRIDGE, K. (1970). *Landscape and Antiquity.* Oxford, Clarendon Press, 304 p.

V

PATRONAGE AND PROBLEMS: BANKS AND THE EARTH SCIENCES

Abstract

Banks's involvements with the Earth Sciences were on two planes. On the "public" front, his enthusiasm for geology and mineralogy seems never to have been more than lukewarm. As an explorer or promoter of exploration he seems to have taken little interest in these subjects. But as a private individual with estates in Derbyshire and Lincolnshire, he needed geological expertise and his geological patronage was both well informed and crucial to the development of geology.

When geology became institutionalised by the foundation of the Geological Society of London in 1807, Banks's earlier patronage of the newly professional and "practical" mineral surveyors caused serious tensions with the "gentlemanly" geologists of that Society, who marginalised the contributions of the mineral surveyors. The tensions have misled historians into thinking that advances in British geology in the Banksian era were largely "gentlemanly".

A "public" involvement: the years to 1792

"His knowledge and attention is very much confined to one study, Botany; and his manners are rather coarse and heavy." Joseph Farington's diary, 21 January 1796.[1]

If Botany was indeed Banks's passion, there is ample evidence that he also took an astute interest in the earth sciences. But, in dealings with the history of science, we need to separate carefully the *priority* of an individual's achievement against the *influence* of that same individual. This has become particularly necessary in the earth sciences, where debates about the relative contributions made by, for example, Abraham Werner (1749–1817) in Saxony and William Smith (1769–1839) in England have failed to make this vital separation. While there is no evidence that Banks has any priority to geological "discovery" —indeed one is "hard put to come up with any single scientific accomplishment to attach to the name of Joseph Banks"[2] — it is clear that Banks's contribution to the development of geology was both influential and seminal.

Banks took an interest in geological matters while still a student at Oxford as witnessed by his membership of the "Fossil Club at Tittup Hall" near the Headington quarries outside Oxford in 1762.[3] On his southern English tour of 1767 however, Banks had little to say of geological interest; a cave near Cheddar

FIGS. 1 & 2. Views of Staffa drawn on the spot in 1772 by John Cleveley junior.[120] Reproduced courtesy of the British Library.

V

which he entered "had nothing at all in it worth the trouble of stopping".[4] But a special visit was made to study Alexander Catcott's famous collection of fossils and minerals at Bristol.[5] The same pattern followed on Banks's later 1767 tour to Wales and then visits to Wednesbury and Dudley.[6] Banks's observations on the fossils of Oxford[7] say little beyond noting the particular fossils occurring there.

Geology also, and perhaps understandably, seems to have occupied little time on the *Endeavour* voyage of 1768–1771, despite the 1768 "hints on minerals and fossils" offered to the expedition by James Douglas (1702–1768), president of the Royal Society.[8] These offered prescient observations on the need to search alluvial materials to learn of the geology of hinterlands. But as an Australian historian has observed, these hints were "overlooked" on the *Endeavour* voyage — "there are no observations, let alone collections, of rocks and minerals to stand with the wealth of material relating to the animal and vegetable kingdoms as souvenirs. Rocks... did travel on *Endeavour*, [but] as ballast".[9]

Banks's next expedition was more geological and it became accidentally more so when, on 12 August 1772, Banks and his Icelandic party reached Staffa and next day saw Fingal's Cave. They were led there by local report that pillars like those of the Giant's Causeway in Ireland occurred. The Irish examples had long been known;[10] and, as far back as 1694, that these columns were made of "*Lapis basaltes*". A "battle of the basalts" about their origins started in mid century. The Frenchman Jean Etienne Guettard (1715–1786) demonstrated the existence of extinct volcanoes in the Auvergne in 1751.[11] This became a "Vulcanist" explanation. Rev. Richard Pococke (1704–1765) instead deduced that these pillars were formed by repeated precipitations from water or mud to give a "Neptunist" view.[12]

In May 1771 Nicolas Desmarest (1725–1815) read to the *Académie des Sciences* in Paris his famous paper on polygonal basalt columns. He had suspected they were volcanic in origin in 1763 and his conclusion that they were, was announced in 1765 and published in 1768.[13] This reached the Royal Society in 1770 when R.E. Raspe confirmed that similar basalt columns near Cassel in Germany were volcanic in origin.[14] This, and oral reports of the 1771 paper from Paris, seem to have inspired Banksian interest in such phenomena and aided the choice of Iceland for his 1772 expedition.

Banks reported in some detail on Staffa. He noted the pillars were "of lava-like material of a coarse kind of basaltes".[15] His detailed description was not published in 1771[16] nor was it, as in an earlier claim, "a phenomenon till then unobserved by naturalists".[17] Banks does however deserve credit for having first brought the wonders of Staffa to the proper attention of "philosophers". Figures 1 & 2 are of Staffa drawings taken on the spot in 1772 by John Cleveley junior.[18] Joseph Farington's observation that "*accuracy* of drawing seems to be a principle recommendation to Sir Joseph" — diary entry 12 December 1793[19] — seems entirely confirmed. It is sad that the value of the party's detailed observations on volcanic columnar basalts was dissipated by the "volcanic illusion" which Daubeny[20] was still able to discuss so eloquently 50 years later.

The expedition to Iceland had a true mineralogical dimension. Uno von Troil (1746–1803), the Swedish priest, was a member and took a real interest in such matters. It was his account of Iceland that was published, not Banks's; supplemented with remarks by Torbern Bergman (1735–1784) who discussed volcanic effects in Iceland and the origins of basaltic pillars. Bergman took these

52

to be an effect of moist substances which had burst while drying to cause contractions.[21] Banks again used rocks merely as ballast and many of his Icelandic lava specimens were supporting moss gardens at Kew by 1784![22]

Between 1781 and 1820, i.e. during most of Banks's presidency of the Royal Society, Carter noted that only 3.6% of papers published concerned geology. Even taking a broader view of Earth Sciences, only up to 7% can be so considered.[23] Banks's personal involvement with such matters up to 1792 was equally episodic.

Banks's involvements with Australian exploration from 1788 were legion but again one notes the strange lack of interest in things mineral: on *Endeavour* [Solander's] "attention was reserved.... for plants and animals".[24] There was a similar lack of any real interest in things mineral on the HMS *Investigator* expedition. Banks instructed Robert Brown in 1801 that "Geology and Mineralogy must be considered by you as subsidiary pursuits and you will be required to do in them no more than is compatible with a full attention to Botany, Entomology, Ornothology etc".[25] Likewise when mineralogists went out to South America (John Mawe in 1804) and Australia (Robert Townson in 1806)[26] there is little evidence of any Banksian enthusiasm for their activities, although Banks was involved with both projects. In a *laissez-faire* society they went out as *individuals* in the eyes of Banks. All this, for two recent writers "betrays the [then] limits of Banksian vision in science".[27] This vision was soon to change.

A "private" involvement: Banks and mineralogy, 1792 to 1801

"*The Gregory Mine into which I twice descended actually passes under [Sir Joseph's] house and several veins of lead are exposed to view in his gardens. Overton Hall therefore may be called a Mining Villa and the fit residence of a mineralogist.*"[28]

In 1792 Banks's private attitude to geology was forced to change. He inherited estates at Overton near Ashover,[29] which had come into the Banks family through inter-marriage with the Hodgkinsons.[30] Up to this time Banks had had limited contact with geology. London long after 1792 was still thought a place where the study of geology was impossible, since flint was "almost the only branch... that can be practically studied" there.[31] The Banks estates at Revesby in Lincolnshire were similarly thought to be in an "uninteresting" region for geology. But Derbyshire was different. Lead had been mined at Ashover since at least the seventeenth century[32] and the Overton mines and estate revenues so intertwined that Banks's income depended on them. One historian has claimed that for Banks "the mineral kingdom was no more than a source of income".[33] If this was ever entirely true, it is surely most true of this decade.

The Gregory Mine at Ashover had been the county's richest and most famous mine. The "clear profit at Gregory Mine to the Proprietors [of whom Banks was one] from the year 1758 till Xmas 1806 ... was £101,535".[34] But between 1783 and 1788 profits dropped by nearly 60% and by 1792 the mines at Overton were becoming a liability. John Milnes noted "from Lady Day 1790 till Xmas 1803 there was a loss paid as per quarterly reckonings of £23,398"[35] One of Banks's first actions on inheriting was to draw up "memorandums made at

V

Overton — March 1793."[36] [John] Nuttall [fl.1765–fl.1830] the local Matlock land surveyor was to make a map of the parish, to survey Banks's lands at Alton "where coal is supposed to be" and then to suggest how such coal might be proved geologically. Clearly Banks was being forced to widen his mineral horizons with the help of his local mineral agent William Milnes II (c. 1757–1814).

A letter Sir Charles Blagden wrote to Banks on 8 September 1794[37] provides further evidence of Banks's new search for better mineral information. It notes that "the Duchess of Devonshire[38] said she had recommended to you Mr Watson, who makes the tablets representing the strata of Derbyshire and she speaks in very high terms of the talents and mineralogical skill of Mr Barker and Mr French, two young gentlemen of that county". Banks had already made contact with White Watson (1760–1835), whose commonplace book[39] notes that Banks first called on him on 17 August 1794 when they had breakfasted together with "Mr Milnes of Ashover". Thomas Barker (1767–1816), lead merchant of Ashford Hall, Bakewell, had been a pupil of Abraham Werner in Freiberg in Saxony in 1790 and 1791.[40] Dr Richard Forester French (1771–1843) of Derby had helped Erasmus Darwin with some of his experiments as early as 1787.[41] French had, in 1792, just graduated M.B. He changed his name to Forester in 1797.[42] He played little further part in advancing Derbyshire geology, although elected an Honorary Member of the Geological Society of London in 1809.[43]

Charles Hatchett (1765–1847), a further visitor to Overton in June 1796, provided vital information of what was known of Ashover geology at that time. His diary[44] records the exposed downward stratigraphic sequence of grit, shale, limestone overlying toadstone in a sketch (Figure 3). This shows that these rocks were then known to occur in a domed structure which had been split by the river Amber. Concepts of such domes — later to be named anticlines — were already familiar, if unnamed, by 1760.[45] Denudation by subsequent erosion was equally clearly known. Hatchett also confirmed the financially unpromising nature of some of the local lead mines in 1796.

The following year saw the first recorded visit to Derbyshire by the man who, with Banks's vital patronage, subsequently helped revolutionize the study of both British and Derbyshire geology: John Farey senior (1766–1826). Farey noted that he first visited Derbyshire in 1797 when examining bogs near Buxton.[46] In June 1798 Farey, who was then estate steward to the Duke of Bedford at Woburn, first met Banks. Farey, who at that time had little real interest in geology, explained to Banks "the extensive system of drainage and irrigation" he was supervising on the Duke's estates.[47] In 1800 Farey first heard of William Smith (1769–1839) the geologist[48] and met him in October 1801, when the relationship which led to Farey being called "Smith's Boswell" commenced.

In the same year one of the last of the old school of strictly mineralogical geologists visited Banks at Overton; the "Neptunian" John Hawkins (?1757–1841) of Cornwall who had also studied at Freiberg under Werner, in 1786 and again in 1793. He wrote to fellow mineralogist Philip Rashleigh (1729–1811) from Buxton on 14 September giving his impressions of Overton. He had met there the "Plutonian" Scotsman Dr Thomas Hope (1766–1844) but they had been unable to resolve their differences about the origins of the toadstone exposed at Ashover, which John Whitehurst had claimed in 1778 was volcanic in

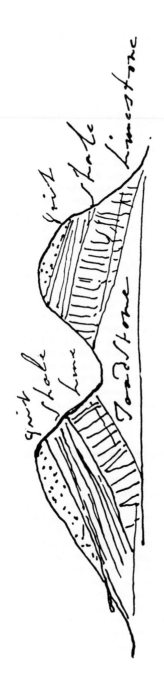

FIG. 3. Sketch of the stratification at Ashover by Charles Hatchett. 1796.[121]

origin. But Hawkins *had* been able to study the relations of the lead veins to both the enclosing limestone and the toadstones. He saw how the high dips of rocks made life difficult for mineral adventurers at Ashover when seeking lead below the overlying shale cover. This was one of the reasons Hawkins thought "the state of mining industry here is much on the decline. The produce of the Derbyshire mines being reduced to one half of what it was ten years ago". In attempts to improve mining output John Milnes (c. 1770–1838), William's brother, prepared a detailed "section of the strata at Gregory's Mine" in June 1801 which he improved up to 1806[49] and, in about 1803, a map of veins and mines in the parish of Ashover.[50]

Banks's private and "public" involvements in geology now came together, since it was John Hawkins who provided the Geological (or as he called them "Mineral Geographical") Instructions which the crew of H.M.S. *Investigator* took to Australian waters in 1801.[51] The intentions of this expedition were chiefly hydrographic and botanical. So the "Instructions" started off in defensive mood, "it would be wrong not to pay some attention to Mineralogy" but conceded that "this department of natural History promises fewer discoveries than the two others [animals and plants] which are ... the objects of the expedition". The influence of Banks is easy to see. It may have been during Hawkins's September 1800 visit to Overton that these instructions were drafted. If so, Banks may have played a part in writing them. John Mawe (1766–1829), the London mineral dealer, was also involved in proffering advice to the *Investigator* expedition.[52]

In order to pay lip service to the need for *some* mineral expertise, Banks had been instrumental in renewing negotiations for a "practical miner" to join this expedition in January 1801. John Allen (born Ashover 1775) was the man chosen[53] but he had only a subsidiary role, working under the direction of naturalists in collecting rocks. He was not initially expected to make trials below the surface, although Banks had changed his mind on this by June 1801. The limitations of sending such a man, however capable a miner, were revealed by the trained mineralogists attached to the French *Baudin* expedition the following year.[54]

A private involvement: Banks and stratigraphy, 1802 to 1811

While efforts were made to save the Ashover mining industry from the terminal decline which finally struck in October 1803, Banks, as we have seen, had come into contact with John Farey (Figure 4) and his "master" William Smith. The chronological connection between this decline and Banks's espousal of their "new technology" of mineral surveying is so close that it seems one was a direct consequence of the other. Proof in the face of the wide or total dispersal of manuscripts of all three protagonists is more difficult. But between 1800 and 1804 we note a total swing in Banks's allegiances from Wernerian "mineral geographers", like Hawkins, to native "mineral surveyors". The close connections between mineral wealth and industrial opportunities meant that Banks could hope for some real financial rewards.

Relations between all three men have been described by Eyles (1985). Banks first met Farey in 1798, while Banks and Smith first met in the summer of 1801; when Banks "favoured Smith with an interview, and from this time till his death remained a steady friend and a liberal patron of his labours".[55] Smith had just published his abortive but widely circulated *Prospectus* in June 1801. The Royal Society copy is annotated by Banks "sent my name to Debret". But Smith's plans to publish, and Sir Joseph's hopes to subscribe, were set back when John Debrett (died 1822), Smith's intended publisher, was declared bankrupt in October 1801. Smith was now entangled in the financial problems which beset him for the next 30 years.

FIG. 4. Silhouette of John Farey, probably drawn by White Watson, in 1807.[122]

V

FIG. 5. Portrait of Sir Joseph Banks in 1802 by Rembrandt Peale (1778–1860).[123]
Reproduced courtesy of the Library, The Academy of Natural Sciences of Philadelphia.

Banks's view of the significance of Smith's discoveries was greatly stimulated by Farey, who on 11 February 1802 wrote Banks a significant letter urging the *importance* of what Smith had discovered.[56] Figure 5 shows a newly located portrait of Banks from this same year. Farey had just returned from a triangular geological "tour of the strata" through Buckinghamshire and Bedfordshire early in 1802, with Smith and Benjamin Bevan (1773–1833), another of Smith's important pupils. This tour had demonstrated to Farey the importance of Smith's discoveries.[57]

Smith had made two advances of great significance for geology. The first was to document the *sequential* order of British rocks. The scale of Smith's achievement here, in building on what little was previously known, can be best seen from the chart published by Challinor.[58] The second was Smith's discovery of the means to *identify* individual strata with that sequence by the organised fossils found in, and often characteristic of, particular rock units.

Banks's response to Farey's letter was characteristically helpful. In May 1802 Smith noted in a letter to his relative Samuel Collett[59] "I have been obliged to have recourse to an uninterrupted pursuit of my subject [land and mineral surveying] with all my plans and papers together in this place [Bath] and shall call on Sir J. Banks in London to settle abt bringing my Papers before the Publick in a much better form than if they had appeared last year. I am now confident they are correct & my map begins to be a very interesting History of the Country".[60]

Banks and Smith attended the annual sheep-shearing meeting at Woburn in June 1802 when "Smith ... exhibited his map now in very considerable forwardness, of the strata of different earths, stones, coals & which constitute the soil of this island ... he was particularly noticed by Sir Joseph Banks".[61] Smith next wrote to Banks at Revesby in October 1802 outlining what little progress he had made. On 21 April 1803 Smith showed Banks "my plan of strata" in London.[62]

In June 1804 the annual Woburn sheep-shearing was again held.[63] Banks, realising the financial plight Smith was in, subscribed £50 as a starting subscription towards the Geological map Smith now hoped to publish.[64] The undated *Proposals* for publishing this, which Smith then circulated, survive in the Bedford papers[65], in Smith's hand. At the Smithfield Cattle Show in December 1804 "Mr Smith... shewed his map of the Strata of England, which is preparing for Sir Joseph Banks, in whose library it will soon be exhibited for the information of the curious".[66] On 29 January 1805 Smith again saw Banks in London according to his diary. He was clearly now having considerable problems struggling to earn a living while finding time to complete his map. His problems also involved adjusting to literary life.[67]

John Farey realised how acute these problems were, and so on 21 May 1806 wrote to the *Philosophical Magazine* to publicise Smith's work and the "want of sufficient public encouragement" that Smith had received. Farey now published "the rules... for ascertaining the relative position... of each distinct stratum, however thin, with regard to those above and below it in the series [of British rocks]" which Smith had discovered. The first was "by the knowledge of its relative position with other known strata in its vicinity" [what geologists would call superposition]. The second "by the peculiar organised remains imbedded in it and not to be found in the adjoining strata". The third, to be used when all else

V

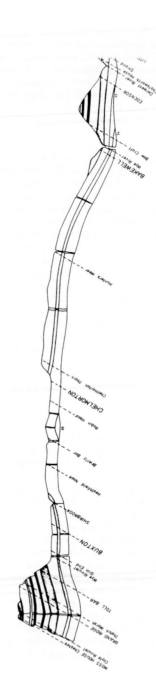

A Section of the STRATA of DERBYSHIRE through BUXTON and BOLSOVER. By
After Mr JOHN FAREY'S Survey of

V

BOLSOVER, By WHITE WATSON, Statuary & Mineralogist, BAKEWELL F.L.S. & c.

FAREY'S Survey of the County 1807

FIGS. 6 & 7. Farey's first geological section across Derbyshire, which he allowed White Watson to copy in November 1807.[124]

61

had failed, relied on the unreliable; "the peculiar nature and properties of the matter composing the stratum itself" [its mere lithology].[68] Ominously Farey wrote to Smith only two days later to note Banks's wish that Smith's work should be completed.[69] But Smith continued in financial difficulties; as he noted to Richard Crawshay on 27 August 1807 the "subscription which Banks had opened in 1804 had not been so readily encouraged".[70]

It was against this background that Banks turned to Smith's better placed and London-based pupil, John Farey with his personal patronage. Banks's first commission was in July/August 1806 when he asked Farey (whose expenses he met) to undertake a "section of the earth from London to Brighton". This was finished and dedicated to Banks early in 1807,[71] but never published in either's lifetime. Banks then asked Farey to make some calculations for the use of his lead mining agent in Derbyshire", as his introduction to Derbyshire. Things were complicated when, later in 1807, Richard Phillips (1767–1840) introduced Farey to Sir John Sinclair (1754–1835), President of the Board of Agriculture. Two parallel projects, both involving Farey and Banks in Derbyshire, now developed.

The first started in August 1807 as a geological survey of Derbyshire "at the instance of [Banks] worthy President of the Royal Society in order to examine minutely its Stratification and Mineral Treasures". At the beginning of September 1807 Farey joined Banks on his annual visit to Overton for a week. The first product of this work was a section of Strata across Derbyshire which Farey allowed White Watson to copy in November 1807 (Figures 6 & 7). Word soon spread about Farey's work for Banks. A.B. Lambert (1761–1842) wrote to William Cunnington (1754–1810) on 23 December 1807 noting; "the last time I was in Soho Square Sir Joseph showed me a curious and interesting drawing that has just been finished by a pupil of your friend Smith, of all the Strata of Derbyshire on Smith's new principles and Sir Jos. was much delighted with it".[72] The section was then sent in by Banks to be exhibited at the second meeting of the new Geological Society of London (at which Banks was elected a member) on 1 January 1808.[73]

Farey was soon also busy on a second and more detailed stratigraphical section right across England from the Lincolnshire coast through Banks's estates at Revesby to end at Overton. Farey moved from Overton to start work at the eastern end of this section, examining the strata near Boston and Revesby in October 1807.[74] Here Farey witnessed another of the many abortive attempts to find coal in strata which merely and superficially resembled coal-bearing Coal Measures and which misled the "adventurers" concerned. Such trials were frequent before the work of the newly professional mineral surveyors like Smith and Farey had established a scientific basis for mineral prospecting. The true geological horizon of this trial near Raithby was identified, nearly correctly, by Farey using "the proper extraneous fossils" he found in these strata, as Smith's Clunch Clay; merely one of many rock units much higher in the British sequence above the Coal Measures which "resembled" coal-bearing beds.[75]

This long and detailed stratigraphic cross section, from the Lincolnshire coast to Overton, Farey finished on 17 February 1808 and dedicated to Banks. On it Farey styled himself Smith's pupil. The section was 3 metres long.[76] Four contemporary copies survive.[77] It was exhibited at Lord Somerville's Spring Cattle Show in London on 29 February 1808.[78] Clearly it was widely distributed, despite not being published. In the following month, members of the Geological Society of London visited Smith, and Farey, who had been present on this visit, opened his correspondence with G.B. Greenough — the president.[79] All parties were hoping to advance the science of geology.

A third fruit of Banks's Derbyshire commission to Farey was a coloured geological map of the NW portion of Derbyshire dated September 1808 of which the original MS also survives in the Sutro Library,[80] with a sketch explaining faults in the "great Limestone District" in Derbyshire.[81] Farey's now improved "section of the Strata of the Great Mineral Limestone District and its bordering Strata in Derbyshire" dated September 1808 also survives.[82] None of these were ever published, but the "mineralogical map by Mr Farey" was exhibited to the Geological Society by the President who had received a copy from Banks on 2 December 1808. His improved September 1808 Derbyshire "mineral section" was also exhibited to the Geological Society at Banks's request on 3 February 1809. But Banks resigned from the Society the following month.

The second collateral Derbyshire project Farey had agreed to undertake for Sir John Sinclair. He "had previous to my [Farey's] setting out on that [Banks] Survey engaged me to collect at the same time, the necessary facts and particulars for a *Report to the Board* [of Agriculture], on the Agricultural and Rural Concerns of the County".[83] The details emerge from letters.[84] The first is a copy of Sinclair's reply to Farey, accepting Farey's terms; the second is Sinclair's explanatory letter to Banks. Sinclair now agreed that Farey enter into "greater details concerning minerals and soil in Derbyshire than had been normal with earlier *County Agriculture Reports*". Sinclair reported to Farey that Banks "seems much impressed" with the idea that Farey should be commissioned to do the Derbyshire *Report* and it was now agreed that Farey be commissioned to do this, for £300 "in full of all Farey's demands". Sinclair sent a copy to Banks with a covering letter noting "if the Board says the allowance is too much, I shall shelter myself under the *Banks* of literature". Banks merely annotated this letter on receipt "not a syllable in my letter has a reference to the increased price offered to Mr Farey" and continues "I think he will deserve it, if he is able to give a distinct account of the Stratification of Derbyshire but whether he is or not remains to be proved". It was impressive that Farey was so soon able to answer Banks's fears.

The Survey of Derbyshire, which the Board of Agriculture had started to take off Banks's hands, now commenced in earnest, and from the late summer of 1807 for two years Farey was busy with his Geological and Agricultural Survey. By a new agreement with Sinclair in April 1810 it was agreed that the Board of Agriculture should purchase, for £150, much of the research which Banks had originally commissioned for incorporation into the *Derbyshire Report* which would now include a general summary of the stratification and mineral concerns of the county as the first volume of the *Report*.[85] This was to have become the first in an intended series of *County Mineral Reports* to accompany the *Agricultural Reports*. By 20 November 1810 the first chapter of Farey's *Derbyshire Report* —covering geology — was completed. It comprised the whole of one volume; an octavo which gave a pioneering survey of British Strata, published in June 1811 (see Figure 8). It broke new ground with a long discussion on "terrestrial stratification", announced Smith's major results and listed the 21 strata down to the Red Marl — the highest unit found in Derbyshire

V

GENERAL VIEW

OF THE

AGRICULTURE

AND

MINERALS

OF

DERBYSHIRE;

WITH

OBSERVATIONS ON THE MEANS OF THEIR IMPROVEMENT.

DRAWN UP FOR THE CONSIDERATION OF

THE BOARD OF AGRICULTURE

AND INTERNAL IMPROVEMENT.

VOL. I.

CONTAINING A FULL ACCOUNT OF

The Surface, Hills, Valleys, Rivers, Rocks, Caverns, Strata, Soils, Minerals, Mines, Collieries, Mining Processes, &c. &c.

Together with some Account of the recent Discoveries respecting the Stratification of England; and a Theory of Faults and Denudated Strata, applicable to Mineral Surveying and Mining.

ILLUSTRATED BY FIVE COLOURED MAPS, AND SECTIONS OF STRATA.

By JOHN FAREY, Sen.

MINERAL SURVEYOR,

OF UPPER CROWN STREET, WESTMINSTER.

LONDON:

PRINTED BY B. McMILLAN, BOW STREET, COVENT GARDEN:
SOLD BY G. AND W. NICOL, BOOKSELLERS TO HIS MAJESTY, PALL-
MALL; SHERWOOD, NEELY AND JONES, PATERNOSTER-ROW;
DRURY, DERBY; BRADLEY, CHESTERFIELD; AND
TODD, SHEFFIELD.

1811.

FIG. 8. Title page of Farey's 1811 Mineral *Report on Derbyshire*, volume 1.[125]

— which had been elucidated. The strata found below in Derbyshire were then sequentially discussed and a significant section on Faults with coloured diagrams included.[86] Finally Farey "sincerely hoped that such a desire may speedily be excited, for the publication of ... [Smith's] valuable Maps and Papers, and descriptions of his Fossils, illustrative of the British Strata as would induce him to lay by his professional engagements, in order to publish them".[87] This hope was sadly to be dashed; although Farey's complete *Report* was published in three volumes over 1811, 1813 & 1817 totalling over 1900 pages for a payment to Farey of £450. This was despite the bankruptcy of the publisher in November 1810 and Sinclair's financial crisis in 1815. Farey's *Derbyshire Report* has rightly been called "magnificent" by Riden.[88]

A final act of this decade was the reading to the Royal Society in March 1811 of Farey's letter to Banks dated 31 January. It described "the great Derbyshire Denudation", and demonstrated the geological structures Farey had uncovered in Derbyshire.[89] But it twisted a knife in the wounded relationship between the Royal Society and the fledgling Geological Society founded in 1807. This wound was made when Banks resigned from the Geological Society in March 1809.[90] It continued to fester for many years after Banks's death.

The Final years: Banks in decline, 1812–1820

This period was overshadowed by Banks's ill health[91] which allowed him fewer opportunities to support the work of "his" mineral surveyors. That they needed help is clear. A letter from Farey to G.B. Greenough of 16 September 1810[92] shows that Farey was already at work on an intended paper for volume 1 of the *Transactions of the Geological Society*. This was to be a modified version of the original Banksian commission; a "minute Mineral Survey of the parish of Ashover and its environs".[93] A second letter of 27 May between the same parties shows that the Ashover map and section could not be read before the Society until the explanatory memoir had been written, which Farey was then busy writing. Farey and his son William had restarted this project in August 1811,[94] after publication of the *Derbyshire Report*.

By 2 December 1812 the large mineral map of Ashover was ready and it was shown to both Banks and Greenough. By 25 December 1812 a diminished version was also ready and good progress had been made with the memoir and the large map and section with the help in Ashover of William Milnes III (1785–1866). The memoir was delayed in December 1812 until Farey had seen the Cuvier & Brongniart memoir which was "not yet in Sir Joseph's library". By 1 January 1813 all was finished, apart from a detailed description of the 24 strata exposed in the Ashover area. The tragedy is that this Ashover work was never published and has nearly all been lost, like most of Farey's many other manuscripts. The only fragment to survive is the reduced map reproduced here as Figure 9. It is a miracle of detailed geological mapping for its date, December 1812, on a scale of $1\frac{1}{2}$ inches to a mile.[95] 24 separate strata are separately coloured geologically.

The Geological Society Council, however, took a less favourable view of this work, as did a historian of the Royal Society.[96] After noting that Farey had not been previously acquainted with Wernerian geognosy and that his work was

V

NOTE: Unfortunately it was not possible to reproduce this illustration in colour in this reprint.

independent, Thomson noted that Farey's stratigraphic observations "certainly do him credit as an observer but are unfortunately too circumstantially minute for common use. General principles stripped of all useless details are much more attractive and much more easily understood and remembered than a multitude of minute observations". The scale of the problem Farey faced in getting this paper published is revealed by his letter to Greenough of 23 January 1813 which refers to further sections of the text having been removed by officers of the Society. It was this version which was formally read in February.[97] By 8 April 1813 the paper could only be published if it was further shortened by the Society, and Farey pleaded with Greenough that his three years work should not be so badly mutilated. If it was to be, Farey asked, on behalf of himself and his patron Banks, that it be returned as soon as possible. But by 29/30 May 1813 a four to one abridgement had been made. Farey complained that it meant this was a new paper; "a stranger to me and my subject". By June 1813 all negotiations had failed and Farey asked for, and eventually was granted, the return of his paper. Farey's correspondence with Greenough now ended. The referee who had been given the job of "seeing it through the press" was Henry Warburton (1784–1858). One wonders if the real reason it was never published was a vendetta against Banks for his resignation in 1809?

A letter of 7 July 1813 from Farey to Sowerby shows he now hoped to publish his Ashover paper "rejected thro' the intrigues of a few individuals by the Geological Society", with another Report he had made on the Alum Shales of Yorkshire, as the first volume of an intended new series of *Mineral Reports* "if I can meet with any bookseller willing to undertake it". But Farey could not find a publisher and in one of several outspoken attacks wrote of those at the Geological Society; "hostile to the cause of real Geological Science, as to those persons engaged in practical and untheoretical investigations of the facts of British Stratification", who had aborted his paper. His failure to achieve separate publication showed it "could not be published at all in this country", such was the lack of interest in supporting such projects.[98] With Banks's ill health, interest in such projects was limited, especially when vetoed by the gentlemen geologists of the Geological Society or plagiarised by others (like White Watson in Derbyshire).[99]

FIG. 9. Farey's remarkable 'mineral map' of Ashover,[126] finished in December 1812. The original scale of 1½ inches to 1 mile has been reduced for this publication (see scale bar on map). The sequence of all 24 strata mapped by Farey (many are identified round the periphery, where *cs* = clay-shale, *gr* = Grit) can be identified as follows from below.

1) *red-brown* [in centre of the Ashover anticline[127]] = Toadstone [Tuff]; 2) *green* = [Carboniferous Limestone] (with Overton Hall on its outcrop); 3) *brown* = [Head & Boulder Clay]; 4) *yellow* = [Ashover Grit]; 5) *grey* = [Ashover Grit]; 6) *lighter brown* = 2nd [Chatsworth] Grit; 7) *grey* = 2nd clay-shale; 8) *pink* = 3rd [Crawshaw Sandstone] Grit; 9) *grey* = 3rd clay-shale (note the coal pits marked at Alton); 10) *red* = 4th Grit; 11) *grey* = 4th clay-shale; 12) *yellow* = 5th Grit; 13) *grey* = 5th clay-shale; 14) *brown* = 6th Grit; 15) *grey* = 6th clay-shale; 16) *pink* = 7th Grit; 17) *grey* = 7th clay-shale; 18) *red* = 8th Grit; 19) *grey* = 8th clay-shale; 20) *yellow* = 9th Grit; 21) *grey* = 9th clay-shale; 22) *brown* = 10th Grit (with Wingerworth Hall on its outcrop); 23) *grey* = 10th clay-shale; 24) *pink* = 11th Grit.

[Beds 9 to 24 are now classed as Lower Coal Measures; a series of interbedded sandstones and shales, often of more limited lateral extent than Farey realised in 1812]

V

The lack of publication outlets for mineral surveyors must be taken into consideration by historians. The debt of later members of the Geological Society to the mineral surveyors has simply not been acknowledged. The *eight* different charts of the "Order of Superposition of Strata in the British Islands" which William Buckland produced between 1814 and 1821 are a prime example. One historian has claimed "it was precisely in seeking to transcend local descriptive stratigraphy that the intelligentsia distinguished themselves, ... [this] becoming one of the hallmarks of the gentlemanly geologist distinguishing him from the practical geological surveyor".[100] This ignores the fact that the latter had laid the groundwork for descriptive stratigraphy in England! Farey's 1812 map reproduced here shows at last the abilities of such people and the remarkable detail of which they, alone then in Europe, were capable.

Banks put his finger on the true problem in September 1811 when writing to the French geologist Faujas de St Fond; "Geology becomes more & more a fashion. I hope we shall before long advance somewhat the Limits of that Science. We have now some Practical men well versd in stratification who undertake to examine the subterraneous Geography of Gentlemens Estates in order to discover the Fossils likely to be useful for Manure for fuel etc... if employment begins to be given to these people the Consequence must be a rapid improvement if the Labour in this great work can find means".[101] But no further *County Mineral Reports* were ever published by the Board of Agriculture, which found itself in serious difficulties because of the recession at the end of the Napoleonic Wars.[102] This badly affected business openings for the mineral surveyors and meant that Banks's aspirations for them remained unfulfilled.

The tensions between Banks and Greenough also need examination. Banks who "determined never to enter Parliament"[103] was landed and above all utilitarian. Greenough, first President of the Geological Society, on the other hand was Member of Parliament for the rotten borough of Gatton (with only one voter), and *nouveau-riche* and polite. Greenough's wealth had come not from land but from patent medicines!

Such tensions have left a fertile field for revisionist historians who have not ensured that all sides are equally represented. One group published fully, the other did not. Some of the divisions are across that most destructive of English barriers, Class; with Gentlemen against Players; "Practical Men" versus "Cabinet Philosophers"; or "the Establishment" against dissent. Jack Morrell claims that there has been too much "emphasis on gentlemanliness in Victorian English science"[104] and the situation regarding Banksian times is the same.

The years 1812–1820 were tragic ones for the mineral surveyors. Smith was given a further advance of £50 by Banks on 18 January 1814.[105] This and several visits Smith made to Banks in 1814 and 1815 were to help "soften the dire aspect of his utter poverty".[106] The publication of Smith's great Geological Map in August 1815, dedicated to Banks; "the most general promoter of science... by his particular encouragement advanced to its present state of perfection", did little to soften Smith's burden of debt, since sales were so soon killed by the rival Greenough version of 1820. Banks subscribed to Smith's *Stratigraphical System of Organised Fossils* in 1817, having opened his magnificent library to aid in its compilation. But this too never proceeded beyond part one, due to a lack of subscribers, despite Banksian urgings.[107]

From 1814 Farey was forced, when writing in the *Philosophical Magazine*, to do so under a cloak of anonymity, in obvious ostracism for his war of words with the gentlemen geologists. The task of lead writer on Geology for Rees's *Cyclopaedia* had already, by 1811, gone to Charles Konig (1774–1851) — "a foreigner holding place of profit here", as Farey wrote.[108]

Banks's final attempt to achieve justice for Smith and Farey was on 30 November 1817 when members of the Geological Society met Smith and Farey at a Banks *Conversazione*. Next day Farey drafted a document outlining Smith's discoveries.[109] William Henry Fitton (1780–1861), whom Banks had earlier helped to establish in medical practice in Northampton,[110] was the Society's mediator. But it was an unsuccessful mediation, and animosity over the issues had reached new heights within the Geological Society by the time of Banks's death.[111] In 1822 Farey could refer to the Society as the "*Anti-Smithian Association*" in Bedford Street. I have however put their vile attempts *on record* and will yet more effectively do so, please God I live".[112]

Smith had been forced to sell his fossil collection to an uninterested British Museum between 1815 & 1818. This final (and present) resting place was due to Banks's crucial intervention,[113] since the keeper Charles Konig was a man who in the opinion of Miss Etheldred Benett had "showed an excessive contempt for fossils which so much affronted me on my first acquaintance with him".[114] But it failed to solve Smith's financial crisis, and he was in the midst of a ten-week stint in a debtor's prison when Miss Benett wrote thus to Greenough. By 1824 Farey had been reduced to offering himself as a copyist to James Sowerby at a rate of one shilling an hour.[115]

Conclusion

It seems paradoxical that the Banks who so perceptively patronised Smith and Farey is so well "patronised" today; whilst they are neglected or denigrated.[116] Farey in particular is a polymath who deserves remembrance. In final irony, he was buried in St James Church, Piccadilly, opposite the present home of the Geological Society which had ostracised him. His son, John Farey junior (1791–1851), regarded by some in 1837 as "the best consulting engineer in England",[117] was blackballed from the Royal Society in 1847[118] as if to show that class divisions remained a critical facet of English history. Engineers were tradesmen. Excluding tradesmen was one of the first "reforms" that Banks had instigated at the Royal Society in 1778.[119]

Acknowledgements

I owe grateful thanks to Stuart Band, Julia Bruce, Harold Carter, Roger Flindall, Beryl Hartley, Jean Jones, Oliver and Myra Morgan, Stella Newton and Mick Stanley for kind assistance. Staff at the Sutro Library in San Francisco, the Cornwall and Derbyshire Record Offices and the Derby Local Studies Library provided every assistance. BP Exploration gave financial support without which this contribution would have been impossible.

V

Notes

(1) K. Garlick and A. Macintyre (eds.), *The Diary of Joseph Farington*, New Haven, 1978, vol. 2, 478.

(2) A.H. Dupree, *Sir Joseph Banks and the Origins of Science Policy*, Minneapolis, 1984.

(3) H.B. Carter, *Sir Joseph Banks 1743–1820*, London, 1988, 26.

(4) S.G. Perceval, '[Banks's] Journal of an excursion to Eastbury and Bristol 1767', *Proceedings of the Bristol Naturalists Society*, n.s.(1899), **9**, 18.

(5) M. Neve and R. Porter, 'Alexander Catcott: glory and geology', *British Journal for the History of Science* (1977), **10**, 37–60.

(6) Carter, op. cit. (3), 49, 53–4.

(7) Ibid., 54.

(8) J.C. Beaglehole, *The Voyage of the Endeavour 1767–1771*, Cambridge, 1955, 518–9.

(9) T.G. Vallance, 'Sydney earth and after: mineralogy of colonial Australia 1788–1900', *Proceedings of the Linnean Society of New South Wales* (1986), **108**, 150.

(10) S. Tomkeieff, 'The basalt lavas of the Giant's Causeway district of Northern Ireland', *Bulletin Volcanologique*, ser. 2 (1940), **6**, 89–143; M. Angelsea and J. Preston, 'A philosophical landscape': Susanna Drury and the Giant's Causeway, *Art History* (1980), **3**, 252–73.

(11) F. Ellenberger, 'Précisions nouvelles sur la découverte des volcans de France', *Histoire et Nature* (1978), **12–13**, 3–42.

(12) R. Pococke, 'A farther account of the Giant's Causeway', *Philosophical Transactions of the Royal Society* (1753), **48**, 230.

(13) K. Taylor, 'Nicolas Desmarest and geology in the 18th century', in *Toward a History of Geology* (ed. C.J. Schneer), Cambridge, Mass., 1969, 346–9.

(14) R.E. Raspe, 'A letter... containing a short account of some basalt hills in Hassia', *Philosophical Transactions of the Royal Society* (1772), **61**, 580–583; A.V. Carozzi, 'Rudolf Erich Raspe and the basalt controversy', *Studies in Romanticism* (1969), **8**, 235–50.

(15) In T. Pennant's [Second] *Tour in Scotland* in 1772 published in 1774, reprinted in J. Pinkerton, *A General Collection of the best and most interesting Voyages and Travels*, London, 1809, vol. 3, 171–569, and R.A. Rauschenberg, 'The journals of Joseph Banks' Voyage up Great Britain's West Coast and to the Orkney Isles, July to October 1772', *Proceedings of the American Philosophical Society* (1973), **117**, 186–226.

(16) R. Porter, *The making of Geology*, Cambridge, 1977, 162, 266.

(17) Anon., 'Sir Joseph Banks', in *Public Characters of 1800–1801*, London, 1801, 380.

(18) British Library, Add. MS. 15510, 22, 34.

(19) Garlick and Macintyre, op. cit. (1), vol. 1, 113.

(20) C. Daubeny, *A Description of ancient and extinct Volcanoes*, London, 1826, 449–51.

(21) J. Pinkerton, *A General Collection of the best and most interesting Voyages and Travels*, London, 1808, vol. 1, 622–3, 730–1.

(22) B. Faujas de Saint Fond, *A journey through England and Scotland to the Hebrides in 1784* (ed. A. Geikie), Glasgow, 1907, vol. 1, 82–3.

(23) Carter, op. cit. (3), 572.

(24) Vallance, op. cit. (9), 151.

(25) T.G. Vallance and D.T. Moore, 'Geological aspects of the voyage of HMS *Investigator* in Australian waters 1801–5', *Bulletin of the British Museum (Natural History), Historical Series* (1982), **10** (1), 5.

(26) H.S. Torrens, 'Under royal patronage: the geological work of John Mawe (1766–1829) and the background for his "Travels in Brazil"', in *O Conhecimento Geologico na America Latina* (eds. M.M. Lopez and S. Figueiroa), Campinas, 1990, 103–113; T.G. Vallance and H.S. Torrens, 'The Anglo-Australian traveller Robert Townson and his map of Hungarian "Petrography"', in *Contributions to the History of Geological mapping* (ed. E. Dudich), Budapest, 1984, 391–8.

(27) Vallance and Moore, op. cit. (25), 2.

(28) John Hawkins to Philip Rashleigh, 14 September [1800], Cornwall County Record Office, DDR 5757/1/109.

(29) *Derby Mercury*, 22 November 1792, 4c.

(30) Anon, 'The family of Hodgkinson, of Overton Hall, in Ashover', *Reliquary* (1872), **12**, 254–5.

(31) H.S. Torrens, 'A Wiltshire pioneer in geology and his legacy — Henry Shorto III (1778–1864)', *Wiltshire Archaeological and Natural History Magazine* (1990), **83**, 176–7.

(32) G.G. Hopkinson, 'Lead mining in 18th century Ashover', *Journal of the Derbyshire Archaeological and Natural History Society* (1952), **72**, 1–21; S. Band, 'Lead mining in Ashover', *Bulletin of the Peak District Mines Historical Society* (1975–6), **8**, 113–5, 129–39.

(33) T.G. Vallance, 'Jupiter Botanicus in the Bush: Robert Brown's Australian field-work 1801–5', *Proceedings of the Linnean Society of New South Wales* (1990), **112**, 51.

(34) J. Milnes, 'Section of the Strata at Gregory's Mine, Ashover, Derbyshire June 26 1801' improved to 1806, Stuart Band collection, Ashover, from an original MS. in Clay Cross Company records.

(35) Ibid.; S. Glover, *The History and Gazetteer of the county of Derby*, Derby, 1833, vol. 2, 52.

V

(36) California State Library Sutro Branch [hereafter Sutro], MS. Coal 1: 30.

(37) Natural History Museum, London, Dawson Turner copies, vol. 9, 101.

(38) Georgina, a keen mineral collector at nearby Chatsworth, D. King-Hele, *The Letters of Erasmus Darwin*, Cambridge, 1981, 327.

(39) MS. in private hands.

(40) A. Raistrick, *The Hatchett Diary*, Truro, 1967, 7, 11, 65.

(41) King-Hele, op. cit. (38), 174, 267.

(42) J.A. Venn, *Alumni Cantabrigienses*, Cambridge, 1944, part 2, vol. 2, 576.

(43) H.B. Woodward, *The History of the Geological Society of London*, London, 1907, 272.

(44) Raistrick, op. cit. (40), 63–5.

(45) J. Challinor, *A Dictionary of Geology*, Cardiff, 1978, 12–3.

(46) J. Farey, 'Geological observations on the County of Antrim', *Philosophical Magazine* (1812), **39**, 361.

(47) J. Banks, 'Effect of the *Equisetum Palustris* upon Drains', *Communications to the Board of Agriculture* (1800), **2**, 349–50; H.B. Carter, *The Sheep and Wool Correspondence of Sir Joseph Banks*, Sydney, 1979, 305.

(48) H.S. Torrens and T.D. Ford, 'John Farey (1766–1826): an unrecognised polymath, in *General View of the Agriculture and Minerals of Derbyshire* (J. Farey), Matlock, 1989, vol. 1, [reprint, orig. 1811].

(49) Milnes, op. cit. (34).

(50) Copy in the Local Studies Library, Derby, see Band, op. cit. (32), 136–8.

(51) Vallance and Moore, op. cit. (25), 39–43.

(52) Ibid., 3.

(53) S. Band, 'John Allen, miner: on board H.M.S. *Investigator* 1801–4', *Bulletin of the Peak District Mines Historical Society* (1987), **10**, 67–78.

(54) Vallance and Moore, op. cit. (25), 4–5, 9.

(55) J. Phillips, *Memoirs of William Smith*, London, 1844, 39.

(56) J.M. Eyles, 'William Smith, Sir Joseph Banks and the French Geologists', in *From Linnaeus to Darwin* (eds. A. Wheeler and J.H. Price), London, 1985, 37–50.

(57) P. Thompson, *Collections for a topographic and historical account of Boston*, London, 1820, 297–8; W.H. Fitton, *Notes on the progress of Geology in England*, London, 1833, 42–3.

(58) J. Challinor, 'The progress of British geology during the early part of the nineteenth century', *Annals of Science* (1970), **26**, opp. 178.

(59) Oxford University Museum, Smith archive.

(60) Eyles, op. cit. (56), 43.

(61) Anon, 'Agriculture' [report on the Woburn sheep-shearing], *Agricultural Magazine* (1802), **6**, 466.

(62) Eyles, op. cit. (56), 43-4.

(63) Anon, 'Woburn sheep-shearing', *Holly leaves* (1949), Christmas, 12-3.

(64) Phillips, op. cit. (55), 45; L.R. Cox, 'New light on William Smith and his work', *Proceedings of the Yorkshire Geological Society* (1942), **25**, 15, 37, plate 5; Carter, op. cit. (3).

(65) Bedfordshire Record Office, 2114/456.

(66) Cox, op. cit. (64), 38.

(67) Ibid., 18.

(68) H.S. Torrens, 'The transmission of ideas in the use of fossils in stratigraphic analysis to America 1800–1840', *Earth Sciences History* (1990), **9**, 109.

(69) Cox, op. cit. (64), 21.

(70) Ibid., 18.

(71) T.D. Ford, 'The first detailed geological sections across England by John Farey 1806–8', *Mercian Geologist* (1967), **2**, 41-9.

(72) Devizes Museum, Cunnington MS.

(73) Geological Society of London, Minutes of the Society, MS.

(74) Thompson, op. cit. (57), 293–302.

(75) J. Farey, 'On the supposed fresh-water origin of the Gypsum Strata in the environs of Paris', *Philosophical Magazine* (1810), **35**, 259.

(76) Ford, op. cit. (71).

(77) British Geological Survey, 1/1313; Oxford University Museum; Natural History Museum, London and Sheffield Central Library, Oakes deed 1221.

(78) Anon, [note of exhibition of Farey's section]. *Agricultural Magazine* n.s. (1808), **2**, 229.

(79) M.J.S. Rudwick, 'The Foundation of the Geological Society of London', *British Journal for the History of Science* (1963), **1**, 325-55.

(80) Sutro, M 2: 24.

(81) Sutro, Geol. 1: 2a.

(82) Sutro, M 2: 22.

(83) J. Farey, *General View of the Agriculture and Minerals of Derbyshire*, London, 1811, vol. 1, v.

(84) Sinclair to Farey, Sinclair to Banks, 14 August 1807, Sutro, Ag 3: 43/44.

(85) J. Farey, 'Notes and observations on.... Bakewell's *Introduction to Geology*', *Philosophical Magazine* (1814), **43**, 334.

V

(86)   W.R. Dearman and S. Turner, 'Models illustrating John Farey's figures of Stratified Masses', *Proceedings of the Geologists Association* (1983), **94**, 97–104.

(87)   Farey, op. cit. (83), vol. 1, 116.

(88)   P. Riden, 'Joseph Butler. Coal and Iron Master 1763–1837', *Derbyshire Archaeological Journal* (1984), **104**, 87–95.

(89)   J. Farey, 'An account of the Great Derbyshire Denudation', *Philosophical Transactions of the Royal Society* (1811), part 2, 242–56.

(90)   Rudwick, op. cit. (79).

(91)   Carter, op. cit. (3), 532.

(92)   University College, London, Greenough MS.

(93)   J. Farey, *General view of the Agriculture and Minerals of Derbyshire*, London, 1813, vol. 2, ix.

(94)   Farey to James Sowerby, 20 August 1811, Bristol University Library, Eyles MS.

(95)   Sutro, M 2: 25.

(96)   T. Thomson, *History of the Royal Society*, London, 1812, 212.

(97)   Anon, 'Report of Mr John Farey's paper on the Ashover denudation', *Philosophical Magazine* (1813), **41**, 303–5.

(98)   J. Farey, *General view of the Agriculture and Minerals of Derbyshire*, London, 1817, vol. 3, vi–vii.

(99)   W. Bainbridge, [Plagiarism of Farey's section by White Watson], *Monthly Magazine* (1818), **45**, 10, 218.

(100)   D.P. Miller, Method and the micropolitics of science, in *The Politics and Rhetoric of Scientific Method* (eds. J.A. Schuster and R.R. Yeo), Dordrecht, 1986, 239.

(101)   G. De Beer, *The Sciences were never at War*, London, 1960, 191.

(102)   Carter, op. cit. (3), 514–7.

(103)   Ibid., 537.

(104)   J.B. Morrell, 'Professionalisation', in *Companion to the History of Science* (ed. R.C. Olby), London, 1990, 988.

(105)   According to Smith's diary (Oxford University Museum).

(106)   Phillips, op. cit. (55), 76

(107)   Cox, op. cit. (64), 57–8.

(108)   Farey to Greenough, 15 June 1813, University College, London, Greenough MS.

(109)   J. Farey, 'Mr Smith's geological claims stated', *Philosophical Magazine* (1818), **51**, 173–80.

(110)   W.R. Dawson, 'Supplementary letters of Sir Joseph Banks', *Bulletin of the British Museum (Natural History), Historical Series* (1962), **3** (2), 63.

(111)   H.S. Torrens, 'The scientific ancestry and historiography of "The Silurian System"', *Journal of the Geological Society of London* (1990), **147**, 659.

(112)   Farey to Sowerby, May 1822, Smithsonian Institution, Washington, MS.

(113)   J.M. Eyles, 'William Smith: the sale of his geological collection to the British Museum', *Annals of Science* (1967), **23**, 209–10.

(114)   Etheldred Benett to G.B. Greenough, 22 June 1819, Greenough MS.

(115)   Farey to Sowerby, 26 March 1824, Eyles MS.

(116)   R. Laudan, *From Mineralogy to Geology*, Chicago, 1987, 168.

(117)   B. Bowers, *Sir Charles Wheatstone*, London, 1975, 111.

(118)   Royal Society, London, Archives, Mss. certificates.

(119)   J. Barrow, *Sketches of the Royal Society*, London, 1849, 33, 39.

(120)   British Library, Add. MS. 15510, 22, 34, through the kindness of Beryl Hartley.

(121)   Raistrick, op. cit. (40), 63.

(122)   Derby Local Studies Library.

(123)   Academy of Natural Sciences, Philadelphia.

(124)   Copy from Derby Local Studies Library, MS 9626, through the kindness of Mick Stanley.

(125)   Author's collection.

(126)   Sutro, M2: 25.

(127)   Notes [thus] are from the 1 inch British Geological Survey map Chesterfield Sheet no. 112, reprinted 1971.

VI

JOHN FAREY (1766-1826)
an unrecognised polymath

Trevor D. Ford & Hugh S. Torrens

Farey was the son of John Farey I (1728-1798) who, though born in Woburn, Bedfordshire, had been a builder and carpenter in Westminster, London, until August 1763 when he married and returned to settle at his birthplace. His mother was Rachel Wright (1732-1804) born at Collingham between Wetherby and Leeds in Yorkshire, who had joined the Wesleyan Methodists at the age of 15. In Bedfordshire the Fareys became tenant farmers of the Duke of Bedford: first at Woburn, where John Farey II was born on 24 September 1766 and received his common school education, then from 1773 at nearby Potsgrave.

In 1782, aged 16, John II was sent to the Halifax Academy started there in 1779 by Robert Pulman (died 1789), writing master and land surveyor. Here "Penmanship, English, Classics, French, Drawing, Merchants' Accounts and Mathematics" were all taught. Farey proved himself a star pupil and Pulman, who was a good mathematician, gave him gratuitous instruction in mathematics and philosophy (including what we would today call the rudiments of science). Farey also studied drawing and surveying, and "was recommended" to, and must have met, John Smeaton (1724-1792), the famous engineer who lived at nearby Austhorpe. More significantly, Farey here started to observe and his (and later his eldest son's) subsequent publications refer several times to steam engines, strata and industrial techniques he had observed in his two years at Halifax (**15***, 208; **127**, 102). About 1784 Farey moved to London where he is first found working in Westminster, probably at his father's old trade. In 1790 he married, at St Pancras, Sophia Hubert (1770-1830). This marriage brought him brothers-in-law who were variously a coal merchant, an architect — Thomas Cundy (1765-1825) (for whom see the *Dictionary of National Biography*, hereafter *DNB*),

(*) Numbers in Bold thus, **15**, refer to items in the Bibliography.

and the surveyor to the Sun Fire Insurance Company in London. The eldest son of the marriage, John Farey III (1791-1851), who became a famous, if now neglected, engineer (see *DNB*), was born in Lambeth in March 1791. There were eight other children. Two died very young, one emigrated to France and three to the United States of America, where descendants of the youngest surviving son, Henry (1800-1858), still live.

John Farey's life is difficult to assess as it spans a truly polymathic range of interests and abilities, quite beyond the competence of today's specialists. Over 250 published books, articles and notes right across this range are recorded in the following Bibliography. If mathematics was a first interest, Farey became very active with a second while in London, singing as a tenor with the Surrey Chapel Society. This met weekly in Southwark to practice choral music. In August 1791 it amalgamated with the newly formed Choral Fund to perform music and to "relieve decayed musicians" and John Farey became the first Secretary and Librarian to the Fund (223, 66). His London musical interests continued after he returned to Woburn, as a *Musical Directory* of 1794 (Doane 1794, 22) records him as still a member of these Societies as well as of the Cecilian Society and a group which performed Oratorios at Drury Lane during Lent. Music and musical theory, which he believed capable of "rigid mathematical treatment", remained a life-long interest, his "favourite source of amusement" outside his professional work (223). Farey's musical work was partially surveyed by Kassler (1979 vol. 1, 329-43). It is not considered further here.

Farey's return to Woburn, after October in 1792, was on his appointment as land steward to Francis Russell (1765-1802), the fifth Duke of Bedford (see *DNB*), who had large estates in Bedfordshire. This was a result of the death of William Jones, the previous steward. Farey became also warden of Woburn parish church. Here he carried out the wide range of duties of his post, assisted by his brother Benjamin Farey (born 1776) and started

to publish both on agriculture, which now became a third
interest (from 1796 — 1), and on his earlier interest in
mathematics (from 1797 — 2). He was a highly organised
and methodical man, good at keeping complex accounts,
skills which he later used as an inveterate indexer. In June
1798 (the year his father — who by now described himself
as a yeoman — died) Farey first met Sir Joseph Banks
(1743-1820), patron of British science and agriculture and
soon Farey's patron too, during the Duke of Bedford's
annual sheep-shearing at Woburn. Banks then examined
and was highly impressed by, the extensive land drainage
and irrigation works Farey had been supervising on the
Duke's estates since 1793, and which first brought Farey
face to face with the local soils and underlying rocks.
This work here is described in volume two of his *Report*
on Derbyshire.

In 1800 Farey first heard of William Smith (1769-
1839) (165, 334), who in June 1801 attended the Woburn
sheepshearing in person. In July 1801 (while Farey was
away studying drainage methods in Northamptonshire)
and again in October, Smith, a land drainer and surveyor
just starting his work as a mineral surveyor and geologist,
again visited Woburn. He was now engaged by the Duke
to carry out further land drainage work here, on boggy
meadows, from mid October to mid November 1801. It
was then that Smith and Farey first met and Farey now
started to develop his fourth, and most significant,
interest: in geology. John Farey soon became Smith's
champion and most important advocate, both for the
novelty and the practical value of Smith's stratigraphic
discoveries, made while based in Somerset between 1791
and 1802. Further visits by Smith to Woburn late in
November 1801 allowed Smith and Farey to examine
the local strata together and in January 1802, with
another of Farey's friends Benjamin Bevan (1773-1833)
of Leighton Buzzard, and the financial support of the
Duke, they set out on a fifty mile "Journey . . . to Investigate the Local Strata". On this tour Smith effectively
demonstrated his geological results in the field to both

men (**63 – d**), and Farey reported enthusiastically on the expedition to Joseph Banks in February 1802 (see **224**, **297**; Phillips 1844, 39; & Eyles 1985). Both Farey and Bevan thereafter became speedy converts to, and advocates of, Smith's stratigraphic methods; Farey in his work as a land surveyor and Bevan as a rising canal engineer. In addition Farey became a close friend of Smith.

But in March 1802 the fifth Duke suddenly died and his brother John (1766-1839), who became the sixth Duke, for reasons which are not at all clear, dismissed Farey from the land stewardship he had held for 10 years (Bevan 1802). During this period, Farey's 112 account books show he had paid out nearly £470,000 and received £247,000, in at least 500,000 transactions during his stewardship, according to a letter to Smith. The financial imbalance relates only to those aspects of the vast Bedford estate management that Farey was involved with and not to any irregularity! Farey's first thought after his dismissal was to lease or rent a 250 – 500 acre farm, as his father had with a Ducal farm, but the new Duke had none vacant and Farey was unable to find another suitable. He turned instead to a new career as a land surveyor and, following Smith's lead, mineral surveyor and agent, taking offices at 12 Upper Crown Street in Westminster, London. Here he rescued Smith's papers from the Charing Cross office Smith had taken in 1803 on first moving to London, from a major fire there in February 1804 and was soon able to negotiate the suitability and rent of a new office for Smith at 15 Buckingham Street (Cox 1942). Smith and Farey often attended agricultural meetings together during this period when Smith's geological and drainage work was much discussed (Anon 1804).

A major boost to Farey's newly independent career came in 1805, when he was awarded the Silver Medal of the Society for the Encouragement of Arts for his earlier experiments on the growth of timber at Wavendon in Bucks (**16–19**). In December 1806 another long family connection started when he became the salaried Secretary of the Smithfield Club, which had been established in 1798 to improve standards of cattle breeding. This brought him into continual contact with the country's leading agriculturalists (Anon 1807). His son William followed him as its Secretary from 1826 to 1836 (Bull 1926).

In 1805 Farey commenced work for the *Cyclopaedia,* a major publication started in 1802 by Abraham Rees (1743-1825) which culminated in 45 volumes containing over 40 million words on completion in 1820. As Farey's contributions are nearly all anonymous, there are major problems in listing the articles for which he was responsible (see **20 to 42**), in volumes which were neither paginated nor dated when published. The first Prospectus (Bodleian library, Oxford) was published late in 1801, while Farey was still working for the Duke of Bedford. This named only Arthur Aikin (Torrens 1983) as the author for Mineralogy and gave no separate author for Geology. Charles Burney (1726-1814) was likewise noted as the sole author for Music. The original covers for the parts as issued, preserved in a copy at the British Museum (Natural History), also name contributors. These first list "Mr John Farey" in part 10, issued on 26 December 1805, as "Agent in the late Duke of Bedford's Rural Affairs". Part 24. of 22 May 1809, still names Farey as a contributor as "late of Woburn" but now adds the name of his eldest son, John junior. The latter contributed many beautiful drawings, starting at the age of 14 with his father's first contribution, and later major articles on technical subjects. Such father and son contributions have added to the confusion, as some articles, like the major article on Steam Engines, have been wrongly attributed (e.g. in the *DNB*) to the father rather than the son (Ferguson 1968).

1806 saw the first, of the many, citations of Smith's work that Farey was to publish (**20** in a drastically shortened article on Canals, **46 & 51**) and in July and August of this year Farey started work on his first original piece of geological research. His brother Benjamin, who had been dismissed with him from Woburn, had found employment with Thomas Pelham (1756-1826), Earl of Chichester of Stanmer Park, at Fulmer near Brighton. Farey reported to Smith on 29 September 1806 that he had spent the summer visiting his brother in Sussex "on the Coach & returned the same way, minuting every appearance of the strata as I went along, while at my Brother's I traversed the South Downs near Brighton in all directions & made two excursions northward to trace the outcrops of three or 4 strata from under the Chalk, returning by different routes. Since this I went from London to near Portsmouth, noting every thing as I went along, & spent two days in riding over the Chalk and clay which covers it, . . . from [Stansted Park] I went on the Coach to Brighton & observed the top of the Clay etc all the way: from Brighton I made an excursion with Earl Chichester (Ben's Master) & Ben to a great number of places between there . . . and Hastings: after examining the Cliffs here I went along the Coast to Bexhill, & saw the quixoit [sic – quixotic] coal works and returned to near Brighton by a different route: from whence I went NE to near Maresfield & after riding about, a day at Sheffield Place, I returned home on the Coach thro' Godstone by a new way: these excursions have given me a complete knowledge of the Strata to be seen in the road to Brighton of which I have sketched a section". Farey found this "charming country for investigation, scarcely a vestige of alluvial matters to disguise or hide the strata . . . but [I] have been able to collect but very few extraneous fossils from Sussex to what I expected".

A further long visit to his brother in February 1807 allowed Farey "to much extend my ideas on the faults and dislocations of the Strata" here. His sketch of Sussex had now been improved and "verified by observations across the country for many miles both east and west" of the London to Brighton line. As Banks reported to John Lloyd (1748-1815) in August 1807, Farey "is so much master of Smith's means of detecting the Stratification of a Country as he rides over it that he has made a section of the Earth under the road from London to Brighton". A fair copy of this version improved to that date, had been given in 1807 to Banks, who had paid Farey's time in preparing it at the latter's request and to whom it was dedicated, and another went to G. B. Greenough (1778-1855), President of the new Geological Society of London. By 1810 copies were "in the hands of many" (**104, 130**). In this section, over five feet long at a scale of one inch to one mile. Farey recorded the stratigraphic sequence in incredible detail, as well as the anticlinal or "denuded" structure of the area and introduced a series of 25 faults between the North and South Downs, many of which have been confirmed by later geological surveying where he placed them. These faults undoubtedly influenced him later to postulate widespread faulting in Derbyshire as well.

John Playfair (1748-1819), founding Honorary Member of the Geological Society, scornfully wrote of Farey's "section of . . . strata [made] between London and [Brighton] . . . [with] which the author . . . became acquainted in three journeys that he made from London to [Brighton], on the top of the mail-coach" (1812, 385). Bakewell (1813a, 124) too sneered at Farey's "stagecoach geology"; to which Farey, with total justification, angily responded (**143, 167-8**). As his letters to Smith make abundantly clear, his work in Sussex had been based on an enormous amount of field work, all carried out unpaid and in his spare time. Ford (1967) has discussed and reproduced a scaled-down version of this section and its significance. From this we can see that Farey had been his own worst enemy in captioning his section, as this suggested it was based on three *single* journeys only. The description which Farey prepared to accompany the section does not seem to have survived.

Farey's work in publicising Smith's work continued, from 1807 in the *Monthly Magazine* (**52**) and from 1808 in Dickson's *Agricultural Magazine* (**92**). Early in 1807 Joseph Banks, who had patronised Farey in preparing the London to Brighton section now asked Farey "to make some calculations for the use of his Lead-mining agent in Derbyshire". Later in the same year Richard Phillips (1767-1840), the London bookseller soon to be knighted (and to go bankrupt!), recommended Farey to the President of the Board of Agriculture, Sir John Sinclair (1754-1835) who asked him to take on the task of preparing the "reprinted" new edition of the *Report on the Agriculture of Derbyshire* for the Board. Farey had already written to Sinclair in May and July 1806 about Smith and the value of geological research (51). Thomas Brown's previous report on Derbyshire of 1794 had been a slim inconsequential affair, with which the Board had had particular problems. At first Farey refused, because of the low financial inducement offered him. Meanwhile Banks, who had been so impressed with Farey's Sussex section and who had a Derbyshire seat at Overton near Ashover and another estate at Revesby in Lincolnshire, asked Farey to visit and survey these estates in the summer of 1807; to report on "the State of the outcropping Strata on my [Derbyshire] Estate for the Purposes of Agriculture & I mean to send him on to Revesby" (Carter 1987, 398) and to look over his woods and estates. The result of this commission was another fine geological section by Farey, now nine feet long, "the earliest known across England" (Sherborn 1929), from Trusthorpe on the Lincolnshire coast to Overton in Derbyshire, which Farey prepared in February 1808 and again dedicated to Banks. A copy soon went to Greenough, and the Banks' copy and two others are known to survive. It has also been reproduced and described by Ford (1967). Sinclair, learning of these new activities, now raised his terms for Farey to undertake the Derbyshire *Report* and on 14 August 1807 Farey now agreed to do it and "combine as much of the knowledge that Mr. Smith has imparted to me, and a few others, respecting the Stratification of the Island, with the inquiries usually made by the Reporters for the Board . . ." and to include a Geological map.

Smith was at first irate, both with the Board and understandably to an extent with Farey, whom he felt had usurped his position. He sent a blank refusal to the request for help which Farey had sent. But their differences were quickly resolved (Cox 1942, 40-3). Farey started on his now joint data-gathering exercises in Derbyshire both for the mineralogical survey of Banks' estates at Ashover and for the *Report* for the Board of Agriculture (Carter 1987) late in August 1807, though he had first visited the county in 1797 (**128**, 361). Farey spent four field seasons in Derbyshire, often working on both projects in parallel, from August – September 1807 and the springs and/or summers of 1808, 1809 and 1810. For the first three seasons work for the Board he was paid £150 (**152**, 334). He was paid a total of £450 for his survey in 1815, making Derbyshire one of the two most expensive surveys undertaken by the Board of Agriculture (Harrison 1955). The resulting three volumes, which the Board published in 1811 and 1813 with the third much delayed volume in 1817 (**124**), became his best known work. Only the first volume is reprinted here. Farey's whole *Report* was by far the largest ever published by the Board and it totalled 1901 pages!

At an early stage, in November 1807, Farey called on the leading Derbyshire experts, including White Watson (1760-1835) who had for the previous 20 years been active as a mineral dealer and fossil collector in Bakewell. Watson's early work is best characterised by the Inlaid Marble Tablets he first made in September 1787. These expounded the stratigraphic sequence then known in Derbyshire, in an understandably crude form, but imaginatively used the actual materials of which the rocks were composed (Ford 1960). Watson was undoubtedly very familiar with the detail of Peakland geology, and, through Werner's pupil Thomas Barker (c.1767-1816), a native of Bakewell, with the Wernerian view of geology. There has been debate about the debts Farey and Watson owed each other. The problem of deciding is not made any easier by the fact that both had modified their initial

9

views on the structure and stratigraphy of Derbyshire by the time their respective books were both published in 1811 (**125**, 27). Volume one of Farey's *Report* was published in June 1811 (**205**, 179).

New material now makes it clear that Farey's arrival in Derbyshire completely revolutionised Watson's thinking, both about the detail of the known stratigraphic sequence in England and its extrapolation to Derbyshire. John Farey's letter to G. B. Greenough of 5 March 1808, which accompanied a Sale Catalogue of Fossils Watson had had for sale in 1805 (Watson 1805), makes clear this was a period before Watson "had any knowledge of Mr Smith's discoveries or was aware of the great number of Derbyshire Strata above the Limestone. besides the 5 which he enumerates". All Watson's publications up to 1805 used, as his standard stratigraphic sequence. merely the 12 units which John Whitehurst (1713-1788) had elucidated within the Carboniferous Limestone and Millstone Grit of the Peak District (1786). Both Watson and Farey were further in debt to Whitehurst in following his lead that Derbyshire toadstones were ancient lavas. a fact which Watson specifically emphasized in 1809 with the preparation of a new Tablet. This showed the affinities of these Derbyshire toadstones with basaltic lavas from Iceland and Vesuvius.

In November 1807 Farey personally gave Watson one of two "hasty" sections he had already prepared across Derbyshire. another across Lincolnshire. as well as details of the stratigraphic sequence he had previously worked out in Sussex. and which were both interpolated with Smith's standard sequence as worked out near Bath. The Derbyshire section Watson copied out over 20-25 November. for him to use in making new improved inlaid tablets accordingly (29 — j; **124** vol. 1, 163). The first of Watson's new "strata tablets of the whole county" was then commenced straightaway on 30 December 1807 and the strata part finished on 27 January 1808. It was presented to the Duke of Devonshire on 20 February 1808. The enormous change from Watson's earlier

version is made very clear by comparing the originals of
both. What is even more clear is the lack of an acknowledgement of the debt Watson owed to Farey when he
came to publish his *Delineation of the Strata of Derbyshire* in 1811 and which undoubtedly justifies a charge
of plagiarism (see **125**, 27; Bainbrigge 1818). By
September 1810 Elias Hall (1764-1853) of Castleton was
also busily helping Farey with his Derbyshire survey. He
was later more careful to acknowledge his debts to Farey.
Farey responded by recommending Hall's Models showing
the Strata of Derbyshire which Hall was producing by mid
1813 **(142)**.

In March 1808 Farey. who had started an enthusiastic
correspondence with the President of the newly formed
Geological Society in London (but of which neither Farey
nor Smith were members) G. B. Greenough, arranged a
visit to Smith's house for members of this Society to
examine his stratigraphically arranged collections. Farey.
from January 1810. also presented specimens and sections
to the Society and from its beginning also disseminated
details of Smith's results **(131,** 425) to the rival
Greenough Geological map of England published in 1820
(213 & 218).

Farey's first Derbyshire volume covered a fair part of
what was then known of the stratigraphic sequence in
Britain, down to the Red Marl or Ground and gave a first
reasonably detailed record of the known sequence working downwards, before Smith had himself published on it.
Farey's discussion of the sequence stops at the troublesome unconformity below the Red Ground (= Trias),
though the Carboniferous rocks are amply covered elsewhere in the volume. One of the outstanding matters
discussed in Volume 1 of the *Report* is the nature and
effect of faulting in relation to denudation in Derbyshire.
After the winter of 1807-8 when he had worked on his
Sussex section, and certainly by the spring of 1808, Farey
had started to postulate "A Great Fault" near Buxton to
explain stratigraphic relationships **(123 & 125)**. This is
shown on unpublished sections and geological maps of

Derbyshire made by Farey in September 1808, which have been recently re-discovered in California. The cause of such faults, which he had postulated first in Sussex, Farey thought to have been satellite attraction or comets which had disrupted the strata (58); such ideas were well within the context of their times (Schaffer 1980).

Farey's problem in Derbyshire was undoubtedly a partial result of his Smithian background. The unconformable nature of the Red Ground (now known as Triassic) overlying Carboniferous rocks in the Bath area caused Smith enormous problems in working out the correct sequence across it and then both he and Farey faced further problems in tracing this and other unconformities across England. Such problems help explain Farey's postulation of faulting as an explanation of stratigraphic relationships in Derbyshire rather than unconformity. That this is an understandable mistake is clear from the history of investigation of the so-called "Red Rock Fault" (Challinor 1978) where this very problem is still with us. If the sequence across an unconformity is not correctly known and the unconformity thus unrecognised. one can just as well postulate a fault contact there as an unconformity. It is only when an unconformity is later revealed by the "gap" becoming filled in areas away from it, that the "truth" is revealed.

But Farey was undoubtedly also guilty of somewhat jumping to conclusions. He regarded a large part of the limestone/shale contact round the margins of the Peak as a series of complex faults. White Watson, with his greater local knowledge derived from the mining community, pointed out (1811) that miners had demonstrated the continuation of limestone beneath shale, at least on the eastern margin, and that the contact here was a normal "basset" outcrop of the feather edge of the shales resting on the limestone. Farey later accepted this, but still continued to insist on a Great Bakewell Fault to explain the sudden disappearance of some toadstone outcrops south of Bakewell. In his text book Robert Bakewell (1813b), born in Nottingham, also disagreed with Farey over some interpretations and an exchange of views occupied many pages of the *Philosophical magazine* (for Farey's contribution see **141-145, 147-150, 152**). Forty years later the Geological Survey still followed Farey's line and inserted a complex series of faults along the western margin of the limestone outcrop, where an unconformity is now known to be the correct explanation, showing how complex these problems are.

Farey's *Report* listed the topographical features of the county and specified what stratum each hill was composed of and what each river crossed. He listed the caverns and mines and said what stratum each penetrated, giving vital historical data otherwise quite lost. Much was doubtless obtained in the field and from conversations with miners and the many helpers Farey listed in this and subsequent volumes. Much was also gleaned by correspondence. It was all systematised into 1st Limestone, 1st Toadstone etc downwards, which was developed from Whitehurst's description as used by Watson in the interim. The Millstone Grit sequences were treated in the same way but Farey numbered these upwards in contrast to Watson who worked downwards, a sure way of introducing confusion! The deductions of both have largely stood the test of time, as can be seen by comparing their sections with current British Geological Survey sheets. In a rather crude way Farey recognised that the eastern half of the limestone outcrop differed from the western. The boundary is roughly where we now draw the outcrop limits of Brigantian (D 2) strata resting on Asbian (D 1).

Reaction to this first volume was mixed. There were some enthusiastic reviews, in which Smith's part was again brought to the fore. But Marshall (1818) wrote a rude review of Farey's first two volumes complaining of the extent to which they dealt with minerals and geology, rather than agriculture. This completely ignored the fact that Sinclair had all along intended to issue county mineral reports one day (Sinclair 1797; Tilloch 1811). Derbyshire was the first, but in the end the only, county

to have had both County Agricultural and Mineral
Reports published (see **124**, vol. 1, vi). These were com-
bined with the approval of both Presidents of the Board
of Agriculture and of the Royal Society. Comparison with
other County Reports is thus hardly appropriate. Of the
geology in this volume, Geological Society member
Leonard Horner (1785-1864) wrote, to Greenough in
September 1811, that Farey "seems to proceed as a
geologist without the aid of science and to adapt nature
to a theory of his own built upon the most insufficient
materials. His sections [of faults] are quite enough to
stagger the faith of anyone who knows the first outlines
of geology". John Hawkins (1758-1841) wrote to Samuel
Lysons (1763-1819) in 1817 in similar vein, that Farey's
plates of faults were "purely hypothetical. I make this
assertion not only because there is nothing in any part of
Europe which confirms these observations of Mr Farey,
but because I can find among the notes which I made
some years ago above & below ground in Derbyshire, no
example whatever recorded of these strange and unnatural
dislocations of the Strata. I suspect therefore that Mr
Farey has made every fact bend to a preconceived
hypothesis" (Steer 1966, 35-9). Posterity however is in
no doubt that Farey's discussion of faulting in this
volume, with 30 classes of faults illustrated with fine
hand-coloured block diagrams, broke quite new ground in
British geology and entitles him to be regarded as a true
pioneer of structural geology (Dearman and Turner 1983),
even though some of the classes of faults would today be
seen as only variants and some of his geometrical effects
are impossible. In any event Farey later modified his own
views on these Derbyshire faults (**124**, vol. 2, 410).

All the time the Derbyshire survey was in progress for
the Board of Agriculture and being written up, Farey,
often now with his talented children as assistants, was
busy on other commissions apart from that for Banks at
Ashover, continually meeting other geologists and
comparing the sequences he now saw in new locations
with those he had worked on already. In 1815 he

estimated his geological travels had involved nearly 20,000 miles by stage coach (**176**, 385). His fee for such work until 1814 was 2 guineas a day, with expenses. In 1809 he was busy in Essex and in the Black Country. In 1810 he visited David Mushet in the Forest of Dean, while working in South Wales. In 1811, when he read his paper on the Great Derbyshire Denudation to the Royal Society on March 28 (**123 & 125**), he reported on estates at Lythe near Whitby (**192**, 251).

In September 1811 he ceased writing for Rees' *Cyclopaedia* both on geology (**231**, 129) and on music (**137**, 7). Geology had undergone great changes in this decade and authors rapidly came into, and went out of favour. The Geological Society had, since its foundation in 1807, encouraged the importation of what Farey saw as wholly inappropriate Wernerian stratigraphic names (**169** etc). His stance against these meant that Rees was soon under pressure to replace him as author on geology, by a more conformist view. Farey was not an advocate for the Huttonian camp as Pestana claims (1979, 358). Pestana in his survey also stated that "Farey seems to have stopped writing for the *Cyclopaedia* after his article Denudation in part 22" (published in December 1808). But Farey was still named as a contributor on the cover of part 24 published six months later. Farey himself said in a letter dated June 2 1812 (**133**, 513) that he wrote the Geology articles from Clay to the end of letter I (which then included the letter J as the relevant volume and the numbering of the gatherings in the volumes themselves show). Letter J was reached with part 37 published on 14 September 1811. Farey repeated in 1815 that he had written on geology up to this time and the article Joints (**165**, 335). So there is clear evidence confirmed by the articles themselves (**20 to 42**) that Farey's connection with the *Cyclopaedia* was longer than realised. The definitive notice of it (Anon 1820) merely recorded that Farey had written on "Canals, Geology [by which the subject rather than the specific articles of this title is meant], Measures, Music and Trigonometrical Survey".

From September 1811 to early in 1812 Farey was trying to finish the very detailed but long-delayed Geological Survey of the parish of Ashover for Banks, work which had started with his first invitation to Derbyshire in 1807. This was to have formed part of a detailed paper in large part on the Ashover denudation which was read in April 1813 (Anon 1813) to the Geological Society, with two large scale maps, a detailed section over more than seven miles and a Memoir of great length. All this was to have supported this Derbyshire *Report* (as he notes in the preface to this volume, where he refers to his "intended Mineral History and large map of the district") but it was never published, being rejected "through the intrigues of a few individuals" by the Society (see **141**, 55 & **124**, vol. 3, vi-x, 207) and it has not survived. One cannot help wondering if the fact that it had been commissioned by Joseph Banks, who resigned with so much indignation against the Geological Society in April 1809 (Rudwick 1963, 349) that helped fan the officers' enmity against both this paper and against Farey, and through this against Smith, who had also been patronised by Banks? We should note that no county map of Derbyshire was ever issued by William Smith in his maps of English Counties, to make up for the loss.

In April 1812 Farey prepared another section from Petersfield in Hampshire to New Church, near Newport in the Isle of Wight (**148**, 120). This once again was never published, although a number of copies exist. It predates Thomas Webster's published work on the Isle of Wight. Farey also gave early, and continued, support for the Sowerby family publication on *Mineral Conchology*, from the very first fossil described in this in June 1812 until his death, supplying stratigraphic information (**157 & 215**), specimens which he collected all round England, Scotland and Wales on his surveys and finally locality indices (**168**; **207**; **233 & 240**) and stratigraphic indexes (**158**; **204**; **232 & 239**) to the first four volumes. In July 1812 he visited Shropshire and Wales and collected such specimens en route for Scotland (**141**). In Scotland Farey worked for the Marquis of Stafford reporting on the latter's estates and coal field mined at Brora in Sutherland (Waterston 1982). This work took him a long way from his former field areas and it is instructive to discover that he was not able to elucidate the true [Jurassic] age of the Brora coals, despite assiduously collecting the fossils he found here. The ranges of the relevant fossils were simply not yet known with sufficient accuracy to allow such long range correlations, and Farey understandably preferred to regard them as evidence that the ranges of what we now know to be Jurassic fossils simply extended down into the Carboniferous!

His route home took him via Newcastle and Durham, to Leeds and then Ashover, where he continued his survey for Banks. In April 1813 he was working for the Commissioners of Sewers in the London area. In the same year he reported to Lord Mulgrave on his "Alum Shales and Coal near Whitby". This report, which again does not survive, was another major piece of work and in July 1813, after the publication of his detailed Derbyshire paper had been rejected by the "Wernerian faction" at the Geological Society, he was hoping to publish that and this Whitby report as volume one of a projected series of *Mineral Reports,* if he could only find a publisher to take the series on, according to a letter he wrote to James Sowerby. Unfortunately he never did and so these reports remained unpublished and, worse, have disappeared. Volume two of his Derbyshire *Report* was published in June 1813. In October he was working on Angelsey and proposing a Mineral Survey of North Wales to Banks' friend John Lloyd, a project interrupted by Lloyd's death in 1815. In November 1814, after he had raised his fees to "all new employers to three guineas a day with expenses" (185), he reported on a supposed coal occurrence near Welshpool.

In 1815 Farey's main surveying works were a series of commissions which now started for Charles Scott (1772-1819), Duke of Buccleuch, on his Scottish estates. Farey reported on lead veins in Dumfriesshire for the Duke in

August and earlier in the same year he had reported on the Coal Field of Dumfriesshire (215). Back in London in the same year he was elected Treasurer of the Smithfield Club. This job, with his existing Secretaryship, now carried an annual salary of 40 guineas (Bull 1926, 40). It was Farey too, who became the secretary of a Public Subscription organised in 1815 (which brought in promises of over £1,750) for the former President of the Board of Agriculture Sir John Sinclair (1754-1835) who now faced financial ruin! (Mitchison 1962). In March 1816 Farey moved to a new home at 37 Howland Street, near Fitzroy Square, London (179, 356). Work for the Duke of Buccleuch continued and Farey's journal of mineral observations in the counties of Selkirk and Roxburgh made in the autumn of 1816 for the Duke still survives. In 1818 he prepared two major reports for the Duke on Water Supply for the City of Edinburgh and on the Duke's Coal properties in the nearby Midlothian coal field. Any future commissions (and a speedy settlement of Farey's bills to the Duke!) were however interrupted by the Duke's early death in April 1819.

Yet another of Farey's interests, quite outside the fields of music and geology, is one in which he has unexpectedly achieved eponymous immortality. This is in mathematics and number theory. In 1816 he published a paper, undoubtedly inspired by his work on musical temperaments and scales and the mathematics of sound, which discussed a "curious property of vulgar fractions". Farey had observed that if all the proper vulgar fractions in their lowest terms, having both numerators and denominators not exceeding a given number n, were arranged in order of magnitude, then each fraction was equal to the fraction whose numerator and denominator are respectively equal to the sum of the two parts of the fractions on either side of it in the series (Glaisher 1879 & Dickson 1919). Such series are now called Farey Series after him, although he was not the first to observe this property, and published no proof. From this follow the Farey Point and the Farey Dissection of the Circle and

Farey Fractions, Numbers and Arcs. The history of Farey Series needs to be investigated. The remarks of the few mathematicians who have commented, with the exception of Regener (1973, 114-5) show great ignorance of the history of John Farey, if not of mathematics, wrongly calling him a "mineralogist" and an "indifferent mathematician" who "attached no importance to his Series".

A significant source for John Farey's later years is a series of diaries of his younger son Henry, taken to the USA in the middle of the last century. Those for 1816 — which, for example, records his father's return from Scottish surveying for the Duke of Buccleuch, 1817-1819 (see Craver et al. 1938 — where the usual confusion between father and son is again evident) and 1820 still survive, in the hands of Arthur Farey in California.

In the third volume of his Derbyshire *Report*, which was considerably delayed in the press and, although printed by June 1816, not published until July 1817 because of Sinclair's financial crisis, Farey considered questions of weights, measures and money. In view of the delay and what he saw as the importance of his ideas, early in 1817 he circulated and published his ideas on total decimalisation of British currency (**186**), ideas which had occupied him since 1795, but which had to wait another 150 years before they were accepted!

In 1818 and 1821 Farey made two very detailed reports (only the first and a part of the second of which survive) on the Black Lead or graphite mine at Borrow-dale, in the Lake District for Henry Bankes (1757-1834), a relative of his patron Sir Joseph Banks, who also held a share in this mine. Here he met Jonathan Otley (1766-1856), the pioneer of Lakeland geology, whom he encouraged to reissue his topographic maps of the Lakes now coloured geologically. These first appeared in 1823. In March 1819 he appeared as a witness, with his brother Benjamin, who had by now been the surveyor of the Whitechapel Turnpike roads for nine years, before the Select Committee on Highways (**216**). Both brothers advocated paving. In 1820 he commented on, and revised, Westgarth Forster's book which had first appeared in 1809 and which was published in a new edition, with Farey's corrections and comments, in 1821 (Forster 1821). In 1822 he was employed by the Commissioners of His Majesty's Woods and Forests to investigate and report on slate quarries in the Bangor area, a report which was one of the few by Farey ever to be published (238). But later in 1822 demand for his professional services seems to have diminished and he now spent much time making detailed indices of the newly appearing books on geology, and offering his services as a copyist (at one shilling an hour!) to James Sowerby. Farey's last known geological activity was a month long stay on geological business somewhere in Ireland in February and March 1825. Later in 1825, after the sudden paralysis of his son Joseph (1796-1829), John Farey was forced to take over his family business, which provided technical assistance, models and drawings for patentees and inventors. But this could not last long as Farey senior died at his home in Howland Street on 6 January 1826, and was buried in St James, Piccadilly.

It is a pity none of Farey's early sections were ever published, as they alone would have established his claim to geological fame. While they were in circulation they could be and were used by others, but they were not so easily credited to him by historians, only used to assessing publications (Torrens 1988, 87). Being up to nine feet long they presented a major technical problem to publish anyway! In preparing them Farey certainly brought the idea of a systematic stratigraphic sequence before the leading geologists of the day well before Smith's own sections were published in 1817. Cox rightly observed (1942, 39) that Farey's first section was probably better executed than any Smith had then prepared, but Farey was always careful to credit where his ideas had originated. His major work remains the 1811 *Report* reprinted here (for which additions or errata in the two later well-indexed volumes of the *Report* should also be checked). This may be claimed as the first equivalent publication to what later became the standard Geological Survey Memoir, wherein the details of strata, quarries, mines and minerals are given systematically. Although Farey thus seems to have set a significant pattern he does not seem to have been given credit for it by historians. Unlike modern memoirs his *Report* was not illustrated by numerous diagrams of the relationships of strata etc and only one small-scale geological map is included (although as we have seen more were intended). Even so this is one of the very first detailed geological maps of a region of Britain and the MSS maps of Derbyshire now known to have survived give us an even better view of his considerable attainments as a geological mapmaker.

Some more theoretical concepts also appear in the 1811 *Report:* the demonstration of the necessity of tracing outcrops across country and of what could be learnt from the pattern of such outcrops; an early recognition of the effects of denudation on outcrops particularly with respect to faults, and an early description of an area later to be recognised as of Pre-Cambrian rocks, in Charnwood Forest. In these rocks he makes a very early allusion to slaty cleavage (124, vol. 1, 155) introducing the term Stratula for it, in which he later included cross-bedding as well, in another perceptive observation (152, 338). The first concept was in effect how a geological map was made, based on the principles Farey had learnt at first hand from Smith. The second concept of denudation, a term he claimed to have introduced to British geology, by which erosion removes parts of the earlier stratigraphic formations to leave the patterns we see today, was implicit in the work of James Hutton from 1785. A major influence here was again Smith's recognition of outliers in the Bath area (104, 134 & 118, 441), which Farey correctly extrapolated as the converse of his denudations or inliers. The relationships of faults to valleys is also clear from Farey's block diagrams but here there is evidence that he was understandably influenced by Whitehurst's older vision of gulfs full of broken rock (even though Farey specifically took issue on this in the Matlock area; see **90)**. Farey also deduced that at least some types of faults were due to tension and others to compression, but he was at a loss to explain this. Similarly he recognised that some hills were of upfolded strata, or anticlinal in structure, but he went further and, at least in his early days, believed that such were due to satellite attraction. Watson did not agree and his later book (1813) was largely directed against Farey's satellite theory: Watson used Masson Hill and Grange Hill near Matlock as evidence that "Conical Hills" had been raised by volcanic pressure from below.

Little of Farey's personal nature comes through a study of his publications, even when the full list presented here is considered. These publications however form a marvellously detailed source for the development of British Geology over the critical period of 1806-1825, although they have hardly been used. He "was a man of most laborious research, and of very retiring habits: rarely mixing in society, but pursuing his studies with incessant application, impelled by a thirst for knowledge rather than by the desire of wealth or fame" (Anon 1826). He was clearly advantaged by his early employment by the Duke of Bedford, which allowed him a more free entry into aristocratic and agricultural circles than was given to Smith. He was transparently honest and open about both the value of improving Society and in giving credit to others where it was due. He believed he was doing them a service by helping to get their ideas into print, with the greater facility he wielded with his pen. His cross-fertilization of his own and others' ideas places him in a well-earned position as a pioneer British geologist. Contrary to the acerbic power of his pen, he seems to have been rather reticent in taking credit to himself, because he was shy. He was deeply interested in political reform, and he also emerges as a pacifist, sick of the years of war in Europe which had been such a feature of much of his adult life (**228**), and as a man with a deep concern for the welfare of his fellow men.

Of the vast collections of manuscripts and specimens he had made personally by the time of his death (Anon 1826), nothing seems to have survived. His latter "collection of geological specimens formed during his professional life as a mineral surveyor" was offered to the British Museum by his widow in July 1828, an offer rejected out of hand by the German-born keeper Charles Konig, who had been earlier involved in replacing Farey as a more Wernerian author on Geology for Rees' *Cyclopaedia* in 1810 and who was not interested in fossils! The problem may be that nobody has searched. Sherborn (1929) first suggested that, because of a fire at his son's residence, supposedly in 1850, little or nothing of the manuscripts of the father could be expected to have survived. Other writers have since followed this without investigating. The truth is that there was a terrible fire, in which four died, at his son John's house in London on 21 December 1844 (Baddeley 1845, 179) but there is no evidence that either the manuscripts or geological collections of John Farey senior, the geologist, were ever involved. Some of the manuscripts of John Farey junior are known to have survived this fire (Farey 1847; Woolrich 1985) and contemporary reports specifically say many books and manuscripts were saved (*Times* 30 December 1844, 6). What must be first established is whether John Farey senior's library and collections were even in the house at the time of the fire. Since his personal, and heavily annotated, copies of William Smith's and James Parkinson's books have survived to the present (in Bristol University Library and in private hands respectively) we should at least expect, and should now start to look for, manuscript material which may also have survived and not simply assume it lost in a fire which may never have involved it. John senior's will (Prerogative Court of Canterbury, Public Record Office, London), dated 14 April 1823, was proved on 3 April 1826. It simply left all his property to his wife Sophia. She died in 1830.

VI

ACKNOWLEDGEMENTS

Our first debt is to Arthur Farey in California, senior member of the Farey family, for his help and encouragement over many years. Tony Woolrich of Huntworth, who has been collaborating on the life and work of engineer John Farey junior, has been of continual assistance.

REFERENCES

Anon 1804 Report of the Woburn Sheep Shearing of 1804. *Agricultural Magazine* **10**, 466-7.

Anon 1807 Report of the Smithfield Cattle Show of 1806. *Monthly Magazine* **22**, 595-7.

Anon 1813 Report of John Farey's paper on the Ashover Denudation to the Geological Society. *Philosophical Magazine* **41**, 303-5.

Anon 1820 Notices respecting new books — *The Cyclopaedia* . . . by Abraham Rees. *Philosphical Magazine* **56**, 218-24.

Anon 1826 Mr John Farey. *Monthly Magazine*, 430-1.

Baddeley W. 1845 London fires in 1844. *Mechanics Magazine* **42**, 177-87.

Bainbrigge W. 1818 [Analysis of Heage Mineral Water and Remarkable Oak]. *Monthly Magazine* **45**, 10-2 & 216-8.

Bakewell R. 1813a In Reply to Mr. Farey, on the Great Derbyshire Fault. *Philosophical Magazine* **42**, 121-6.

Bakewell R. 1813b *An Introduction to Geology*. London: Harding.

Bevan B. 1802 [Meteorological Observations]. *Monthly Magazine* **14**, 1-2.

Bull L. 1926 *History of the Smithfield Club from 1798 to 1925*. London: Smithfield Club.

Carter H. B. 1987 *Sir Joseph Banks*. London: British Museum (Natural History).

Challinor J. 1978 The "Red Rock Fault", Cheshire: a critical review. *Geological Journal* **13**, 1-10.

Cox L. R. 1942 New light on William Smith and his work. *Proceedings of the Yorkshire Geological Society* **25**, 1-99.

Craver H. W., Dickinson H. W. & Jenkins R. 1938 The Farey diary, 1819. *Transactions of the Newcomen Society* **17**, 215-9.

Dearman W. R. & Turner S. 1983 Models illustrating John Farey's figures of Stratified Masses. *Proceedings of the Geologists Association* **94**, 97-104.

Dickson L. E. 1919 *History of the Theory of Numbers*. Volume 1. Washington: Carnegie Institution.

Doane J. [1794] *A Musical Directory for the year 1794*. London: Westley.

Eyles J. M. 1985 William Smith, Sir Joseph Banks and the French Geologists, pages 37-50 in *From Linnaeus to Darwin: Commentaries on the History of biology and geology*. London: Society for the History of Natural History.

Farey J. [junior] 1847 Letter. *Mechanics Magazine* **46**, 379.

Ferguson E. S. 1968 Cast Iron Aqueduct in Rees's *Cyclopaedia*. *Technology and Culture* **9**, 597-600.

Ford T. D. 1960 White Watson (1760-1835) and his Geological Sections. *Proceedings of the Geologists Association* 71, 349-363.

Ford T. D. 1967 The first detailed Geological Sections across England by John Farey 1806-08. *Mercian Geologist* 2, 41-9.

Forster W. 1821 *A Treatise on a section of the Strata from Newcastle-on-Tyne to the Mountain of Cross Fell, in Cumberland.* Alston: Pattinson (for the author).

Glaisher J. W. L. 1879 On a Property of Vulgar Fractions. *Philosophical Magazine* (5) 7. 321-36.

Harrison W. 1955 *The Board of Agriculture 1793-1822.* London University: M.A. thesis.

Kassler J. C. 1979 *The Science of Music in Britain 1714-1830.* Two volumes. New York & London: Garland Publishing.

Marshall W. 1818 *The Review and Abstract of the County Reports to the Board of Agriculture.* Volume 4. Midland Department. York: Wilson.

Mitchison R. 1962 *Agricultural Sir John: The Life of Sir John Sinclair of Ulbster 1754-1835.* London: Bles.

Pestana H. R. 1979 Rees's *Cyclopaedia* (1802-1820): a sourcebook for the history of geology. *Journal of the Society for the History of Natural History* 9. 353-61.

Phillips J. 1844 *Memoirs of William Smith, LL.D.* London: Murray.

Playfair J. 1812 Review of Cuvier & Brongniart's *Geographie Mineralogique des environs de Paris. Edinburgh Review* 20, 369-86.

Regener E. 1973 *Pitch Notation and Equal Temperament; a formal study.* Berkeley etc: Univ. of Los Angeles Press.

Rudwick M. J. S. 1963 The Foundation of the Geological Society of London. *British Journal for the History of Science* 1, 325-55.

Schaffer S. 1980 The Great Laboratories of the Universe: William Herschel on Matter Theory and Planetary Life. *Journal for the History of Astronomy* 11, 81-111.

Sherborn C. D. 1929 The earliest known Geological Section across England. *The Naturalist* December 1, 393-4.

Sinclair J. 1797 General View of the Inquiries essential for the Internal Improvement of the Kingdom, with a Plan for reprinting the Agricultural Surveys. *Communications to the Board of Agriculture* 1, lxviii-lxx.

Steer F. W. 1966 *The letters of John Hawkins and Samuel & Daniel Lysons 1812-1830.* Chichester: West Sussex County Council.

Tilloch A. 1811 Proposed Mineral Surveys of the British Counties: Mr. Kirwan's Opinions on this subject. *Philosophical magazine* 37, 8-10.

Torrens H. S. 1983 Arthur Aikin's Mineralogical Survey of Shropshire 1796-1816, and the contemporary audience for geological publications. *British Journal for the History of Science* 16, 111-53.

Torrens H. S. 1988 Hawking History – a vital Future for Geology's Past. *Modern Geology* 13, 83-93.

Waterston C. D. 1982 John Farey's Mineral Survey of south east Sutherland and the Age of the Brora coalfield. *Annals of Science* 39, 173-85.

Watson W. 1805 *Catalogue of a Collection of fossils etc . . . to be sold by auction at the Rutland Arms, Bakewell on Monday 4 February 1805.* Derby: Drewry (printer).

Watson W. 1811 *A Delineation of the Strata of Derbyshire . . . designed from a Tablet.* Sheffield: Todd.

Watson W. 1813 *A Section of the Strata forming the Surface in the Vicinity of Matlock-Bath in Derbyshire.* Chesterfield: Ford (for the author).

Whitehurst J. 1786 *An Inquiry into the Original State and Formation of the Earth.* Second Edition. London: Bent.

Woolrich A. P. 1985 John Farey [junior] and the Smeaton Manuscripts. *History of Technology* **10**. 181-216.

JOHN FAREY BIBLIOGRAPHY

Compiling a bibliography of the writings of John Farey senior is a difficult task. He was enormously prolific across a polymathic range of subjects encompassing agriculture, geology, mathematics, music and politics. Secondly there is the problem of separating his writings from those of his eldest son, also John (1791-1851), and who also published widely. But perhaps the major problem is that Farey often published anonymously, particularly from 1815 on, partly in obvious ostracism for his outspoken views on the treatment of himself and William Smith by officers of the Geological Society.

Those anonymous items which can with certainty be ascribed to John Farey senior are included in this list [within square brackets thus].

The list is certainly still incomplete, more so for his many agricultural and musical items than for those in scientific fields.

Abbreviations used are:

AP = *Annals of Philosophy*
GM = *Gentlemans Magazine*
MM = *Monthly Magazine*
NJ = *Nicholson's Journal*
PM = *Tilloch's Philosophical Magazine.*

Isolated numbers in **Bold** refer to numbered items in this Bibliography.

1. 1796 On Top Dressings, in the neighbourhood of Dunstable. *Annals of Agriculture* **25**, 66-76.

2. 1797 Question 731 answered. *Gentleman's Diary or the Mathematical Repository* **57**, 42-3 (see also pages 34-6 for his answers – not published – to questions 721-3).

3. 1798 Question 742 answered. *Gentleman's Diary or the Mathematical Repository* **[58]**, 37-8 (see also pages 34-6 for his answers – not published – to questions 737 & 740).

4. 1798 New Mathematical Questions 753 & 754 to be answered *Gentleman's Diary or the Mathematical Repository* **[58]**, 46 (see also vol. **59**, 2).

5. 1800 Abstract of Crops produced 1795-1800 on estates of Duke of Bedford. *Annals of Agriculture* **37**, 347.

6. 1800 Question 780 answered. *Gentleman's Diary or the Mathematical Repository* **60**, 38 (see also p. 35 for his answers – not published – to questions 775 & 776).

7. 1803 On Salmon's claim to the mode of transferring paintings. *MM* January, 477.

8. 1804 On the Mensuration of Timber. *PM* **19**, 213-22.

9. 1804 Mercurial and Spirit Thermometers compared. *MM* **17**, 213-4.

10. 1804 [given as Tho. Rafey – corrected in the index] State of the Grand Junction Canal. *MM* 17, 228-9.

11. 1804 On Malthus' Principle of Population. *MM* 18, 188-90.

12. 1804 [wrongly given as John Farcy] The great fiery Meteor of Nov. 13 [1803] and on other subjects. *NJ* 7, 66-7.

13. 1804 On certain Properties of Plane Triangles. *Gentlemans Mathematical Companion* for 1805. no. 8. 1-8.

14. 1804 Questions 129-30 answered. *Gentlemans Mathematical Companion* for 1805. no. 8, 30-1.

15. 1805 On blasting with Gunpowder. *PM* 20, 208-9.

16. 1805 Silver medal awarded to, for experiments on the growth of timber trees. *Transactions of the Society for the Encouragement of Arts etc.* 23, 112.

17. 1805 Minute admeasurement of 108 trees. *Transactions of the Society for the Encouragement of Arts etc.* 23, 126.

18. 1805 A Plantation for profit should be of one kind of trees. *Transactions of the Society for the Encouragement of Arts etc.* 23, 142.

19. 1805 Plan of a wood at Wavendon. Bucks. in respect of which John Farey was awarded a [silver] prize in 1805. reproduced in Hudson D. & Luckhurst K. W. 1954 *The Royal Society of Arts.* London: John Murray.

20 to 42. 1806-11 The following contributions to A. Rees *The Cyclopaedia*, which was published over 1802 to 1820 (for dates of publication see Anon 1820), can be credited with certainty to Farey senior. although all were published anonymously:

Article	Date of Publication	Pages
a) Canal	2.1806	142 pp.

(much shortened from Farey's original manuscript version: see his annotation to the offprinted version in British Library 435 k 19 and 165. 335)

Article	Date of Publication	Pages
b) Clay Balls	8.1807	column
c) Clay Strata	8.1807	2 pp.
d) Coal (in part see 104, 114)	8.1807	16 pp.
e) Colliery	8.1807	7 pp.
f) Concentricity of Strata	11.1807	column
g) Continent	11.1807	5 pp.
h) Crop out	7.1808	paragraph
i) Deluge	9 & 12.1808	12 pp.
j) Denudation	12.1808	2 pp.
k) Encroachment of the Sea	8.1809	2 pp.
l) Endings of the Strata	8.1809	column
m) Excavation of Valleys	11.1809	column
n) Extraneous Fossils	11.1809	2 pp.
o) Fullers Earth (part author)	10.1810	2 pp.
p) Glossopetrae	10.1810	2 pp.
q) Grand Ridge (see 125, 33)	1.1811	2 pp.
r) Gravel in Geology	1.1811	2 pp.

| s) Ice-Borne | 8.1811 | 2 pp. |
| t) Joints in Mining | 9.1811 | column |

Farey was also busy as the author of articles on the more mathematical and theoretical aspects of music, commencing with that on

u) Concert pitch

(see **89**, 4; Scholes 1948 & Kassler 1979, 1200-4). Farey's own comments in **137**, 7 suggests that he stopped writing on Music when the article Interval in Music was reached and thus at the same time as he ceased to write on Geology.

His other known articles are on

v) Barometric Measurement of Height

w) Trigonometrical Survey

(teste Taylor 1966)

43. 1806 [given as by Mr Henry Fary but corrected in *MM* **22**, 147] The late Meteor. *MM* **22**, 103-4.

44. 1806 On shooting-stars, meteors, and meteoric stones with calculations and remarks relative to the meteor of 17 July last. *MM* **22**, 144-7.

45. 1806 On shooting stars. *MM* **22**, 444.

46. 1806 On the Stratification of England; the intended Thames Archways, etc. *PM* **25**, 44-9.

47. 1806 On music. *PM* **26**, 171-6.

48. 1806 [Anon] Review of *"Observations on the Utility, Form and Management of Water-Meadows"* by William Smith, 1806. *Literary Panorama* **1**, 70-71.

49. 1806 [Anon]. Review of *"The Elements of Land Surveying"* by A. Crocker, 1806. *Literary Panorama* **1**, 71-3.

50. 1806 [Anon]. Review of *"A Treatise on the Teeth of Wheels, Pinions etc."* by M. Camus, 1806. *Literary Panorama* **1**, 257-62.

51. 1806 Letter dated 16 July 1806 to Sir John Sinclair, of the Board of Agriculture, on the State of Public Roads in Britain in *Second Report from the Select Committee on Acts regarding the use of Broad Wheels, and other matters relating to the preservation of the Turnpike Roads and Highways of the Kingdom.* In British Parliamentary Papers. Ordered by the House of Commons to be printed 18 July 1806 (pp. 51-3).

52. 1807 On the means of obtaining water. *MM* **23**, 211-2.

53. 1807 On Correcting the Anomalies of the Atmosphere by Art. *MM* **23**, 314-5.

54. 1807 On the Stanhope Temperament of the Musical Scale. *PM* **27**, 191-206.

55. 1807 On different Temperaments of the Musical Scale. *PM* **27**, 313-22.

56. 1807 On the Means of Ascertaining the Nature of Soils etc. and on the Finding of Coal. *Agricultural Magazine (Dickson's)* **(3) 1**, 115-7.

57. 1807 On a new Mode of equally tempering the Musical Scale. *PM* **28**, 65-6.

58. 1807 On the dislocations of the Strata of the Earth. *PM* **28**, 120.

59. 1807 On the Stanhope Temperament of the Musical Scale. *PM* **28**, 140-43.

60 to 85. 1808-1818 or 1819 The Following articles can be credited to Farey in David Brewster's *Edinburgh Encyclopaedia.* This commenced publication in 1808 and finished eighteen volumes later in 1830 (for dates of publication see Sherborn 1937). In an introductory note later bound in to volume 1 in 1830 (p. xi) "The late Mr John Farey senior's" authorship of major articles is listed and the note added that his other writings in this work are identified by the Greek lower case letter zeta. Those seen are listed here; the great majority are on Music.

Article	Date of Publication	Pages
a) Bearing Notes in Music	1810	3. 368
b) Beat, Beatings and Beats	1810	3. 368-70
c) Bedford	1810	3. 391-3
d) Bedfordshire	1810	3. 393-7
e) Chromatic	1813	6. 399-401
f) Chronometer	1813	6. 461
g) Comma [in Music]	1813	7. 18-21
h) Commensurable Intervals	1813	7. 21-22
i) Common medium [recte measures]	1813	7. 31-33
j) Concert pitch	1813	7. 53-55
k) Concorde	1813	7. 107-09
l) Diatesseron	1814	7.
m) Diesis [in Music]	1814	7. 737-39
n) Diminished Intervals	1814	7. 744-45
o) Discord [in Music]	1814	7. 751
p) Enharmonic	1815	9. 56
q) Euharmonic Organ	1815	9. 225-6
r) Farey's Temperament	1815	9. 273-4
s) Farey's Notation	1815	9. 274-6
t) Gases, Sounds produced by	1816	10. 120-21
u) Harmonics [etc]	1816	10. 638-42
v) Hyperoche [in Music]	1817	11. 598
w) Intervals [in Music]	1817	12. 175-9
x) Isotonic System	1817	12. 327-8
y) Liston's Scale	1818 or 1819	13. 41-2
z) Literals in Music	1818 or 1819	13. 42

86. 1808 Proceedings of the Smithfield Club. *Farmer's Magazine* **9**, 82-5.

87. 1808 On the Stanhope & other Temperaments of the Musical Scale. *PM* **29**, 345-9.

88. 1808 reprint of no. **51**. Ordered to be reprinted 8 March 1808.

89. 1808 On the 2 systems of Musical Temperament recommended by Earl Stanhope, & Mr Hawkes's System etc. *PM* **30**, 3-8.

90. 1808 On the Stratification of Matlock in Derbyshire, pointing out a mistake of the late John Whitehurst, and on the Transmutation of Lime into Silex. *PM* **31**, 36-41.

91. 1808 Building en Pisée. *MM* **25**, 8.

92. 1808 On the Finding of Coal in the South Eastern Counties of England. *Agricultural Magazine (Dickson's)* **(3) 2**, 22-31.

93. 1808 On Burning Clay for Manure, and on Merino Mutton. *Agricultural Magazine* **new series 3**, 385-6.

94. 1809 Merino Mutton not Morbid Scrophulous Carrion, in reply to the pert Apothecary of Loughborough. *Agricultural Magazine* **new series 5**, 163-4.

95. 1809 On the supposed universal Distribution of Fossil Coal, in Reply to Mr B. Cook; and on the Nature and Situations of the extraneous fossil (Belemnite) analysed by Mr J. Acton, under the Denomination of a "Crystal" called a Thunderpick. *NJ* **22**, 68-70.

96. 1809 On the Conversion of French weights into English. *NJ* **22**, 337-8.

97. 1809 Observations on a late paper by Dr William Richardson, respecting the basaltic District in the North of Ireland, and on the Geological Facts thence deducible; in Conjunction with others observable in Derbyshire and other English Counties: with the application of these facts to the Explanations of some of the most difficult Points in the Natural History of the Globe. *PM* **33**, 257-63.

98. 1809 A reply to Earl Stanhope, on his defence of certain principles & facts erroneously stated in his stereotyped *"Principles of the Science of Tuning Instruments with Fixed Tones"*. *PM* **33**, 292-9.

99. 1809 On the intended Thames Archway between Rotherhithe and the Limehouse. *PM* **33**, 372-83.

100. 1809 Geological Observations on the Excavation of Valleys and local Denudations of the Strata of the Earth in particular Districts etc, in reply to Mr John Carr's letter. *PM* **33**, 442-8.

101. 1809 Geological Observations on the Excavation of Valleys, the supposed Existence of numerous Lakes at former Periods where Valleys now exist, which the Streams flowing through them are said to have broken down, etc. in reply to Mr John Carr's letter. *PM* **34**, 49-53.

102. 1810 On organs and Fiorin Grass. *MM* **29**, 115-7.

103. 1810 On a pretended musical discovery. *MM* **29**, 413-4.

104. 1810 Geological Remarks and Queries on Messrs Cuvier & Brogniart [sic]'s *Memoir on the Mineral Geography of the Environs of Paris*. *PM* **35**, 113-39. [The translation of the above memoir in the same volume on pages 36-58 also by Farey].

105. 1810 On M. Bemetzrieder's erroneous Calculations of the Magnitudes of certain Musical Intervals. *PM* **35**, 175-6.

106. 1810 On the supposed Fresh-water Origin of the Gypsum Strata in the Environs of Paris; on the Geological Characters and Relations of the Alum Shales on the Northern Coasts of Yorkshire; and on the Orbicular Blocks of Sienite on Mount-Sorrel Hill, in Leicestershire. *PM* **35**, 256-61.

107. 1810 A list of about 500 Collieries in and near to Derbyshire. *PM* **35**, 431-8.

108. 1810 6 Theorems containing the chief Properties of all regular douzeave Systems of Music etc. *PM* **36**, 39-53.

109. 1810 Information, that a further Publication of the late Mr. Smeaton's Engineery Designs and Papers is in hand – Copy of a list of the principal British Strata, by the late Rev. John Michel, (of whose posthumous Papers on Geological Subjects, further Information is requested:) with some Experiments of Mr Smeaton's on Limestones, – and Queries respecting Mr. Tofield. *PM* **36**, 102-6.

110. 1810 A further set of 15 corollaries to the musical Theorems |in item **108** above) etc. *PM* **36**, 374-5.

111. 1811 On the musical Sounds of the Gases, – on the meteorologic Solution of Water in Air. – Electricity etc. – on Water Pressure Engines for Mines. – on the Confusion arising from various Meanings to the same Words and Marks used in Science. *PM* **37**, 3-6.

112. 1811 On Dr A. Walker's Opinion, respecting the general Deluge, the Formation of Mountains, the Ruptures of the Strata etc. by the approach of a Comet to the Earth. *PM* **37**, 35-9.

113. 1811 A List of about 280 Mines of Lead, – some with Zinc, Manganese, Copper, Iron, Fluor, Barytes, etc. in and near to Derbyshire. *PM* **37**, 106-11.

114. 1811 A List of about 700 Hills and Eminences in and near to Derbyshire, with the Stratum which occupies the Top of each, and other Particulars, – and the Answers received, to Inquiries in our last Volume, respecting Mr Michell and Mr Tofield's Geological Manuscripts. *PM* **37**, 161-76.

115. 1811 On a grand practical Improvement in the Harmony of Musical Instruments, by the Introduction of the Rev. Henry Liston's Patent Euharmonic Organ: with the names of the 60 distinct Sounds which it produces in each Octave, from 20 Pipes, and their Intervals calculated, *PM* **37**, 273-8.

116. 1811 Reply to Mr. John Taylor on Water-Pressure Engines for Mines. *PM* **37**, 309-10.

117. 1811 A table of the Beats on Mr William Hawkes's Patent Organs & Piano-Fortes, calculated by the Rev. C. J. Smyth. *PM* **37**, 321-3.

118.   1811   Geological Observations on unstratified Mountains, and on the Use and Abuse of Geological Theories. *PM* 37, 440-3.

119.   1811   Geological Remarks and Queries on Dr Campbell's Map and Account of the Stratification of Lancashire. *PM* 38, 336-9.

120.   1811   Theorems for calculating the temperaments of such regular Douzeaves as are commensurable, or defined by a certain number of equal parts, into which the octave is divided. *PM* 38, 434-6.

121.   1811   On Mr. Broadwood's method of Tuning. *MM* 32, 238.

122.   1811   Mr. Farey's reply to Mr. Broadwood. *MM* 32, 424-5.

123.   1811   An Account of the Great Derbyshire Denudation. *Philosophical Transactions of the Royal Society* 101, 242-56.

124.   1811   *A General View of the Agriculture and Minerals of Derbyshire.* Volume 1 (also reissued in 1815 with a new title page) pp. xlvii, 532, (extracts published in 1812 in *PM* 39, 191-208, 253-62).   1813 Volume 2 pp. xx, 522.   1817. Volume 3 pp. xxvii, 725. London: Board of Agriculture.

125.   1812   An Account of the Great Derbyshire Denudation. *PM* 39, 26-35.

126.   1812   [Anon]   On the cause of audible sound in vibrating strings, tuning forks etc; on the use of Hawkes's mouth tuning-forks; on Earl Stanhope's proposed steel piano-forte strings, etc. *PM* 39, 37-9.

127.   1812   Geological Observations, in Correction of and in Addition to the Paper on the Great Derbyshire Denudation, and the Report on Derbyshire, etc., relating principally to Coal-measures near to the Chalk Strata; the Course of the third and fourth Grit Rocks and Crowstone through Yorkshire, and the Termination of its Coal-field Northward; the Limits of the Yellow Lime Rock, and the Existence of Red Marl, Gypsum Beds, Strontian, etc. between its Rocks, etc. *PM* 39, 93-106.

128.   1812   Geological Observations on the County of Antrim, and others in the North-east part of Ireland, in an Attempt to arrange the numerous Facts, stated by Dr. William Richardson to the Royal Irish Academy, and to the Royal Society, and those recently published in the Rev. John Dubourdieu's *Statistical Survey of Antrim*, by Dr William H. Drummond in the Preface and Notes to his Poem, *"The Giant's Causeway"*, etc., and to refer each of them to one of the four principal Strata, separating such as belong to the Alluvia: with incidental Facts and Observations respecting other Districts, etc. *PM* 39, 266-82, 353-62.

129.   1812   On the Rev Mr Liston's Euharmonic Organ, & on his *"Essay on Perfect Intonation"*, just published, for explaining fully the principles of tuning, and of performing upon this organ with perfect harmonies, in almost every possible variety of keys & passages. *PM* 39, 373-6.

130. 1812 Further remarks on the Rev. Mr. Liston's *"Essay on perfect Intonation"* and his scale with 59 notes in the octave; and on other scales etc. *PM* **39**, 414-23.

131. 1812 Correction of an erroneous Statement in the Account of Mr. Bakewell's lectures, as to his originality in exhibiting a Geological Map of England: with Remarks on the Geological Questions, whether the lower Derbyshire Strata anywhere else appear in England?; and How were Caverns formed by subterraneous Currents of Water? and How were Minerals Veins opened and filled? *PM* **39**, 425-8.

132. 1812 Objection to converting the Thames into Docks. *MM* **33**, 3-4.

133. 1812 Smithfield Club prizes. *MM* **33**, 209-19.

134. 1812 Mr Farey in reply to M. De Luc. *MM* **33**, 513-7.

135. 1812 On the Nature of those Meteors commonly called Shooting Stars. *NJ* **30**, 285-6.

136. 1812 On the apparent Streaks of Light, left sometimes by falling or shooting Stars; and on their apparent rectilinear Courses in the Atmosphere. *NJ* **32**, 269-71.

137. 1812 Mr Farey on his Notation of Musical Intervals. *MM* **34**, 7-8.

138. 1813 Observations on Peeling Oak Timber. *Communications to the Board of Agriculture* **7**, 177-84.

139. 1813 Prizes distributed by the Smithfield Club. *MM* **35**, 31-2.

140. 1813 On Chemical and Musical Numbers. *MM* **36**, 217-9.

141. 1813 Cursory Geological Observations lately made, in Shropshire, Wales, Lancashire, Scotland, Durham, Yorkshire NR. and Derbyshire. Some Observations on Mr. Bakewell's Geological Map, and on the supposed Identity of the Derbyshire Peak and the Craven Limestones. *PM* **42**, 53-9.

142. 1813 Observations, in Objection to some new Arrangements, and Simplifications of the Strata of England proposed, by Mr. Bakewell. A defence of the Reality and Circumstances stated, respecting three great Faults or Dislocations of the Strata in and near Derbyshire. On Mr. Silverwood's intended Section of all the Derbyshire Strata. On Mr. Hall's Survey and Models on the High Peak of Derbyshire. The Slate of Charnwood Forest not stratified, etc. *PM* **42**, 103-16.

143. 1813 Reply to Mr. Bakewell's Letter on the great Derbyshire Fault. Mr. B's lectures. Stage-coach Geology. The great Southern Denudation. Limestone resting on Slate. The great Limestone Fault. etc. *PM* **42**, 164-71.

144. 1813 Notes and Observations on the Introduction and three first Chapters of Mr. Robert Bakewell's *Introduction to Geology*, embracing incidentally several new Points of Geological Investigations and Theory. *PM* **42**, 246-61.

145. 1813 [Notes and Observations on the 4th, 5th and part of the 6th Chapters of Bakewell's *Introduction to Geology*]. *PM* **42**, 356-67.

146. 1813 On the connection between Shooting-Stars and large Meteors, and proceeding both from terrestrial and satellitulae. *NJ* **34**, 298-300.

147. 1814 [Notes and Observations on the remaining part of the 6th and parts of the 7th Chapters of Bakewell's *Introduction to Geology*]. *PM* **43**. 27-34.

148. 1814 [Notes and Observations on the remaining part of the 7th [and 8th] Chapters of Bakewell's *Introduction to Geology*]. *PM* **43**, 119-27.

149. 1814 [Notes and Observations on the 9th Chapter of Bakewell's *Introduction to Geology*]. *PM* **43**. 182-90.

150. 1814 [Notes and Observations on the 10th and part of 11th Chapters of Bakewell's *Introduction to Geology*]. *PM* **43**. 252-61.

151. 1814 [An Engineer] On Fire Damp in Coal Mines. *PM* **44**, 303.

152. 1814 [Notes and Observations on part of the 11th and the 12th Chapters. and Appendix of Bakewell's *Introduction to Geology*]. *PM* **43**, 325-41.

153. 1814 Mr. Marsh's Harmonics; and the Fossil Skeletons. *MM* **37**, 23-4.

154. 1814 Architectural models. *MM* **37**, 227.

155. 1814 [Reply to Mr. G. (recte C.) Hall]. *MM* **37**, 395.

156. 1814 Intonation. *GM* **84** (1). 135-7.

157. 1814 [Letter on the Stratigraphic range of Belemnites] in J. Sowerby, *Mineral Conchology*, Volume 1, page 128.

158. 1815 Supplementary index to James Sowerby's *Mineral Conchology* volume 1 arranging the Shells described therein according to the several Strata in which they are found imbedded, in Sowerby's *Mineral Conchology* volume 1, pages [237-244].

159. 1815 Calculations of the Intervals & Beats of the sounds yielded by various Gases in the corrected Experiments of Messrs. F. Kirby & A. Merrick, recorded in *Nicholson's Journal*. *PM* **45**, 26-8.

160. 1815 [A Constant Reader] Queries, as to Grindstones and Ironstone in Durham, and Shells etc. near Cambridge. *PM* **45**, 108-9.

161. 1815 [An Engineer] On Fire Damps in Mines. *PM* **45**, 116-8.

162. 1815 Short Notices of Geological Observations made in the Summer of 1814, in the South of Yorkshire, and in North Wales, and of some Inferences therefrom, as to the Structure of England and Wales. *PM* **45**, 161-77.

163. 1815 [by a Correspondent – A Constant Reader] An earnest Recommendation to curious Ladies and Gentlemen residing or visiting in the Country, to examine the Quarries, Cliffs, steep Banks etc. and collect and preserve Fossil Shells, as highly curious Objects in Conchology, and, as most important Aids in identifying Strata in distant Places; on which Knowledge the Progress of Geology in a principal degree, if not entirely, depends. *PM* **45**. 274-80.

164. 1815 [by a Correspondent – A Constant Reader] Further Queries as to the proper Places in the British Series of Strata, of the Newcastle Grindstone Rock and its Muscle Shell Ironstone, and of certain organised Remains found near Cambridge. *PM* **45**. 295-6.

165. 1815 Observations on the Priority of Mr. Smith's Investigations of the Strata of England; on the very unhandsome Conduct of certain Persons in detracting from his Merit therein; and the Endeavours of others to supplant him in the Sale of his Maps; with a Reply to Mr. W. H. Gilby's Letter in the last Number. *PM* **45**. 333-44.

166. 1815 An improved Piano-forte. – New logarithmic scales. – Quantity of rain on Blackstone Edge. *PM* **45**. 386-7.

167. 1815 On certain Accidents to which Coal-works are liable, particularly those of Water bursting into the Pits from old Works that are near adjacent, as recently occurred at Heaton in Northumberland; the accidental Explosions of Fire-damp, setting Fire to the waste Coals in the Works, as happened last Summer at Brora in Sutherland; and the spontaneous Firing of loose small Coals and pyritic Dirt, etc. *PM* **45**. 436-52.

168. 1815 An Alphabetical Arrangement of the places from whence Fossil Shells have been obtained, by Mr James Sowerby, and drawn and described in volume 1 of his *Mineral Conchology*. *PM* **46**, 211-24.

169. 1815 A Reply to Dr W. H. Gilby; with some additional Facts regarding the Stratification of Britain, in proof of the Futility and Absurdity of the Attempts, at applying to the same, the Terms and Distinctions of the Wernerian Geognosy. *PM* **46**, 278-85.

170. 1815 On the late Mr Giles Hussey's Drawings. *MM* **38** 508-10.

171. 1815 On a mis-statement respecting Mangel Wurzel. *MM* **39**, 4-5.

172. 1815 Prizes distributed by the Smithfield Club. *MM* **39**, 34-5.

173. 1815 [A Mineral Surveyor] Hilly Ground. *MM* **39**, 210-1.

174. 1815 Tragical Explosion at Newbottle Colliery. *MM* **39**, 523-8.

175. 1815 On the Coal Works in Sutherland. *MM* **40**, 9-11.

176. 1815 Improvement of Stage Travelling. *MM* **40**, 384-6.

177. 1815 Musick. *GM* 85 (2), 208.

178. 1816 [by a Correspondent – A Constant Reader] Geological Queries regarding the Coal Strata of Northumberland and Durham and the Appearances of such in Lincolnshire. *PM* 47, 12-3.

179. 1816 A letter from Dr William Richardson to the Countess of Gosford (occasioned by the Perusal of Cuvier's *Geological Essay*), describing the Arrangement of the Strata for 60 miles on the South and as many on the North of Gosford Castle, in Armagh County in Ireland. *PM* 47, 354-64.

180. 1816 On a curious Property of vulgar Fractions [i.e. Farey numbers]. *PM* 47, 385-6 & 48, 204. (see also *PM* 49 345 & 458).

181. 1816 [no. 180 on Farey numbers reprinted]. *Bulletin de la Société Philomatique de Paris* (3) 3, 112.

182. 1816 On preventing Fire-damp Explosions in Coal-pits. *MM* 41, 32-5.

183. 1816 Prizes distributed by the Smithfield Club. *MM* 41, 195-6.

184. 1816 Remarks and Suggestions, for further improving and applying to Use the Government Trigonometrical Survey of Great Britain. *PM* 48, 427-31.

185. 1817 On the Mineralogical Description and Mineral Map of the County of Perth, which was in the Contemplation of Lord Gray and others who proposed to subscribe thereto, in 1814. *AP* 9, 219-21.

186. 1817 Remarks and Suggestions for improving the British Coin and the keeping of Money Accounts, preparatory to the entire Introduction of Decimal Money. *PM* 49, 16-23.

187. 1817 Mr. Farey's Correction of his Remarks in our last Number, regarding a Geologist being attached to the Government Trigonometrical Establishment. *PM* 49, 55-6.

188. 1817 On the indispensable Necessity of perfectly ventilating Coal-pits, and the Insufficiency and Danger of Safety-lamps as Substitutes for such Ventilation. *PM* 49, 57-61.

189. 1817 [by a Correspondent – A Constant Reader] Geological Queries, regarding the Coal Strata, Basaltes, and Red Marl of Northumberland and Durham, and on the Appearances of Coal etc. in Lincolnshire. *PM* 49, 122-5.

190. 1817 *To the musical professors & Amateurs, who may attend to try or hear Mr Liston's Patent large Euharmonic Organ, with the compound stops, exhibiting at Messrs. Flight & Robson's room, in St Martin's Lane* [London]. [Broadside at British Library].

191. 1817 [Anon] On the Exhibition and Harmonic effects of the Rev. Mr. Liston's Euharmonic Organ. *PM* 49, 213-5 [reprints no. 190 above].

192. 1817 [by a Correspondent – A Constant Reader] Answers to the Geological Queries by N. J. Winch Esq. with some Remarks, and further Queries proposed to that Gentleman and to other practical Investigators of the Strata of the North of England. *PM* 49, 250-6.

193. 1817 A Supplementary Table of Musical Intervals, for supplying the Omissions in Plate V of our xxviiith volume etc. *PM* 49, 360-1.

194. 1817 On the Nomenclature of Musical intervals, & the advantages of a set of symbols or characters, by which the mutual relations of the principal ones can be expressed, in the form of simple equations. *PM* 49, 362-7.

195. 1817 On Mr Liston's, or his euharmonic scale of musical intervals, extended to his tuning process, from 59 to 612 notes in the octave. showing thus, a division of the octave into 612 equal parts, or, as nearly so, throughout, as experiments in harmonics, or the most refined musical performances seem to require. *PM* 49, 442-8.

196. 1817 [by a Correspondent – A Constant Reader] Geological Queries to Mr Westgarth Forster, Mr Winch. Mr Fryer etc regarding the Basaltic and other Strata of Durham. Northumerland etc. *PM* 50. 45-50.

197. 1817 [by a Correspondent – An Engineer] On the Cases of Injustice which Authors sometimes suffer from other Writers. and from Annotators; particularly by the late Mr John Williams. Author of the *"Mineral Kingdom"*. *PM* 50. 116-21.

198. 1817 [by a Correspondent – A. C[constant]. R[eader]. Geological Queries regarding the Strata of the Vicinity of Bridlington; and some Acknowledgements to Nathaniel John Winch Esq., etc. *PM* 50, 200-4.

199. 1817 On forming Collections of Geological Specimens; and respecting those of Mr. Smith in the British Museum. *PM* 50. 269-74.

200. 1817 [by a Correspondent – A Constant Reader] Acknowledgements to Mr Westgarth Forster; further Geological Queries, on the Basaltic Strata of Durham and Northumberland: and suggestions regarding the Situation of the Granite Patches of the North of England, in its Series of Strata. *PM* 50. 358-62.

201. 1817 [Anon and in third person] Discoveries in the Basaltes, Greenstone, etc. *MM* 43, 36-7.

202. 1817 On searching for Coals. *MM* 44, 107-8.

203. 1817 [Anon – A Traveller] A Whyn-Dyke cut by a Stratum of Limestone. *MM* 44, 409-10.

204. 1817 [Stratigraphical Index for Sowerby's *Mineral Conchology*] idem for volume 2 in Volume 2 pages 240-51.

205. 1818 Mr. Smith's Geological Claims stated. *PM* 61. 173-80.

206. 1818 Mr. W. Smith's Discoveries in Geology. *AP* 11, 359-64.

207. 1818 [Alphabetical Index of places in Sowerby's *Mineral Conchology*] idem for volume 2. *PM* 52, 348-63.

208. 1818 On the very correct Notions concerning the Structure of the Earth, entertained by the Rev. John Michell as early as the year 1760; and the great Neglect which his Publication of the same has received from later Writers on Geology, and regarding the Treatment of Mr. Smith by certain Persons. *PM* 52, 183-95, 254-70 & 323-41.

209. 1819 On Wheel Carriages and their effects upon Roads. *PM* 53, 102-3.

210. 1819 On the Importance of knowing and accurately discriminating Fossil-Shells, as the means of identifying particular beds of the Strata, in which they are enclosed; with a List of 279 Species of Varieties of Shells, of which the several Stratigraphical and Geographical Localities are mentioned, which seem to require the particular and minute attention of the Collectors and Examiners of Fossil Shells in their natural Deposits. *PM* 53, 112-132.

211. 1819 A letter to Professor Jameson. *PM* 53, 275-6.

212. 1819 On Wheel Carriages and the Incapacity of most roads to sustain the Wear of very heavy Loads. *PM* 53, 276-8.

213. 1819 Free Remarks on the Geological Work of Mr. Greenough. *PM* 54, 127-32.

214. 1819 A Stratigraphical or Smithian arrangement of the Fossil Shells which were described in Latin by Martin Lister in 1678. *PM* 54, 133-40.

215. 1819 [Letter on Closeburn Lime quarry, Dumfriesshire] in J. Sowerby, *Mineral Conchology*, Volume 3, pages 82-3.

216. 1819 Evidence of John Farey, mineral surveyor and engineer (pages 41-5) in *Report from the Select Committee on the Highways of the Kingdom with the Minutes of Evidence taken before them*. British Parliamentary Papers ordered by the House of Commons to be printed, 25 June 1819.

217. 1820 On the alleged Plagiarisms of Frenchmen: on the Originality of the musical Instrument called the Sirene; and on the Pitch and Scale of the Notes of a French Standard Harmonica, which are said to have been ascertained thereby. *PM* 55, 321-3.

218. 1820 Free Remarks on Mr. Greenough's Geological Map. *PM* 55, 379-83.

219. 1820 [by a Correspondent – A.B.C.] Reflections on the Noachian Deluge and on the attempts lately made at Oxford for connecting the same with present Geological appearances. *PM* 56, 10-4.

220. 1820 On the recent Alterations said to be made by some Tuners of Musical Instruments, in the Places of the Wolves, or Largely tempered Concords, on common 12-stringed or Douzeave Keyed-Instruments. With some Queries thereon, to Musicians. *PM* 56, 341-2.

221. 1820 On the Specific Gravities of the Gases, and the different Musical Sounds which they occasion in the same Organ-Pipe. *PM* 56, 412-5.

222. 1820 [Anon] Large Organic Remains. *PM* 56, 459-60.

223. 1820 On different modes of expressing the magnitudes and relations of Musical Intervals; with some remarks, in commendation of Professor Fisher's Proportionally-tempered Douzeave. *American Journal of Science* 2, 65-81.

224. 1820 Letter dated 24 February 1808 addressed to Sir Joseph Banks [on the Geology of Lincolnshire], pages 293-300 in P. Thompson *Collections for a topographic and historical account of Boston*. London: Longman and Co. (republished in 1856 in the same author's *The History and Antiquities of Boston*. London: Longman and Co.).

225. 1821 A Series of Queries addressed to Dr Burney of Gosport, regarding Shooting Stars and Meteors, with some Suggestions on the same Subject to the Astronomical Society of London etc. *PM* 57, 346-51.

226. 1821 Remarks and Suggestions as to the State and Progress of the Government Trigonometrical Survey, with regard to the Dimensions, Figure and Structure of the Earth. *PM* 58, 54-7.

227. 1821 On Shooting Stars and Meteors which throw down Meteorolites, as distinguished from fiery Appearances low in the Atmosphere etc. *PM* 58, 183-6.

228. 1821 War destructive of the Liberty of Europe. *MM* 51, 126-7.

229. 1821 On the over-burning of Limestone. *MM* 51, 310-1.

230. 1821 [An Engineer – but Farey according to the index] Strictures on the Divining Rod. *MM* 52, 18-9.

231. 1821 Barometric Measurements near to Canals. *MM* 52, 129-30.

232. 1822 [Stratigraphical Index for Sowerby's *Mineral Conchology*] idem for volume 3 in Volume 3 pages 187-94.

233. 1822 [Alphabetical Index of places in Sowerby's *Mineral Conchology*] idem for volume 3. *PM* 59, 321-35.

234. 1822 [Anon] Examination of the north western slope of the Snowdonian range of Mountains. *MM* 53, 250-1.

235. 1822 On overflowing Wells and Boreholes. *MM* 54, 35-7.

236. 1822 On Procuring Fresh Water on the Sea Shore. *MM* 54, 202-3.

237. 1822 On Mr. Cumberland's Theory. *MM* 54, 300-2.

238. 1823 *Report of Mr John Farey, Mineral Surveyor and Engineer, of 37 Howland Street, Fitzroy Square, London, on various matters relative to the Rocks and Quarries of Slate belonging to the Crown, in the Commons of the parish of Llanllechid, in the county of Carnarvon*. dated 20 March 1822 (pp. 8-38 with a

letter). In British Parliamentary Papers relating to Slate Quarries on the Crown's Estate on Llanllechid Common in the County of Carnarvon. Ordered by the House of Commons to be printed 11 April 1823.

239. 1823 [Stratigraphical Index for Sowerby's *Mineral Conchology*] idem for volume 4 in Volume 4 pages 153-60.

240. 1823 [Alphabetical Index of places in Sowerby's *Mineral Conchology*] idem for volume 4. *PM* 61, 333-47.

241. 1823 On different Modes of Working Coals, and of ventilating the Works. *PM* 61, 99-101.

242. 1823 On the unconformable Position of the Pontefract Rock of Sandstone, with respect to the subjacent Coal-measures, as shown in the new *Geological Map* of Yorkshire. *AP* [2] 5, 270-8.

243. 1823 Some Particulars regarding the Ashmolean Catalogue of Extraneous Fossils published in Latin by Mr Edward Luid (or Llwyd); and recommending a Translation of the same to be made and printed. *AP* [2] 5, 378-80.

244. 1823 Reply to Mr. Luckcock and Britannicus [on production and consumption of agricultural produce]. *MM* 55, 308.

245. 1823 [Anon] Notice of volumes 1 to 4 of Sowerby's *Mineral Conchology*. *MM* 55, 543.

246. 1823 In answer to Mr. Fitch and Capt. Layman on procuring sea water in the Sea-Sand. *MM* 56, 37-40.

247. 1823 On Artesian Wells and Boreholes. *MM* 56, 309.

248. 1824 On the velocity of Sound and on the Encke Planet. *PM* 64, 178-81.

249. 1824 [Anon] Smith's Geological Atlas part 6. *MM* 57, 546-7.

250. 1824 [Anon] Smith's Geological Atlas part 6. *PM* 63, 447-9.

251. 1824 [Anon] Need for Smithian principles in boring for Coal. *MM* 58, 240.

252. 1824 Spirit and Mercurial thermometers compared. *MM* 58, 389-90.

253. 1824 On Concert-pitch. *Harmonicum* 2, 176-8.

254. 1825 On the comparative Expenses of Toll Roads in different Counties and Queries on M'Adamizing Streets. *MM* 58, 486-8.

255. 1825 On Hazel Nuts found in Peat Bogs. *PM* 66, 314-5.

256. 1825 Defence of Captain Scoresby. *MM* 59, 102-3.

257. 1825 Joint Stock Companies. *MM* 59, 145-52.

258. 1825 [Improvement of our Metropolis]. *MM* 60, 312.

VI

REFERENCES

Anon 1820 Notices respecting new books – *The Cyclopaedia* . . . by Abraham Rees. *PM* 56, 218-24.

Kassler J. C. 1979 *The Science of Music in Britain 1714-1830.* Two volumes. New York: Garland Publishing.

Scholes P. 1948 *The Great Dr Burney.* Two volumes. Oxford: University Press.

Sherborn C. D. 1937 Brewster's *Edinburgh Encyclopaedia.* Issued in 18 vols from 18 - - [1808] to 1830. *Journal of the Society for the Bibliography of Natural History* 1, 112.

Taylor E. G. R. 1966 *The Mathematical Practitioners of Hanoverian England 1714-1814.* Cambridge: University Press.

Coal hunting at Bexhill 1805–1811:

HOW THE NEW SCIENCE OF STRATIGRAPHY WAS IGNORED

This paper describes the lengthly attempts made to find coal at Bexhill, East Sussex, between 1805 and 1811 in hope of reviving the Wealden iron industry. The chief promoter of this Sussex Mining Company, William James (1771–1837), was convinced true coal was easily available in Sussex. The London-based mineral surveyor John Farey (1766–1826), on the other hand, from 1806 correctly urged that it was impossible to find true coal here, on the stratigraphic grounds taught him in the field from 1801 by William Smith (1769–1839). Farey knew that the Sussex adventurers had first, confused pieces of lignite for seams of coal and second, were hunting many thousands of feet above the geological horizon at which Smith had demonstrated that the main deposits of English coal occurred. Farey supported his view by articles, some printed in agricultural journals, and a unique newspaper advertisement. His advice was ignored. The project failed, at a total cost of well over £30,000.

INTRODUCTION

T he Income . . . would be immense . . . from the Value [these Coal Mines] will give to the Surface of the [Bexhill] Estate by the Establishment of an Harbour and of Furnaces, Foundries and other Manufactories which prevail in a Country abounding, as I conceive this does, with valuable Minerals. Then we may say to our political Enemy we also have a *Coast of Iron* (W. James, Report to the Duchess of Dorset, November 1805).

Until the 1760s, the Weald of Kent, Surrey and Sussex was the leading iron-making centre in Britain, based on locally mined iron ore and locally produced charcoal. Thereafter it lost out to competition from other areas, especially Scotland, which used coal and new technology. By 1800 Ashburnham was the sole surviving furnace here, and that closed in 1813.[1] It was natural, though, that local people should hope that the industry was not finally lost, but could be revived by finding in the Weald the fuel which had taken it elsewhere. Meanwhile coal had also been increasingly substituted for furze and underwood for domestic and industrial purposes, with imports to Sussex rising fourfold between 1780 and 1807.[2]

The first reports that 'coal' occurred in Sussex had been promoted in 1800 at Ashdown Park and Newick and 1801 at Heathfield and in St Leonards

Forest,[3] but Bexhill became the first, and only, Sussex location at which serious exploration was to be made. The Revolutionary and Napoleonic Wars made their greatest impact on the Sussex coast following the breakdown of the Peace of Amiens, as Napoleon amassed his army of invasion at Boulogne in 1804. The Government put in hand a major programme of defence, building Martello towers backed by barracks. The towers around Bexhill were still being built in 1808.[4] Four brickfields had also been established, probably firing the bricks in large open clamps which used a by-product of coal, town-ash.[5] Bexhill was in the midst of this activity, with a barracks for 3000 men built in 1804 north-west of the village, with brickfields a couple of miles to east and west at Bulverhythe and Cooden,[6] and twelve Martello towers sited between Bulverhythe (number 43) and Rock House Bank (number 54).[7] The manor of Bexhill had long been possessed by the Sackville family, and from the estate of the infant Duke of Dorset land for the barracks was compulsorily purchased and the land for the brickfield at Cooden was requisitioned.[8]

The main driving-source behind the Bexhill coal-hunt, William James, later noted that it was on 30 May 1805 that he had first 'perused letter from Mr Neale about the existence of Coals' on the Dorset estate.[9] Certainly on 17 August 1805, Josias Routledge, a copyholder of Bexhill manor, wrote to

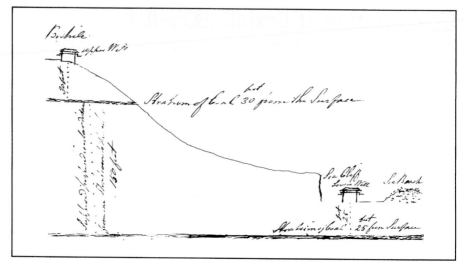

Fig. 1. Josias Routledge's sketch of the situations of coals at Bexhill, August 1805. That in the upper well was 30 feet below surface, that in the lower 25 feet, with the supposed perpendicular distance between them 150 feet (CKS U269 E173/2).

Thomas Neale or Neill, steward to the Duke's mother, the dowager Duchess of Dorset, with a sketch reproduced here as Figure 1, that:[10]

> The Coal . . . found here, has been discovered by Wells, . . . sunk for the accommodation of the Troops stationed here, and . . . at the Sea Side, by Wells that have been sunk for the use of the Martello Towers building by the Sea . . . The Stratum in which the Coal lies is nearly similar in both Wells . . . The thickest stratum of Coal that was found in the upper Well was about the thickness of your hand and the piece now sent the thickest of any in the lower one . . . There were several strata of Coal about a foot apart from each other above these, of less thicknesses all laying in the same strata.[11]

Routledge had clearly been the first to comment on the supposed coals found in these excavations. His second surviving letter to Neale asked, if five or six were to subscribe £50 or £100 each in searching for coal (Routledge not hesitating to be among them), would the Duchess of Dorset join them? If they then found coal, the first profits would naturally go to repay the expenses incurred. But would the Duchess allow these same parties to have exclusive rights to work any coal found thereafter?[12] It seems to have been John Forster, the solicitor who handled the

settlement of the Duchess's Bexhill land transactions with the Government,[13] who involved the most important figure in the saga, William James, since Forster was then a partner with James in Staffordshire coal-working.[14]

WILLIAM JAMES (1771–1837)

James is best known, and achieved his place in the *DNB*, as a railway pioneer. But he was also a highly successful land-agent and surveyor of Wellsbourne, Warwickshire, and 14 Carey Street, London, and, until his bankruptcy in 1823, a major coal-owner of West Bromwich, Staffs.[15] In a sycophantic biography his daughter claimed that 'as a mineral surveyor his fame appears to have been universal' and that, 'as a geologist and mineralogist, Mr James can take rank with the first men this country has ever produced', from his many undertakings 'to demonstrate the existence of coal mines on the estates of [his] friends in those situations . . . contrary to the general opinion of all other miners', because of 'all the noblemen and gentlemen [who] placed great reliance upon his judgement in respect both to the value and management of mineral as well as landed property'.[16] More realistically, Robert Stephenson (1803–1859) who knew James well

VII

through their railway projects, instead thought he was 'a ready, dashing writer, but no thinker at all on the practical part of the subject he had taken up . . . His fluency of conversation I never heard equalled, and so you would judge from his letters'.[17]

Some such letters survive of those he wrote to the geologist William Smith (1769–1839).[18] James had been one of the first people to receive copies, in 1799, of Smith's pioneering stratigraphic record of the 'Order of the Strata in the Vicinity of Bath'.[19] On 7 October 1800 James wrote to Smith 'there is not a doubt of your making a Fortune, if you will make proper exertions and not spend your time *Gratis* . . . No man has worked with more industry, or to less purpose than yourself. Beware of democratic principles'. His last known letter to Smith, dated 25 January 1805, noted further:

> you have been long acquainted with the similarity of our Views and Labors . . . rest assured that however great may have been your labors, and extensive your Observations you have yet very much to learn, and I can . . . only believe that you have as yet a Glimmering Knowledge of . . . the Arrangement of Strata. I assure you that I have with great Attention and in most parts of this kingdom, considered the subject of your Pursuit and Study, and I have made very little Way towards a general arrangement.

How little, Smith's pupil, John Farey, was very soon to demonstrate to him.

Commissioned by the Duchess of Dorset, James started his 'mineralogical View of the Estate at Bexhill and its Neighbourhood' on 22 October 1805 and reported on the 27th that:

> A Miner pretending to offer an Opinion in a New Country on viewing one Spot only, it is an airy Dream. With infinite Care and much Labour, I have completed my View, which extended over many Miles of Country, and the Result is, that I can deliberately state my thorough Conviction of the Existence of Strata of Coal in your Grace's Estate.[20]

His view had involved 'examining the range of Strata from Robertsbridge, Battle and to the east of Hastings', and:

> the crops of Rocks along the Beach at Bexhill and collecting specimens of secondary strata indicative of Coal, and in viewing and investigating the Lie and Disposition of the Strata along the Beach from Hastings to Bexhill. In traversing the Ravines and Brook

Courses behind the Priory to Crowhurst Estate and thence to Bexhill. Attending Routledge about the researches made by him for Coal . . . and journeying along the Coast completing the Investigation of Specimens on the Beach as also examining for 9 miles to the extent of the Estate towards Pevensey. Examining the Interior of the Estate and the Ravines and Brook Courses and taking particulars of the Crop of the Rocks and Strata . . . and delivering my Sentiments on the existence of Coal and advising . . . how to form a Company to explore the Estate.

On 25 October James explored the wells already sunk and with Routledge traced the strata to Ashburnham and the ironstone working there and then to Battle. The next day was spent examining the country adjacent to Ashburnham, but he could 'not discover the Crop of any indicative Strata similar to the Ironstone found at Bexhill'.

On 10 November James sent his 16-page *Report on the Strata indicative of Coal at Bexhill in Sussex and its Neighbourhood* to Her Grace.[21] According to the Report, the 'Material Structure of this Island' was produced by 'three Great Causes'. First, 'the hand of the Creator at the Creation . . . in the Composition of those Saxa . . . considered by Miners *Primitive Rocks*, void of organic bodies as Granite, Schistus, Chalk [sic] &c'. Second, these were then disrupted 'at some subsequent period by *Volcanic Effects*, and the introduction of a new Genera of Saxa . . . and deposits of decomposed Primitive Strata'. Third, came 'the Creation of the Secondary Strata, formed of the minute parts of the decomposed primitive Rocks and an amalgamation of Animal, Vegetable and Marine Fossils . . ., such as Argillacious and Calcareous Gritstone, Greys, Penant Stone, secondary Schistus, Limestone and Chalk, Clays, Marls, Bines, Ironstone, Clunch, White Fluae, Peldron, Coal &c'. It was these last which James had 'researched'. He also discussed dip and the occurrence of faults or breaks which threw strata 'to Day', to appear on the surface. When this did not happen, as in Sussex, one was forced to 'discover the Existence of subterranean Minerals from the superficial Indications and God knows, at present our knowledge on that subject is so very limited that the wisest Man and most experienced Miner must confess *he is just beginning to learn*'.

James continued:

> Bexhill is situated in a District of Secondary

VII

Strata, which is terminated by the Chalk Hills . . . Coal being considered by Chemists and Miners to be an accumulation of Vegetable . . . Substances, . . . the strata indicative of Coal are those which contain Vegetable Fossils. The Strata next the surface at Bexhill, lying nearly horizontal . . ., [their] internal structure cannot be so accurately determined as tho' the Angle or Dip was greater, but those Strata, which I have traced . . . indicate most conclusively that Strata of Coal are deposited under this Estate. These strata he identified in order downwards:

1 Argillaceous *Grit Stone* with an Ochery Appearance,
2 a *Steatite* called *White Fluae*
3 the *Cliff* or Argillaceous Schistus with Vegetable Impressions
4 two thin Bines of *Argillaceous Ironstone*
5 Argillaceous Strata in Rotchy Rock, called *Grey Fluae*
6 thin seams of inferior *Fire Clay*
7 *Batt* containing Vegetable Impressions
8 *Strong Clunch Rocks* with Lissums or Seams of Coal and Cannel . . . and Impressions of Vegetables
9 *Ironstone, Bines* & *Cliff*
10 seams of *Batt* with Vegetable Impressions.[22]

James also noted that 'on the beach and in the crop of the strata out at Sea, I found specimens of *Strong Clunch Rocks, Peldron* and a very valuable measure of Argillacious Ironstone, more than six inches thick . . . On the Land Side below the Camp at Bexhill is a strong Spring highly impregnated with Iron, unquestionable percolating thro . . . Ironstone Strata'. 'These several Appearances' James thought were:

conclusive evidence of the Existence of Coal in this Estate, but whether that Coal is sufficiently thick to be recovered at a profit it is impossible for me to determine. At all events, I think the Indications are so strong, the situation so inviting, and this Mineral so valuable, that a fair prospect may be seen by Speculators to induce them to sink pits and prove the Country.

James had 'good reason to think that at about 60 yards on the Beach a Stratum of Coal will be met with below the Peldron rock, but where there is scarce any obliquity [dip] in the strata my Opinion on the subject is altogether hypothetical'.

James' *Report* also had sections on *Proof of Mines* and *Royalty and Prospect of Advantage*. In the first he suggests proving the area 'to the Depth of One

Hundred Yards at the Least', and that 'there are three situations which ought to be tried: at the Beach [Site 1, half a mile SE of the village], on the Downs [Site 2, at the NE corner of Bexhill Down], and near the west Martello tower [on the Dorset estate, and later numbered 51 — Site 3]'.[23] James recommended that Routledge and his friends form a partnership to treat with the Duchess for a grant of mines for 21 years. As to any royalty, 'in this case where no Coal is recovered within 300 miles Coastways [i.e. where none occurs nearer than that] and where all the Risk and Expence are to be defrayed by the Speculators, the Royalty ought to be low as an inducement'. James concluded 'it is impossible to conceive in any Situation prospects more flattering than what present themselves on the supposition that a good Coal shall be found at Bexhill. At a Royalty of 1/ 10[th on] the selling price, the Income arising from this Source would be immense . . ., with other royalties on clays, ironstone etc . . . most considerable'. In his touching finale, James was 'so thoroughly convinced of the Existence of the Coal, that I am ready to take any Share in the Company to be formed for the proof and Working thereof'. All the similarities which James had used throughout this *Report* to base his opinion upon were merely 'superficial indications'. This was the crucial point in James's methodology. He completely failed to use any knowledge of stratigraphic ordering which Smith had certainly passed onto him from 1799.

James' bill for the view and report was £95. As he anticipated substantial increases in surface land values, James was also retained to undertake valuations of the Stoneland and Bexhill estates and for these he was paid £200 in the year ending 25 March 1807 and £300 in each of the following three years.[24] James was still acting as land-steward of the Bexhill estate in December 1810.

AN ACT OF PARLIAMENT

At the end of November James was in London consulting the Duchess of Dorset, her husband Lord Charles Whitworth, and their solicitor John Forster, on how to proceed after such an enthusiastic report.[25] They agreed that an Act of Parliament should be obtained to enable mining leases to be granted. James and Forster drafted the Bill, which was examined by a House of Lords Committee. On 24 April 1806, 'Mr William James, Land agent' duly appeared before it and reported:

that to the best of his knowledge & belief there are under the said Manor & Lands valuable Mines, Veins, Layers & Strata of Freestone, Clay, Sand, Ironstone & other valuable Substances. That within the said Manor & Lands there are good situations for building Houses, Warehouses & Manufactories & for making Wharfs, Docks & Harbours. And that there are persons of respectability willing to treat for the working of the said Mines & for making the said Buildings [etc.] . . . And being examined, says, that he viewed the Lands about two months ago, & there was an idea there were Mines & that Coal & Ironstone might be found from the appearance of Lissums or Laminae of Shale in the Wells upon the Duke's Estate — that he has not examined beneath the Surface, that the Land has been viewed by no other person that he knows of — that he is not the least able to form any Estimate of the increases of the value of the Estate, but that they have had offers to treat for the payment of a given Royalty — offers for Leases of 40 or 50 years, & to pay them, a Royalty per Ton of a Tenth and Twelfth of the produce, & which he considers as very advantageous to the Estate.

Finally James certified the acreage of Bexhill manor was 1124, with an annual rent £430,[26] in a notably less enthusiastic report than the one he had earlier given to the Duchess. In the Commons the Bill was committed to John, 'Mad Jack', Fuller (c. 1756–1834)[27] and General Charles Lennox (1764–1819),[28] MPs for Sussex, for their consideration. On 19 May Fuller reported that they also found the allegations true, and the Bill was enacted unamended four days later. Significantly, the printed Act's reference to 'Valuable mines, Veins, Layers and Strata of Freestone, Clay, Sand, Ironstone, Minerals, and other valuable Substances' at Bexhill, now added Minerals to the list earlier given by James under oath.[29] He had clearly been less certain in his evidence before Parliament than in the euphoric *Report* prepared for the Duchess.

PARTNERS IN THE SUSSEX MINING COMPANY

Of the Sussex Mining Company, little is known. A report in 1809 noted that there were eleven partners but named only three. Nine can be identified and a

tenth (Bill) suggested. It is always possible that more than one share was held by one of the partners.[30]

1. John Bagnall (1759–1829), iron and coal master of West Bromwich.[31]
2. Samuel Bill (c. 1773–1847), coal and timber-merchant of West Bromwich, James's coal exploration manager in Sussex, may also have been a partner. He was James's agent at Pelsall Colliery, Walsall from 1813,[32] but he went bankrupt in 1821,[33] and died in 1847.[34]
3. Arabella Diana, Duchess of Dorset (1769–1825), left on her first husband's death in 1799, 'an accumulation of wealth as had scarcely ever been vested among us, in a female, and a widow'.[35]
4. Samuel Fereday (1758–1839), banker, coal-owner and ironmaster of Sedgley and Bilston, Staffs. who also went bankrupt, in both 1817 *and* 1821[36] and fled to Boulogne, France, where he died.[37]
5. John Forster (1752–1834), of Lewisham and Lincoln's Inn, London, the Duchess of Dorset's and the company's solicitor.[38]
6. William James, company treasurer and chief instigator, bankrupted 1823.
7. 'Mr Payton or Peyton', named in the 1809 report.
8. Josias Routledge (fl. 1791–1822), from 1791 of Bexhill and London, who in 1805 prompted the Dorset estate to call in William James. His address in 1822 was in Dieppe, France, which must be the result of his near or actual bankruptcy.[39]
9. Nicholas Vansittart (1766–1851), MP, then Secretary to the Treasury 1806–7 and later Chancellor of the Exchequer 1812–23,[40] and partner with James in the Balls Hill and Golden Hill collieries, near West Bromwich, Staffs.[41]
10. The Duchess' second husband Lord Charles Whitworth (1752–1825).[42]

Another, with knowledge of the Midland coal fields, who was also involved was Matthew Boulton (1728–1809) steam engineer and entrepreneur,[43] perhaps in connection with the supply of steam engines. An undated 'extract of a letter from Messrs Boulton and Watts, Birmingham' reads:[44]

Our Mr Boulton had not an opportunity of forming a conclusive opinion as to the existence of Coals at Bexhill but the cursory observations which he was enabled to make incline him strongly to think that there are Coal Measures at Bexhill, the stratification of the Grounds, both in the parts where the Trials have been made as well as in the adjoining Country, is very analogous to that of the

VII

principal Coal Districts and as far as any Inference can be drawn from this analogy, there are very good grounds for concluding that coal will be found at Bexhill.

EXPLORATION FOR COAL STARTS

The Company did not wait for the passage of their Act but had already started their trial borings. Their first, euphoric, press report appeared on 2 June 1806:

A discovery was last week made near the sea coast, in this county, which will probably prove of great national importance: — A vein of exceedingly fine coal about four feet thick, and of considerable extent, was discovered and proved, on an estate the property of the Duke of DORSET, at Bexhill; and some hundreds of miners, with proper engines for raising the coals, we understand, are engaged for that purpose. By the above important discovery, the fine iron of the county may probably be again wrought with vast advantage to the public, as well as to individuals; divers manufactories may be successfully established, and the agricultural interests of the county, by the increased facility and reduced expence in burning lime, be materially assisted. Veines of coal have been discovered . . . in other parts of our county, where, had the research been pursued with as much spirit and perseverance as at Bexhill, the result would, probably, have been as successful.[45]

Further news followed on 23 June:

the persons engaged in the coal works on the estate of the Duke of Dorset, at Bexhill . . ., have met with so much encouragement through the whole progress of their laudable pursuit, that they have determined on sinking a shaft for raising the coal immediately, and the whole county must feel an interest in the success of their operations. We expect shortly to hear of miners being employed in a similar research, not many miles from this town [Lewes].[46]

This first site, in the close by the sea shore as shown in Figure 1, was near the present Ashdown Road (NGR TQ 754077).[47] Only the first 27 feet of strata here had so far been sunk, and all the strata below, to a total depth of 164 feet, had instead been bored.[48] At this depth, the borers penetrated Bed 32, a 'Strong Coal, 3 feet six to eight inches thick'; the 'vein of

coal' announced on 2 June 1806. Sinking shafts, large enough for two men to work in, was expensive, while boring, with thin iron rods which percussed and pulverized the strata, was much cheaper, but gave much less reliable data.[49]

The local paper also continued to announce how this trial was now stimulating others elsewhere in Sussex:

we are glad to find that the success which attended the research for coal at Bexhill, has enabled others to similar pursuits, in situations, perhaps, equally promising. At Rotherfield several men are actively employed in boring; at Maresfield, we understand, some good specimens have been obtained . . . [while those] of good coal have been drawn on the estate of John Newnham Esq., at Maresfield: and the men employed, we understand, are got down to a stratum of considerable promise.[50]

Samuel Bill, Bexhill exploration manager for James, was certainly involved in boring at Rotherfield,[51] and in December 1807 he also was offering advice to George Shiffner of Coombe Place in Hamsey, on a design of tramway to bring chalk from the pit at Offham Hill, near Lewes, to a wharf on the River Ouse. This was an alternative to that which William Jessop had proposed. This project had been put forward in 1807 by the local civil engineer Cater Rand, who will reappear in this story.[52]

JOHN FAREY ARRIVES

During July and August 1806 the geologist and polymath, John Farey, was busy drawing up a stratigraphic cross 'section of the earth from London to Brighton' for Sir Joseph Banks (1743–1820), President of the Royal Society, and making regular visits to Sussex.[53] His section, over five feet long, gave details of all the strata that Farey had recognized in the Weald working downwards from a 'marker' stratum, the Chalk of the North and South Downs. During his Sussex fieldwork Farey stayed with his brother Ben, steward to the Earl of Chichester at Stanmer. On 12 September he made an excursion to the Bexhill workings. Farey described this visit in an anonymous letter to the *Agricultural Magazine*, which he acknowledged as his, although James seems also to have been involved. It reported that William James was:

a miner of the first repute. These works have

proceeded with a degree of spirit and enterprize, which has placed all the eastern parts of the county on the tip-toe of expectation as to the vast benefits they are to receive, not only in the supply of coal for domestic use, but as the means of again opening their dormant iron furnaces. So little doubt of success is entertained that extensive stabling have been built of brick, in the most substantial manner, and horses [?*recte* houses] for the superintendants and workmen in the intended mines, on a spot where formerly no buildings were standing. Two wells or shafts have been sunk, each about eighty feet deep, principally through sand or soft sand-stone rock, some of the layers of which are said to contain impressions of vegetables, like Feras [*recte* ferns], considered in most parts of England as a certain indication of coal veins being at no great distance. No other appearance of coal have yet, it seems, been met with in sinking the shafts, but the principal expectations are formed on the report of some experienced practical miners who bored in this place some months ago, and reported that their auger passed through a four feet vein of coals, at one hundred and sixty five feet deep. The water comes in so plentifully that the steam engine working in one of the pits, and a horse gin, with buckets in the other, to assist it, were barely able to keep down the water some days ago. A second steam-engine is about to be erected, . . . and no expence whatever will be spared, in exploring a treasure so valuable for this part of the county, as a four foot vein of coals, and doubtless the gaining of this, would secure other and thicker veins below it. We sincerely hope that no circumstance will occur to damp the ardour of the parties in this interesting search after an article of such general interest as fossil coal.[54]
From this it is clear that work had now been going on for some time at the second Bexhill sinking, at a site above the town on the edge of Bexhill Down (also shown in Fig. 1 — about NGR TQ 737 083),[55] whereas the first shaft was soon to be drowned out by sea water entering it.[56] That two expensive shafts, instead of exploratory borings, were now being sunk provides the best proof of how high hopes for the Sussex Mining Company had become. Farey had seemed enthusiastic in print. But to his friend (and correspondent of William James) William Smith on

29 September, he described, in much more guarded terms, his visit to these 'quixoit[ic] coal works' — implying that he already saw the Sussex scheme as impractical.[57] His letter continued

I was surprized to find various slight *vegetable impressions* some like Fearns in a soft red grit rock in Hastings Cliff E of the Town, & plenty of detached pieces of *bituminous wood*: they shewd me the same fearny leaves from their Coal Shaft at Bexhill as a certain sign of Coals, but said I 'one swallow don't make a summer'. They begin to sink at highwater mark & will never get down to the pretended 4 foot vein of Coals which they *bored thro'* at 165 feet, as I expect, for at 80 feet they employ a Steam-Engine & a horse-gin bucketing nearly all the time, & all below them is sandy or grit rock I expect.[58]

Farey first discussed the significance of William Smith's work and how 'our newly acquired knowledge of the stratification . . . has rendered the expectation vain of digging coals in all these parts [south of London] notwithstanding the confident assertions in your magazine [which had reprinted the reports of the previous June] to the contrary by certain speculators in Sussex' in an article dated 16 February 1807 published in the *Monthly Magazine*.[59] Farey was now on record with his opinion that it was impossible to find any true coal at Bexhill.

Nevertheless, the local newspaper still reported in June 1807:

The success which has attended the operations of the miners, in search of coal at Bexhill, in this county . . . has been quite equal to the expectations of those most immediately concerned in the laudable undertaking, and that a lamb was in consequence roasted whole for an entertainment given one day last week.[60]

The next report, a month later, ominously made reference to materials *other than* coal having now been found, since:

The miners employed in search of coal, at Bexhill have lately met with a stratum of earth, which it has been discovered, contains a large portion of SALT of a very excellent quality . . . it is conceived, from specimens which have been produced, that it may be extracted, by a very simple process, to good advantage; but if not, a soil so highly impregnated with saline matter, must be found extremely valuable as a manure.[61]

VII

Farey now felt forced to enter the debate in earnest. He published a new letter, 'On the finding of Coal' dated 9 August 1807, inspired by the report of additional 'Kenal Coal' being found between Heathfield and Waldron in Essex, in the *Agricultural Magazine*. Farey pointed out that these places were in fact in Sussex and noted 'the avidity with which some ignorant or interested persons circulate stories, respecting the finding of fossil *coal*, in situations where our present knowledge of the strata of the British island, utterly preclude the expectation'. He referred to his recent articles 'Coal' and 'Colliery' just being published in Abraham Rees's *New Cyclopaedia*,[62] and noted how this new, supposed coal discovery in Sussex, had yielded:

> several pieces of bituminated wood . . . a few months ago, lodged in greyish white clay. A box full of these supposed pieces of coal were sent up to London to the proprietor of the wood, John Fuller Esq. one of the Members [of Parliament for Sussex] . . . who did me the honour to consult me thereon. I can confidently state, both from the inspection of these specimens, and from a practical examination of this very neighbourhood, which I made during a mineralogical tour last summer that nothing can be more dissimilar, than these bituminated woods, and indeed all the other fossils of Sussex, are to the coal and accompanying strata of Newcastle, and every part of England where regular fossil coal is dug. I could point out perhaps fifty places at least, where a white or pipe-clay stratum might be found; and in which, in all probability, detached pieces of this bituminiated wood might, and, indeed, repeatedly for ages back, have been found in digging ditches, pits, wells &c in this stratum: as every curious person's cabinet will there testify: it is the more surprising, therefore, that the finding of such, should now be trumpeted forth as new and extraordinary discoveries. One of Mr Fuller's pieces of wood-coal, which he had the intention of presenting to the Mineralogical Cabinet of the Royal Institution, was about ten inches long, seven inches broad, and four inches thick; exhibiting the grain and fracture of a piece of wood, some parts of which appeared still in that state, while others of its lamina were so highly bituminized, as to seem like pitch. It appeared . . . to be a fragment of

a very large tree, and to have been entirely surrounded by the clay, some of which was adhering to it.[63]

Farey's *Cyclopaedia* article 'Colliery' also referred to the Sussex trials. It noted that he had brought:

> specimens of a reddish soft sand-stone last summer from the foot of the cliff on the sea beach, about two miles east of Hastings in Sussex, from the vicinity of a cottage called the Grovers,[64] which contained so many detached pieces of bitumenized wood, that were an augre-hole to be bored into it, and supplied with water, &c. something like the appearance of penetrating a coal vein, might be had in the borings; and it is this stratum dipping under Bexhill, situate about 6¹/₂ miles to the westward, which . . . has been there mistaken in the borings for a seam of coal, but which the improved boring apparatus of Mr Ryan,[65] . . . would have detected, and saved, perhaps, a most unparalleled waste of money in the measures now pursuing.[66]

Farey's August 1807 article drew a powerful response from the Lewes schoolmaster, engineer and surveyor, Cater Rand (1749–1825). Rand had been a school and writing master, scientific lecturer, accountant and bookseller until his bankruptcy in 1784.[67] Thereafter he became active as patentee, land-surveyor and civil engineer all round Lewes.[68] Rand, who, as 'C. Rand Lewis Esq. Sussex', had been a confusing subscriber to one of the first works to bring aspects of British stratification to public attention in 1778,[69] had pronounced favourably on both the 'coal' found in the earliest 1800 discovery at Newick,[70] and on that first found on Fuller's land between Heathfield and Waldron in December 1801,[71] but which was only drawn to public attention between July 1807 and February 1811.[72] He was probably involved with our Bexhill speculators from the early days. Rand had ordered the last edition (1792) of Whitehurst's book for the Lewes Library Society in August 1803, with other books on 'Subterraneous Surveying' and the 'Analysis of Minerals' in 1805, but none of the books he had ordered for this Society by 1807 gave any details of the new stratigraphic results which Smith and Farey had by then worked out.[73]

Writing as 'Sussexiensis', Rand had addressed the Editor of the *Agricultural Magazine*, but this reply to Farey appeared only in the *Sussex Weekly Advertiser*. He first accused Farey of 'lugging in what he does

VII

not seem to understand . . . in a most illiberal, invidious and ungentlemanly stile'. Rand thought the hunt for coal in Sussex, that 'truly useful and valuable article', was 'laudable'. He was astonished that Farey could declare that Sussex contains none. He thought it contained an 'abundance of good coal . . . if sought for judiciously under the direction of an able Engineer'. Rand, confusing Rees's earlier edition of Chambers' *Cyclopaedia*, which was 'at his elbow but with not a single word to be found relative to the subject', with Rees's *New Cyclopedia* (for which Farey was then busy writing), thought that 'a man who can deliberately . . . declare his knowledge of the whole fossilated strata of Sussex to an hitherto imperforated depth, and a surface of more than a THOUSAND SQUARE MILES from a hasty superficial survey of a solitary parish or two' must be a fool and a 'Sussex Pudding Head'. Rand's diatribe concluded that 'our best mineralogists' were in favour, since 'fine specimens of Coal have been drawn from Sussex' already, whatever the opinion of Farey, our 'Sussex mineralogical Tourist'. Rand thought 'the works now carrying on at Bexhill, with so much spirit in exploring a run of coal, has every flattering prospect of success from the appearance of the accompanying strata abounding in the usual vegetable impressions'. It is fascinating to see Rand's unfair criticism of Farey as a 'tourist' in 1807 mirrored by others, who instead criticized Farey's 'stage coach geology', in 1812 and 1813.[74] Rand gave final evidence of his total ignorance of Farey's new stratigraphic results by concluding that, since in the Newcastle coalfield they had had sometimes to reach twice the Sussex depth before good working seams were found, they should persevere at Bexhill.[75]

FAREY RENEWS HIS ATTACK

John Farey was absent from London from September to December 1807, and heard of Cater Rand's letter only on his return. He immediately set to work to reply, in a long letter which reprinted Rand's letter, made 47 detailed comments and summarized his reasoning against any true coal occurring in Sussex. It was a devastating reply and is a fascinating, as well as historic, document. The article is dated 4 January 1808 and appeared in the January 1808 issue of Dickson's *Agricultural Magazine*. In the hope of influencing local opinion, and redeeming his reputation among the original readers of Rand's letter, Farey also advertised in the newspaper which

had printed it, under the date of 13 January 1808.

This announced that Rand had greatly misrepresented him, because there were 'the most invincible arguments . . . against the probability of finding useful and real COAL, in any of the south eastern counties of England'. Farey intended to reprint Rand's letter with his answers in a forthcoming publication in 'hopes that his motives for wishing to avoid the discussion of a question of SCIENCE in a newspaper will be seen and approved, by all who are capable of understanding the subject'.[76]

Farey's article expressed amazement that Rand should be unaware 'that a great and scientific Dictionary [Rees's *New Cyclopaedia*] has been some years publishing' [since 1802]. When the old *Dictionary* which Rand cited was published, in 1786–88, 'little was known of the *stratification* of the British Islands, that could apply satisfactorily to . . . the probability of finding Coal in the South-eastern Counties'. But this old *Dictionary* had carefully separated Bovey Coal from common Staffordshire

FOR THE LEWES AND BRIGHTHELMSTON JOURNAL.

SUSSEX COAL

MR. FAREY, finding lately on his return from a journey, that some person under the signature of SUSSEXIENSIS, in this paper of the 5th and 19th of October last, has greatly misrepresented his observations in Dr. DICKSON's AGRICULTURAL MAGAZINE for August, particularly, by replying to remarks on a pretended DISCOVERY in ESSEX, and representing the same to have been said of SUSSEX; and by making reference therein, to CHAMBERS's DICTIONARY, edited by Dr. Rees, THIRTY YEARS AGO, instead of DR. REES's NEW CYCLOPÆDIA, NOW PUBLISHING, which was expressly quoted, and wherein (vol. viii. part 2.) it is presumed, that the most invincible arguments are to be found, against the probability of finding useful and real COAL, in any of the south eastern counties of England. He takes this method of informing all whom it may concern; that the LETTER OF SUSSEXIENSIS, has, at his request, been reprinted in the AGRICULTURAL MAGAZINE, to be next published (for January), and that thereto he has subjoined AN ANSWER. Mr. F. presumes to hope, that his motives for wishing to avoid the discussion of a question of SCIENCE in a Newspaper, will be seen and approved, by all who are capable of understanding the subject.
12, Upper Crown-street, Westminster, 13th January 1808.

Fig. 2. John Farey's announcement of January 1808 regarding Sussex Coal.

or Pit Coal, the two sorts that Rand had 'so laboured to confound'. Their distinction, Farey said, was the principal issue. 'Regular Coal occured in *seams* or strata while the *Bituminated Wood* of the pipe clay stratum in Sussex and elsewhere is lodged in *casual and detached masses* only.' The '*stratification* of the country' confirmed 'that *the South-eastern Counties of England contain no Fossil Coal*, likely to be of use as a substitute to that supplied by the mines from Somersetshire to Durham or counties to the west'.[77]

Farey emphasized the 'importance of the facts, and principles of *stratification*, discovered by William Smith and others, which are contained in Vol. 8 part 2 and have no where else been published', that is, in his own 1807 articles in the *Cyclopaedia*. He had traversed Sussex for 'several hundred miles, for verifying the observations, and perfecting myself in the theory taught me by Mr Smith, and that from materials and specimens thus collected, I have prepared a *Section* of its principal Strata, which has now been some months in the hands of the President of the Royal Society'. Farey recorded that 'to Mr *Fuller*, also, I stated in my report (on his consulting me as I have mentioned) the principles, somewhat at length, on which I recommended him not to listen to the delusive prospects held out to him, as had in so many instances been done to proprietors, not in Sussex only, but in every other county, where no Fossil Coal was likely to be found'.[78] Farey ended:

in all the numerous trials for Coals in the South-eastern Counties which have been related to me . . . scarcely one of them was deemed by the Coal-finder or the credulous populace, to be *conclusive* — either the [boring] rods broke, or were maliciously destroyed — the owner, a mean spirited person, grew tired, and would advance no more money — the miners were bribed by some rival Coal-owner — or, forsooth, some evil-minded person, by his words or writings, *checked* the Ardour of the undertakers.

Farey felt it was very important that assertions relating to the occurrence of *vegetable impressions* at Bexhill be confirmed, as:

in all the country surrounding Bexhill, [Farey had] found no vegetable forms, wood perhaps excepted; it is true, that when visiting the intended Coal-shaft there, on the 12th of September, 1806, I was shewn, and took specimens, of what the Superintendent of the

works with great confidence produced, as minute *vegetable impressions*, that were dug up at fifty feet below the surface, but on inspecting these afterwards, they were found to be only ramifications of a ferruginous substance . . . with no *form or characters of a vegetable*, or of any other organised remain.

Farey asked that, if any such have indeed been found, that they be forwarded to John Martin Cripps of Lewes for study. Cripps (1780–1853), Farey's local informant, was a knowledgeable mineralogist,[79] and another, local, man who had now sided against these Sussex Coal Adventurers.

Farey continued to advise against the Bexhill trial. In 1809 he noticed the 'error which has occasioned the useless expenditure of hundreds and sometimes of thousands of pounds, in numerous instances, as some in the vicinity of Boxhill [sic] in Sussex can testify, on recent experience'.[80]

FAREY'S ADVICE IS IGNORED

The Bexhill trials continued despite Farey's best efforts. At the meeting of the 'acting Partners of the Sussex Mining Co.' on 13 July 1809, Samuel Bill listed the strata recently bored at Cooden to a depth of 451 foot 5 inches.[81] These had now been bored through at a third site, the first which James had himself suggested, on the coast 'near the western Martello Tower' on the Dorset estate, later numbered 51.[82] The minutes of this meeting note how the Dorset estate had now been proved to the depth to which their Company had engaged and that one of the shareholders, John Forster, had now 'notified . . . Mr James his Determination not to incur individually any [further] expences in Boring'.[83] It was resolved that he and any other gentleman were at liberty to withdraw and that any that did would be 'indemnified from that date from all further Calls and Expences' and would receive a share of the value of the property of the Company from those partners who did continue the Works, at the end of 12 months, or sooner if the works were abandoned. Clearly there was now dissent amongst the ranks. It seems already to have been the public perception that the venture had failed: Mary Frewen writing from Northiam on 8 May 1809, to thank her brother for the cocoa nuts, wondered whether he was tempting her to have a hothouse, as 'if the Bexhill Colliery had success it might have been an additional inducement'.[84]

At a general meeting on 12 August 1809, the

value of the 'Stock' costed only up to July 1808, was estimated to be £11,399, leaving a balance against the Company of £5031 with a surplus of £6369. Stocks of timber, bricks and iron had all been included and the [steam] engines valued at nearly their original costs. The sinking of the shaft at the Down site (no. 2) and all the expenses of the establishment had also been estimated at cost price. The cost of coal for sinking and drawing water at the Down had been not less than £120 a week. Since that sinking 'most of the stock has been employed & consumed, the Engines have become deteriorated & th[at] work abandoned', but calls had now been made upon the Company to the amount of £700 per share, being £7700 on 11 shares. The total expenses at Bexhill to 8 July 1808 were noted as £30,754 . . . The August 1809 minutes concluded:

the view of the present Measures [still] Boring through [at a new fourth, but unlocated, site] being very promising, and the Expences on that account only amounting to £22 per week. Resolved that the Borings be continued and the Miners employed till next General meeting. Resolved that the Treasurer do make such calls as he may think necessary for paying Debts & prosecuting the works. Resolved that in Case at the boring a stratum of Coal be bored into, the operation do instantly cease, and a Special Meeting be called of all the Partners to attend the perforation.

Hope clearly still sprang eternal! This August 1809 meeting resolved to adjourn until 16 October 1809.

The last heard in any actual search for coal here is a receipt from William James, dated 25 March 1810, on account of the Sussex Mining Company. It reads 'received of Her Grace the Duchess of Dorset as Guardian to the Duke of Dorset, the sum of Two Hundred and Seventy two pounds on account of the Sussex Mining Co. as per account for [two years advanced] Rent returned to them on account of the abandonment of Works'.[85] The Dorset estate at least had abandoned its involvement.

But if these partners had done so, James was not yet so ready to give up. This remarkable notice (which shows the care with which newspaper notices should be taken as historical sources) appeared in the *Monthly Magazine* in 1811:

SUSSEX . . . The individuals who have engaged in the expensive mine works at Bexhill, will be amply rewarded for their enterprise, having sunk through a valuable mine of most

excellent coal 10$^{1}/_{2}$ yards thick, on their estate, which mine is now at work. This will be of great public advantage, as the works are over the main fault, in a situation where, till now, the most experienced miners considered no mine of coal could exist; and it proves the extent of mine land to be greater by many hundred acres than it was before supposed to be.[86]

Notices referring to this same 'Sussex Coal Mine at Bexhill' appeared elsewhere.[87] The original source, the *Sussex Weekly Advertiser*, had instead additionally reported that it was 'some of those spirited individuals who [had] prosecuted the expensive mine works at Bexhill, and [who] afterwards proceeded into Staffordshire [i.e. James and his partners there, Bagnall, Fereday, Forster and Vansittart who] have been amply rewarded for their enterprize'.[88] They had there discovered new deposits of the famous 10 yard Coal, in the West Midlands, not in Sussex.[89] This was where many of the Sussex Mining Company's partners had come from, and whither they now returned.

But this same notice continued, to show how obtuse these speculators still remained in their Sussex aspirations, 'The above Company, we understand, intend to re-commence their works at Bexhill, in about a twelvemonth, by which time the Staffordshire mine, it is expected, will produce a very large income'. But, despite such terminal optimism, nothing more is heard of the Sussex Mining Company.

Farey made his last comment on the Bexhill trials in 1812, when he admitted 'his too confident and hasty expressions that no distinct small *vegetal impressions* like those of the Coal-measures were to be found in the British Series [of Strata] above the Lias and Red Marl'. He noted his call to produce to Cripps any such specimens from the 'disastrous scheme of sinking for Coals at Bexhill', had failed to produce a single response. Farey now thought these 'imperfect accounts of *Wood-Coal* or bituminated Wood in the Pipe Clay Stratum ([which is] below the Chalk and not above it as I now understand the clay of Purbeck [Dorset] to be)' were at a different and somewhat lower stratigraphical level [in Sussex]; but 'without much altering my opinion of the improbability of discovering even one *useful seam of Coal* at Bexhill, or any other part of Sussex'.[90] This shows the problems Farey still faced in correlating these Wealden strata, having been the first to

VII

unravel their stratigraphic order in Sussex, and his ability to change his mind when new data became available.

James had 200 copies of a 'specification of estate at Bexhill', printed by Richard Taylor and Co. on 17 July 1812.[91] No copy of this survives but it must relate to the final sale of James's own estate at Bexhill, where he 'possessed a large house'.[92] The notice a month later of the sale of a freehold estate at Bexhill may relate to the same property, and to James' final departure from the town.[93]

POSTSCRIPT[94]

Local, as opposed to national, comment on these Sussex trials was very muted. In 1815 a Hastings *Guide* noted acidly, and rather inaccurately, that 'Bexhill . . . was once thought to have been fertile in Coals till some speculative gentlemen at a very considerable expense ascertained the contrary'.[95] W. D. Conybeare and William Phillips noted in 1822 how Smith's Ironsand Formation (the stratum to which these Wealden rocks were then assigned) 'much resembles, in some places, . . . the great coal formation. These circumstances have led to expensive but abortive attempts to prove [coal] from these beds near Bexhill, attended with so great an expense'.[96] Thomas Webster in 1826 pointed out that 'it was from the abundance of the iron, the beds of clay and shale with vegetable impressions and the fragments of charcoal in the sandstones, that the expectations had been formed of finding coal in this formation, before the difference between lignites and true coal was generally understood'.[97] This assessment highlights Farey's truly original contribution to the debate, as it was he who had first correctly concluded, by early 1807, that the complete *difference* between lignite and true coal, and their separate English stratigraphies, were indeed the crucial questions.[98]

William Fitton later tried to claim that it was he and his fellow workers at the Geological Society who had been the first to shed light on the stratigraphy of Sussex, from the 1820s onwards. He wrote in 1833 how

> the assemblage [at Bexhill] is very nearly the same in mineral composition with that of the coal measures. . . differing from it only in geological place and the character of its fossils. It is not surprising therefore at a time when the geological relations of the groups in

England were less understood than at present, these carboniferous portions of the Wealden group should have excited hopes of discovering coal . . . the borings, which some years ago were conducted . . . at Bexhill, were much more excusable than has been supposed.[99]

This gentlemanly judgement ignores the ungentlemanly contribution of John Farey, who had argued on these very same, scientific, grounds for the abandonment of the Bexhill and other Sussex attempts, while they were in progress from early in 1807, well before the Society was founded in November 1807. The early members of the Geological Society were interested in disputing 'the nature of coal . . ., not where to find it',[100] so that when this later became a matter of interest to them, they happily rewrote history to advance their own, later, contributions. Rupke has rightly emphasized the lowly image of economic geology in this English school of geology at that time, when its 'economic aspect was . . . thought not to merit academic rank'.[101]

Such polarized history should make us re-examine the contributions made by such men as Farey and Smith to the advance of geology and ask how fairly such 'practical' geologists were treated by the 'gentlemen geologists' of the soon-to-be-formed Geological Society of London, and how their 'practical' achievements have fared at the hands of 'academic' historians. It was only in 1875 that William Topley (1841–1894) noted the remarkable role Farey had played in Sussex.[102]

The stratigraphic emphasis that Farey had originally so encouraged led eventually to the discovery of true Carboniferous Coal, lying unconformably beneath Mesozoic rocks, in Kent nearly a century later.[103] The first thoughts of this had come in 1855 when Robert Godwin-Austen (1808–1884) read a paper on the possible extension of such coal fields in the south-east of England. The 1871 exploratory boring near Battle by the Sub-Wealden Exploration Committee encouraged further efforts and a historically misinformed article, full of hindsight, about Wealden Coal, but which reported an industrial archaeology survival from the 1805 attempt.[104] The later cored boring by the South Eastern Railway Company near Dover, which discovered coal there in 1890, equally inspired another such 'historical' article on James's doomed, and without hindsight misguided, attempts to mine coal in Sussex.[105]

VII

Acknowledgements

This work has been financially, and appropriately, supported by BP Exploration. I also owe real thanks to the staffs of the Record Offices in Chichester, Lewes, Liverpool, Maidstone, and the House of Lords, of the Public Library, Brighton and at Bexhill Museum, as well as to Ben Bather (London), Stella Brecknell (Oxford), John Cooper (Brighton), John Farrant (Lewes — who very kindly edited a first version), John Fuller (Tunbridge Wells), William F. Hedger (Bexhill — who equally helpfully read and made many comments on this first draft), Vicky Haworth (Newcastle-on-Tyne) and Stella Pierce (Wincanton), for much help and encouragement. Documents from the Sackville archives are quoted, and Figure 1 reproduced, by kind permission of the Trustees of the Knole Estate.

NOTES

Abbreviations

CKS   Centre for Kentish Studies, Maidstone
DNB   *Dictionary of National Biography*
ESRO East Sussex Record Office, Lewes
GM   *Gentleman's Magazine*
GSL   Geological Society, London
SA   *Staffordshire Advertiser,*
SAC   *Sussex Archaeological Collections*
SWA   *Sussex Weekly Advertiser.*

1   H. Cleere & D. Crossley, *The Iron Industry of the Weald* (Cardiff: Merton Priory Press, 1995), 208–11.
2   J. H. Farrant, 'The seaborne trade of Sussex, 1720–1845', *SAC* **114** (1976), 111.
3   These early Sussex coal 'expectations' will be fully discussed in a future paper.
4   *SWA*, 23 May 1808, 3.
5   M. Beswick, 'Bricks for the Martello towers in Sussex', *Sussex Industrial History* **17** (1987), 20–27.
6   A. Hudson, 'Gazetteer of barracks in Sussex during the Revolutionary and Napoleonic Wars 1793–1815' (1986, typescript in Sussex Archaeological Society Library), 3. L. J. Bartley, *The Story of Bexhill* (Bexhill: Parsons, 1971), 120–21.
7   Numbering follows the coastal section published by W. H. Fitton, 'Observations on some of the strata between the Chalk and Oxford Oolite in the south-east of England', *Transactions of the Geological Society of London* (2) **4** (1836), 103–400, *see* pls. Xa–b.
8   CKS, U269 E173/2, J. Howarth to the Duchess regarding compulsory purchase, 10 & 29 August 1805.
9   CKS, U269 A364/3, Original Voucher no. 172.
10 C. J. Phillips, *History of the Sackville Family,* **2** (London: Cassell, 1929), 305–6. CKS, U269 E173/2, Routledge to Neale, 17 August 1805.
11 CKS, U269 E173/2, Routledge to Neale, 17 August 1805, his sketch (fig. 1) is also preserved.
12 CKS, U269 E173/2, Routledge to Neale, August [after 17th, 1805].
13 CKS, U269 E173/2, undated [1805].
14 E. M. S. P[aine], *The Two James's and the Two Stephensons* (Dawlish: David & Charles, 1961), 24.
15 *SA*, 19 July 1823, 2.
16 P[aine], 15, 23–4, 93, 98.
17 Robert Stephenson, in S. Smiles, *The Lives of the Engineers,*

3 (London: Murray, 1862), 190.
18 Oxford University Museum, Smith archives.
19 J. Farey, 'Mr Smith's geological claims stated', *Philosophical Magazine* **51** (1818), 173–80 (178).
20 CKS, U269 E173/2, 10 & 27 October 1805.
21 CKS, U269 E173/1, 10 November 1805.
22 Much of James's language here is highly arcane. The trade skills and private language then used by such coal seekers had already been reported in 1789 to be their 'grand arcana': J. Brand, *History and Antiquities of Newcastle on Tyne* **2** (London: White, 1789), 679. For some of this language *see* W. J. Arkell & S. I. Tomkeieff, *English Rock Terms* (London: Oxford University Press, 1953).
23 There have been such changes at all these sites since then that nothing of industrial archaeological significance is now to be seen at them.
24 CKS, U269 A364/3, Original Voucher 1806–7 no. 172. U269 A140, General Estate Accounts, vols 2, 3, 4, 6 and 7, 1806–1810.
25 CKS, U269 A364/3, vouchers nos 170 and 171.
26 House of Lords Record Office, Committee Book, **51** (24 April 1806), 120–22.
27 J. Lawrie, 'John Fuller Esquire of Rose-Hill', *Proceedings of the Royal Institution of Great Britain,* **44** (1971), 331–57. G. Hutchinson, *Fuller of Sussex: a Georgian Squire* (Hastings: private, 1993). R. G. Thorne, *The House of Commons 1790–1820,* **3** (London: Secker & Warburg, 1986), 845–8.
28 Thorne, **4**, 414–15.
29 46 Geo III liv.
30 CKS, U269 A364/3, voucher no. 171 notes that early in 1806 James met 'Fereday, Bagnall and other Miners in Staffordshire to get Members of the Company'. P[aine], 13, notes the involvement of 'the late Lord Whitworth, Duchess of Dorset, Mr Vansittart, and others'.
31 *SA*, 28 November 1829, 4.
32 P[aine], 95, 102.
33 *SA*, 22 September 1821, 2.
34 *SA*, 23 & 30 January 1847, 5.
35 V. Sackville-West, *Knole and the Sackvilles* (London: Lindsay Drummond, 1947), 192, 200, 208.
36 *SA*, 24 May 1817, 2 & 10 February 1821, 2.
37 R. P. Fereday, 'The Career of Richard Smith 1783–1868' (unpub. M.A. thesis, Univ. of Keele, 1966), 168–76.
38 *The Times*, 3 December 1834, 6.
39 ESRO, ADA 164–6 (kindly supplied — with so much else — by William Hedger, who also located the baptisms of three of Routledge's children at Bexhill 1791–95).

[40] Thorne, **5**, 437–41.

[41] Liverpool Record Office, 385 JAM 6/1.

[42] Phillips, **2**, 277–302.

[43] *DNB*.

[44] CKS, U269 E173/2.

[45] *SWA*, 2 June 1806, 3, and repeated in *Monthly Magazine*, **21(1)** (July 1806), 584–5.

[46] *SWA*, 23 June 1806, 3. *Bath Chronicle*, 26 June 1806, 3.

[47] ESRO, AMS 5819, plan of the Manor of Bexhill drawn up by James in 1808 shows this first site as 'the Engine'. A redrawn and modified extract of this map, also showing this first site, is in W. H. Mullens, *A Short History of Bexhill* (Bexhill: private, 1927), facing p. 19. CKS, U269 A140/6 1808–9, and A364/8 for payment of James' bill for . . . perambulation and Survey of Bexhill manor and fair plan thereof £341-6-6 and his voucher.

[48] Three versions of the measures sunk and bored through here survive: CKS E 173/2 (MSS watermark 1805); GSL, QP Misc 76 (MSS watermark 1804) donated 5 May 1809 by Dr John Macculloch, 1773–1835; and in Gideon Mantell, *The Fossils of the South Downs* (London: Relfe, 1822), 35–6. A modern re-interpretation appears in F. H. Edmunds, *Wells and Springs of Sussex* (London: Memoirs of the Geological Survey, 1928), 57.

[49] H. S. Torrens, 'Some thoughts on the complex and forgotten history of mineral exploration', *Journal of the Open University Geological Society* **17(2)** (1997), 1–12. The boring rods used at Bexhill were provided by the Birmingham engineer William Whitmore (1747–1819) and he or Boulton & Watt may also have provided the steam engines used, see P[aine], 12.

[50] *SWA*, 30 June & 7 July 1806, 3; reprinted in *Monthly Magazine* **22(2)** (August 1806), 94–5.

[51] CKS, U269 A364/6, Bill's bill for expenses in 1807, paid 18 June 1808.

[52] ESRO, SHR 1966. *Monthly Magazine* **27** (April 1809), 309. M. Robbins, 'The first Sussex railway', *Railway Magazine* **117** (July 1971), 355–7.

[53] H. S. Torrens, 'Patronage and problems: Banks and the earth sciences', in R. E. R. Banks *et al.* (eds), *Sir Joseph Banks: a Global Perspective* (London: Royal Botanic Gardens, 1994), 49–75.

[54] Anonymous, 'Sussex, September 20, 1806', *Agricultural Magazine* 2nd ser., **1** (September 1806), 211–12. Farey later acknowledged having written this, *Agricultural Magazine* 3rd ser., **2** (January 1808), 31.

[55] ESRO, AMS 5819 also shows this second site, as 'Engine Pit'. Another 'Plan of Bexhill' by J. Andrews of Epsom dated 1808 in Bexhill Museum marks this site as 'Coal pits'.

[56] Mantell, 35–6.

[57] *See* H. S. Torrens & T. D. Ford, 'John Farey (1766–1826): an unrecognised polymath', in J. Farey, *General View of the Agriculture and Minerals of Derbyshire* **1** (1811, reprinted Matlock: Peak District Mines Historical Society, 1989), 1–28.

[58] Oxford University Museum, Smith archives.

[59] J. Farey, 'On wells and springs', *Monthly Magazine* **23** (April 1807), 211–12.

[60] *SWA*, 29 June 1807, 3.

[61] *SWA*, 27 July 1807, 3.

[62] *The Cyclopaedia* (London: Longman etc.) **8**, part 16, articles 'Coal' and 'Colliery', published 10 August 1807.

[63] J. Farey, 'On the finding of coal', *Agricultural Magazine* 3rd ser., **1** (1807), 115–17.

[64] Shown as the Govers, east of Hastings, on the section by Thomas Webster, 'Observations on the strata at Hastings, in Sussex', *Transactions of the Geological Society of London* 2nd ser., **2(1)** (1826), 31–6, pl. 5.

[65] James Ryan patented his boring apparatus, to recover oriented cores from borings for the first time, in 1805. Farey's is one of the first published statements of its potential; *see* H. S. Torrens, 'James Ryan (*c*. 1770–1847) and the problems of introducing Irish "new technology" to British mines in the early nineteenth century', in P. J. Bowler & N. Whyte (eds), *Science and Society in Ireland: the Social Context of Science and Technology in Ireland, 1800–1950* (Belfast: Institute of Irish Studies, 1997), 67–83.

[66] 'Colliery', *The Cyclopaedia* **8**, part 16.

[67] *GM*, **54(2)** (1784), 559.

[68] J. H. Farrant, 'Civil engineering in Sussex around 1800, and the career of Cater Rand', *Sussex Industrial History* **6** (1974), 2–14.

[69] John Whitehurst, *An Inquiry into the Original State and Formation of the Earth* (London: Bent, 1778).

[70] MSS Coal 1:29 (dated 1800) in Sutro library, San Francisco, California. *SWA*, 30 June 1806, 3. Mantell, 34.

[71] *Brighton Guardian*, 30 June 1830, 4. P. Lucas, *Heathfield Memorials* (London: Humphreys, 1910), 91–4.

[72] *SWA*, 13 July 1807, p. 3. *MM* **31** (February 1811), 92.

[73] ESRO, Lewes Library Society Minute Book, R/L11/1/4 (kindly supplied me by John Farrant).

[74] Torrens & Ford.

[75] *SWA*, 5 & 12 October 1807, 4.

[76] *SWA*, 18 January 1808, 3.

[77] J. Farey, 'On the finding of coal in the south-eastern counties of England', *Agricultural Magazine* (Dickson's) 3rd ser., **2** (Jan. 1808), 22–31, dated 4 January.

[78] Farey's report to Fuller seems not to have survived.

[79] *DNB*.

[80] J. Farey, 'On the supposed universal distribution of fossil coal . . .', *Nicholson's Journal of Natural Philosophy* **22** (1809), 68–70.

[81] CKS, U269 E173/2 (watermark 1808).

[82] At Tower 51 on the coastal section published by W. H. Fitton, 'Observations on some of the strata between the chalk and Oxford oolite in the South-East of England', *Transactions of the Geological Society of London* 2nd ser., **4** (1836), 103–400, see pls. Xa–b. For the geology here *see* R. D. Lake, 'The stratigraphy of the Cooden borehole, near Bexhill, Sussex', *Institute of Geological Sciences Report* 75/12 (London, 1975).

[83] CKS, U269 E173/2, minutes dated 13 July to 12 August 1809.

[84] ESRO, FRE 2225 (a reference kindly sent me by Philip Bye).

[85] CKS, U269 A364/9, voucher 213.

[86] *Monthly Magazine* **31** (May 1811), 392.

[87] *The Tradesman, or Commercial Magazine* **6** (1 June 1811), 502.

[88] *SWA*, 4 March 1811, 3.

[89] *Victoria County History, Staffordshire* **17** (London: Oxford University Press, 1976), 40. James's work, in this known coalfield, had earlier drawn the remarkable comment that 'entrepreneurs like William James of West Bromwich . . . were men as isolated as they were outstanding': *Victoria County History, Staffordshire* **2** (London: Oxford University

Press, 1967), 101.

90 J. Farey, 'Geological observations . . .', *Philosophical Magazine* **39** (1812), 93–106 (100).

91 St Bride Printing History Library, London, R. Taylor & Co., 1812 Ledger p. 164.

92 P[aine], 97.

93 *SWA*, 24 August 1812 (from William Hedger).

94 The fallout of these trials at the London Geological Society, founded in November 1807, is discussed in a paper in press in *Annals of Science*.

95 An Inhabitant, *The Hastings Guide*, 4th edn (London, 1815), 50.

96 W. D. Conybeare & W. Phillips, *Outlines of the Geology of England and Wales* (London: Phillips, 1822), 137.

97 Webster, 31.

98 W. Topley, *Geology of the Weald* (London: Longmans, 1875), 51, 59, confirms the frequent occurrence of lignite in the Bexhill beds.

99 W. H. Fitton, *Geological Sketch of the Vicinity of Hastings*

(London: Longman etc., 1833), 49.

100 R. Porter, 'The Industrial Revolution and the rise of the science of geology', in M. Teich & R. Young (eds), *Changing Perspectives in the History of Science* (London: Heinemann, 1973), 323.

101 N. Rupke, *The Great Chain of History* (Oxford: Clarendon Press, 1983), 18, 200.

102 Topley, 10–12, 348. Details of modern Wealden stratigraphy will be found in W. Gibbons, *The Weald* (London: Unwin, 1981) or R. W. Gallois, *British Regional Geology: the Wealden District*. 4th edition (London: HMSO, 1965).

103 G. Tweedale, 'Geology and industrial consultancy: Sir William Boyd Dawkins (1837–1929) and the Kent Coalfield', *British Journal for the History of Science* **24** (1991), 435–51.

104 Anon., 'Under the Wealden', *Engineer* **34** (2 August 1872), 65, with references to earlier 1868 articles also of interest.

105 Anon., 'A Sussex coal mine', *Bexhill Chronicle*, 9 April 1889, reprinted in *The Standard*, 20 April 1889, 3.

VIII

James Ryan (c.1770–1847) and the Problems of Introducing Irish 'New Technology' to British Mines in the Early Nineteenth Century

INTRODUCTION

The life and work of the Irish-born mining surveyor and engineer James Ryan throws light on the problems encountered by early nineteenth-century inventors trying to interest the commercial world in their work. Ryan invented a boring device which for the first time recovered cores and so gave superior information about underlying rock strata. This invention could also be used to ventilate mines. His work enjoyed only partial success in Ireland, and he encountered much opposition when he moved to England later in his career. Ryan's experiences show how even important inventions can be rejected on the grounds of short-term expediency. It is also apparent that his Irish origins generated a certain amount of prejudice against him among the already-suspicious English mine owners.

RYAN'S IRISH ORIGINS

From the commonplaceness of his name, Ryan's early history must remain unknown. He was certainly born in Ireland in about 1770 (from his age at death). Conceivably a Tipperary land surveyor and grocer of the same name, recorded as active from 1750 might be related.[1] A later claim that Ryan hailed from Donegal relates only to his work there in 1814 (see below).[2]

Ryan later cryptically noted that 'whilst endeavouring, since 1792, to gain a living in Britain, I adopted mining as a calling'.[3] This introduces a second problem for the historian, namely the papyrophobic nature of much mining activity. Ryan noted in one of the few pieces of auto-biography that he wrote that he had 'from a youth, a powerful pre-dilection for the study of minerals and their various geological character and position'.[4] This brought him his first post in Ireland in 1800, a date confirmed by his 1831 note that he had been '30 years as a miner'.[5] Ryan later acknowledged that he then 'became noticed by some partial friends who had attached great importance to the systematic arrangement of my ideas'. Among these was the celebrated Irish scholar Richard Kirwan, who had published *Observations on Coal Mines* in 1789.[6] Since Ryan's birthplace is unknown, whatever schooling he received is equally uncertain. Ryan's own copy of Samuel Cunn's London edition of *The Elements of Geometry* dated 1754 which survives, may be a relic of his school days.[7]

Ryan's first mining employment was as 'mineral surveyor' working for the Grand Canal Company of Ireland (GCI) from 1800.[8] This company soon started a new and expensive mining venture in 1803, to build up trade on the Canal, by leasing some collieries near Castlecomer.[9] By April 1804 Ryan was based at these Doonane collieries, north-east of Castlecomer on the borders of the then counties of Kilkenny and Queen's County (now Laois). This was in an area of considerable technical innova-tion in an Irish context, both for canals and collieries. A new canal from Monastereven to Castle Comer had been proposed in 1800, with a branch to 'the coalpits'[10] and at these Doonane pits both the first Newcomen steam engine in Ireland had been erected, in 1740, as well as the first separately condensing Boulton and Watt steam engine, in 1782–83.[11] But the output of the Doonane collieries had not been able to justify the high and, with yearly premium payments, recurring costs of this last innovation and they had gone bankrupt in 1791.

GCI archives show Ryan was busy exploring for coal by boring at Doonane late in April 1804.[12] He was soon in dispute with his English superior, Israel Rhodes, perhaps because Rhodes 'does not seem to have had any mining experience'.[13] The GCI Board supported Ryan over Rhodes in July 1804 and this may have precipitated Rhodes' return to England in November 1804. In the following months Ryan was quarrelling with David Aher (1780–1841) who replaced Rhodes.[14] The matter in dispute was whether the GCI should stop exploring and start working some of their coal pits. Otherwise Ryan could see the expense would accumulate and ruin the company to 'the disgrace' of those involved earlier.[15]

By this date Ryan was also busy in North Wales. He had been employed here by the coal owner Edward Roscoe at a Bagilt colliery and nearby by Sir Thomas Mostyn, Bart (died 1831). Sometime later in 1804 he was also 'employed by Rigby & Hancock at Llanwarder Colliery, near Bagilt' again in North Wales.[16]

RYAN'S CORE-BORING INVENTION

Ryan's most significant invention, his new boring apparatus, is first heard of early in 1804. At a meeting of the Dublin Society on 19 April 1804 with antiquary General Charles Vallancey (1721–1812) of the Royal Engineers in the Chair (whose help Ryan later acknowledged[17]), it was noted that 'Mr James Ryan, having laid before the Society a core, brought up by a new borer of his invention, which appears to them to have great merit, and that Mr Ryan is deserving of public encouragement.' It was then resolved 'that Mr Ryan be applied to for information, if he will furnish the Society with such a borer of his invention, to sink 40 feet: and what will be the expense of the same'.[18] On 22 November 1804 'Mr James Ryan [again] attended the Society, and informed them that in compliance with their requisition . . . he had made a boring instrument, for which he had obtained a patent, and was ready to furnish the Society with one of six feet diameter, made exactly according to the tenour of the patent.'[19]

Ryan here claimed to have patented his boring apparatus by 22 November 1804 but this clearly only referred to the fact that he had instigated patent proceedings. His English patent was set in motion for him between 24 January 1805 and 12 February 1805 by an attorney, Walter Henry Wyatt of Hatton Garden, London, while Ryan was still in Ireland. He was named as 'engineer to the Undertakers of the Grand Canal', which company made him first a loan of £120 and then 'paid the entire expense' to allow him to take out this patent.[20] The patent was granted on 28 February 1805,[21] and included a plate with detailed drawings of all the comprehensive elements of his new equipment.[22]

Details of the patent were circulated in both literary and technical literature in England. The first commented that 'as the soil to be bored is of various consistencies in different places, and, at different depths, often times in the same place, Mr Ryan has contrived various bits to be attached to the boring-rod' and concluded, 'by some of the above-mentioned tools, cores or solid cylinders of the soil may be extracted, from one to twenty inches in length, and from one to twenty inches in diameter, by which the dip of the different strata met with in boring may be ascertained, as well as the nature of minerals and other substances which occur.'[23] The technical press also commented favourably that Ryan's patent provided a model, that 'fairly and distinctly' described his invention, unlike so many others which were often 'exhibited to conceal.'[24] The patent was also noticed in German.[25]

The first to publish his observations on Ryan's novel invention was Richard Lovell Edgeworth (1744–1817) of Edgeworthstown, Co. Longford, long a member of the Lunar Society and now an enthusiastic supporter of Ryan's endeavours, as Ryan again acknowledged.[26] Edgeworth wrote in 1806:

> I take this opportunity of mentioning a trial that I lately made of Mr Ryan's patent Boring Machine, for exploring the strata of mineral countries. This

machine acts like the surgical *trepan*, and cuts a circular hole, leaving a *core* in the middle which is drawn up from time to time by a pair of self-closing tongs. I found that this gentleman's machine, from his want of knowledge how to push his own invention, had not obtained due credit; I therefore invited him to try his machine at my house, that I might witness the result of the experiment. Two men, relieved from time to time, cut a truly circular hole, five inches and a quarter in diameter, through a block of hard limestone, leaving a *core* a little taper of four inches and a half diameter and six and a three quarters in length, which core is now in my possession. It is as true and as smooth as if turned and polished in a lathe, and the under surface shews exactly the fracture by which it was detached from the block at bottom. By this contrivance mines may be ventilated at small expense, the specimens of strata that are bored through may be brought up whole and unmixed, no deception can take place; and not only the dip, but the fracture, lap, and accidents to which each stratum is liable, may be determined at any depth. True vertical and horizontal sections may be previously obtained of any spot where it is proposed to sink shafts; and the subterraneous topography of a whole district may be laid down upon a map with confidence before any great expense is hazarded on mere speculation.[27]

Comments agreeing with Edgeworth soon followed: 'We wish [Ryan's invention] more success than it has hitherto met with; for it would be found extremely useful in ascertaining the quality of minerals and other substances, as well as the dip of the strata; at the same time that it is applicable in sinking wells.'[28]

At least two others had tried out Ryan's invention in Ireland, for mineral prospecting. Both wrote letters dated 1806 which were first used in a printed Testimonial for 'J. Ryan, Mineralogical Surveyor, Ventilator and Director of Mines &c', of circa 1812.[29] The first was Samuel Perry (1765–1829) of Woodroof, near Clonmel, County Tipperary,[30] an Irish barrister and land owner who had graduated from Trinity College Dublin in 1786. He 'made several trials on my estate at Woodroof, in search of coal. I found the Patent Engine of your invention vastly to surpass the old system of boring with the chisels and much more satisfactory: your Engine not only bringing up the Cores entire, but it also shews the layer of each stratum as it goes through; whereas, with respect to the chisel, as it cuts every thing to pulp, nothing . . . can be ascertained to satisfaction.' The second, L. [recte John von Prebeton, Count] Van Wilmsdorf Richards, was a Hannoverian migrant who married into the Richards family of Mac Mine, Wexford in March 1802.[31] He took the name Richards in May 1802.[32] He thus inherited estates at Rathspeck [Rathaspick], three miles Southwest of Wexford and had 'given over further trial on my estate, because of meeting pudding-stone (a substance supposed to exclude coal) . . . [but] I am perfectly satisfied, if any [coal] had been there, by trying with your Patent Engine, I could not have missed it as the cylinders came up perfect, and enabled any person to judge of their properties.'

Edgeworth's first announcement had made it clear that Ryan's invention was already seen to have two main uses, for mineral prospecting (by cutting cores of the strata penetrated) and for ventilating mines (by boring passages). Richards, by 1806, had also used Ryan's device in successful drainage work, suggesting a third potential use for the invention.

In August 1807, the geologist and polymath John Farey (1766–1826) confirmed that Ryan's invention

> consists in using a cylindrical cutter, something like the surgeon's trepan-instrument, by which a core, or solid and unbroken piece of each stratum, is cut, and by other tools brought vertically to the surface, in the exact position as to the cardinal points, in which it stood in the strata, and thus the quantity and direction of the dip, as well as the exact nature of the strata or measures, are correctly ascertained.[33]

Farey was clearly struck with the novelty of this device by which the crucial dip of strata could be monitored underground.

Ryan had been told by the GCI on 15 April 1805, that 'they will have no further use for his services after 1 May', the GCI having employed Archibald Cochrane (1749–1831), ninth Earl Dundonald to visit and report on the Doonane Collieries on 18 April, with Richard Griffith (1784–1878), later famous as an Irish geologist.[34] Cochrane's long report was very dismissive of Ryan's work, some of whose borings were underneath 'strata known to lay under the Coal' and of his invention.[35] Borehole G which was 35 yards deep had been 'performed with Ryan's large borer . . . in very hard rock . . . and had hitherto cost upwards of £13 per yard, a most enormous price . . . more than double the price at which a Pit could be sunk'. Furthermore Lord Dundonald claimed that he

> does aver that by the old method of boring the strata . . . may be ascertained with the greatest precision and at the same time much less expense than can be done by Mr Ryan's method of boring, which was practised in Scotland 25 years ago and discontinued from its not having been found under many circumstances to answer equally well as the old plan of boring. Lord Dundonald's authority is a Mr Telfer . . . who is now in Dublin.

William Telfer was a mathematical instrument-maker based in Glasgow who had taken out two patents for flax preparation.[36] When James Millar (1762–1827) published his second edition of John Williams' *Natural History of the Mineral Kingdom* in 1810, he confirmed this earlier use in Scotland, but instead noted that it was 'Mr Scott of Ormiston in East Lothian [who] had . . . long employed [such an instrument] for the purpose of extracting a core or cylinder of the coal . . . But I do not know that it was ever applied to rocks in general, or in any other way but to determine the thickness of the coal *when it is discovered by the common apparatus* [emphasis added] . . . Mr Ryan's exclusive privilege may perhaps be considered as perfectly entire.'[37] This confirms that Ryan was the first, at least in Britain, to realise the need for, and to supply a means whereby, cores of strata could be examined when bored through in prospecting for minerals. Ryan's priority is confused by a recent erroneous claim that his invention was developed in the 1820s.[38]

The scale of the potential advance that Ryan had provided can be seen by studying the contemporary alternative 'common apparatus' for boring.[39] This was both old, having then been in use for centuries, and primitive, in that it reduced the rocks penetrated by the borer to fragments by percussion, from which little could be learnt. Ryan's method completely removed the great disadvantage of this old system which was, as Samuel Perry's testimonial of 1806 noted, the way the chisels it used 'pulped' all the strata penetrated and so enormously reduced the quality of any data retrieved. But the old system did have the enormous advantage, in the eyes of conservative British coalowners and of Lord Dundonald, of being cheap. This last 'advantage' allowed it to remain in use into its third century until after the British Coal industry was nationalised in 1945![40]

RYAN LEAVES IRELAND

Such views of the value of 'cheapness' extended to Ireland. Ryan was dismissed from his employment by the GCI in May 1805. He had had a fortnight's notice but on 26 April was told he could now 'stay until 24 May if he likes.' The GCI Board 'thought he would wish to make use of his patent in England', which they could now use in Ireland, having paid for it, 'without the expense of his salary'! Ryan, in a reply to the GCI dated 6 May 1805, noted 'the system of boring, invented by me, has been the only one that the Irish could tell Foreigners that they could [not] be done without.' Ryan claimed 'its expenses must be less than any other as the two [Irish] men that operates [it] does not get one fourth of the wages of the Foreigners. I have proof of sixteen different false reports being made in the Kilkenny & Queen's County Collieries by [old style] boring, since proved by sinking.'[41] All such economies in using Irish workmen in Ireland were however soon found to evaporate when English labour was used in England. The major problem at this date for Irish members of some of the new professions, like mineral surveying, was the lack of openings for them in Ireland.

From this point onwards, Ryan spent most of his time in England. However, he did not cease all contact with Irish mining. On 20 January 1814 he wrote from 'Sudley Mine, Donegal', as Mine agent to the metalliferous mines owned here by the third Earl of Arran, Arthur Saunders Gore (1761–1837). Ryan was 'mine agent to the Earl for nine months' of each year.[42] In the summer of 1814 Ryan was also in Belfast, in contact with the local geologist Dr. James Macdonell (1762–1845).[43]

RYAN AND MINERAL SURVEYING

Edgeworth's note that Ryan's device had two uses is confirmed by the 'schizophrenia' which greeted it when introduced to England. The first was in improving mineral prospecting, where it was more efficient but certainly more expensive. When Ryan arrived in England to further its promotion in the heartland of the Industrial Revolution, most mine owners were interested in costs, not in 'efficiency gains.' So his invention seems to have been hardly put to the use to which members of geologist William Smith's school at least, thought it should have been, namely in prospecting for stratified minerals.

Ryan actively tried to promote this first use in various ways. In April 1807 he wrote to the London-based Board of Agriculture about the use of his invention 'in draining experiments'. In January 1808 his paper 'on his Auger' was referred to its general committee and Davies Giddy (1767–1839) reported on it in July 1808.[44] Sadly the board's further records have not survived but John Farey confirmed that

> in April, 1807, Mr Ryan presented a complete set of his apparatus to the Board of Agriculture in London, and bored a hole of some depth therewith near Kensington, under the inspection of some of its members; the cores or borings therefrom being exhibited to the Board, and lodged with the apparatus in their repository, they voted a pecuniary reward to Mr Ryan. From the apparent importance of this discovery to mining, but to coal-finding in particular, we were induced to wish, to give an accurate description and drawings in this place of Mr Ryan's apparatus . . . [but] under the article MINING we shall endeavour to give them in the further state of perfection, in which practice will doubtless then present the same.[45]

Sadly Farey's problems with the editor of the Rees' *Cyclopaedia*, for which he ceased to write from September 1811, meant that this promise was never fulfilled.[46]

By June 1807 Ryan had also demonstrated his boring apparatus, to the forgotten ancestor of the London Geological Society (founded November 1807), the British Mineralogical Society. Their Secretary was the quaker social reformer William Phillips (1770–1843). His testimonial noted that 'after a careful inspection and examination of the Instrument . . . they are persuaded that it affords results much more satisfactory than any of the methods now in use; since by bringing up the different Strata in solid Cylinders, it supplies the means of a more accurate knowledge of their depth and quality, while it indicates, at the same time, their dip and inclination'.[47]

Later the same year, 1807, Ryan was back in Cumberland, then one of the most technologically advanced areas of coal mining in England. Moreover it provided the great proportion of the coal then imported into Ireland. At Workington the new Isabella Pit was sinking, having started early in 1807. It must have been then that Ryan was given a manuscript section of the strata penetrated during sinking of the pit, down to 168 feet. This Ryan later donated to Trinity College Dublin where it survives.[48] The coal owner here, John Christian Curwen (1756–1828), provided a testimonial on 30 September 1807 that Ryan's boring apparatus had been successfully used there, down to eight fathoms and that he 'had no hesitation in stating it as my opinion, that it will be found highly serviceable to the mining interests of the country'. Earlier the same month Ryan visited the nearby Seaton Iron Works whose manager also provided a highly satisfied testimonial.[49]

Ryan also returned, less successfully, to Whitehaven where he demonstrated his boring apparatus in August at Mirehouse Farm,[50] and late in October 1807 near Hope Pit, at the latter to a depth of 102 feet [=31 metres].[51] The owner of these mines was William Lowther, first Earl of Lonsdale (1757–1844). His agent was James Bateman (1749–1816) who wrote to Lord Lowther on 10 August 1807

> James Ryan the Irish Patent borer who wrote to your Lordship in London & and whose letter you sent me, we have employed near Myrehouse for the last three weeks in Boring, but he has only bored about 29 feet which at Mr Rawlings [then the best old style borers in the north[52]] price (being the price I agreed to pay him) comes to 29/-. His two men at 1 guinea each per week for three weeks will cost him 6 guineas and his own time and rods ought to make him as much [profit]. From the above statement your Lordship will see he has no chance to bore at the Rawlings prices. We have advanced him three Guineas on account, he wanted more but I told him he must earn it first. I expect he will leave us soon, as he must sink money very fast.[53]

This confirms that here Ryan's 'new technology' was simply seen as slower and more expensive. The fact that it could provide much better quality data for potential prospectors (as Farey had urged) was not thought relevant. In the context of a known mining area, like Whitehaven, we should perhaps not expect it to have been. But Bateman's letter ended 'we think him [Ryan] a great braggadochia.' This implies that Bateman also thought Ryan was full of empty promises and that he, and other members of the English mining fraternity, were prejudiced against such an Irishman, whom they feared had kissed the Blarney Stone too often.

The laissez-faire system of patronage then operative in Britain often confused the price of a scientific advance with its value. A particularly abortive trial for coal was then under way at Bexhill in Sussex, in hope of restoring the long faded iron industry there. This used old boring technology (supplied by the Birmingham engineer William Whitmore) under the authority of an Act of Parliament. But over several years it completely failed, despite an expenditure of £80,000 and a shaft many feet deep, simply because it was sited much too high up the stratigraphic series that Smith and Farey had worked out. It was later quoted as a classic example of the value of science in lowering the price of mining ventures.[54] Farey investigated this Bexhill attempt in person in the summer of 1806 and in August 1807 wrote of the specimens he collected east of Hastings which contained many detached pieces of bitumenised wood

> that were a [old style] augre-hole to be bored into it, and supplied with water, &c. something like the appearance of penetrating a coal vein, might be had in the borings; and it is this stratum, dipping under Bexhill, situate about 6½ miles to the westward, which in the opinion of Mr Farey has been there mistaken in the [old style] borings for a seam of coals, but which the improved

boring apparatus of Mr Ryan . . . would have detected and saved, perhaps, a most unparallelled waste of money, in the measures now pursuing.[55]

In 1808 Ryan became involved with the Thames Archway Company, attempting to bore a first tunnel under the Thames at London, under the direction of Richard Trevithick (1771–1833). Trevithick's attempt was successful up to December 1807, when water and quicksand broke into the tunnel workings. In April 1808 a meeting of the directors reported the opinions of two eminent northern mining viewers William Stobart of Durham and John Buddle (1773–1843) of Newcastle-on-Tyne. This meeting then directed Ryan to make exploratory borings on the north shore.[56] The outcome of these borings is unknown as the tunnel was abandoned in 1809, due to the technical difficulties that continued to be met. But the choice of Ryan's apparatus shows that some were now choosing it for the good quality borehole data it gave, only then available by using Ryan's device, which was noted particularly for its ability to bore through 'gravelly soils'.

On 11 April 1808, Ryan demonstrated his apparatus to potentially its most important audience. This was a selection of 19 members of the Royal Society, including its President Sir Joseph Banks (1743–1820) and the Geological Society of London, including its President George B. Greenough (1778–1855). The demonstration was held near the house of the naturalist and artist James Sowerby (1757–1822) in Lambeth, near London. Here Ryan successfully bored 10 feet down with an eight-inch diameter corer. The list of those who witnessed the trial survives as does the detailed log of the strata penetrated.[57]

This meeting was also significant as Sowerby must then have introduced Ryan to the new methods of William Smith and John Farey who had been using fossils to identify particular strata against the Natural Order of rocks which they had previously elucidated. Smith had introduced himself to Sowerby the previous month when Sowerby became an enthusiastic convert to Smithian methods, unlike many of the gentlemen geologists of the Geological Society.[58] Smith's stratigraphic advances had already demonstrated the stupidity of some misguided attempts to find coal.[59] Ryan, probably guided by Sowerby, became an enthusiastic proponent of these new methods which brought some science to the 'art' of prospecting for stratified minerals. From June 1808 Ryan sent fossil specimens, letters and geological sections, including materials he had collected on his travels in Scotland, Ireland and at Coalbrookdale to James Sowerby,[60] then busy starting to compile his new work on the fossils of Britain.[61]

Ryan and Sowerby must also have entered into some form of business agreement as Ryan's later advertising broadsheets of about 1812 and 1817 note that orders for his services and the use of his Patent Boring Apparatus were to be placed at the 'British Mineral Collection, 2 Mead Place, St George's Fields, Lambeth', Sowerby's home address. Ryan had also by 1812 'formed a company of itinerant Miners, Drainers &c [to] execute orders in any part of the United Kingdom; make Estimates and Surveys of Estates, depicting their Mineral and Fossil contents on Maps or Models, contract for exploring Royalties by Boring; undertake to clear Coal Mines of inflammable or other Gas, however dangerous'.[62]

Ryan, probably less aware of the tensions then existing between the working class 'mineral surveyors', that he represented, and the gentlemen geologists of the Geological Society, also sent material to this society. His presents comprised some of the first stratigraphic collections that the society received. A particular collection of specimens in 'description of the Stratification extending from London to Stourbridge in Worcestershire' given, through the president, on 3 August 1808 was accompanied by a descriptive catalogue.[63] The latter survives to show both how well and how soon Ryan had espoused Smithian methods.

RYAN AND MINE VENTILATION

Edgeworth had noted in 1806 that there was a second potential use of Ryan's invention, to create passage ways to ventilate coal mines. This proved a highly political, rather than scientific, matter, in an England which was soon to be shamed into doing something about the massive mortalities in coalmines which yearly resulted from explosions. As a result of this situation, Ryan's device was soon 'highjacked' into the vitriolic debate which developed.

Ryan had first gone to Newcastle in May 1806 to try to get his device used there in coal prospecting, and John Buddle, the most eminent viewer there, even agreed to become an agent for it. But Ryan's attempts to also encourage its use for the better ventilation of coal mines, by using it to bore gas drains to rid the most affected mines there of mine damp, failed. Buddle refused to support the use of Ryan's new technology for ventilation in the North East,[64] retorting that there were very few deaths from such mine damp and that the existing ventilation system was adequate.[65]

In 1808 Ryan tried again under rather different circumstances in the South Staffordshire collieries. Here Ryan's method worked well. The thick coals of South Staffordshire allowed easier ventilation by his methods than the thinner and more faulted coal seams of the North-East which were worked over greater areas. Ryan was first employed here by Lord Ward and Dudley to clear his Netherton mine at Dudley. This brought Ryan to Dudley for the first time, which became his home for the rest of his peripatetic life. Ryan cleared this mine with two men and two boys within 20 days, between 3 and 27 December 1808. So successful was Ryan's system here that it was used throughout South Staffordshire and certificates were issued in 1811 recording Ryan's success in cutting gas-ways with his borer. One read

we have no hesitation in saying that during 2½ years in the most dangerous works, without gas firing lines [previously used here to try and remove gas] or other expensive precaution Mr Ryan did not lose one life.[66]

Ryan's main supporters here were Lord William Ward (1750–1823) of Himley Hall, third Viscount Dudley & Ward and a major coalowner in the area and self-made Samuel Fereday (1758–1839) of Ettingshall Park, Sedgeley, a major iron and coal master and banker, a man both made by the Napoleonic War and broken by its concluding Peace in 1815.[67]

On 1810 Ryan lectured on his system at the Royal Institution in London, an organisation which was soon to become embroiled in the political debate on mine safety which involved scientists of the prestige of Sir Humphrey Davy.[68] An explosion in May 1812 at Felling colliery on Tyneside caused 92 deaths and brought a new urgency to the search for a solution. The Society for Preventing Accidents in Coal Mines was founded in Sunderland in October 1813, with Buddle still wholly opposed to the introduction of Ryan's methods.[69] Davy's invention of the safety lamp drew from the President of the Royal Society, Sir Joseph Banks, one of his most effusive letters.[70] The history of the safety lamp has involved many such strong opinions, and some myth making in the long war between science (Davy) and the practical man (George Stephenson).[71] The safety lamp was cheaper and thus seemed a more satisfactory solution than the improved mine ventilation advocated by Ryan. Ryan's own experiments showed that the Davy lamp could be dangerous and made to explode.[72] Posterity has duly confirmed how the introduction of the safety lamp generated a rise, not a decline, in the number of fatalities from gas explosions in English coal mines.[73]

A contemporary referred to the 'rejection of Mr Ryan's plans in the North' and the 'prejudices and mistaken interests which had coalesced in the North' in rejecting them. He noted that there were 'viewers who systematically oppose the introduction of invention' and how there 'are strong deeply-rooted prejudices here of more than fifty years' undisturbed growth, in favour of the existing system of ventilation, which the influence of any individual, be his genius what it may, can never remove'.[74] He specifically noted John Buddle, who opposed Ryan and supported the development of the Davy lamp.[75] Great prejudice continued in the North East against Ryan. The Rev. John Hodgson wrote in 1816 of having had to listen to 'three hours of Ryan's Irish eloquence' at a public lecture in Newcastle.[76] As late as 1828 Buddle noted to Hodgson that 'our friend Ryan is again amongst us . . . The best way will be, probably to treat him with silent contempt, and allow him to exhaust his venom. The trade will not again be humbugged by him.'[77] The North East led British coal technology and such attitudes were taken as authoritative.

In 1816 the polarised politics of mine ventilation and safety erupted between the Royal Society and the Royal Institution (which favoured the Davy lamp) and the Society of Arts (which favoured Ryan). In 1816 the latter rewarded Ryan with their prestigious Gold Medal and the largest premium they had ever awarded, of 100 guineas.[78] Ryan published a *Letter* explaining his system in 1816[79] followed by an *Appeal* in 1817.[80]

In 1818 Ryan moved to Shropshire and leased mines at Middletown Hill in Montgomeryshire. He was elected a member of the Salopian Lodge of Freemasons based in Shrewsbury, as a 'Director of Mines', in hopes of new patronage.[81] But the mines caused him major financial embarrassment and he was still involved in litigation in 1840.[82] While at Middletown, Ryan erected at his own expense a school 'for instructing young Men in my system of Mining'. This was between 1819 and 1831 and must have been the first purpose-built mining school built in Britain.[83]

In 1824 Ryan published a new *Appeal*[84] and continued to urge the value of his ventilation system. In 1831 his first notice appeared in the *Mechanics Magazine*, whose editor noted that 'Mr Ryan and his system deserve more public consideration than they have hitherto received.'[85] On 6 July 1835 Ryan was called as a witness before the *Select Committee on Accidents in Mines* which the Government had now set up. This gave his history of his efforts with mine ventilation.[86]

The last years of Ryan's life were spent promoting his system of mine ventilation. The *Report of the South Shields Committee to investigate the Causes of Accidents in Coal Mines* of 1842 had been very favourable to his ideas and his work was now taken up by the *Mining Journal* which published a letter by another early pioneer in mine safety, Dr John Murray (?1786–1851), stating that

> we want ventilation, and a scientific system of working coal mines – not safety-lamps . . . In the *Report of the South Shields Committee appointed to investigate the Causes of Accidents in Coal Mines*,[87] we have an honest, honourable, and faithful tribute to the merits of Mr Ryan's plan. The award of the Gold Medal and 100 guineas, by the Society of Arts, in 1816, to Mr Ryan, was founded on the ample testimony, by practical men, of its triumphant success; and M. Boisse, the distinguished director of the Belgian mines, lauds the 'avantages incontestables' of the system propounded by Mr Ryan. What further evidence do we require of the excellence of his plan?[88]

The Belgian referred to had been involved in a concourse held in 1840, to discover the best means of avoiding mine explosions.[89]

On 28 September 1844 a mine disaster at Haswell, near Durham took 95 new lives and inspired a new commission of inquiry under Charles Lyell and Michael Faraday. Ryan attended the inquest, coming all the way from Derbyshire, but was not allowed to speak by the coroner who recorded a verdict of 'accidental death'. Another disaster followed at Coxlodge Colliery in Northumberland in October 1844 after which Ryan's methods were again cited.[90] Ryan attended this inquest also, now at the expense of the Birmingham banker and philanthropist Benjamin Attwood (died 1874) who had been impressed by the value of Ryan's ideas. Once again Ryan was not allowed to speak at the inquest.[91] In a lecture at the Royal Institution in January 1845 Faraday paid tribute to Ryan '[whose] principle of withdrawing gas, I am glad to find, is not new among the coal-owners. Mr Ryan's method of ventilating mines is one which essentially depends upon drawing or draining of the gas from the mine. To my mind his principle seems very beautiful.'[92]

On 21 July 1847 Ryan died aged 77 at Dudley.[93] He was buried at St Thomas Church on 25 July.[94] He had latterly been receiving a yearly pension of £50 a year from the revenues of Lord Ward's mines.[95] All his papers and correspondence were left to the mining engineer Henry Johnson (1823–1885) of Dudley. Johnson was the founder in 1844 of the firm of Johnson, Poole and Bloomer, geotechnical engineers of Stourbridge and a few of Ryan's books and Henry Johnson's diaries still survive in their care. Johnson paid tribute to Ryan in 1862:

> happily with the introduction of the Davy many years ago, and the constant application of the late James Ryan, who was better known amongst the colliers by the significant cognomen of 'Count Sulphur', ventilation has vastly improved. His great theme was, 'remove the cause and the effect ceases', and by adopting his recommendation in this district of driving the air-heading on a level with the roof of the gaitroad, all the gas liberated is immediately carried off by the top air-heading. Previous to this recommendation, which there is not a shadow of a doubt emanated from him (as all his papers and correspondence, left with me at his death, clearly testify), the air-heading was driven universally in the benches, i.e. on the very floor of the mine.

Johnson concluded that Ryan was

> a departed genius, who, unhappily, in his day, was all heart and soul in endeavouring to alleviate the sufferings of the workmen, increasing the wealth of the coal owners, and yet, withal, did so little earthly good for himself or family, for his last moments were comparatively those of a pauper.[96]

A more recent historian in 1928 rightly noted he was a 'celebrated Irish mining engineer and one of the remarkable omissions from the *Dictionary of National Biography*'.[97] Ryan was clearly also a very brave man, as William Mathews noted in 1860:

> the present mode of ventilation is unquestionable the offspring of his genius. The courage and perseverance with which Mr Ryan prosecuted his system were deserving of the highest praise, and the danger which he personally encountered and the resolution which he displayed were such that he was familiarly known amid the colliers by the name of 'hell-fire Jack'. He may be remembered by many coal owners of the present generation by the importunity with which he continually urged upon them the righteousness of coroner's juries finding a verdict of wilful murder in all cases of deaths from explosions in those collieries in which his system of ventilation was not acted upon.[98]

Ryan was the victim of polarised attitudes and geographies. He was popular among colliers but unpopular amongst mine owners, as his innovations involved expense. He was regarded as a genius in his adopted Black Country but as a liar, a charlatan and 'Irish' elsewhere. His truly original invention of the first boring apparatus which could recover cores from boreholes (now vital technology all over the world in search of minerals)

80

was soon forgotten because, as Robert Bald (1776–1861) the Scottish mining engineer wrote in 1830:

> The impression which the public has at present regarding [his] mode of boring is, that it is very expensive . . . It is, however, but too well known, how much mankind are attached to old plans, strongly prejudiced against new ones, and that it is no easy matter to change particular habits; this may have operated against Mr Ryan's invention and have prevented success attending it.[59]

Such are the problems which have always faced the true innovator.

ACKNOWLEDGMENTS

The staff of the Cumberland Record Office, Carlisle, the Durham Record Office and the North East Institute of Mining and Mechanical Engineers in Newcastle provided all possible assistance. Ruth Heard (Dublin) gave much appreciated help in getting me both details and access to GCI records. I thank Gordon Herries-Davies (Nenagh), Valerie Ingram (Dublin), Colin Knipe (Brierley Hill), Nick Lee (Bristol), Linde Lunney (Dublin), Colain Macarthur (Letterkenny), John Thackray (London) and Patrick Wyse-Jackson (Dublin) for their kind help.

NOTES

1. R.V. & P.J. Wallis, *Index of British Mathematicians Part III* (Newcastle-upon-Tyne, 1993), p. 119.
2. R.L. Galloway, *Annals of Coal Mining* (London, 1898), p. 411.
3. In a letter to Josiah Wedgwood junior dated 6 September 1831, Wedgwood archives 21880–29, Keele University Library.
4. Ryan's printed flyer 'To the Coal-Owners of the Tyne and Wear' dated 15 November 1843, Bell collection, North East Institute of Mining and Mechanical Engineers, Newcastle.
5. Memorandum on mining, Wedgwood Archives 21874–29, accompanying his letter to Josiah Wedgwood junior dated 3 August 1831, 21878–29, Keele University Library.
6. *Transactions of the Irish Academy*, 2 (1789): pp. 157–170.
7. Archives of Johnson, Poole & Bloomer, Brierley Hill.
8. *Report from the Select Committee on Accidents in Mines* (London, 1835), p. 204 (answer 2830).
9. Ruth Heard, *The Grand Canal of Ireland* (Newton Abbot, 1973), pp. 143–7.
10. W.Tighe, *Statistical Observations relative to the County of Kilkenny* (Dublin, 1802), plate IX.
11. G. Bowie, 'Early Stationary Steam Engines in Ireland', *Industrial Archaeology Review*, 2 (1978): pp. 168–74, p. 168.
12. GCI Minute Book, volume 28, entry for 24 April 1804. The earlier volume (27) does not survive.
13. Heard, *The Grand Canal of Ireland*, p. 144.
14. Obituary in *Proceedings of the Institution of Civil Engineers*, 3 (1844): pp. 14–5.
15. GCI Minute Book, volume 30, entry for 27 December 1804.
16. *Report from the Select Committee on Accidents in Mines*, p. 204 (answers 2827–9).
17. Ryan, 'To the Coal-Owners of the Tyne and Wear'.
18. *Proceedings of the Dublin Society*, 40 (1803–4): p. 83.

VIII

19. *Proceedings of the Dublin Society*, 41 (1803–4): p. 15.
20. Ryan, 'To the coal-Owners of the Tyne and Wear'.
21. Number 2822.
22. C.J. Jackson, *A History of the Development of Drill Bits and Drilling Techniques in Nineteenth Century Britain* (Open University Ph.D., 1983), pp. 215–8.
23. *Monthly Magazine*, 19 (1805): pp. 368–9.
24. *The Retrospect of Philosophical, Mechanical, Chemical . . . Discoveries*, 1 (1806): p. 85.
25. *Magazin aller neuen Erfindungen*, 6 (1806): pp. 223–7 and plate 4.
26. Ryan, 'To the Coal-Owners of the Tyne and Wear'.
27. William Nicholson's *Journal of Natural Philosophy etc*, 15 (1806): p. 85.
28. *The Retrospect of Philosophical, Mechanical, Chemical . . . Discoveries*, 2 (1806): p. 410.
29. Copy in Bell papers, volume 6, p. 162, British Geological Survey archives, Keyworth.
30. B. Burke, *The Landed Gentry* (London, 1871), pp. 1081–2.
31. B. Burke, *The Landed Gentry* (London, 1871), p. 1164.
32. *Dublin Gazette*, 8 May 1802.
33. A. Rees, 'Coal', in *The Cyclopaedia*, (London, 1807).
34. *GCI Minutes*, volume 31, entry for 15 April 1805.
35. *GCI Minutes*, volume 31, entry for 4 May 1805 (pp. 229–45).
36. Patent numbers 2469 (1801) and 2607 (1802).
37. James Millar, *The Natural History of the Mineral Kingdom by John Williams* (Edinburgh, 1810), volume 2, p. 356.
38. Michael Flinn, *The History of the British Coal Industry*, II (Oxford, 1984), p. 72.
39. H.S. Torrens 'The History of Coal Prospecting in Britain 1650–1900' in *Energie in der Geschichte* (Dusseldorf, 1984) pp. 88–95 and 'The History of Coal Prospecting in Britain – a neglected subject', *Geology Today*, 2, no. 2 (1986), 57–8.
40. Francis G. Dimes, 'Correspondence', *Geology Today*, 2 no. 5 (1986), 138.
41. GCI Minutes, volume 31, entries for 15 April to 9 May 1805.
42. Tyne and Wear Archives, 1589/102–6.
43. Anne Plumptre, *Narrative of a Residence in Ireland . . . in 1814 and 1815* (London, 1817), p. 98.
44. Board of Agriculture, Register of letters received, B XII, and Minute Book fair copy, B VII, University of Reading, Institute of Agricultural History. See also Ryan, 'To the coal-Owners of the Tyne and Wear'. The Board's testimonial is reprinted in Ryan's 1812 testimonial cited above, note 29.
45. Rees, 'Coal'.
46. H.S. Torrens & T.D. Ford, Introduction to the reprint of John Farey's 1811 *General View of the Agriculture and Minerals of Derbyshire* (Matlock 1989).
47. Printed Broadsheet of *c.* 1817, of 'J. Ryan, F.A.S. Mineralogical Surveyor, Director of Mines &c' in the author's collection.
48. MSS in Dept of Geology, Trinity College Dublin.
49. Testimonial cited above, note 29.
50. Cumberland Record Office, D Lons. W, Whitehaven district, Boring journal 1776–1842.
51. Cumberland Record Office, D Lons. W, 'Journal of Incidental Borings not connecting with the Whitehaven Coal or Lime Field', no. 39.
52. Flynn, *History of the British Coal Industry*, p. 72.
53. Cumberland Record Office, letter of Bateman to Lowther, 10 August 1807.
54. John F.W. Herschel, *A Preliminary Discourse on the Study of Natural Philosophy* (London, 1831), p. 45.
55. A. Rees, 'Colliery', in *The Cyclopaedia*, (London 1807).
56. Francis Trevithick, *Life of Richard Trevithick* (London, 1872), volume 1, p. 269.

VIII

82

57. James Sowerby archive, Natural History Museum, London.
58. L.R. Cox, 'New Light on William Smith and his Work', *Proceedings of the Yorkshire Geological Society*, 25 (1942): pp. 1–99, pp. 53–4.
59. H.S. Torrens, 'William Smith's "New Art of Mineral Surveying" and the "Brewham Intended Colliery": a failed attempt to find coal in Southern England between 1803 and 1810' in G. Gohau, ed., *Livre Jubilaire Francois Ellenberger* (Paris, 1996), in press.
60. Four of James Ryan's letters to Sowerby, dated 1808, 1809, 1830 and undated, are in the Eyles archive, Bristol University Library.
61. See James Sowerby, *The Mineral Conchology* (London, 1812–1846), 7 vols.
62. Testimonial cited above, note 29, and the broadsheet, note 47.
63. Geological Society archives MUS 1/94 and 'Donations to the Cabinet of Minerals', *Transactions of the Geological Society of London*, 1 (1811): p. 409.
64. *Tracts on the Necessity of Legislative Interference in protecting the Lives and Health of the Miners against Colliery Explosions and the Injurious Effects of Badly Ventilated Mines* no. 2 (8 December 1849), p. 13 and ref. 38, p. 135.
65. *Report from the Select Committee on Accidents in Mines*, answer 2834.
66. Testimonial cited above, note 29.
67. Fereday fled to France in 1821 where he died an uncertificated bankrupt in 1839 (*Staffordshire Advertiser*, 6 April 1839, p. 3).
68. M. Berman, *Social Change and Scientific Organization: The Royal Institution 1799–1844* (London, 1978), pp. 175–182.
69. J.H.H. Holmes, *A Treatise on the Coal Mines* (London, 1816), pp. 146–155.
70. T.G. Vallance, 'Jupiter Botanicus in the Bush', *Proceedings of the Linnean Society of New South Wales*, 112 (1990): pp. 49–86, pp. 53–4.
71. A.R. Griffin, 'Sir Humphrey Davy: his Life and Work', *Industrial Archaeology Review*, 4 (1980): pp. 202–13, p. 202.
72. J.H.H. Holmes, 'On Safety lamps for Coal-Mines', *Annals of Philosophy*, 8 (1816): pp. 129–131.
73. David Albury and Joseph Schwartz, *Partial Progress* (London, 1982) and A.F.C. Wallace, *The Social Context of Innovation* (Princeton, 1982), p. 115.
74. Holmes, *A Treatise on Coal Mines*, pp. 88, 140 & 153.
75. T.Y. Hall, *On the Safety Lamp for the Use of Coal Mines* (London, 1854), p. 14.
76. Durham Record Office, NCB I/JB/1496, letter to Buddle, 17 June 1816.
77. J. Raine, *A Memoir of the Rev. John Hodgson* (London, 1858) I, pp. 170–1.
78. 'The Gold Medal and One hundred Guineas . . . to Mr James Ryan . . . ', *Transactions of the Royal Society of Arts*, 34, (1816): pp. 94–121.
79. *A Letter from Mr James Ryan . . . on his Method* (London, 1816).
80. *The Appeal of James Ryan . . . to Proprietors of Collieries . . .* (Birmingham, 1817).
81. A. Graham, *A History of Freemasonry in The Province of Shropshire* (Shrewsbury, 1892), p. 232.
82. *Mining Journal*, 10 (no. 245), 2 May 1840, p. 138.
83. Keele University Library, 21874–29.
84. *The Appeal of James Ryan . . . to Proprietors of Collieries* (Stoke-upon-Trent, 1824).
85. *Mechanics Magazine*, 15 (1831), p. 461.
86. *Report from the Select Committee on Accidents in Mines*, answers 2824 to 2940.
87. Reprinted by James Mather, *The Coal Mines, their Dangers and Means of Safety* (London, 1858), pp. 23–72.
88. *Mining Journal*, 13 (23 December 1843), p. 419.
89. A.-A.-M. Boisse, 'Memoire sur les Explosions dans les Mines de Houille' pp. 35–140 of *Des Moyens de Soustraire l'Exploitation des Mines de Houille aux Chances d'Explosion* (Bruxelles, 1840), pp. 62–8, 130.
90. *Times*, 17 October 1844, p. 6e.
91. *Times*, 1 November 1844, p. 6d.

92. *Civil Engineer and Architects Journal,* 8 (April 1845), p. 118.
93. *Mining Journal,* 17 (July 1847), p. 346.
94. Parish Register, Dudley Library.
95. Dudley Archives Office, Dudley Estate Archive, V/2/4.
96. H. Johnson, 'On the Mode of Working the Thick or Ten Yard Coal of South Staffordshire', *Transactions of the North-East Institution of Mining Engineers,* 10 (1862): pp. 183–96, p. 194.
97. A.J. Hawkes, *Jubilee Exhibition of Early Mining Literature* (Wigan, 1928), p. 34.
98. 'On the Ten Yard Coal of South Staffordshire and the Mode of Working', *Proceedings of the Institution of Mechanical Engineers,* (1860): pp. 91–120, p. 105.
99. Robert Bald, 'Mine' in D. Brewster, ed., *The Edinburgh Encyclopaedia,* 14 (1830): pp. 314–378, pp. 330–1.

IX

ARTHUR AIKIN'S MINERALOGICAL SURVEY OF SHROPSHIRE 1796–1816 AND THE CONTEMPORARY AUDIENCE FOR GEOLOGICAL PUBLICATIONS

Introduction

IT has become almost traditional for historians of geology to claim that Roderick Murchison (1792–1871) 'opened to view for the first time'[1] the fossiliferous rocks below the Old Red Sandstone which Murchison described in his monumental work *The Silurian System* published in 1839. Murchison himself claimed in the introduction to this work 'no-one was previously aware of the existence below the Old Red Sandstone of a regular series of deposits, containing peculiar organic remains'.[2] Professor John Phillips expressed the traditional view well when he wrote of the larger area of which Shropshire forms a part: 'practically before the Summer of 1831 the whole field of the ancient rocks and fossils . . . was unexplored but then arose two men . . . Adam Sedgwick and Roderick Murchison and simultaneously set to work to cultivate what had been left a desert'.[3] Against this we must set the statement of George B. Greenough (1778–1855), first president of the Geological Society of London, as reported in 1841.[4] He had 'frequently expressed a conviction, as a result of his own observations . . ., that adequate enquiry alone was wanting to prove the existence of a succession of strata in the west of England, and in Wales—not less regular than that which had been demonstrated in the centre and east of the Island.'

The difficulties historians face in assessing these claims are made greater by the fact that the intended second part of W. D. Conybeare and W. Phillips' classic text *Outlines of the geology of England and Wales*,[5] which was to cover the stratigraphic sequence below the Old Red Sandstone, was never published. A similar fate befell another planned publication on these ancient rocks in Shropshire. This was by another of Murchison's predecessors, Arthur Aikin, who issued *Proposals for a mineralogical survey of the county of Salop and of some adjacent districts* before Murchison began work. This is a three-page quarto printed pamphlet accompanied by an

[1] J. Thackray, 'R. I. Murchison's *Silurian System* 1839', *J. Soc. Biblphy nat. Hist.* 1978, *9*, 61.
[2] R. I. Murchison, *The Silurian System*, London, 1839, 4.
[3] in A. Geikie, *Life of Sir Roderick I. Murchison*, 2 vols., London, 1875, *1*, 179.
[4] by [W. H. Fitton] 'Review of the Silurian System . . . by R. I. Murchison'. *Edinb. Rev.* 1841, *73*, 7.
[5] part 1 was published in 1822.

112

engraved 'Mineralogical map and section' and a further three-page explanation of this map. It was printed by 'Richard Taylor and Co., Shoe Lane, London', but bears no date. This work, despite containing an engraved map and a geological cross section, is not cited in Bassett's[6] or Cowling's[7] bibliographies. In this paper I discuss the significance of Aikin's work in Shropshire, its dates, the reason why the survey of Shropshire was abandoned unpublished, and Murchison's subsequent use of Aikin's results. An appendix lists and identifies all the known subscribers to the survey; from this list conclusions are drawn about the nature and size of the contemporary audience for geological publications. The Shropshire part of this audience is of particular interest because of the area's special place in the history of technology. The East Shropshire coalfield, centred on Coalbrookdale, has been called the cradle of the Industrial Revolution because of the series of technological innovations made there, starting in 1709.[8] An analysis of the extent to which geology was encouraged in this area may show to what extent the 'usefulness' of geology, especially to mining and agriculture, was one of the most important determinants in its development in Britain between 1750 and 1820. This relationship has been much debated.[9]

Arthur Aikin (1773–1854)

His grandfather, the Rev Dr John Aikin (1713–1780),[10] was a dissenting minister who taught classics and later divinity at the dissenters' Academy at Warrington from 1757 to 1780.[11] Arthur's father, also Dr John (1747–1822), was in medical practice at Warrington from 1771 to 1784. He lectured on chemistry and natural history at the Academy where he had been a student, and no doubt introduced his young son to the delights of natural history. John Aikin maintained his interest in natural history after his move to Yarmouth.[12] He is, however, better known as a man of letters and as a natural historian than as a physician,[13] and when he moved again,

---

[6] D. A. Bassett, *Bibliography and Index of Geology and allied sciences for Wales and the Welsh Borders 1536–1896*, Cardiff, 1963.

[7] G. C. A. Cowling, *A descriptive list of the printed maps of Shropshire, 1577–1900*, Shrewsbury, 1959.

[8] B. Trinder, *The Industrial Revolution in Shropshire*, 2nd edition, London, 1981.

[9] S. Tomkeieff, 'James Hutton and the Philosophy of Geology'. *Proc. R. Soc. Edinb.* 1950, *63*B, (4), 389. J. G. C. M. Fuller, 'The industrial basis of stratigraphy, John Strachey (1671–1743) and William Smith (1769–1839).' *Bull. Am. Ass. Petrol. Geol.* 1969, *53*, 2256–2273. R. S. Porter, *The making of geology: Earth Science in Britain 1660–1815*, Cambridge, 1977, 131–2. I. Inkster, 'Science and Society in the Metropolis: A Preliminary Examination of the Social and Institutional Context of the Askesian Society of London,' 1796–1807. *Ann. Sci.* 1977, *34*, 1–32. P. Weindling, 'Geological controversy and its historiography: the prehistory of the Geological Society of London,' pp. 248–271. in L. J. Jordanova & R. S. Porter (editors). Images of the Earth. Essays in the History of the Environmental Sciences, *Brit. Soc. Hist. Sci. Monog.* 1979, *1*, 282 p.

[10] Pedigree in J. Hunter, 'Familiae minorum gentium' (editor J. W. Clay), vol. 1 *Publications of the Harleian Society* 1894, *37*, 183.

[11] W. Turner, *The Warrington Academy* with an introduction by G. A. Carter, Warrington, 1957.

[12] See his article in *Gents. Mag.*, 1786, *56*, (1), 34–35.

[13] *D.N.B.*, and R. Frankenberg, 'John Aikin (1747–1822). Doctor and Philosopher'. *Mem. Proc. Manchr. lit. phil. Soc.* 1964, *106*, 20 p. (offprint).

to London in 1792, he played an active part in the Hackney circle of Unitarians. He also became editor of several journals including the well known *Monthly Magazine*, which ranged across the spectrum of politics, literature and general science. In 1794 he was elected a member of the Linnean Society of London. He exerted a crucial influence on his son Arthur.

Arthur was born at Warrington on 19th May 1773 and spent the first ten years of his life there. He attended the Free School at Warrington from the age of six, and from 1784 a school at Palgrave on the Norfolk-Suffolk border, directed by his aunt Anna Laetitia Barbauld (1743–1825). The major stimulus to his interest in science, especially chemistry, came with a visit to his father's friend Dr Joseph Priestley (1733–1804) in Birmingham when he was twelve. A further result of this visit was that Arthur became one of the first students at the Unitarian Academy at Hackney which opened in September 1786. Here he was taught history and chemistry by Priestley.[14]

Aikin at first chose to follow in his grandfather's footsteps as a Unitarian minister and it was to further this career that he was introduced to the county of Shropshire. Non-conformity in Shrewsbury, the county town, has a long tradition and the High Street Church there was opened in 1691.[15] In April 1793 its, by then Unitarian, minister Rev John Rowe (1764–1833), wrote to inform the subscribers to the church 'that he found it necessary to decline in future undertaking the whole duty as sole pastor of the Society'.[16] Rowe asked Rev Dr Andrew Kippis (1725–1795), one of the leading tutors at Hackney, to recommend a suitable candidate to be his assistant. After Rev John Corrie (1769–1839), an assistant tutor at Hackney College, had been unsuccessfully approached

> the Rev Arthur Aikin son of John Aikin M.D. was then requested to preach as a candidate and in consequence received an unanimous invitation to supply the vacancy occasioned by the partial resignation of Mr Rowe, which he accepted, and at Michaelmas 1793 he entered on his office.[17]

The printed registers of the Shrewsbury High Street Church[18] record Aikin's ministry there from 29th September 1793 to June 1795, when he left the ministry altogether. Whilst there he 'secured the general esteem and attachment of his congregation and formed many valuable friendships'.[19] We know that Aikin's salary during his ministry at Shrewsbury

[14] B. Rodgers, *Georgian Chronicle: Mrs. Barbauld and her family*, London, 1958, and H. McLachlan, *English Education under the Test Acts*, Manchester, 1931, 246–255.

[15] R. F. Skinner, *Nonconformity in Shropshire 1662–1816*, Shrewsbury, 1964.

[16] R. Astley MSS. Shrewsbury Public Library.

[17] R. Astley, History of the Presbyterian Meeting House, Shrewsbury. London, (reprinted from the *Christian Reformer* N.S. *3*), 1847, 22.

[18] G. E. Evans (editor), *Shropshire Parish Registers. Nonconformist Registers part 1*. Shrop. Par. Reg. Soc. 1903 (includes Shrewsbury High Street Church Registers, 1692–1812), vii.

[19] obit. of A. Aikin in *Christian Reformer* 1854, N.S. *10*, 379 and G. M. Ditchfield, *Some aspects of Unitarianism and Radicalism*. Ph.D. thesis, Cambridge University, 1968, 327.

114

was £32.10.0. a quarter, the same as the senior Minister John Rowe.[20] This was a handsome salary and allows us to discount the idea that Aikin left the ministry for financial reasons. It seems clear that he left for reasons of conscience and 'doubts about the truth of revealed religion',[21] although it is possible there may also have been some disagreement over the political activities of the Unitarians in Shrewsbury.[22]

Arthur then began a second career devoted to literary and scientific work, writing, lecturing and travelling. In August 1795 he visited William Roscoe in Liverpool.[23] He soon became a reviewer for the prestigious *Monthly Review*, contributing to it from November 1795 to January 1799.[24] He spent at least part of the winter of 1795–1796 in Edinburgh,[25] attending lectures at the University, although he never matriculated or graduated there.

In 1796 Aikin settled in London,[26] but he spent that summer in a pedestrian tour of North Wales and Shropshire accompanied by his brother Charles Rochemont Aikin (1775–1847) and a cousin called Charles Kinder. The principal purpose, as Aikin stated in his published *Journal* of the tour, was 'as a supplement to the mineralogical studies of the author', as he

> wished to proceed to the investigation not of minute detached fragments but of masses of rock in their native beds; to observe with [his] own eyes the position and extent of the several strata, the order observed by nature in their arrangement and the gradual or more abrupt transitions of one species of rock into another.[27]

He also wished to see the operations of mining, extracting and refining metallic ores in North Wales.

It was after reading H. B. de Saussure's *Voyages dans les Alpes*[28] that he decided to undertake this tour, in order to attempt something similar in North Wales and the Borders. The party started from Shrewsbury on 25th July 1796 and proceeded into Wales, returning to Shrewsbury on 22nd August. Extracts of his journal appeared in the *Monthly Magazine*,[29] then edited by his father, before publication of the book.[30] James Dallaway in his

[20] Church accounts preserved at the Unitarian church, Shrewsbury.
[21] Rodgers, op. cit (14), 162–3.
[22] J. Money, *Experience and identity: Birmingham and the West Midlands*, Manchester, 1977, 225.
[23] G. Peacock, *Memoir of Dr. Thomas Young*, London, 1855, 74.
[24] B. C. Nangle, *The Monthly Review, 2nd series 1790–1815*. Indexes of contributors and articles. Oxford, 1955, 29.
[25] D. L. Emblen, *Peter Mark Roget; the word and the man*. London, 1970, 29, and A. J. C. Hare, *The life and letters of Maria Edgeworth*, 2 vols., London, 1894, *1*, 43.
[26] *Gents. Mag.* 1854, *197* (2), 194.
[27] A. Aikin, *Journal of a Tour through North Wales and Part of Shropshire with observations in Mineralogy and other branches of Natural History*. London, 1797, v.
[28] Published Neuchâtel 1779–1796 in 4 vols.
[29] 1796, vol. 1, 15–8, 104–7, 191–4.
[30] Extracts also appeared in [*Nicholson's*] *Journal of natural philosophy, etc*, 1797, *1*, 220–5, 367–72, so it received wide publicity.

review of the *Journal*[31] said it contained 'much solid and useful information . . . communicated to the lover of the beauties of Nature picturesquely considered and of the scientific investigation of her mineral and vegetable Kingdoms'. A more accurate modern appraisal[32] states that the *Journal* demonstrates his then 'superficial views' of the geology of the area by comparison with his later more 'sophisticated geological memoir' of 1811. The most important sections of the published journal are chapters XVIII, chiefly on the geology of the Plain of Salop (pp. 187–212), and XIX, a summary of his geological observations on the tour (pp. 213–231). These will be discussed briefly when describing his mineralogical survey of Salop.

In 1797 Aikin again went on a mineralogical tour, this time to the Highlands of Scotland in the company of fellow Unitarian George Dyer (1755–1841), author and eccentric.[33] Some details of this tour are given in a poem written by Dyer and published in the *Monthly Magazine* in February 1798.[34] The poem was entitled 'to Mr Arthur Aikin on taking leave of him at Dunkeld in Perthshire after a pedestrian tour'. It also appeared in the following month in the *Edinburgh Magazine*.[35] The poem reveals again that 'the leading object of Mr A.'s tour into Scotland was a mineralogy survey of the country', and records of Aikin,

> Thy task is toil and patience to survey.
> The form, position and proportions due
> Of mountains, and their natures thence deduce
> Hence shall determine well the distant eye
> What treasures sleep within, or slates or lime,
> Granites or porph'ries; nor shall vain ascent
> Thy feet beguile; to thee research shall bring
> Its pleasures due, to other profit bring.

The same tour must have included a trip to see the geology of Portsoy near Banff on the Moray Firth. The Winch correspondence contains a long letter from Aikin to Nathaniel John Winch (1768–1838), fellow geologist, about his visit, which was submitted in 1798 to the Newcastle-on-Tyne Literary and Philosophical Society but never published.[36]

In December 1798 the *Monthly Magazine*[37] announced Arthur Aikin's commencement as a public lecturer with a course of lectures on the Theory and Practice of Chemistry to start in February 1799, assisted by his brother C. R. Aikin, at their house 4 Broad Street Buildings, London. The courses

[31] *Monthly Review* 1797, *23*, 386–8.
[32] Porter, op. cit (9), 235.
[33] *D.N.B.*
[34] vol. 5, 121–3.
[35] vol. 11, 223–5.
[36] MSS at Linnean Society, London. Aikin's *Observations on the stratification . . . of Portsoy* were to have been accompanied by a suite of specially collected specimens which however miscarried see *A historical sketch of the Transactions of the Literary and Philosophical Society of Newcastle upon Tyne*. Newcastle on Tyne, 1807, xxii–xxiii.
[37] vol. 6, 455.

on chemistry continued for several years at this house or at the Aldersgate Street General Dispensary,[38] and Aikin was still giving chemistry lectures as late as 1851 with Dr Alfred S. Taylor, F.R.S. The syllabus to the 1799 lectures was published, by the two Aikin brothers,[39] as was the 1851 syllabus.[40] It is for his work in chemistry that he is best remembered today.[41]

Chemical analyses were an integral part of mineral analyses at this time, so when the British Mineralogical Society was founded in April 1799[42] the Aikin brothers were elected early members: Charles Aikin on 27th June 1799 and his brother Arthur on 17th October 1799.[43] Arthur was also President of this Society from 1801 until December 1806[44] and a regular attender at its meetings. The history and aims of this significant Society have only recently been examined by Paul Weindling.[45] The Society was first established to provide analyses of British native ores and minerals,[46] but later also included the analysis of soils.[47] Having acquired a number of corresponding members in various parts of the country, the Society, during Arthur Aikin's presidency, had set itself the ambitious additional target of gathering 'materials upon which to found a general history of the mineral topography of the island'.[48]

Aikin continued his geological work in Shropshire during this period. He was in Shrewsbury on 7th September 1800 when he wrote to John Pinkerton (1758–1826), geographer and fellow student of mineralogy.[49] He wrote that he hoped to call on Dr Robert Townson (1762–1827) who then lived at Lydley Hayes, Cardington, south of Shrewsbury. Townson had travelled very widely on the continent and had studied the geology and mineralogy of Shropshire from about 1785. He had moved to Shropshire with his family and brother-in-law in 1777. How much help Townson was able to give Aikin with his later work in Shropshire is not clear, although Aikin had been approached to analyse geological material for Townson in 1804.[50] It is perhaps significant that Aikin's map and section later published in his *Proposals for a Mineralogical Survey of Shropshire* were centred on much the same area as that where Robert Townson had

---

[38] Inkster, op. cit. (9), 8–9.

[39] Rodgers, op. cit (14), 289.

[40] preserved in the Wills Library, Guy's Hospital, London.

[41] *D.N.B.* and A. Kent, 'Arthur Aikin (1773–1854) and other presidents.' *Proc. chem. Soc.* 1962, April, 133–134.

[42] L. Bradshaw, *Life of William Allen with selections from his correspondence*, 3 vols., London, 1846, *1*, 45.

[43] Minute book of the Society. Mineralogy Dept. Library, British Museum (Nat. Hist.), London.

[44] W. W. Watts, 'Fifty years of work of the Mineralogical Society.' *Mineralog. Mag.* 1926, *21*, 108–9.

[45] P. J. Weindling, 'The British Mineralogical Society: A Case-Study in Science and Social Improvement.' in I. Inkster and J. B. Morrell (editors), *Metropolis and Province: Science in British Culture 1780–1850*, London, 1983, 120–50.

[46] W. H. Pepys, 'British Mineralogical Society,' [*Nicholson's*] *Journal of natural philosophy etc.* 1799, *3*, 138–141.

[47] [*Tilloch's*] *Phil. Mag.* 1801, *9*, 282–3.

[48] [*Tilloch's*] *Phil. Mag.* 1802, *12*, 285.

[49] D. Turner (editor), *The Literary correspondence of John Pinkerton, Esq.*, 2 vols., London, 1830, *2*, 188.

[50] Townson's letter to Rev. W. Turner of 18 January 1804 in Winch MSS. Linnean Society, London.

been resident and of which he had already published a mineralogical account.[51]

In the summers of 1801 and 1802 Arthur Aikin was again touring, collecting materials for a mineralogical map of Great Britain, according to a letter from John Farey (1766–1826) to William Smith (1769–1839).[52] Aikin's companion on these tours was Wilson Lowry (1762–1824), artist and engraver and also fellow student of geology and mineralogy and a Member of the Geological Society of London from 1808.[53] The relevant extract of Farey's letter reads as follows:

> Mr Lowry the famous engraver is now at Woburn making drawings of agricultural implements for Dr. Rees's new Encyclopaedia, he called here on Tuesday evening last and in the course of conversation I learnt that he had been out this and the two last summers for several weeks on mineralogical tours with Mr. Aikin, a skilful mineralogist and chemist, and their object had been to collect materials for a mineralogical map of Great Britain; he had understood that I was acquainted with you, and he told me that he much wishes to see you, he requested that I would inform you, and said it was his wish to try and unite your scheme and theirs in one. . . .
>
> Crown Street, Westminster
> 1st October, 1802.

The tour in July 1802 included a visit to North Wales to which Aikin referred in a second letter to John Pinkerton, then in Paris, dated 26th August 1802.[54] In it Aikin mentions a 3 week stay in North Wales concentrating on the area of Cader Idris and Snowdon. This letter also introduces us to another of Aikin's activities, namely editorial work for others, which started to demand more of his attention from 1802. He was then engaged in editing for Pinkerton *An Abridgment of Mr Pinkerton's Modern Geography* (London 1803). He also translated Vivant Denon's *Travels in Upper and Lower Egypt* (London 1802, 3 vols.). Even more time consuming was the new *Annual Review or Register of Literature*, a strongly unitarian review of the publications of the year, which Aikin edited from 1802, the first volume being published in 1803, until 1808.[55] From January 1802 he was also involved with writing for Abraham Rees' *Cyclopaedia* and in the same year he edited with his brother, and contributed to, the second volume of *Annals of Philosophy, Natural History etc.* published in London. In addition 1805 saw the appearance of a fourth edition of his book for

[51] R. Townson, A sketch of the Mineralogy of Shropshire pp. 158–203 in *Tracts and Observations in Natural History and Physiology*. London 1799 and op. cit. (4), 4.

[52] Wm. Smith, MSS. Geology Department, Oxford University Museum. The Royal Society of Arts in London had, from 1802, offered their gold medal or a premium of 50 guineas for a *Mineralogical Map of England and Wales*. Aikin and Lowry may have considered submitting an entry.

[53] *D.N.B.* and H. B. Woodward, *The History of the Geological Society of London*, London, 1907, 270.

[54] Original in Stoke Newington Public library, printed in Turner, op. cit. (49), *2*, 229–30 and Rodgers, op. cit. (14), 223–4.

[55] P. H. Le Breton. *Memoirs, miscellanies and letters of Lucy Aikin*. London, 1864, 163–4 and T. Rees & J. Britton, *Reminiscences of Literary London from 1779 to 1853*. London, 1896, 53–5.

IX

118

children *The natural history of the year*, first published in London in 1798[56] and which reached its seventh edition in 1834.[57]

Nonetheless Aikin did find time for some scientific work. In 1802 he published a Description of Schieferspath,[58] and he was a contributor of Shropshire plant records to Dawson Turner and Lewis Weston Dillwyn's *Botanist's guide*.[59] In 1805 Aikin also became an original proprietor of the newly founded London Institution, a breakaway group from the earlier formed Royal Institution.[60] The London Institution later subscribed for a copy of his survey (see p. 144).

Two important events in Aikin's career took place in 1807, firstly the publication of the *Dictionary of chemistry and mineralogy* jointly with his brother C. R. Aikin, and secondly in November the foundation of the Geological Society of London. He came to play an important role in the Society and his *Proposals for a mineralogical survey* was intimately connected with it. That Aikin should have been involved in the foundation of the Society is natural in view of his close connection with the earlier British Mineralogical Society. It has been claimed that Aikin was also a leading member of the Askesian Society of London, founded in 1796,[61] but there is no evidence that he was anything more than a visitor to the meetings of this Society.[62]

The history of the formation of the Geological Society of London has been related in the official centenary history[63] and more recently by Rudwick.[64] Aikin was present at the inaugural meeting, and it is clear from Rudwick's account that Aikin's influence, among others, was crucial in directing the new Society's attention to the wider study of geology rather than to mineralogy alone. Greenough had carried out field work in Ireland in the summer of 1807 and Aikin had again been on field work in Shropshire and the mountains of Wales in the same summer, and both had argued that geology was 'a more attractive and engaging study than mineralogy'. Happily, the journal of part of Aikin's summer tour of 1807 has survived and been published.[65] The Shropshire portion of the journal starts at Ludlow and continues westward to Bishops Castle. The stratigraphic data given in this journal are as rudimentary as those in the *Journal* of 1797. We may especially note Aikin's observations on fossils. At Ludlow he merely records 'the hill opposite the town on the other side of the river

[56] A. A. Lisney, *A Bibliography of British Lepidoptera*. London, 1960, 293–6.
[57] copy in Stoke Newington Public Library.
[58] [*Tilloch's*] *Phil. Mag.*, 1802, *14*, 293.
[59] published in 1805, London in 2 vols.
[60] J. Cutler, *The London Institution*. Ph.D. thesis, University of Leicester, 1976, 1–16, 213.
[61] Inkster, op. cit. (9), 8, 16, 18–9.
[62] Weindling, op. cit. (45).
[63] Woodward, op. cit. (53).
[64] M. J. S. Rudwick, 'The foundation of the Geological Society of London: its scheme for co-operative research and its struggle for independence.' *Br. Jl Hist. Sci.* 1963, *1* (4), 325–355.
[65] Anon, 'Arthur Aikin in Wales 1807 from Ludlow to Dolgelley.' *Notes and Queries*, 1920, (12), *7*, 122–125.

[is] composed of beds of calcareous flagstone . . . abounding in shells'. There is no change of emphasis here from his earlier observation of August 1802 of a 'specimen of argillite full of shells at the very summit' of Snowdon.[66] On this, as on earlier tours, Aikin is still more interested in the composition and declivity of his Shropshire rocks than in fossils.

In March 1808 a small booklet entitled *Geological Inquiries* was issued by the Geological Society as its first publication, compiled by Greenough and Aikin.[67] This was widely circulated and reprinted in books and journals in England, India and America,[68] and has been reprinted in part by Hawkes more recently.[69] It is of prime importance for any understanding of the early work of the Society. In it the authors note the close dependence of geology on mineralogy and urge the importance of making local geological observations which the Society would collect and put together. This point was also stressed by Francis Horner (1778–1817), brother of Leonard (1785–1864) then one of the secretaries of the Geological Society of London, in a letter of September 4th 1811 to Lord Webb Seymour (1777–1819).[70] Most significantly Greenough and Aikin express the hope that by this activity, 'Mineralogical maps of districts which are now so much wanting may be supplied'. Attention is also directed to the organic remains or fossils found in stratified rocks by their series of eleven questions, which were presumably prompted by the several visits made by some of the Society's officers in 1808 to view William Smith's collection of fossils on display at his London home.[71]

The Geological Society next formed a 'committee for the construction of mineralogical maps, models, etc.' on April 7th 1809.[72] Laudan has pointed out that this committee enshrined the main mission of the new society—the preparation of a mineralogical map or maps.[73] By 14th June 1810 Arthur Aikin had been appointed to serve on this 'Committee of maps and sections' together with his companion on his early tours, Wilson Lowry.[74] Aikin's *Proposals* came as a direct result of the formation of the Committee and was Aikin's contribution to its work. The importance of making geological maps to the new Geological Society was further emphasised in the first printed report of its Council to the Annual General Meeting of 10th July 1810 which noted: 'The want of geological maps

[66] Turner, op. cit. (49), *2*, 230.

[67] Rudwick, op. cit. (64), 334.

[68] including [*Tilloch's*] *Phil. Mag.* 1817, *49*, 421–9; *Monthly Mag.* 1817, *43*, 436–9; *Am. Mineralog. Jl* 1810, *1*, 43–52, and sources quoted in J. M. Eyles, 'First Publication of the Geological Society,' *Nature*, 1942, *149*, 442 and Weindling, op. cit. (9), 270.

[69] in *Q. Jl geol. Soc. Lond.* 1942, *98*, Proceedings, xiii–xv.

[70] L. Horner (editor), *Memoirs and correspondence of Francis Horner, M.P.* London, 1843, *2*, 100.

[71] T. Sheppard, *William Smith: his maps and memoirs.* Hull, 1920, 216, and Weindling, op. cit. (9), 261, 269–70.

[72] Woodward, op. cit. (53), 30.

[73] R. Laudan, 'Ideas and Organisations in British Geology: A case study in Institutional History,' *Isis*, 1977, *68*, 532.

[74] R. S. Porter, *The making of the Science of geology in Britain 1660–1815*, Ph.D. thesis, University of Cambridge, 1974, 460.

having been greatly felt, and an opinion being entertained that much valuable information might be procured by collecting sections and models of particular districts, the Committee of maps were appointed, with instructions to direct their attention to these points'.[75]

The Proposals for a Mineralogical Survey of Shropshire

The *Proposals* has previously been very diversely dated, Bassett[76] giving 1797 and the British Library catalogue, being the most misleading, dating the work as ?1800. This, without the query, has been followed by Rodgers[77] and Laudan,[78] although the latter elsewhere also dates it as 1802. The Shrewsbury Public Library copy was formerly catalogued as *c.* 1830–1835. The printed catalogue of the Geological Society Library[79] is more cautious and merely states that it is undated. Extravagant claims for the priority of Aikin's work have been made as a result of some of these dates which could easily have been dispelled by study of the watermarks in the paper used. The eight copies of Aikin's *Proposals* examined all carry watermarks between 1805 and 1809.

The correct date of publication is revealed in the earliest ledger[80] of the printers R. Taylor and Co.[81] On page 185 headed 22nd June 1814[82] are details of the printing of Arthur Aikin's book *A manual of mineralogy* crown 8vo among others, and at the foot of the same page, but added later, are details of Aikin's *Proposals* in 4to, as follows:

'1810 5th May. Proposals for Mineral Survey of Salop, a sheet Sm[all] pica 4to.

500 of half sheet, the other 400 with alterations and paper	£5. 2.0.
Sewing 400 extra with map	£4.14.0.
Total:	£9.16.0.'

This clearly shows that the binding was completed by the above date and that publication was indeed in May 1810, after the 5th, and this is confirmed by contemporary references.[83] Fitton's claim many years later that they were issued about the close of 1809[84] can be rejected.

[75] Geological Society, *Report of the Council to the Annual General Meeting of July 10 1810*, London, 1810.
[76] *A Source-book of Geological . . . maps for Wales and the Welsh Borders (1800–1966)*, Cardiff. 1967, 79.
[77] Op. cit. (14), 289.
[78] R. Laudan (née R. Bush), *The development of Geological Mapping in Britain between 1790–1825*, Ph.D. thesis, University of London, 1974, 129, 273 and 110–12.
[79] J. Dallas, *Catalogue of the library of the Geological Society of London*, London, 1881, 9.
[80] now preserved at the St. Bride Printing Library. London.
[81] N. Barker, 'Richard Taylor—a preliminary note,' *Jl Printing Hist. Soc.* 1966, *2*, 46.
[82] A confusion with this date led to Aikin's *Proposals* being wrongly dated to 1814 in B. B. Woodward (ed.), *Catalogue of the books, manuscripts, maps and drawings in the British Museum (Natural History)*. 5 volumes, London 1903–1915, *1*, 21.
[83] Anon, 'On the impropriety of assigning new meanings to the established marks used in science, and on observing the directions and dips of strata.' [*Tilloch's*] *Phil. Mag.*, 1811, *38*, 356–7, and J. Farey, 'Notes and observations on part of the eleventh and twelfth chapters and appendix, of Mr. Robert Bakewell's *Introduction to geology*'. [*Tilloch's*] *Phil. Mag.* 1814, *43*, 334.
[84] op. cit. (4), 5.

The full title of the *Proposals* is *'Proposals for a mineralogical survey of the county of Salop, and of some adjacent districts'*. In this prospectus Aikin appeals for subscribers, and notes the existing lack of surveys of the mineralogy of English counties and that in the previous works devoted to the counties generally 'the practical miner or philosophical geologist would search in vain for a connected description of the mineral beds'. He records that 'of late years . . . it has been shown that the crust of the earth . . . instead of exhibiting those signs of ruin and confusion which a superficial examination might at first suggest, partakes in a very eminent degree of that order and regularity by which every other class of natural objects is character-ized'.

He draws four general conclusions: firstly that most of the earthy minerals are formed into strata, secondly that these strata occur in a determinate order of superposition, thirdly that veins 'differ materially in their contents according to the relative age of the strata within which they are enclosed', and fourthly that some unstratified rocks are also found within the great natural series of rocks. He then points out the usefulness of the study of mineralogy to many different categories of people, the 'Landed Proprietor, the Agriculturalist, the Planter, the Miner, the Manufacturer and the Builder' especially, in a county 'so well deserving of investigation or so well fitted for a specimen of geological topography' as Shropshire, which yields 'iron, lead, copper, zinc, limestone, freestone, slate, various clays, granular quartz for china and finer pottery ware, coal, petroleum and common salt'.

The only way to communicate such information to others, he says, is by full descriptions accompanied by accurate maps of the county, to which he says he was drawn by 'local attachments and accidental circumstances'. He records that Shropshire abounds in Secondary rocks [i.e. bedded rocks in Wernerian terms], is not wholly deficient in Primitive rocks, and again abounds in rocks Transitional to these two. It is also peculiarly rich in unstratified and unconformable rocks belonging to the Trap Formation 'the origin of which still continues a subject of such animated controversy'.

Aikin gave details of the information he would record for each of the Shropshire strata. He would detail for each the visible limits or superficial extent, its direction, its rise and dip, its thickness and general height above sea level, the principal fractures which each may have suffered, the nature and names of the substances of which each is composed 'as well as of those minerals and fossils which it may accidentally contain' (the latter still hardly a central element to his survey), the economic uses to which each has or may be applied, the soil into which each decomposes, and finally 'a list of those vegetables growing naturally on [each] surface which appear to be properly characteristic'. The mines of the county and the methods of extracting both the ores and their metals were also to be described.

As a sample of his methods and style Aikin gives a map of the county between the Longmont (Longmynd) and Corve Dale, geologically engraved, on a scale of 1 mile = 1 inch which is reproduced here as Figure 1. It shows the means whereby the different rock types were to be distinguished. Colour was not used at all but a series of engraved 'parallel lines for the stratified rocks, drawn in the direction of the real bearings of the strata . . . while the unstratified rocks are represented in the usual manner'. In other words these lines are strike lines for each stratum. The order of superposition is further indicated 'by drawing on the *upper* edge of each stratum small arrows, the heads of which point towards the next stratum lying immediately beneath "at right angles to the strike"' a practice for which he was castigated by an anonymous reader in the following year[85] who pointed out that it was conventional to record the dip of rocks and not their rise[86] as he claimed Aikin had done.

The map was accompanied by an engraved transverse section of the geology drawn along a north-west to south-east axis in which colours have been used in some copies to distinguish the different rocks. The map and section have an added importance for the history of cartography in view of Aikin's close connection with the Geological Society since they give us a view of graphic representation in English geology in 1810, before the publication of the first volume of the Society's *Transactions* (issued August 1811)[87] and before Cuvier and Brongniart's seminal *"Carte géognostique"* of the strata around Paris.[88] The importance of the early work of the Geological Society in encouraging visual expression of geological research has been emphasised by Rudwick.[89]

Aikin's map and section together reveal how English geological maps and sections might have evolved, but for the influence of Cuvier and Brongniart, with the use of an inadequate series of engraved conventional signs to separate strata rather than the use of colours. We can see that the rise of rocks rather than their dip was then being recorded, as also in Aikin's cross section through the Wrekin published in 1811.[90] However, Rudwick's suggestion that it was again Cuvier and Brongniart who instigated the parallel use of geological map and traverse section together into British geological publication via the Geological Society of London seems unlikely. Aikin's *Proposals* shows that they were in use by a member of the Society's Committee of maps the year before the French publication, and the recent publication of the lost drawings for James Hutton's *Theory of the*

---

[85] op. cit. (83), 356.
[86] For discussion of the terms 'dip' and 'rise' see J. Challinor, *A dictionary of geology* 5th edition, Cardiff, 1978, 87, 262.
[87] Rudwick, op. cit. (64), 354.
[88] In *Essai sur la Gôgraphie Minéralogique des Environs de Paris*. Paris, 1811.
[89] M. Rudwick, 'A visual language for Geology.' *Hist. Sci.* 1976, *14*, 158, 195.
[90] A. Aikin, 'Observations on the Wrekin and on the great coal field of Shropshire'. *Trans. geol. Soc. Lond.*, 1811, *1*, 191–212, and unnumbered plate.

Mineralogical Plan published in Aikin's Proposals 1810 of 'part of the county between Corve Dale and the Longmont' Shropshire. 'Scale 1 inch to a mile. The names (unless otherwise expressed) are of the Hills. Q stands for Quarry.'

124

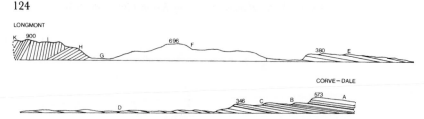

Geological Section along the line marked on Figure 1 redrawn from the version published by Aikin in his Proposals 1810. Scale 1·5 inches to a mile. 'The figures denote the barometrical height [Sic] above Eaton brook.' Reduced.

Earth shows the parallel use of map and cross section as far back as around 1785.[91]

Aikin's *Proposals* shows clearly his correct interpretation of the geological structure of that part of Shropshire which he depicted, as he was able to divide it into three distinct series of strata. One was 'composed of recent stratified rocks, another of primitive rocks, while between the two extends a great mass of unstratified rock' of uncertain origin of formation. This essentially correct interpretation is confirmed by the cross section of the area he gives, and reproduced here as Figure 2. This was drawn along the line marked on the map from the south-east where the uppermost stratum is lettered A, to the north-west where the most westerly stratum is lettered K. Strata A–E were assigned to Werner's Newest Floetz limestone formation. Stratum F was an unstratified mass which formed Caer Caradoc, Garstone, Hope Bowdler and the Ragleath hills, mainly of very indurated compact 'felspar' whose petrography is described in further detail. Aikin assigned it to one of the more recent Trap formations. The more western part of the section was again composed of stratified rocks but 'differing greatly in both their age and direction' from those in the east. These rocks dipped in general to the east and the oldest was G overlain by H–K belonging to Werner's Primitive Series completely lacking in fossils. That Aikin was right to subdivide the rocks of the area into these three groups, however misguided the assignment of Wernerian formational names may now seem, can be seen from the following tabulation which shows Aikin's lettered strata and the thickness and basic lithology he recognized for each, against the lithostratigraphic names used in the recent geological memoir of the Church Stretton region.[92] More recent lithostratigraphic names for some of the Shropshire Silurian sequence such as the 'Much Wenlock Limestone Formation' have yet to achieve recognition and are not used here.

Aikin's record of Strata A, B and E yielding fossil bivalves should be noted. Even allowing for the fact that brachiopods, which are the commonest fossils in these strata, would then have been called bivalves,

[91] G. Y. Craig (ed.), *James Hutton's Theory of the Earth: The Lost Drawings*. Edinburgh, 1978, 40.

[92] D. C. Greig et al. 'Geology of the country around Church Stretton, Craven Arms, Wenlock Edge and Brown Clee.' *Memoirs of the Geological Survey of Great Britain*. London, 1968, 380 p.

Aikin letter YOUNGEST	Lithology	Thickness	Recent name
A	limestone, almost wholly composed of bivalves and other fossils, alternating with slate-clay with corals	200′	Aymestry Limestone
B	limestone and slate-clay the former softer than that in A but also yielding bivalves	300′	Lower Ludlow Shales
C	as A but conformable with B	500′	Wenlock Limestone
D	blue slate clay with marine fossils	1400′	Wenlock Shales to Acton Scott Group inclusive
E	reddish brown sandstone with bivalve shells mostly pectinites [sic]	400′	Cheney Longville and Chatwall sandstones
F	Unstratified mass mainly of tile red compact felspar	?	Uriconian Volcanic suite
K	Purple clay slate		Stretton Shale Group
I	Greenstone and Greenstone slate veined with quartz		
H			
G	Primitive clay slate		More recent Longmyndian rocks

Spanning labels in table: FLOETZ LIMESTONE FM (A–D), TRAP FM (F), PRIMITIVE SERIES (K–G); ORDOVICIAN & SILURIAN STRATA (A–E); PRE CAMBRIAN (K–G).

OLDEST

The dip or rise and thicknesses of the group of rocks K–G, were, he noted, not always easy to determine.

there is no doubt from Aikin's record of pectinites in Stratum E that he has, here at least, misidentified brachiopods as pectenid bivalves. Brachiopods are the commonest faunal element in both the Cheney Longville and Chatwall members, especially orthids which superficially resemble pectenids.[93] He had also misidentified brachiopods from the 'die earth' of the

[93] op. cit. (92), 110–114.

126

Coalbrookdale coalfield as 'bivalves chiefly of the genus *Cardium*.'[94] The die earth here is, according to Symonds,[95] Wenlock Shales, or Bed D of the above classification in part. These are salutary reminders of the contemporary state of the knowledge of fossils, especially of brachiopods. There is no reason to think Aikin was merely a worse palaeontologist than most of his contemporaries.

The term *Pectinites* for *Pecten*-like fossil shells can be traced back to early English authors on fossils like Plot[96] and Lhuyd.[97] This pre-Linnean usage was not continued by Linnaeus himself in his *Systema naturae*, 1758, 10th edition, but the name *Pectinites* continued to be used until at least 1820 by German authors. James Sowerby, the most influential of early nineteenth century English authors on fossils however preferred to dispense with the previously-used suffix '*-ites*' for fossilised examples of shells,[98] and regarded *Pectinites* as a synonym of *Plagiostoma*.[99] *Cardium* is a generic name for Bivalvia used by Linnaeus in 1758.

The major problem for Aikin and his contemporaries was the uncertain state of brachiopod studies in 1810. David Ure[100] had, in 1793, described and figured a number of Scottish Carboniferous Productid brachiopods under the all-embracing generic name of *Pecten*. Sowerby, when describing *Productus* as a new genus in 1814, wrote: 'No-one would conceive these shells could be in any way related to the genus *Anomia* of Linnaeus but as yet there seemed no other place for them in the system.'[101] The first suggestion that brachiopods deserved separation from other molluscs only came in 1802, and the term Brachiopoda was only first proposed in 1806.[102] English workers for some years however still continued to use Linnaeus' system, and to group brachiopods with true bivalves. The generic name *Orthis* was not proposed until 1827 by the Scandinavian zoologist J. W. Dalman. Despite this unsatisfactory state of bivalve and brachiopod classification, the differences between members of the groups had been recognised by Aikin's time, and Aikin could have separated them. Aikin's difficulties should however remind us that fossils could then only be properly used and discriminated if they had been described and some idea of their geological ranges established, and how crucial the publication of the Sowerbys' *Mineral conchology* was to the advance of British stratigraphy.

Further details of Aikin's work on the rocks labelled A and C in these

[94] op. cit. (90), 199.
[95] W. S. Symonds, *Records of the Rocks*, London, 1872, 139.
[96] R. Plot, *The natural history of Oxfordshire*, Oxford, 1677, 103–4, plate 4, fig. 11.
[97] E. Lhuyd, *Lithophylacii Britannici ichnographia*, 2nd edition, Oxford, 1760, 29–32 (nos. 562–625 etc.).
[98] J. Sowerby, *The mineral conchology of Great Britain*, Vol. 1, London, 1812, vi.
[99] op. cit. (98), 175 (1814).
[100] D. Ure, *The history of Rutherglen and East Kilbride*, Glasgow, 1793, 317–8, plates 14–16.
[101] op. cit. (98), 153.
[102] H. M. Muir-Wood, *A history of the classification of the Phylum Brachiopoda*, London, 1955, 10.

Proposals (the Aymestry and Wenlock Limestones) can be found in his complementary paper in the first volume[90] of the Geological Society's *Transactions* published on 14th August 1811, but possibly written a little earlier than the *Proposals*. This paper discussed the Wrekin and the Great [Coalbrookdale] Coal Field of Shropshire. In it Aikin distinguished a limestone formation he had found to underlie the coal beds to the east of the Wrekin at Steeraway Hill. He named it as (a different) Bed C and it is now known to be unconformable Carboniferous Limestone with the Coal Measures above. Aikin wrongly equated this limestone with the westerly of the two parallel ranges of limestone he had correctly separated elsewhere, but here grouped together running NE–SW to the southwest of the coalfield, and which he had earlier illustrated and briefly discussed.[103] The most easterly of these two ridges, formed by what is now called the Aymestry Limestone, Aikin claimed to be characterised by 'chain corals, pentacrinites, small ammonites [misidentified euomphalid gastropods, a mistake he made also in 1796 and common at the time[104]] and a few bivalve shells,' and to run from Mocktree near Leintwardine along the continuous escarpment to Mogg Forest. In addition he equated with the rocks of this ridge the famous Wenlock Limestone fossil localities of Benthall Edge near Broseley and Lincoln Hill north of Ironbridge, the latter locality one illustrated earlier by John Whitehurst.[105] It is clear from these correlations that Aikin was not yet always able to separate three quite different major fossiliferous limestone units even in this small area. Along the ridges between Mocktree and Lincoln Hill he took too much account of a similarity in dip across what we today know are fault lines. As a result he wrongly equated the rocks and fossils of the northern Wenlock Limestone outcrop with crinoids, presumed gastropods and the chain coral which forms Benthall Edge and is exposed on Lincoln Hill, with those of the Aymestry Limestone to the south which forms the ridge from Mocktree to Mogg Forest. It is likely that if he had realised the significance of the highly characteristic fossil assemblages of the Wenlock and Aymestry Limestones from an earlier period, he would have distinguished the two rocks away from the main Wenlock Edge area. Around Wenlock Edge he was certainly able to separate the Aymestry and Wenlock Limestones on topographic evidence from 1810, and using fossils to some extent from 1812. It is significant that Roderick Murchison continued to confuse these two limestones from 1831 until 1834,[106] a remarkable error at this date but perhaps one traceable to Aikin's original error.

Aikin had however the means to correct his mistake by 1812 (see p.

---

[103] op. cit. (27), 197 and plate.
[104] W. Pitt, *A topographical history of Staffordshire*, Newcastle-under-Lyme, 1817, 191.
[105] J. Whitehurst, *An Inquiry into the original state and formation of the Earth*, 2nd edition, London, 1786, 208–9, pl. 3, fig. 3.
[106] J. C. Thackray, 'T. T. Lewis and Murchison's Silurian System' *Trans. Woolhope Nat. Fld Club* 1979, *42*, 190.

131). In his earliest correlations of these rocks Aikin was still undoubtedly giving overriding significance to their rise and strike and the escarpment and ridge patterns they produced, just as he had done on his 1796 tour.[107]

Progress of the Shropshire survey

There is evidence that Aikin was actively gathering material for his Shropshire survey well before the *Proposals* was issued in May 1810. On 4th July 1809 he visited Hannah Mary Rathbone, the widow of William Rathbone IV (1757–1809) at their home, Greenbank, near Liverpool.[108] She was the daughter of Richard Reynolds of Ketley Bank, Shropshire, and her husband had played a considerable part in the Shropshire iron trade from the 1780s.[109] Aikin may have been seeking introductions to Salopians who could help him with the survey, as on 28th August 1809 Aikin and two of his subsequent subscribers, Dr Thomas Dugard (no. 39) and Archdeacon Joseph Corbett (no. 37), dined together at the latter's house in Longnor, Shropshire, with Corbett's elder sister Katherine Plymley (c. 1758–1829). She recorded this meeting in her manuscript diary thus:[110]

> 28th I dined at my brothers with Dr Dugard and Mr Arthur Aikin, who had requested the Doctor to introduce him, he is the son of Dr [John] Aikin and the nephew of Mrs Barbauld—he was brought up for the ministry among the Unitarian dissenters and was for some time the Pastor of the Unitarian meeting in Shrewsbury, but he became so skeptical that he was no longer easy in his situation and resigned it, having become an unbeliever in revealed religion. Whatever are the notions he has had the misfortune to imbibe he does not intrude them on others as Dr Dugard tells me. He *now supports himself by his writings* [italics here added] and so highly admired my brother's agricultural report for Shropshire [published in 1803] that he was anxious to be in his company. He was in Shropshire for the purpose of making a mineralogical survey and has some thoughts of publishing a mineralogical or geological map with an accompanying treatise on this County. He appears thoughtful and mild, his conversation is intelligent and he expresses himself with much clearness—he looks out of health—I afterwards heard from the Doctor [Dugard] that he was much pleased with the day and thought himself much obliged to my Brother.

In view of this one may ask why the proposals were not issued in late 1809, rather than the following summer. Again, other commitments have to be taken into account, and especially Aikin's involvement with the *Cyclopaedia* issued under the editorship of fellow unitarian Rev Thomas Rees (1743–1825). In the preface to the final volume Aikin is named as having contributed to the articles on chemistry, which appeared in part 14

[107] op. cit. (27), xi, 197.
[108] E. Greg (ed), *Reynolds-Rathbone letters and diaries 1753–1809*. Edinburgh, 1905, 145.
[109] Trinder, op. cit. (8), 40.
[110] Diary no. 79, August 17 to November 29, 1809—Shropshire County Record Office, 567/4, quoted by kind permission of Charles Corbett, Esq.

in February 1807, and on geology written with fellow unitarian Robert Bakewell (1767–1843) in part 31 in November 1810. Aikin also contributed to the article on mineralogy published in 1813.[111] This work, for which he was paid, would have kept him busy over this period from 1802 onwards.[112] Aikin's involvement with the Geological Society's 'Committee of Maps' in 1810 probably provided the final stimulus for the issue of the *Proposals*.

After it was issued we know of Aikin's continuing activity in the field in Shropshire that year only from the manuscript diary of the geologist John Macculloch (1773–1835).[113] Entries show that Macculloch, fellow member of the Geological Society of London since 1808, was touring Shropshire with Aikin in September 1810. The tour was presumably undertaken because of their joint membership of the Society's Committee of maps and sections. Macculloch's particular research at this time was however directed to finding a British limestone suitable for millstones for gunpowder. He toured widely in England in 1809 and 1810 in this search, which had a more utilitarian purpose than Aikin's work.[114] On 19th September Macculloch and Aikin dined together at the Shrewsbury house of John Wicksteed, later to be named as a subscriber (no. 59) to Aikin's *Proposals*. The next day they visited the Hope Lead Mines, southwest of Minsterley. On 27th September they made a joint excursion via Buildwas Abbey to Coalbrookdale. They stayed that evening with another of Aikin's subscribers, P. H. Witton (no. 61) of the Lightmoor Iron Works, and the following day 'spent a profitable day amid the quarries of Lincoln Hill and Benthall Edge and in various speculations which the whole of this very interesting scene affords.'

Information about the progress of the mineral survey of Salop after this comes from a number of sources. The most important is the long notice inserted by Aikin in the *Salopian Journal*, the Shrewsbury newspaper printed by William Eddowes (1754–1833), also the local agent named in the *Proposals* to receive subscriptions for him in Shrewsbury.[115] The notice appeared in the issues of 25th September 1811 and 2nd October 1811. A subscription list published in a newspaper is an interesting example of such a listing and one of a type not mentioned by Wallis in his survey.[116] It begins by repeating some of the paragraphs of the *Proposals* about the intended work, and then asks for help with the undertaking from 'those gentlemen who direct the various mining establishments of the County'. Especially

[111] Anon, 'Notices respecting New Books. The Cyclopaedia . . . by Abraham Rees . . . 39 vols.' [*Tilloch's*] *Phil. Mag:*, 1820, *56*, 219.

[112] He is already named as a contributor in the prospectus for the first part in 1802. Copy in British Library collection, 11902 c. 26 (77), 1802.

[113] Transcripts from this were kindly provided by David Cumming of the University of Glasgow.

[114] D. Flinn, 'John Macculloch M.D., F.R.S. and his geological map of Scotland: his years in the Ordnance, 1795–1826' *Notes Rec. R. Soc. Lond.* 1981, *36*, 83.

[115] L. C. Lloyd, 'The Book Trade in Shropshire. Part 1' *Trans. Shrops. archaeol. nat. Hist. Soc.* 1935, *48*, 105–110.

[116] P. J. Wallis, 'Book subscription lists.' *The Library* 1975, (5), *29*, 255–286.

130

Aikin seeks 'to secure the active support of the man of science in his undertaking' which will help him 'to enter upon mining speculations with a reasonable prospect of success or at least to avoid the delusions too often practised against him by ignorant or designing adventurers'.

In this notice Aikin stated he had been busy on the survey during the summers of 1810 and 1811 but 'without attempting to extend the knowledge of his plan much beyond the circle of his personal acquaintance', a statement not perhaps easily reconciled with the number of copies of the *Proposals* known to have been printed in 1810. 300 subscribers at 6 guineas each were needed to publish the survey, and he both appealed for additional subscribers and named the 68 who had come forward in the year and a half since the *Proposals* was first issued to subscribe for only 70 copies in total. It is not known what success this appeal had.

He also gave details of his plans for publication of the survey which would cover the whole of the county. The entire work he stated would comprise one volume in Quarto accompanied by a Folio of Plates. The plates would included a complete geological map of the county on a large scale, sections of strata, profiles of the mountains and plans, views and sections of the principal mines. There is no doubt Aikin planned an impressive publication, aimed as much at the Salopian as the geologist, and one considerably larger in scope than the Geological Society of London would be likely to publish.

There is evidence that Aikin's mineralogical survey of Salop both continued for a few years after the issue of these appeals and was adequately publicised on his behalf. The influential Board of Agriculture in London patronised it and Sir John Sinclair (1754–1835), the President, referred to the survey in a speech delivered on 12 June 1810 which was later printed. Sinclair noted the proposed Shropshire survey as 'an undertaking for accomplishing which he is considered to be peculiarly well qualified and which is the first attempt of the sort on a regular and extensive plan.'[117] John Farey very bitterly refuted this claim when discussing his own work for the same board since August 1807 in Derbyshire.[118] Aikin's survey was also noticed and commended by John Playfair (1748–1819) in a notice published in November 1811.[119] This reviewer 'ardently wished for the success of his undertaking' and Aikin was certainly busy in the summer of 1811 continuing his researches in Shropshire because he then discovered a witherite locality in Shropshire at Snailbeach mine.[120] In 1812 Aikin became one of the secretaries of the Geological Society,[121] an appointment which could only aid his search for subscribers.

[117] Sir John Sinclair, *Address to the Board of Agriculture on the progress made by that Institution in promoting the Improvement of the Country, on Tuesday 12th June 1810*. London, 1810, 4.
[118] op. cit (83), 334–5, 337.
[119] [J. Playfair], 'Review of the Transactions of the Geological Society, volume 1'. *Edinb. Rev.* 1811, *19*, 207–229.
[120] A. Aikin, 'Notice concerning the Shropshire Witherite.' *Trans. geol. Soc. Lond.* 1817, *4*, 438–442.
[121] Woodward, op. cit. (53), 296.

In February 1812 Aikin reported, at a meeting of the Geological Society of London, his discovery of the brachiopod which James Sowerby named *Pentamerus knightii* in August 1813.[122] This was found near Ludlow in the rock later called the Aymestry Limestone. This discovery shows Aikin was by then taking a more active interest in fossils, although his earliest Geological Society publications are always noted as basically mineralogical in character.[123] The report of the Council of the Geological Society to the Annual General Meeting in the same month was also emphatic on the need to study fossils

> The very scanty number of Organic Remains, [in the Society's collections] however, imposes upon the Council the necessity of calling the attention of the Members to that department. Its importance is now generally admitted, not only as illustrating the natural history of our globe, but as affording a valuable character, by which strata may often be identified, where other characters fail.[124]

Sowerby recorded *Pentamerus knightii* from at least two localities in Shropshire as reported by four collectors. This discovery enabled Aikin thereafter to separate the rocks later named Wenlock and Aymestry Limestones at least in the outcrops south of Craven Arms whence the fossil was reported. This brachiopod was at once found to be a very good index fossil at the latter horizon and is now known to be confined to that particular stratigraphic horizon.[125] Aikin also provided Sowerby with other fossil brachiopods collected during his Shropshire survey, including specimens described by Sowerby as other species of *Pentamerus*.[126] Some were from the same horizon as *P. knightii* but from Yeo Edge [= today's View Edge near Stokesay] to the north of Ludlow and described as *Pentamerus aylesfordii* and as nearly resembling *P. knightii*. Aikin also provided the figured syntype[127] of another brachiopod described by Sowerby as *Pentamerus laevis*, a very common species and one recognised by Aikin as characterising a lower limestone horizon below the Wenlock Limestone, and now called the Pentamerus Beds of the Upper Llandovery. These fossils helped him to separate these three limestones (see p. 127) thereafter.

In 1813 further notices of Aikin's intended Shropshire work were

---

[122] Sowerby, op. cit. (98), 73*–74* (August 1813).

[123] See obituary notices of Aikin in *Q. Jl geol. Soc. Lond.* 1855, *11*, Proceedings xli–xlii and *Am. Jl Sci.* 1855, 391–2.

[124] Geological Society, *Report of the Council to the Annual General Meeting of February 7 1812*. London, 1812.

[125] M. G. Bassett, 'The articulate brachiopods from the Wenlock Series of the Welsh Borderland and South Wales.' Part 4. *Palaeontogr. Soc. [Monogr.]* 1977, (4), 172–5.

[126] op. cit. (98) 75*–76*, (August 1813).

[127] There is some uncertainty about the locality whence came Aikin's specimen. Sowerby's text says merely 'from Bildwas', but the claimed still-surviving original in the British Museum (Nat. Hist.) London reg. no. BB 126 is from 'Long Mynd'. See L. R. M. Cocks, 'A review of British Lower Palaeozoic brachiopods'. *Palaeontogr. Soc. [Monogr.]* 1978, 143 and 182.

132

given by Robert Bakewell in his influential textbook[128] and by Joseph Nightingale in his contribution on Shropshire to the *Beauties of England and Wales*. Nightingale acknowledged Aikin's help with material on the mineralogy of Shropshire[129] and noted his mineralogical survey had been in progress from 1810 which 'from his profound knowledge, tried abilities, and indefatigable industry will no doubt possess a just claim to the approbation of the public, while it confirms the solid reputation which the author has already acquired'. In 1814 Farey[130] stated that he believed the field work undertaken in Shropshire for the survey by Aikin was 'yet in hand'. This was a busy year for Aikin as his well-known *Manual of Mineralogy* was published, based on the lectures he had just given to the Geological Society in the winter of 1813–14. The Appendix to the *Dictionary of Chemistry and Mineralogy* of 1807 also appeared, and he spent the summer in Cornwall curating the late Philip Rashleigh's (1729–1811) famous mineral collection at Menabilly.[131]

In later years Fitton,[132] who had in the same article misdated the appearance of the *Proposals* to 1809, stated that Aikin abandoned his survey in 1815. This seems unlikely in view of two surviving letters of this year in which Aikin mentions his survey. The first dated January 3rd 1815 and addressed to his subscriber Dr Dugard at Shrewsbury[133] states 'I shall be in Shropshire in the course of next spring [1815] in order to complete my Survey when I shall doubtless have the pleasure of seeing you'. The second letter dated September 5th 1815 is addressed to James Watt junior (1769–1848) Esq., Soho [Birmingham].[134] It reads as follows:

Dear Sir,

It being my intention to include in my "Survey" chemical analyses of the principal varieties of Shropshire iron ore (especially of that from Lightmore) together with the several qualities of bar and cast iron manufactured therefrom. I shall be much obliged to you for a specimen of the best Shropshire bar and cast iron. About $\frac{1}{2}$ a lb. wt. of each will be amply sufficient.

Yours very truly,

Arthur Aikin

It is clear from the above that Aikin was still actively prosecuting his survey in the Autumn of 1815. In an article on Shropshire published in volume 32 of Abraham Rees' *Cyclopaedia* in December 1815[135] it was stated

[128] R. Bakewell, *An Introduction to Geology*, London, 1813, 294.
[129] Rev. J. Nightingale, *Shropshire—The Beauties of England and Wales*, London, 1813, *13*, parts 1–2, viii, 33 and in list of Salop books [1207].
[130] op. cit. (83), 334.
[131] A. Russell, 'Philip Rashleigh of Menabilly, Cornwall and his mineral collection,' offprint from *Jl Royal Inst. Cornwall*, 1952, 9.
[132] op. cit. (4), 5.
[133] in Beaumont MSS. Warrington Reference Library.
[134] in Muirhead MSS. Box IV A—Birmingham Reference Library.
[135] A. Rees (editor), Article 'Shropshire' in *The Cyclopaedia or Universal Dictionary of Arts, Sciences and Literature*, London, 1815, *32*, unpaginated.

that 'Mr Aikin is preparing an interesting publication on the mineralogical stratification of this country', but no further references to Aikin's survey have been found. Fitton's claims many years later that the *Proposals* was issued in 1809 and the survey abandoned in 1815 seem essentially correct, though misdated at each end by one year, the true dates being 1810 and 1816.

The Abandonment of the Survey

More than one reason for the abandonment of the survey can be put forward. One possibility is that Aikin's new commitment from early in 1817 first as candidate for and then as Secretary of the London Royal Society of Arts[136] forced its abandonment. This seems unlikely if the survey (as suggested above) was already abandoned.

The most likely explanation of the abandonment of the Shropshire survey is a financial one, a general consideration that has been largely ignored by those writing on the development of geology at this period. The original 1810 *Proposals* stated 'the price of the work will be for each copy on common paper six guineas and for the same on large paper with the first impressions of the plates twelve guineas, half the money to be paid at the time of subscribing', both considerable sums of money. On 17th May 1813 Aikin was to write to Greenough thus 'Hitherto I have followed Geological pursuits only as the occupation of my leisure hours deriving from other sources all the income required for the supply of my wants and wishes'. By the time Aikin was interviewed for the post of Secretary to the Royal Society of Arts in London—to which he was elected in February 1817—he recorded he was then occupied in drawing up patents and in advising on scientific matters, without mentioning his geological activities as a source of income.[137] As Inkster[138] has said, scientific activity for men like Aikin was an important source of income, a fact too often ignored by historians. It is clear from the 68 subscribers who responded to the 400 copies of his *Proposals* in the year and a half after it was issued, that Aikin's Shropshire work was not viable financially. Robert Townson's projected work on Yorkshire[139] in which 'the leading subjects will be Geology, Mineralogy, Natural History in all its different branches' was finally abandoned in 1806 after four years' work, again for lack of subscribers.

There is no doubt that Aikin was with hindsight most unfortunate to have chosen Shropshire for his survey. As Trinder has pointed out the wartime boom in the Shropshire iron trade began to ebb in 1812 and there followed years of considerable economic depression in Shropshire, with the

---

[136] Rodgers, op. cit. (14), 175 and Le Breton, op. cit. (55), 106–8.
[137] Greenough MSS, Cambridge University Library MSS. Add 7918 and H. T. Wood, *A History of the Royal Society of Arts*, London, 1913, 336.
[138] op. cit. (9), 32.
[139] Final Prospectus [1803] in M. Boulton MSS, T 40, Birmingham Reference Library.

134

trough reached in 1816.[140] This was the year of the abandonment of Aikin's survey. The nationwide depression which followed peace in 1815 was also blamed for some of the difficulties which attended the publication of William Smith's Geological Map in 1815 by its author.[141]

An analysis of the 68 subscribers who did come forward will give an idea of the sorts of people and industries to whom a geological survey would prove useful in their own estimation. They are listed in the Appendix in which they are identified and documented.

Of the 24 Geological Society subscribers (35%—Category B) it should be noted that they comprise only 12% of the then cumulative membership of the Society, which suggests that the Society's support for Aikin was minimal, despite his close involvement with it.

An analysis of the 36 Shropshire subscribers (who make up 53% of the total) will best give an indication of the variety of local people to whom Aikin's work appealed, at whom it was most aimed, and the main reason why Aikin sought to publish his survey outside the Geological Society. Of the 36, 19 (53%) were land owners interested in the mineralogical survey to improve the value of their Shropshire estates and mines. Of these ten (53%) were also subscribers to the Shropshire General Agricultural Society instituted in 1810.[142]

Five subscribers (nos. 27, 32, 33, 38 and 53) were ironmasters; two were connected with what we may term engineering (28 and 60), and one (Witton no. 61) was involved in both. Three were physicians (39, 40 and 58), five were tradesmen (30, 31, 47, 59 and 62) and one was a barrister.

Of the religious groupings the great majority were members (as far as is known) of the Anglican Church although only two were clergymen (37 and 43). Aikin's strong unitarian connections were also obviously of great importance in obtaining subscribers to his survey. As many as eight (22%) of the total number of Salop subscribers were involved with the High Street Unitarian Chapel in Shrewsbury, an important unitarian focal point at this time.[143] There are three other Unitarians in category D. These are early examples of provincial Unitarian interests in science, closely analogous to the important unitarian connection with the Manchester Literary and Philosophical Society founded in 1781.[144] Perhaps a unitarian interest in geology is understandable because of their rejection of the literal truth of the Scriptures.[145] One must not however ascribe too great an importance to the unitarian contribution to provincial science in general at

---

[140] Trinder, op. cit. (8), 137, and see J. R. Wordie, *Estate Management in Eighteenth Century England*, Royal Historical Society Studies in History *30*, 1982, 127.
[141] Autobiographical notes dated June 6 1839 in Wm. Smith MSS, Geology Dept., Oxford University Museum.
[142] *Salopian Journal* 28 November 1810.
[143] Ditchfield, op. cit. (19), 304.
[144] A. Thackray, 'Natural knowledge in cultural context: The Manchester Model', *Am. Hist. Rev.* 1974, *79*, 672–709.
[145] O. Griffiths, *Religion and Learning*, Cambridge, 1935, 161–3.

this time.[146] Nor must the Quaker contribution to Shropshire improvements be overemphasised. Aikin's subscribers numbered only one member of the Society (no. 38) and two others whose membership had lapsed (nos. 53, 62).

It seems clear that the numbers who came forward to subscribe were simply insufficient to finance the publication Aikin had in mind. While there is no doubt many people did appreciate the direct utility of geology it is also clear that its value was not yet generally realised even in an area of thriving industry like Shropshire, where in 1811 the Census revealed a total population of 194,298 with 16,993 employed in agriculture and 16,744 in trade and manufacture.[147] Public awareness of geology and what it could achieve was still very limited.

Contemporary Problems in Publishing Geological Maps and Memoirs

Financial problems also beset three contemporary but larger-scale attempts to complete geological maps and memoirs of England and parts of Scotland: those of William Smith (1815), of George Greenough (1820), and of John Macculloch (1819). It seems worthwhile to briefly review these problems in the light of those also experienced by Arthur Aikin to see if any general conclusions can be drawn.

a) Smith's Map

In 1801 Smith issued his first printed prospectus[148] for an intended work on the strata which was circulated in 'great numbers'. Farey, who was one of those originally circulated and would have been well informed of its progress, tells us this failed 'to produce an adequate list of Subscribers to Mr. S's proposed Map and Work and having *received no Money on account thereof, but from two Individuals*, he found himself compelled to lay the same aside, and apply very assiduously to his Enginery and other business, for retrieving his pecuniary affairs'.[149] This is confirmed by Cox who writes 'the history of the next few years [after 1801] was one of repeated attempts on Smith's part to take advantage of his rare intervals of leisure to proceed with his proposed treatise and on the other hand to find some means of financing its publication'.[150] Smith's letters from this period confirm this: 'the expense of such a publication is too great for my circumstances'— Smith to Richard Crawshay 1805;[151] or his letter to the Duke of Bedford of

[146] R. S. Porter, 'Science, Provincial Culture and Public Opinion in Enlightenment England.' *Brit. Jl Eighteenth Century Studies*, 1980, *3*, 20–46.

[147] J. Nightingale, op. cit. (129), [1210].

[148] L. R. Cox, 'New light on William Smith and his work.' *Proc. Yorks. geol. Soc.* 1942, *25*, 13–4. (5 surviving copies have been traced).

[149] J. Farey. 'Mr. Smith's Geological Claims Stated.' [*Tilloch's*] *Phil. Mag.* 1818, *51*, 178 and 'Observations on the priority of Mr. Smith's Investigations of the Strata of England . . . ' [*Tilloch's*] *Phil. Mag.* 1815, *45*, 335.

[150] op. cit. (148), 15.

[151] op. cit. (148), 16.

136

18th May 1804[152] asking for patronage for his work on the strata as 'I have now no prospect of getting any remuneration but through the medium of a publication'. The contributions of Sir Joseph Banks, who paid down £50 at the Woburn Sheep Shearing meeting of June 1804[153] and of Richard Crawshay who also paid down £50 soon afterwards, came nowhere near the sums needed.

Smith's financial problems with his map were not solved until the end of 1812 when John Cary apparently accepted the entire financial risk involving in preparing Smith's geological map and the entirely new topographic map on which it was based. From this point progress was rapid. But Cary's intervention did not solve any of Smith's many other financial problems since Smith was twice arrested for debt in London in 1814.[154] Smith's completed map was exhibited however, despite this, on 8th February 1815. The total number of subscribers was 414[155] but the number of copies actually issued may have been less than this because some subscribers refused to purchase a copy when it appeared, and some had died before the map was finally published at a cost of 5 guineas a copy in its simplest form;[156] a lower figure than that named for Aikin's Shropshire survey. These prices may be compared with those charged for the contemporary volumes of the *Transactions of the Geological Society of London*. Volumes 1–3 issued over 1811 to 1816 together cost seven pounds nine shillings.[157] The fact recorded by Farey,[158] under the name of 'a Constant Reader', that the final list of subscribers to Smith's map would 'be found almost barren of names familiar to us of late years as managers of the Geological, Wernerian and other Societies or writers in their Transactions' is also significant as it reduced the number of his potential subscribers considerably. Of the 68 subscribers to Aikin's survey and the 414 to Smith's map only five names appear in both lists, and there is no certainty in two of these five cases that it is the same subscriber.

The financial results of the rivalry between Smith and Greenough's geological maps are also clear enough. One subscriber to Smith's map, Rev Edward D. Clarke (1769–1822) Cambridge Professor of Mineralogy, and already a correspondent of Arthur Aikin, wrote to John Carey on 13 December 1815 to say he had subscribed to Smith's map on the mistaken assumption that 'it was the map for which the Geological Society have been so long collecting materials. But I desire it to be distinctly understood that if the map you mention be not published by the *Geological Society* and

---

[152] Wm. Smith MSS, Geology Dept., Oxford University Museum.

[153] *Agric. Mag.* 1804, *10*, 469.

[154] Cox, op. cit. (148), 43–44. R. C. Boud. 'The Early Development of British Geological Maps,' *Imago Mundi* 1975, *27*, 73–96 and J. M. Edmonds, 'The First "Apprenticed" Geologist' *Wiltshire Arch. Nat. Hist. Mag.*, 1982, *76*, 145.

[155] Cox, op. cit. (148), 53.

[156] Sheppard, op. cit. (71), 123.

[157] Woodward, op. cit. (53), 311.

[158] 'Further queries as to the proper places in the British series of strata.' *[Tilloch's] Phil. Mag.* 1815, *45*, 295–296.

under their auspices I do not intend to be a Subscriber and . . . Mr. Smith must excuse me for declining the purchase of his Map because I really cannot afford it'. Clarke did however offer to recommend Smith's map for the Cambridge University library.[159]

b) Greenough's Map

Aikin, as a founder member of the Geological Society, was closely involved with the production of this map, which had been in gestation since 1808[160] before Aikin issued his *Proposals* in 1810. Its first draft was submitted in 1812 while Aikin was actively engaged on his Shropshire work. On January 3 1815 Aikin wrote to Dr. Thomas Dugard of it thus: 'Our great map . . . of which you have I think seen the first rough draft is in the hands of the engraver and will be completed with all due dispatch', and when it finally appeared in 1820 Greenough acknowledged that Aikin had provided 'some valuable details on the geology of Shropshire',[161] which received special commendation in Fitton's review.[162]

The support of the Geological Society and the fact that both G. B. Greenough and Henry Warburton provided £1,000 each towards its production[163] meant it was not subject to financial difficulties. Nevertheless two points are worth noting: one is its slow progress; the agreement with the engraver was made in November 1814, but the map was not finally published until May 1820—taking three years longer than Smith's. The other is its poor sale, at a price of 5 guineas to Members of the Geological Society and 6 guineas to other purchasers; Laudan suggests that sales in the first five years after its publication amounted to only about 100 copies,[164] and that the total distributed in this period through all channels could not have exceeded 300 copies.

c) Macculloch's Western Islands

A somewhat similar undertaking, which can also be contrasted with Aikin's, was John Macculloch's *Description of the western islands of Scotland* published in 1819. It is obviously difficult to compare directly a published with an unpublished (and not surviving) work, and Macculloch covered a much larger area than Aikin, ranging from Lewis to the Isle of Man. There were also important differences in attitudes between Macculloch and Aikin, who would surely not in 1820 have referred to 'namby pamby cockleologists and formation men' in the way Macculloch did.[165] Volumes 1 and 2 of Macculloch's work comprised text, covering not just geology but

---

[159] Wm. Smith MSS, Geology Dept., Oxford University Museum.
[160] Woodward, op. cit. (53), 56–60.
[161] G. B. Greenough, *Memoir of a geological map of England*, London, 1820, 5.
[162] Fitton, op. cit. (4) 7, 9, 14–15.
[163] J. Bowen, *A brief memoir of the life and character of William Baker*. Taunton, 1854, 75.
[164] Laudan, op. cit. (78), 247–252.
[165] K. M. Lyell (editor), *Memoir of Leonard Horner F.R.S., F.G.S.* London, 1890, *1*, 174.

IX

138

agriculture, climate, antiquities and inhabitants. Volume 3 comprised ten topographic or geological views, twenty three plates of structural or stratigraphic diagrams and geological cross sections (including some biological and archaeological objects) with ten geological maps of the western islands.

The production of the work has been considered in detail by Cumming[166] who demonstrates that sales did not even cover publication costs. The retail price of the three volumes was £3.3.0, only half that of Aikin's projected work, for 600 octavo pages of text and 43 plates, which were particularly expensive to produce for a number of reasons. Cumming suggests that because the retail price was set at too high a level this restricted the potential market. Aikin's experience with his more detailed, ambitious and expensive but smaller-scale undertaking suggests the market may not have been large enough for works of this sort. The more geological the contents the more the audience for such books diminished.

Thomas Webster's Contribution to Aikin's Shropshire Survey

Murchison[167] in acknowledging some of those who had helped him in preparing his magnum opus published in 1839, *The Silurian System*, wrote as follows: 'In preparing my work I derived much assistance from a valuable original MS. on the Structure of Shropshire by Mr A. Aikin, the earliest modern geologist, who, with his associate Mr T[homas] Webster, worked in this field.' It could be argued, however, (see p. 116) that Dr Robert Townson's earlier work in Shropshire was also 'modern'.

Thomas Webster's (*c.* 1772–1844) connection with Aikin's work in Shropshire is also noted by Edwards[168] who writes that Webster's 'first experience of field geology may have been in Shropshire, while working with Arthur Aikin'. Certainly many drawings were made by Webster for Aikin's intended work in Shropshire[169] and some were used by Murchison in 1839,[170] but while it is certain that these were not the first geological drawings or engravings which Webster had done they may well have introduced him to geology in the field. The notice of Aikin's intended work in the *Salopian Journal* of 25th September 1811 stated that Aikin 'has arrived at the period in which it would be expedient to place some of his drawings and sections in the hands of the engraver'. From this it is clear that if Webster was the artist who had produced these drawings, he had certainly finished some by that date.

Webster joined the Geological Society in 1809.[171] His manuscript

[166] D. A. Cumming. 'A Description of the Western Islands of Scotland, John Macculloch's successful failure.' *J. Soc. Biblphy nat. Hist.* 1977, *8*, 270–285.
[167] R. I. Murchison, 'Anniversary Address.' *Proc. geol. Soc. Lond.* 1842, *3*, pp. 637–687.
[168] N. Edwards, 'Thomas Webster (circa 1772–1844).' *J. Soc. Biblphy nat. Hist.* 1971, *5*, (6), 469.
[169] Fitton, op. cit. (4), 5.
[170] Murchison, op. cit. (2) 255 and woodcuts 24, 26, 28, 36, 40, 45 and lithographs at pages 82, 216, 225, 256, 269, 283, 291.
[171] Woodward, op. cit. (53), 272.

autobiography[172] makes no mention of his work in Shropshire, stating only that over the period 1802–1812 he lived chiefly by landscape painting and teaching. Webster's first letter reporting on his fieldwork for Sir Henry Englefield in the Isle of Wight and Dorset is dated 21st May 1811,[173] but his work with Aikin did take him into the field in Shropshire and their connection seems to have started before Webster's work for Englefield.

Webster's introduction to geology had come through his connection with the Royal Institution where he prepared drawings of geological subjects for Sir Humphrey Davy's lectures there in 1805.[174] Webster had also drawn fossils for John Pinkerton, one of Arthur Aikin's early contacts, which were published on 1st August 1811.[175] It seems likely that Webster and Aikin started work together on preparing drawings for the Shropshire survey in 1810 or 1811. This may well have been one of the introductions by which Webster was appointed as Keeper of the Museum, Librarian and draughtsman to the Geological Society in June 1812.[176]

Murchison's Use of Aikin's Survey

After his Shropshire survey was abandoned Aikin restricted himself to publishing a few papers on his Shropshire work in the *Transactions* (and contributing Shropshire specimens to the Museum) of the Geological Society from 1811 to 1824. These were in continuation of his first paper (1811) which is the most important. He was however still being urged in 1822 to publish his full results,[177] and as late as 1828 W. D. Conybeare was still trying, and observed that Aikin 'wants stirring up'.[178] But between 1832 and 1835 Aikin abandoned all ideas of further publication and passed his Shropshire notes and drawings to Murchison for incorporation in the latter's work on the Silurian System.

When Murchison's *Silurian System* was published (1839) he noted Aikin's projected work in Shropshire in his introduction and stated that Aikin 'had formed a project of describing Shropshire in detail; but having long abandoned his intention he no sooner heard of the progress I was making in the present work, than he placed at my disposal his original notes and drawings illustrative of certain tracts around the Wrekin and the Caradoc'[179] and also the Coalbrookdale Coalfield. This tells us the areas in which Aikin's work was concentrated, although, as Fitton observed,[180] the

---

[172] Webster MSS, Archives of the Royal Institution, London, 121A-B.

[173] Sir Henry Englefield, *A description of the principal picturesque beauties, antiquities and geological phenomena of the Isle of Wight*, London, 1816, 117.

[174] A. M. Ospovat, 'Four hitherto unpublished geological lectures given by Sir Humphry Davy in 1805.' *Trans. R. geol. Soc. Corn.*, 1978, *21*, 70.

[175] J. Pinkerton, *Petralogy. A Treatise on Rocks*. London, 1811, *2*, pls. 1–2.

[176] Woodward, op. cit. (53), 47.

[177] W. D. Conybeare & W. Phillips, *Outlines of the Geology of England and Wales*. London, 1822, Part 1, 424.

[178] J. W. Clark & T. K. Hughes, *The Life and Letters of the Rev. Adam Sedgwick*, 2 vols., Cambridge, 1890, *1*, 324–5.

[179] op. cit. (2), 4–5, 99.

[180] Fitton, op. cit. (4), 10.

area 'examined by Mr Aikin . . . was more extensive than Mr Murchison seems to have supposed'. Of these notes and drawings only a few pages, transcribed into one of Murchison's notebooks, survive.[181] The transcription can be dated from internal evidence to between 1832 and April 1835, showing the period in which it came into Murchison's hands. The notes are, however, too incoherent to allow us to judge the final state of the work that Aikin placed at Murchison's disposal.

A partial judgement can be made from the testimony of historian W. H. Fitton who saw the original notes and drawings which Aikin had made during his survey and later lent to Murchison. Apart from Webster's drawings, some other drawings intended for the survey were made by Aikin's youngest brother the architect Edmund Aikin (1780–1820). Fitton remarked that the drawings by these two 'form a large and very effective portion of the illustrations' in Murchison's work (1839) which suggests that more than those actually credited to Webster were reproduced.

Of the now lost notes Aikin made during his survey we need only quote Fitton verbatim:[182]

> Mr Aikin's notes appear to us to coincide with Mr Murchison's descriptions in so many points of detail, that they must have been of great assistance in his enquiries. On looking over them, with the aid of the Ordnance maps, and of this Silurian volume it now appears that, although the order of superposition was unknown to the writer, the same beds are so correctly identified at many distant points, both by lithological character and by fossils, as to enable a person possessed of the key to connect many of their detached portions. Thus, Mr Aikin recognized the 'Upper Ludlow Rocks' in the vicinity of the Abberley hills. He mentions the concretional structure which characterizes some of these beds. He distinguished the limestone of Yeo Edge and Mocktree Hill, by its 'quadrivalve shell', (*Pentamerus Knightii*), from what he calls the 'nodular limestones' of Wenlock and Benthal Edge; and connected several remoter calciferous rocks (the 'Caradoc' of Murchison) by their peculiar fossils (*Pentamerus laevis* and *oblongus*), to which he had given a temporary distinctive name; indicating, especially the course of the ridges on the west of Wenlock Edge, and their containing those shells. In these notes we find, also, a line of plutonic elevation, precisely agreeing with that of Mr Murchison, traced for some miles south-west of Caer-Caradoc. And on the subject of 'compound sandstone', the following question is proposed, which leads exactly to the views illustrated in this volume with great force of evidence: 'Is not the compound sandstone of Lythe Hill, etc., a mixture of grawacke-slate with greenstone, formed during the deposit or outburst of the latter?'.

Fitton's remarks seem at first ambiguous, especially in his remark 'the order of superposition was unknown to' Aikin. The explanation must be that the complete order of superposition and the exact relationships of his Shropshire rocks to the Old Red Sandstone were never clarified by Aikin.

[181] Murchison MSS, Notebook 78, pages 25–30 and one at end. Geological Society of London.
[182] op. cit. (4), 5–10.

But it is clear that over the areas in which he worked, such as that shown in the engraved map accompanying the 1810 *Proposals* (see fig. 1), Aikin did know firstly that many of the rocks were superposed and secondly what the local order of superposition was to a considerable degree. Fitton shows how indebted Murchison was to Aikin's pioneering work in Shropshire, and how Aikin changed his views on some controversial points during his survey. Of especial importance is the later separation by Aikin of the rocks, subsequently named the Wenlock and Aymestry Limestones, which he had confused in 1811 (p. 127). He was able to do this partly by attention to the relevant fossils which he had recognised by 1812 (p. 131). The only major criticism that Fitton makes of Aikin's work was his inference of unconformity because of a supposed regularity in difference of dip which was not in fact substantiated by later work.

An additional point recently made by Secord[183] of Murchison's work is that most of Murchison's typical sections were in Shropshire like the Caradoc and Wenlock formations. Murchison's Silurian succession was displayed most clearly in Shropshire and Murchison described these Salopian Sections first when he came to describe the succession in detail. This gives Aikin's pioneer work on them an added significance.

Conclusions

Murchison made a quite unjustifiable claim about the demise of Aikin's Shropshire survey:[184] 'In truth at the early period when Mr Aikin undertook the task it was almost hopeless to attempt to unravel the structure of Shropshire; for that County not only contains every sedimentary formation from the lias to the slates inclusive but is also rendered most complex by the numberless dislocations of the strata through the agency of volcanic rocks'. Yet, as we have seen, Aikin's *Proposals* of 1810 already contained a highly creditable sketch of the structure of that part of the country from the Longmynd to the ridge formed by the Aymestry Limestone, and correctly separated the stratified from the unstratified volcanic rocks of the area. Murchison's suggestion that geology was not sufficiently advanced to investigate Shropshire in Aikin's main period of survey over 1809–1816 must thus be rejected—the use of fossils to identify the relevant rocks was already becoming known and was practised by Aikin in Shropshire. It is far more likely that the 'hopelessness' of Aikin's attempt had financial and not scientific causes as inferred by Murchison.

Although Aikin, according to Fitton,[185] 'disclaimed any previous knowledge of the stratigraphic system described by Mr Murchison' in 1839, his work does demand a re-assessment of this claim above, and Murchison's other claim that 'no one was [previously] aware of the

[183] J. A. Secord, 'King of Siluria: Roderick Murchison and the Imperial Theme in Nineteenth Century British Geology.' *Victorian Studies*, 1982, 25, 422.
[184] op. cit. (2), 4.
[185] op. cit. (4), 9.

142

existence below the Old Red Sandstone of a regular series of deposits containing peculiar organic remains'.

Other work contemporary with Aikin's in Shropshire also suggests that Murchison's claims are overstated. John Farey (1766–1826) wrote on June 14 1812:[186] 'Shropshire . . . I have not seen except in the distant horizon', yet within one month he was there in person. He visited Croft Ambrey Park limeworks, southwest of Ludlow, where he collected the index fossil *Pentamerus* [= *Kirkidium*] *knightii* from one of the three limestone rocks he was able to trace in the Ludlow area and which he discovered underlay the Clear Hill [= Clee hills] Coal Measures to the east. More significantly he correctly correlated this Croft Ambrey [= Aymestry] limestone with outliers of the same limestone on Tinkers Hill and Caynham Camp [= Cairbairn Hill] to the southeast of Ludlow. This was achieved within a two or three day visit[187] and it is clear he was able to identify, separate and follow the discontinuous outcrops of limestone rocks later named Carboniferous, Aymestry and Wenlock Limestones in this area in this short time using the same techniques he had used elsewhere on other rocks in England. We must conclude that Greenough's claim in the introduction to this present paper has much to support it from the work of Aikin and Farey alone.

We must also agree with Laudan[188] that the small size of the audiences to which the geological maps and memoirs of Aikin, Smith, Greenough and Macculloch appealed are significant, and note that such projects were financially crippling unless subsidised in some way. We may leave the final word on this to John Farey, writing in January 1817 of an intended Mineralogical Survey of Perthshire to architect William Atkinson (c. 1773–1839): 'The art of mineral surveying is at present so much in its infancy that the public in general are not sufficiently acquainted with its value to give the same extended encouragement to its professors as they do to other arts of longer established importance. On this account a surveyor can expect *no profit* from *the publication* of large mineral maps, but in prudence must look for real employers before commencing such works'.[189] He might well have had Aikin's Shropshire survey in mind while writing this.

When Murchison started work fifteen years later over a much larger area he brought no new techniques to the unravelling of Siluria but boundless energy, sagacity[190] and the necessary financial resources. The *volte-face* that had taken place in the appreciation of geology over these

---

[186] [*Tilloch's*] *Phil. Mag.* 1812, *39*, 427.

[187] J. Farey, 'Cursory geological observations lately made in Shropshire (etc.)'. [*Tilloch's*] *Phil. Mag.* 1813, *42*, 53 and 59.

[188] op. cit. (78), 228 and 253.

[189] J. Farey, 'On the mineralogical description and mineral map of the County of Perth . . .' *Ann. Phil.* 1817, *9*, 219–221.

[190] Geikie, op. cit. (3), *1*, 96.

twenty years is shown by the fact that, instead of Aikin appealing in the newspapers to potential subscribers to come forward in 1811, we find the potential subscribers themselves appealing to Murchison to make his researches available in book form so that they could purchase copies.[191] This was a truly remarkable revolution in the public attitude to geological publication and its financing.

Acknowledgments

In following Aikin's footsteps in Shropshire I have been assisted by a large number of librarians and archivists throughout Britain to all of whom I tender my thanks for the kindness with which all my queries were answered. Special debts which cannot go unacknowledged are owed to Anthony Carr at Shrewsbury (who also found the 1811 subscription list), and his staff in the Local Studies library who all gave me much help and led me to sources I should otherwise never have found. Similar thanks go to Marian Halford and her staff at the Shropshire Record Office.

James Mosley, librarian of the St Bride Printing Library, London, gave particular help in tracing entries in the printing ledgers of Richard Taylor, to which I was initially led by George Lancaster of Taylor and Francis, Ltd. Dr William Wake kindly assisted by sending information from the records of the Shrewsbury Unitarian Church. David Cumming helpfully responded to an appeal by sending diary extracts which shed new light on Aikin's activities in 1810. Professor E. A. Vincent gave permission for quotations to be made from the William Smith archive in his care.

Joan Eyles, Jim Secord, John Thackray, Barrie Trinder and Paul Weindling all read a draft of this paper and suggested a considerable number of improvements and additions for which I am most grateful. Michael Oates allowed me to borrow on very extended terms his personal copy of Aikin's *Proposals*. Finally without the generous hospitality of John and Susan Thackray I could only have spent a fraction of the time I was actually able to spend researching in London.

Joan Cliff kindly typed my manuscript and D. Macdonald drafted Figure 2.

APPENDIX

An analysis of the 68 known subscribers to Aikin's mineralogical survey in 1810 and 1811. The subscribers can be divided into any number of possible categories but it seems appropriate to separate first those with Geological Society connections (B), either as Ordinary (i.e. London based) or Honorary members from outside the capital, from those with predominantly Shropshire connections (C), leaving a few subscribers who are either institutions (A) or family friends and other categories (D).

---

[191] Murchison, op. cit. (2), 6, and Thackray, op. cit. (1), 63.

144

A. Institutional subscribers (2) 3% of total.
1. **The London Institution.** Arthur Aikin was an original proprietor of this institution founded in 1805, which built up a fine library.[1] He was also an unsuccessful applicant for the post of Librarian there.[2]
2. **School Library,** Shrewsbury. This library, known to have been in use by 1596, served not just the school but the whole Shrewsbury community at the time of Aikin's survey.[3]

B. Individual subscribers connected with the Geological Society (24) 35%.
   The following subscribers nos. 3–26 can be identified as subscribers through their membership of the Geological Society of London founded in 1807. In the following list only those who were elected Members by September 1811, the date of the subscribers list, are given. Christian names and other interpolated material are enclosed in square brackets and the following abbreviations are used: F.M. Founder Members; H.M. Honorary Members, i.e. resident outside London; O.M. Ordinary Members, i.e. resident in London; with the year of their election.
   Details of their membership are derived from the lists published by Woodward.[4] One other subscriber Dr Thomas Dugard was an Honorary Member living in Shrewsbury but is given here only in the Shropshire list, (no. 39). It should be noted that although two of these subscribers nos. 5 (Banks) and 10 (Davy) had resigned from the Geological Society in April 1809,[5] they are included here.

3. **Th[omas] Allan,** Esq. F.R.S. Edinb[urgh] HM 1807
4. **W[illiam] Allen,** Esq. F.R.S. London FM 1807
5. **Rt. Hon. Sir Joseph Banks,** Bart, K.B. P.R.S. OM 1808
6. **W[illiam] Babington,** M.D., F.R.S. London FM 1807
7. **R[obert] Bingley,** Esq., F.R.S. London OM 1808
8. **R[ichard] Bright,** Esq. Bristol HM 1807
9. **J[ohn] G[eorge] Children,** Esq. F.R.S. London OM 1807
10. **Professor [Humphry] Davy of the Royal Institution,** F.R.S. FM 1807
11. **B[enjamin] Fayle,** Esq. London OM 1809
12. **R[obert] Fergusson,** Esq., F.R.S., Edinb[urgh] OM 1809
13. **G[eorge] B[ellas] Greenough,** Esq., M.P., F.R.S. London FM 1807
14. **W[illiam] Henry,** M.D., F.R.S., Manchester HM 1808
15. **Leon[ard] Horner,** Esq. London OM 1808
16. **James Laird,** M.D. London FM 1807
17. **W[ilson] Lowry,** Esq., London OM 1808
18. **W[illiam] Macmichael,** M.D. London OM 1808
19. **W[illiam] H[asledine] Pepys,** Esq., F.R.S. London FM 1807
20. **D[avid] Ricardo,** Esq., London OM 1808
21. **W[illiam] Saunders,** M.D., F.R.S. London OM 1808
22. **S[amuel] Solly,** Esq., London OM 1810
23. **H[enry] Warburton,** Esq., F.R.S. London OM 1808
24. **W[illiam] Williams,** Esq. London OM 1808
25. **S[amuel] Woods,** Esq. London OM 1808
26. **J[ohn] Yelloly,** M.D., London OM 1811

C. Individual subscribers with Shropshire connections (36) 53%.
   Names and addresses are given first just as they appear in the printed list of 1811. Any interpolations to these and added dates are enclosed within square brackets.
27. **William Anstice,** Esq., Madeley Wood [1781–1850]. Ironmaster and

partner in the Madeley Wood ironworks and mines from 1803,[6] later very active in geology becoming a Fellow of the Geological Society in 1836 and greatly aiding Murchison with his work in Shropshire from the 1830's, especially through his fine collection of Shropshire geological specimens.[7]

28. **Charles Bage,** Esq., Shrewsbury [1752–1822]. From at least 1778 he was a land surveyor, but had become a wine merchant also of Shrewsbury by 1789, when he was made a Burgess.[8] He later became well known as an architect and the designer of the first multi-storied cast iron framed building, erected in Shrewsbury and completed in 1797.[9] He was Mayor of Shrewsbury in 1807.

29. **T[homas] Beale,** Esq., Heath House [Aston-on-Clun, 1781–1845]. Of a landed Shropshire family for whom see Burke. His sister Anne (died 1857) married Rev. John Rocke (1783–1849) of Clungunford in 1812. In the following year Rocke sent Shropshire fossils to Aikin and the Geological Society of London via Thomas Dugard (no. 39). Rocke was later another who helped Murchison with his Silurian researches.[10]

30. **John Beck,** Esq. Ditto [sic]. [banker of Shrewsbury, 1760–1821].

31. **Peter Beck,** Esq. Ditto [sic]. [banker of Shrewsbury, 1761–1824].

There must be a printer's error here in giving the Beck brothers the same address as Thomas Beale. Peter and John Beck were both baptised at the High Street Unitarian church and were sons of Peter Beck, grocer of Shrewsbury. John was named as a grocer in 1784 and Peter as a wineseller in 1806 (having taken over from C. Bage (no. 28) in 1800) the dates when they became Burgesses of Shrewsbury.[11] But they were also both involved in a banking concern in the town.[12]

32. **Thomas Bishton,** Esq., Kilsall [near Tong, 1785–1839]. Born at Donington 17th July 1785, son of John Bishton (1735–1806) landowner of Kilsall. His father was also operator of coal mines and ironworks in Shropshire and elsewhere and was also the Marquis of Stafford's (no. 56) (q.v.) chief agent from 1790.[13] He was also the author of the original *General Survey of the Agriculture of Salop*, published for the Board of Agriculture in 1794. On John senior's death in 1806 he was succeeded as the Marquis of Stafford's chief agent by his son John (1806–1810) and then a second son George (1810–1812). Thomas a younger son had taken up a share in the Lilleshall Iron Company in 1807 but little is otherwise known of him. He was buried at Donington 27th November 1839.[14]

33. **Thomas Botfield,** Esq., Hopton Court [Hopton Wafers, 1762–1843]. Another man with active interests in geology at the time of Aikin's survey; he had supplied James Parkinson (1755–1824) with specimens of fossil plants from his coal mines in Shropshire before 1804.[15] The coal mines were at Titterstone Clee Hill but the Botfields were also very active and successful as ironmasters and landed gentry elsewhere in Shropshire.[16] Thomas Botfield became a Member of the Geological Society in 1813.[17]

34. **Right Hon. the Earl of Bridgewater [John William Egerton,** 1753–1823. Owner of vast estates including much in Shropshire.[18] He was also the first chairman (1805) of the Ellesmere Canal, owning the whole of Ellesmere itself.[19]

35. **Isaac Hawkins Browne,** Esq., M.P. Badger [S.S.E. of Shifnal 1745–1818]. Best known as an assayist and as M.P. for Bridgnorth.[20] Browne was also a Shropshire landowner who developed his properties industrially with the help of Thomas Botfield's (no. 33) father.[21]

36. **Sir Corbet Corbet** Bart. Adderley Hall [Audlem *c.* 1753–1823]. Shropshire landowner and chairman of County Quarter Sessions.[22] In 1804 the British Mineralogical Society of which Aikin was president had analysed a "red micaceous substance" from his Shropshire estates.[23]

146

37. **Rev. Archdeacon [Joseph] Corbett.** Longnor [S. of Shrewsbury, c. 1759–1838]. He was one of the more important of Aikin's subscribers. He was the only son and heir of Joseph Plymley and under the name of the Rev. Joseph Plymley he wrote for the Board of Agriculture, of which he was an Hon. Member from 1795, their final Report *General View of the Agriculture of Shropshire* on which he started work in 1795 and first published in 1803. This included a number of geological observations sent in by William Reynolds (1758–1803) of Coalbrookdale, the published works and other communications of Robert Townson, of Aikin[24] and other of Aikin's subscribers including his own physician Thomas Dugard (no. 39). In November 1804 he assumed the name of Corbett on the death of his uncle.[25] In 1809 Aikin had visited the Plymley family to discuss his intended mineralogical survey (see p. 128).

38. **Francis Darby,** Esq., Coalbrookdale. [1783–1850]. Eldest son of Abraham Darby III (1750–1789), builder of the famous Ironbridge at Coalbrookdale. Francis became one of the partners in the Coalbrookdale Company after the death of his father, on coming of age, and was one of its managers from 1810–1850 although his role does not appear to have been a prominent one. They were a famous Quaker family, but some of Francis' interests in art, collecting art, and in natural history were unusual for a member of the Society of Friends, of which he was an atypical member.[26]

39. **Thomas Dugard** M.D. Shrewsbury [1777–1840]. Physician in Shrewsbury and the only Shropshire Honorary Member of the Geological Society of London before Aikin's survey started. He was elected in 1807 as one of the first of this category of member. He was born in 1777, son of William a mercer of Newport, Shropshire. He emigrated to North America about 1790 and studied medicine at Columbia College 1794–1795. He returned to England without graduating and in 1796 was appointed assistant to Dr John Evans (no. 40) who was then surgeon to the Ketley Iron Co. In July 1800 he became house surgeon at the Salop Infirmary, Shrewsbury. He was awarded in 1804 an M.D. degree by testimonials from the University of St. Andrews and in 1811 became physician to the Salop Infirmary. He was a knowledgeable geologist, botanist and chemist though he published very little. In 1810 he guided William Buckland (1784–1856) on the first geological tour Buckland[27] made and later was one of the founders of the Shropshire and North Wales Natural History Society in 1835 and one of Murchison's helpers with the production of the *Silurian System*. He died January 19th 1840.[28]

40. **John Evans** M.D. Shrewsbury [1756–1846]. John Evans was born on 4th July 1756 at Llwynygroes, Montgomeryshire, the son of John Evans (1723–1795) well known as a cartographer and map maker.[29] The father's nine sheet map of North Wales published in 1795 on a scale of nearly one inch to the mile was that used by Aikin on his tour in 1796.[30] It was reissued in 1802. The son who subscribed to Aikin's survey and was also a personal friend from 1796,[31] is stated to have attended Westminster school and Oxford University by the *Dictionary of Welsh Biography*[32] but this must be an error, as the Oxonian who graduated BA in 1778 and was awarded his Bachelor of Divinity degree in 1783 was aged 17 when he matriculated in April 1773. Our John Evans must be a different man as he would then have been only 16. In fact he attended Edinburgh University where he graduated MD in 1778. He was elected an ordinary member of the Edinburgh Natural History Society in 1785.[33] He was senior physician to the Salop Infirmary from 1782–1814, physician to the Coalbrookdale Co. at a salary of 20 guineas per year, also physician to the county gaol, founder of the Shrewsbury Public Library with E. Harries (no. 42), author of the paper on Sutton Spa near Shrewsbury published by Joseph Plymley (no. 37) in 1803 (pp. 73–82) and of a number of medical and botanical papers published in journals. He also published a never

completed poem "The Bees" between 1806 and 1813. He left Shrewsbury in 1814 and died 18th January 1846.[34]

41. **Thomas Eyton**, Esq., Wellington 2 copies [1753/54–1816]. Member of a Shropshire landed family[35] who became a Burgess of Shrewsbury in 1776, and High Sherriff of Salop in 1779. He was a partner in the Shrewsbury Old Bank and a very active promoter of Shropshire canals.

42. **Edward Harries**, Esq., Arscott [Great Hanwood, 1743–1812]. One of the leading promoters and major shareholders in the famous Coalbrookdale Iron Bridge in 1775 and part owner of the site since he owned much of the parish of Benthall where he was involved in ironworks.[36] He was Rector of Hanwood 1768 to 1782 and Vicar of Cleobury Mortimer 1768–1779. In 1782 he resigned both livings after conversion to Unitarian views.[37] He contributed much information to Joseph Plymley (no. 37) in 1803 (p. 47–8) especially on the soils of Shropshire, who also described him as "of very considerable property" (p. 119).[38] His monumental inscription in the church at Hanwood is given by Chitty[39] where he is named as Reverend but he dropped this title on resigning from the church.[40]

43. **Rev. Hamlet Harrison**, Rector of the First Portion of Pontesbury [from 1809, SW of Shrewsbury *c*. 1764–1843]. M.A. 1789 Oxon.[41] who in 1792 became Headmaster of Brewood Grammar School in Staffordshire. In 1809 he was accused among other crimes of neglecting his teaching there in favour of farming and other concerns and in 1810 he was evicted. But he refused to leave until Michaelmas 1811 when he departed to Shropshire.[42] His obituarist refers to his owning large property.[43]

44. **W[illiam] Cheney Hart**, Esq., Hope Bowdler [1755–1818]. Born in Shrewsbury and baptised on 31st May, 1755, at the High Street Unitarian Church[44] entered Warrington Academy in 1771[45] the son of Dr Cheney Hart (1726–1784) born at Warrington Lancs. who was physician to the Shrewsbury Infirmary from 1751–1779 and a well known Shrewsbury nonconformist.[46] In 1772 William matriculated at Oxford University and later became a barrister.[47] He entered the Middle Temple in 1773 and was called to the Bar in 1778. In 1789 he was made a Burgess of Shrewsbury. He practised on the Shrewsbury and Salop Sessions 1800–1814 and died in 1818.[48]

45. **Sir John Hill** [3rd] Bart. Hawkstone [Hodnet 1740–1824]. Member of a famous Shropshire landowning family[49] who had been MP for Shrewsbury before the date of Aikin's Survey.

46. **John Hill**, Esq., Hawkstone [Hodnet, 1769–1814]. Eldest son of the above.

47. **Mr W. Hughes**, Shrewsbury [born 1777 fl. 1812]. Two men of this name are shown in printed voters lists for Shrewsbury elections 1807 and 1812.[50] Aikin's subscriber is identified with the William Hughes who was a starchmaker of Dogpole from 1796–1807 and soapmaker of Wyle Cop in 1812 both in St Julian's parish. He was baptised 14th August, 1777, son of John at the Unitarian High Street church.[51] The family soap and starch factory in Shrewsbury was later taken over by a member of the Wicksteed family[52] (no. 59).

48. **R[owland] Hunt**, Esq., Boreatton [Baschurch, 1784–1835]. A member of another famous family of Shropshire landowners,[53] he was elected Hon. Memb. of the Board of Agriculture in 1810[54] and was very active in the Ellesmere Canal Company.[55]

49. **Hon. C[harles] C[ecil] C[ope] Jenkinson** MP, Pitchford Hall [S.E. of Shrewsbury, 3rd Earl of Liverpool, 1784–1851]. Statesman and MP for Sandwich with estates in Shropshire.[56]

50. **Richard Lyster**, Esq., Rowton Castle [Shrewsbury, *c*. 1772–1819]. Shropshire landowner and Colonel and High Sheriff of Salop 1812 and MP for Shrewsbury from 1814 to 1819.[57]

51. **T[homas] N[etherton] Parker,** Esq., Sweeney Hall [Oswestry, 1771–1848]. Shropshire pamphleteer, inventor and landowner.[58] At the time of Aikin's survey he was involved in coal mining speculations in the Morda Coalfield just south of Oswestry which were connected with the Ellesmere Canal.[59] He was Sheriff of Shropshire in 1815. He also later helped Murchison with his geological investigations in Shropshire.[60]

52. **Right Hon. Earl Powis [Edward Clive** 6th Earl, 1754–1839]. Shropshire landowner of Powis Castle & Walcot Park, Lydbury North and Lord Lieutenant of the county 1804 to 1839[61] and a member of the Board of Agriculture from 1793. He was active in canal promotion in the area for the improvement of his estates and quarries.[62] He later assisted Murchison with his work in Shropshire in the 1830's and was active in gaining subscribers for him.[63]

53. **William Phillips,** Esq., Donnington [1763–1831]. Partner in the Donnington Wood ironworks with members of the Bishton family (no. 32). These were later taken over by the Lilleshall Company in 1802, with which he remained connected. He was also involved with William Reynolds (1758–1803), the famous Ketley ironmaster in a glass house at Donnington Wood from 1791.[64] He was disowned by the Society of Friends in the same year.[65]

54. **Charles Rogers,** Esq., Ludlow [1753–1820]. One of the few subscribers from the southern part of the county. A London East India merchant who, on his retirement from business, purchased the Stanage estates west of Ludlow which extended into Radnor, Hereford and Shropshire.[66] He died in Ludlow, where he also owned property, on December 31st 1820.[67]

55. **J[ohn] Stackhouse,** Esq., Acton Scott. [Church Stretton, 1741–1819]. Famous botanist and author[68] whose family had large landowning interests in both Cornwall (where he was born) and Shropshire.[69] From 1804 he spent most of his winters in Bath where he died. He married one of the Actons of Acton Scott in 1773. J. A. de Luc records of a visit to Pendarves in Cornwall on 28th July 1806 where he met Stackhouse; 'he has . . . great concerns . . . in the mines of the neighbourhood. Hence he is very well acquainted with the interior part of the ground wherever it has been opened to seek and follow the loads'.[70]

56. **Most Noble the Marquis of Stafford [George Granville Leveson-Gower,** 1758–1833]. The second marquis, probably the richest man in England at this time—the 'leviathan of Wealth'. His large Shropshire estates were based on Lilleshall where he was connected with collieries and ironworks.[71] Elected a Member of the Geological Society in 1815.[72]

57. **Right Hon. the Earl of Tankerville [Charles Bennet** 4th Earl, 1743–1822]. Owner of extensive estates in Shropshire particularly in Shrewsbury and the lead mining district of the country round Shelve.[73] He had a double interest in Aikin's Survey as after 1774 and before 1806 he took up the study of natural history and built up a magnificent collection of recent shells.[74] His collection of fossils was equally famous and was described by William Buckland (1784–1856) as 'extremely rich' when he visited it at Walton-on-Thames in December 1818.[75]

58. **W[illiam] Tayleur,** M.D. Shrewsbury [1773–1836]. M.D. Edinburgh 1795 and also studied at Göttingen University 1795–96. On his return he settled as a physician to the Salop Infirmary Shrewsbury from 1800–1811 where he was made a Burgess in 1806.[76] He was of a well known Shrewsbury family.[77] His grandfather, also William (1712-1796), became a Unitarian and was its foremost promoter in Shrewsbury and a personal friend of Joseph Priestley.[78] Dr William died in 1836.[79]

59. **Mr [John] Wicksteed,** Shrewsbury [1774–1837]. Another Unitarian baptised at the High Street church on 31st March 1774.[80] He was a long standing personal friend of Arthur Aikin. Dr John Macculloch recorded in his diary for 19th

September 1810 when the three were dining together at Wicksteed's house in Shrewsbury that both Wicksteed and Aikin attended Edinburgh University in 1795–96 with him,[81] although neither Aikin nor Wicksteed matriculated there and must have been attending lectures privately. Wicksteed was a woollen draper in Frankwell, Shrewsbury at the time of Aikin's Survey, and it seems certain he was the unnamed friend who contributed chapter VII 'On the woollen manufacturers of North Wales' to Aikin's published *Journal*.[82] He defended Aikin's name against S. T. Coleridge in 1798.[83] He was also a student of chemistry.[84] His son Thomas (1806–1871) became a well known civil engineer through Aikin's help[85] and it was at his house in Oldford near London, that John Wicksteed died in 1837.[86]

60. **Mr H[enry] Williams,** Hadley Lodge [Wellington, *c.* 1754–1842]. Williams is an interesting member of a profession only starting to flourish by the time of Aikin's survey. He began as an engine erector of Boulton and Watt engines about 1779.[87] In 1782 he entered the service of the Reynolds family and by 1789 he was chief millwright to their Ketley Ironworks and in 1790 was John Rennie's guide round these works when Rennie visited them.[88] In 1794 he became the Shropshire Canal Company's chief engineer and in 1797 also engineer to the Shrewsbury Canal.[89] By 1818 he was of sufficient financial status to become one of the partners in the Ketley Ironworks after they had been relinquished by the Reynolds family.[90]

61. **P[hilip] H[enry] Witton,** Esq., Lightmore [Dawley *c.* 1762–1838]. He was of a West Bromwich Unitarian family.[91] He was in the 1780's a member of the Old Meeting House, Birmingham and in 1786 he set up in business as a buckle maker with his relative and fellow Unitarian Archibald Kenrick (1760–1835).[92] Witton was initially a stamper by trade. The damage caused by the Priestley riots in Birmingham was drawn and described by Witton with Rev. John Edwards in a book published in 1791.[93] Probably in common with many Birmingham Unitarians he was forced to leave the town (like Joseph Priestley). From 1797 to 1800 he was engineer to the Warwick and Birmingham Canal Company, having previously been clerk-accountant to the same company. He is next found at the Lightmoor Iron Works in Shropshire and on 27th September 1810 Dr John Macculloch and Aikin on a field tour together spent the night at his house.[94] These works were then owned by Messrs. Addenbrooke and Pidcock of Stourbridge[95] and Witton seems to have been their manager. By 1814 he was back in Birmingham where he appears in post-1820 directories as a plater. He died in 1838.[96]

62. **Mr G[eorge] Young,** Shrewsbury. 2 copies. [1780– ?). Young was born in Worcester, the Quaker son of a land surveyor, schoolmaster and civil engineer of the same name (1750–1820)[97] who in 1786 was elected a member of the Smeatonian Society of Civil Engineers.[98] His son was elected a Burgess of Shrewsbury in 1806[99] when he was described as a Coal Proprietor of Canal Wharf by which time he had left the Society of Friends. He was also a waggon proprietor and he continues as a coal and latterly iron merchant in Canal Wharf, Shrewsbury, in directories and voters lists until 1835.

D. Subscribers with other connections (6) 9%.

63. **P[eter] Crompton** M.D. Eton [House, Wavertree, Liverpool 1763–1833]. Fellow Unitarian of a Derby landed family.[100] He entered Warrington Academy in 1781,[101] Edinburgh University in 1783 and Leyden University in 1784 where graduated M.D. in 1785,[102] having shared rooms at Leyden with Dr Robert Darwin later of Shrewsbury, Charles Darwin's father.[103] He practised first at Derby where he became a member of the Philosophical Society.[104] He moved to Liverpool in 1798, turned to brewing and became well known as a political figure

150

and parliamentary reformer.[105] He was a family friend of the Aikins,[106] presumably from his days at Warrington Academy.

64. **Perceval Lewis,** Esq., F.A.S. Lymington [*c.* 1757–1821]. Son of Edward of Downton the M.P. for Radnor, he was a barrister of Lincolns Inn assigned to the Welsh circuits. He retired to Lymington about 1802, was elected a Fellow of the Society of Antiquaries of London on 13th June 1811, and died 23rd September 1821.[107]

65. **Paul Panton,** Esq., Plasgwyn, Anglesea [1758–1822]. His father (Paul 1731–1797) was a barrister and antiquary with a keen interest in collieries and mines and according to the Dictionary of Welsh Biography,[108] he followed much in his footsteps. The son went to school in Warrington which may have provided an early contact with Aikin. He also practised as a barrister on the Welsh circuit and took a keen interest in Welsh studies and antiquities which explains why he subscribed to Aikin's intended work. It is also possible he was related to Joseph Corbett's (no. 37) first wife née Jane Panton.

66. **Sir J[ohn Saunders] Sebright** [7th] Bart M.P., F.R.S. [1767–1846]. Land-owner in Worcestershire and Hertfordshire (but not apparently in Shropshire), politician and agriculturalist.[109] It was his latter interest—he was an Honorary Member of the Board of Agriculture from 1796—which explains his interest in Aikin's survey. He was elected a Member of the Geological Society in 1814.[110]

67. **William Smith,** Esq., M.P. London [1756–1835]. Politician; at the time of Aikin's Survey M.P. for Norwich. He was well known as an abolitionist and emancipator who opposed the wars with France.[111] He was a fellow Unitarian and a friend of Arthur Aikin's father which explains his subscription. He had been educated at the Daventry non-conformist Academy.

68. **S[amuel] Wakefield,** Esq., London [? –1835]. Samuel was the brother of Arthur Aikin's former teacher at the Hackney Academy, Gilbert Wakefield (1756–1801).[112] The family connection was further cemented in August 1806 when Gilbert's daughter Anne married Arthur Aikin's brother and co-worker Charles Rochemont Aikin. He was a fellow Unitarian who lived at Hackney and the family connection explains his subscription. He died July 1835.[113]

N.B. Bracketed numbers in BOLD type thus (**53**) refer to footnotes in main paper.

[1] Cutler, op. cit. (**60**) and M. Berman, *Social Change and Scientific Organisation. The Royal Institution 1799–1844*, London, 1978, 92–3.

[2] W. H. Pepys MSS, Royal Institution Library, London.

[3] P. Kaufman, 'The loan records of Shrewsbury School Library', *The Library*, 1967, (5), *22*, 252–256.

[4] Woodward, op cit. (**53**), 268–273.

[5] Rudwick, op. cit. (**64**), 349–50.

[6] Trinder, op. cit. (**8**) 44, 139.

[7] H. S. Torrens, 'The Reynolds-Anstice Shropshire geological collection'. *Archives of Natural History*, 1982, *10*, 429–441.

[8] H. E. Forrest, *Shrewsbury Burgess Roll*, Shrewsbury, 1924, 11.

[9] A. W. Skempton and H. R. Johnson, 'The First Iron Frames', *Archit. Rev., Lond.* 1962, *131*, no. 751, 175–186, and J. Tann, *The Development of the Factory*, London, 1970, 137–44.

[10] John and John Bernard Burke, *A Genealogical and Heraldic Dictionary of the Landed Gentry of Great Britain*, 8th edn., London, 1894, 117, *Monthly Mag.*, 1812, *33*, 298 and Thackray, op cit. (**106**), 193.

[11] Forrest, op. cit. (**8**), 20.

[12] Joseph Morris MSS, Shropshire pedigrees *8*, 4194—Shrewsbury Public Library.

[13] Trinder op. cit. (**8**), 36, 38, 44–5, 118, 122, 133, 230–1 and Wordie, op. cit. (**140**), 53–63, 125.

[14] Joseph Morris, op. cit. (12), *2*, 605.

[15] J. Parkinson, *Organic Remains of a Former World*, 3 vols, London, 1804, *1*, 415.

[16] Trinder, op. cit. (**8**), *Gents. Mag.*, 1811, *81*, (1), 228–9 and C. P. Fendall and E. A. Crutchley, *The Diary of Benjamin Newton, Rector of Wath 1816–1818*. Cambridge, 1933, 22.

[17] B. Botfield, *Stemmata Botvilliana*, London, 1858, 80–81 and R. I. Murchison, *Address delivered at the anniversary meeting of the Geological Society of London on 17th February 1843*, London, 7–8.

[18] G. E. Cokayne, *The Complete Peerage of England, Scotland, Ireland and Great Britain*, ed. V. Gibbs and others, 13 vols. London, 1910–59, *2*, 315–6.

[19] E. A. Wilson, *The Ellesmere and Llangollen Canal*, Chichester, 1975.

[20] *D.N.B.*

[21] Trinder, op. cit. (**8**); a long notice appeared in *Gents. Mag.*, 1818, *88*, (2), 179–182.

[22] *Gents. Mag.*, 1823, *93*, (1), 470 and J. Burke, *A Genealogical and Heraldic History of the extinct and dormant Baronetcies of England, Ireland and Scotland.* 2nd Edn., London, 1844, 134.

[23] Anon, 'British Mineralogical Society'. / *Tilloch's* / *Phil. Mag.*, 1804, *19*, 89.

[24] op. cit. (**27**).

[25] *Gents. Mag.*, 1838, N.S. *10*, 555, J. A. Venn, *Alumni Cantabrigienses* Part II from 1752 to 1900, 6 vols., Cambridge, 1940–54, *5*, 142, and C. Hulbert, *The Manual of Shropshire Biography, Chronology and Antiquities*, Shrewsbury, 1848, 3–4.

[26] B. Trinder, *The Darbys of Coalbrookdale*, Chichester, 1974, J. Randall, *History of Madeley*, Madeley, 1880, 296 and information from Ian Lawley, Ironbridge. His death is noticed in *Gents. Mag.* 1850, N.S. *33*, 556.

[27] W. Buckland, *Address delivered at the Anniversary Meeting of the Geological Society of London on the 19th February 1841*. London, 1841, 78.

[28] Katherine Plymley MSS, diaries—Shropshire Record Office, Joseph Morris, op.cit. (12), *9*, 4614–5 and Gents. Mag., 1840, *169*, 556.

[29] *Dictionary of Welsh Biography down to 1940*. Oxford 1959, 241 and J. B. Harley, 'The Society of Arts and the Survey of English Counties, part 4'. *Jl R. Soc. Arts*, 1964, *112*, 538–43.

[30] Aikin, op. cit. (**27**) x–xi.

[31] op. cit. 5.

[32] op. cit. (29), 242.

[33] *Laws of the Society instituted at Edinburgh MDCCLXXXII for the investigation of Natural History*, Edinburgh, 1803, 27.

[34] R. R. James, 'Medical Men in Practice in Shropshire 1779–1783', *Trans. Shrops. archaeol. nat. Hist. Soc.*, 1919, (4), 7, 209, Shrewsbury Public Library MSS 15492, Gents. Mag. 1846, *180*, 334, and *Salopian Shreds and Patches*, 1886 (31 March), 7, 149–50.

[35] Burke, op. cit. (10), 1952, 17th edition, 790.

[36] N. Cossons & B. Trinder, *The Iron Bridge. Symbol of the Industrial Revolution*, Bradford-on-Avon, 1979.

[37] Ditchfield, op. cit. (**19**), 335–8.

[38] See also Burke, op. cit. (10), 1871, 5th edn. 588.

[39] L. F. Chitty, 'Hanwood Monumental Inscriptions'. *Trans. Shrops. archaeol. nat Hist. Soc.*, 1913, (4), *3*, xv.

[40] Venn, op. cit. (25), *3*, 250.

[41] J. Foster, *Alumni Oxonienses. The Members of the University of Oxford 1715–1886*, 4 vols., London and Oxford, 1887–8, *2*, 616.

[42] D. Thompson, *A History of Brewood Grammar School*. Cannock. 1953.

[43] *Gents. Mag.*, 1843, N.S. *20*, 660–1.

[44] Evans, op. cit. (**18**), 16.

[45] Turner, op. cit. (**11**), 67.

[46] Skinner, op. cit. (**15**), 49.

[47] Foster, op. cit. (41), *2*, 619.

[48] *Gents. Mag.*, 1819, *89* (1), 91 and information from Miss E. McNeill, Librarian of the Honourable Society of the Middle Temple.

[49] John Burke, *Burke's Genealogical and Heraldic History of the Peerage, Baronetage and Knightage*, 105th edn., London, 1970, 1335–6.

[50] in Shrewsbury Reference Library.

[51] Evans, op. cit. (**18**), 25.

[52] C. Hulbert, *The History and Description of the County of Salop*. Shrewsbury, 2 vols., 1837, *2*, 306–7.

[53] Burke, op. cit. (10), 1952, 17th edn., 1320.

[54] *Salopian Journal* 20th June 1810.

[55] Wilson, op. cit. (19).

[56] *D.N.B.*

[57] Burke, op. cit. (10), 1843, 2nd edn., 2 vols., *1*, 782.

[58] Burke, op. cit. (10), 1952, 17th edn., 1508.

[59] Wilson, op. cit. (19), 73.

[60] Murchison, op. cit. (**2**), 142.

[61] Cokayne, op. cit. (18), *10*, 652–3.

[62] C. Hadfield, *The Canals of the West Midlands*, Newton Abbot, 1966.

[63] Thackray, op. cit. (**1**), 63–65.

⁶⁴ Trinder, op. cit. (8), and Monumental inscription in Lilleshall Church.
⁶⁵ Society of Friends, Shropshire Monthly Meeting minutes 16.3.1791 (transcript at Ironbridge George Museum library).
⁶⁶ E. Davies, *A general history of the county of Radnor*, Brecknock, 1905. R. J. Colyer, 'The Hafod estate under Thomas Johnes and Henry Pelham, fourth Duke of Newcastle'. *Welsh Hist. Rev.*, 1977, *8*, 271 dates the sale of Stanage to 1799.
⁶⁷ Gents. Mag., 1821, *91*, (1), 92.
⁶⁸ *D.N.B.*
⁶⁹ Burke, op. cit. (10), 1952, 17th edn., 2005.
⁷⁰ J. A. De Luc, *Geological Travels*, 3 vols., London 1811, *3*, 213.
⁷¹ Cokayne, op. cit. (18) *12*, 201, 564, *D.N.B.*, E. Richards. 'The Industrial Face of a Great Estate, Trentham & Lilleshall 1780–1860'. *Econ. Hist. Rev.*, 1974, (2), *27*, 414–430 and Wordie, op. cit. (**140**) who gives full details of the Marquis' of Shropshire estates at this period with a map (page 282).
⁷² Woodward, op. cit. (**53**), 277.
⁷³ Dr. Barrie Trinder (pers. comm.).
⁷⁴ Gents. Mag., 1822, *92*, (2), 644. J. Greig (ed.), *The Farington Diary*, 8 vols, London, 1922–28, *3*, 273 and Cokayne, op. cit. (18), *12*, 634–5.
⁷⁵ Elizabeth O. Gordon, *The Life and Correspondence of William Buckland, D.D., F.R.S.*, London, 1894, 23.
⁷⁶ Forrest, op. cit. (8), 279.
⁷⁷ Burke, op. cit. (10), 1921, 13th edn., 1719, where he is named as of Teignmouth, Devon whence he later retired.
⁷⁸ Ditchfield, op. cit. (**19**) and *Monthly Mag.*, 1796, *1*, 338.
⁷⁹ *Salopian Journal* 25th May 1836.
⁸⁰ Evans, op. cit. (**18**), 24.
⁸¹ Information from David Cumming.
⁸² Aikin, op. cit. (**27**), 69–84.
⁸³ E. L. Griggs, *Collected letters of Samuel Taylor Coleridge*, 6 vols., Oxford, 1956, *1*, 392–4.
⁸⁴ H. MacLachlan, *Letters of Theophilus Lindsey*. Manchester, 1920, 20.
⁸⁵ *Minut. Proc. Instn civ. Engrs.*, 1872, *33*, 241–6.
⁸⁶ *Salopian Journal* 22nd March 1837. Two of John Wicksteed's grandchildren were christened Arthur Aikin see S. Lawrence, *The descendants of Philip Henry M.A.* London, 1844, 18.
⁸⁷ Trinder, op. cit. (8), 79, 84, 123, 138.
⁸⁸ Rennie MSS, National Library of Scotland Acc. 5111. Rennie notebook no. 4.
⁸⁹ Hadfield, op. cit. (62), 154–5, 164.
⁹⁰ see also J. Plymley, *General view of the agriculture of Shropshire*, London, 1813, 294–6, and his gravestone in Ketley St. Mary's Church.
⁹¹ See pedigree in Hunter, op. cit. (**10**), *1*, 365, where he is the younger of the two of this name.
⁹² R. A. Church, *Kenricks in Hardware: A Family Business 1791–1966*, Newton Abbot, 1969, 19–21.
⁹³ *Views of the Ruins of the principal Houses destroyed during the Riots at Birmingham*, Birmingham, 1791.
⁹⁴ C. Hadfield, *The Canals of the East Midlands*. Newton Abbot, 1966, 167 and John Macculloch's diary for 1810, information from David Cumming. Witton was still resident at Lightmoor in May 1812 see Monthly Mag., 1812, *33*, 586.
⁹⁵ N Mutton, 'An engineer at work in the West Midlands. The diary of John Urpeth Rastrick for 1820'. *Jl West Midlands Reg. Studies*, 1969, Special Publication *1*, 29.
⁹⁶ *Aris' Birmingham Gazette* 30th April, 1838.
⁹⁷ information from Malcolm Thomas of the Library of the Society of Friends, London.
⁹⁸ A. W. Skempton & E. C. Wright, 'Early Members of the Smeatonian Society of Civil Engineers'. *Trans. Newcomen Soc.*, 1972, *44*, 37.
⁹⁹ Forrest, op. cit. (8), 322.
¹⁰⁰ Stephen Glover, *The history, gazetteer and directory of the county of Derby*. Derby, 2 vols., 1829, *1*, 104, 1833, *2*, 578–9, Hunter, op. cit. (**10**), *1*, 23 and Burke, op. cit. (10), 1894, 8th edn., 432.
¹⁰¹ Turner, op. cit. (**11**), 78.
¹⁰² R. W. Innes Smith, *English-speaking students of Medicine at the University of Leyden*, Edinburgh, 1932, 58.
¹⁰³ F. Darwin, *Life and Letters of Charles Darwin*, 3 vols., London 1887, *1*, 8.
¹⁰⁴ R. P. Sturges, 'The Membership of the Derby Philosophical Society 1783–1802', *Midland History* 1979, *4*, 212–229.
¹⁰⁵ I. Sellers, 'William Roscoe, the Roscoe circle and Radical Politics in Liverpool 1787–1807'. *Trans. Hist. Soc. Lancs. Ches.*, 1968, *120*, 45–62 and J. A. Picton, *Memorials of Liverpool*. 2 vols. Historical 2nd edn., London, 1875, *1*, 364.
¹⁰⁶ Rodgers, op. cit. (**14**), 263.
¹⁰⁷ Gents. Mag., 1822, *92*, (1), 89–90 and information from F. H. Thompson, Secretary of the Society of Antiquaries of London.
¹⁰⁸ op. cit. (29), 728–9.

[109]. *D.N.B.* and E. Rees and G. Walters 'The dispersion of the manuscripts of Edward Lhuyd'. *Welsh Hist. Rev.*, 1974, *7*, 155.

[110] Woodward, op. cit. (**53**), 276.

[111] *D.N.B.*

[112] *D.N.B.*

[113] Will in Prerogative Court of Canterbury records—Public Record Office, London.

X

The scientific ancestry and historiography of *The Silurian System*

Historians have pointed out the relationship between the 'heroic age of geology' and the Industrial Revolution, and some have claimed that the emergence of geology was conditioned by contemporary developments in mining and industrialization (Tomkeieff 1950). Industry, they believed, created demands for raw materials which mining then exposed. Such 'exposures' in turn advanced geological investigation. If so, it is a paradox that the English area which most stimulated the Industrial Revolution is now able to celebrate this over a period of 280 years, while The Murchison Symposium was an express celebration of only a 150th anniversary. By 1839, Shropshire industry and the Ironbridge Gorge were involved, not with the innovatory beginnings of iron smelting using coal-based fuels, but declining in innovation if not in scale, as they provided the gigantic iron plates for the new steam ship *Great Britain* (Trinder 1981).

If there was a connection between the rise of geology and of industry, we should surely be able to demonstrate it in an area like Shropshire. We would equally expect the gap between the beginning of industrialization and the beginning of geology in this area to be much less than one of 130 years. Is the size of this gap simply because there was no direct connnection between geology and industrialization or is there some other explanation? These questions are explored, if not always answered, in this paper, with special regard to Shropshire and adjacent areas. These regions are now properly regarded as a 'birthplace' of industry and are also just those acknowledged by Roderick Murchison as having provided the standards for his Silurian sequences, as the subtitle to his *magnum opus* makes clear. This is despite the fact that Shropshire was never 'part of the original *Siluria*' (Secord 1982, p. 422).

2

The Silurian System was a Murchisonian creation (in 1835) and can, strictly speaking, have no pre-history (Secord 1986). There is a real danger of being anhistoric in discussing such concepts. As Ospovat (1979, p. 163) complained when asked to review Abraham Werner's concept of a Basement Complex: 'I cannot discuss [it] because Werner did not have a concept of the basement complex'. But we can and should consider the state of Shropshire geology before Murchison started work:

Shropshire 'geology' before Murchison

There is abundant evidence that the rapid and early industrialization of the Shropshire coalfield encouraged geological activity. The celebrity of the area as a 'tourist resort' was established early on, not only because of the scenery but also because of the sheer scale and power of the industrialization. Trinder (1988) has shown that the area was attracting international attention by the 1750s and he reprints descriptions of the area by 35 visitors up to 1830, when Murchison was about to start his work. Many were of some eminence in science and a significant number were drawn to the area by the geology and collected specimens in the many excavations for coal, ironstone, clay and lime. People like Richard Pococke (1704–1765), Bishop of Ossory and Meath in Ireland, visited the Severn Gorge at Coalbrookdale in 1751 and recorded the fossils of Lincoln Hill, particularly those now called trilobites (Trinder 1988). These discoveries soon contributed to the contemporary debate at the Royal Society about the true affinities of these fossils. In 1755 Emanuel Da Costa (1717–1791) argued correctly that they were both marine and 'of the crustaceous kind' and described and figured one of these 'curious fossile animals' from Coalbrookdale (Da Costa 1755). Da Costa's figure can be recognized as a dalmanitid trilobite of Wenlock age (Fig. 1).

Da Costa highlights a major problem for many in being a 'scientist' at this time and for many years afterwards, since, when his paper was published in January 1755 he was in the Kings Bench Prison, London, for debt (Smith 1821, vol. 2,

p. 482). Further misfortune followed him after he was elected clerk to the Royal Society in 1763, as he was soon dismissed from the Society's employment (in December 1767) and spent the next five years in prison at the suit of the Society (Cockerell 1922). A similar fate befell another significant visitor to Shropshire, Rudolf Erich Raspe (1737–1794), author of the *Singular Travels, Campaigns and Adventures of Baron Munchausen* of 1786. He had been confined briefly in the Fleet prison in 1780 for the same reason (Carswell 1950). Soon afterwards Raspe discovered red lead ore at the Hope and Snailbeach mines, southwest of Shrewsbury (Aikin 1797). But his work in Shropshire did not liquidate his debts, so *Baron Munchausen* had to be written instead, but made no money for its author. Such financial problems seem to have dogged all serious 'Silurian' investigators before Murchison, showing the real importance of the latter's financial independence to the successful outcome of his work.

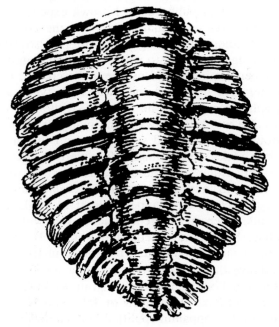

Fig. 1. A trilobite from Coalbrookdale, Shropshire figured by Da Costa (1755), ×2.

4

The first proper 'student of the earth' to have had close Shropshire connections may have been Robert Townson (1762–1826). He had additional problems to contend with, as the illegitimate son of a London merchant who died in 1773 when Robert was only ten (Vallance & Torrens 1984). Robert then moved to Cardington in Shropshire in 1777 to live with his new brother-in-law, who was the vicar there. The powerful surroundings of the Lawley and Caer Caradoc, nearby Hoar Edge and Wenlock Edge, and the whole Church Stretton area had an immediate effect on him for he turned to natural history almost full time, travelling on foot through Europe to Sicily between 1783 and 1787. On his way back he attended lectures on mineralogy in Paris and then studied at the Universities of Edinburgh, where he met James Hutton, and of Göttingen.

On both his returns from the continent, Townson had faced problems of finance, finding no patrons willing to sponsor his scientific studies and so his own major contribution to Salopian geology, *A sketch of the Mineralogy of Shropshire,* was published at his own expense (Townson 1799). This gives a fascinating view of the contemporary state of 'geology'. Lacking any ordered stratigraphical framework against which to work, Townson's observations, however penetrating, could not be and were not related to each other. He described the local rock types and their petrography (a word that he was one of the first to use in English). He was keenly aware that many strata occur here in obviously superimposed sequences, and that many such Shropshire rocks are also highly fossiliferous. But he made no use of either of these realizations to order his observations in any stratigraphical sense. This was an advance that could only come, at least in England, in the next decade when an ordered sequence was both made out by William Smith and others, and was publicized widely. Townson, having failed to find patronage in Britain for his intended investigations of the mineralogy of Canada in 1791, or of India in 1796, decided to emigrate to Australia as one of its first settlers. He arrived in 1807 and was too soon involved in the appalling politics that characterized early Australia. This sadly affected all his antipodean scientific aspirations.

Stratigraphy comes to Shropshire

Whatever the failings of the early years of the Geological Society of London (Miller 1983), it did provide a real forum for the investigation of British geology and the examination of stratigraphically considered sequences. The first such geologist to be connected with both the Geological Society and with Shropshire was Arthur Aikin (1773–1854), who was at first a non-conformist minister in Shrewsbury from 1793 to 1795 and soon became attracted to the mineralogy of the area, making a tour of Shropshire and North Wales in 1796 (Aikin 1797). In 1807 he became a founder member of the Geological Society, and as his contribution to its work he issued in 1810 *Proposals for a Mineralogical Survey of Shropshire,* which he prosecuted actively until 1816 when forced to abandon the whole project. He had been able to find barely a quarter of the subscribers needed to allow him to publish (Torrens 1983). His *Proposals* include a sample engraved geological map and a geological cross-section of the area between Corve Dale and the Longmynd in Shropshire. These, and the short accompanying text, show that his work was no longer simply petrographic or mineralogical, but properly stratigraphical.

For each stratum that he recognized Aikin intended to record and map its extent, direction and rise (as opposed to the dip which we now record) as well as its thickness and the minerals and fossils that each contained. It is quite clear that Aikin had already been able to separate three quite distinct groups of rocks in Shropshire by 1810. These are the stratified rocks that we now place in the Ordovician and Silurian, the unstratified rocks that we now place in the Ordovician and Silurian, the unstratified rocks now known to be Uriconian (Precambrian) volcanics, and another quite separate series of stratified rocks assigned to the Precambrian. He also assessed assiduously the relationships between these three rock groups.

In addition, manuscript and printed sources show that as his Survey progressed Aikin paid more and more attention to the fossils, which had long been known to occur in many of the stratified rocks in Shropshire. This was due undoubtedly to the direct influence of William Smith, both on Aikin himself, since Aikin was already well informed of

Smith's discoveries by October 1802 when Smith's results were certainly well developed (Eyles 1985), and from the visits to Smith's offices and collections made in 1808 by officers of the Geological Society (Torrens 1983). Aikin, in common with all his contemporaries, faced problems in using fossils because of the contemporary state of systematic palaeontology. At first he misidentified brachiopods as bivalves. But by February 1812, as he came to rely on the expertise of others, he could report on the stratigraphical occurrence of *'Pentamerus' knightii* near Ludlow. This discovery allowed him to distinguish the rocks which Murchison later named (and at first confused) the Wenlock and Aymestry limestones. Aikin too had earlier confused these. That Murchison shared this confusion is significant as we shall see.

Other early geological activity in Shropshire

While the work of Townson and Aikin was being prosecuted and geological investigations in Shropshire were moving from 'mere' mineralogy to more stratigraphical investigations, other significant work was in progress there. The massive scale of mineral extraction in many parts of the county had long provided golden opportunities for the fossil and mineral collector, and fine collections were being built up, like that made by the local ironmaster William Reynolds (1758–1803), as well as by visitors. Reynolds had long had a great interest in science (Trinder 1981), and his collection, started at least as early as 1776, passed to his nephew after his death and was then placed at Murchison's disposal for his Silurian work (Torrens 1982).

Not long after this, more public museums were established in Shropshire. That in Ludlow was founded in October 1833 (Lloyd 1983), and that in Shrewsbury, which attempted to cover, however unsuccessfully, North Wales as well, in June 1835 (Torrens 1987). These were focussed respectively round the Ludlow and the Shropshire and North Wales Natural History Societies. A number of members of both societies were of particular assistance to Murchison during his Silurian survey. One in particular, the

Rev. T. T. Lewis (1801–1858) curate of Aymestrey, 'had the honour of conducting Mr Murchison . . . along the path of an old road . . . presenting a continuous section from the Lower Ludlow rock to the Old Red Sandstone . . . in his first visit to Herefordshire [in] July 1831' (Lewis 1866, pp. 99–100). Lewis had begun to classify the stratigraphical sequence here and to collect the fossils characteristic of each formation in 1827, well before Murchison has started any 'invasion of the graywacke' (Geikie 1875, vol. 1, p. 172). Murchison never, however, reciprocated with an adequate acknowledgement of Lewis's contribution to his work (Thackray 1979). Another Murchisonian helper was Dr Thomas Du Gard (1777–1840) of Shrewsbury, one of the founding Honorary Members of the Geological Society of London in 1807 (Torrens 1983). He had guided the Rev. William Buckland from Oxford on the first-ever geological tour that Buckland had made and was no less helpful to Murchison, whose letter to him of 29 July 1832 shows that he was already both medical and local geological advisor to Murchison during his Silurian studies (Anon 1903, pp. 167–168). Dr Thomas Lloyd was another who gave Murchison much help and who is best remembered for his discovery of the Ludlow Bone Bed (Lloyd 1983).

The relationship of these people and of their societies to Murchison and his Silurian work was not a parasitic one but was notably symbiotic, with Murchison providing the project to which they could and did contribute by working out local successions, collecting the fossils of each unit, and tracing outcrops. They deserve to be remembered. But as Lyell wrote to Gideon Mantell on 23 March 1829, there was then a strong tendency for the Geological Society to be 'Metropolitan monopolists' (Mantell letters, Turnbull library, Wellington, New Zealand). This was confirmed the next year by Robert Bakewell (1767–1843), who wrote in the *Magazine of Natural History* (Bakewell 1830), as reported by another provincial with Murchison specifically in mind, that there was then 'a certain prejudice more or less prevalent among the members of scientific Societies in large cities like London and Paris, which makes them unwilling to believe that persons residing in provincial towns or in the country can do anything important for science'

(Samuel Woodward MSS, vol. 4, p. 28, Norwich Castle Museum).

William Fitton on the history of geology and the Smith 'cult'

The first chapter of Murchison's *The Silurian System* included a very short section on the 'previous state of geological knowledge' before his Silurian investigations began (Murchison 1839). William Fitton (1780–1861), one of the first English geologists to attempt to treat history as a properly investigative 'science', was highly critical of this attempt at history (Fitton 1841).

Part of the reason why Fitton objected so strongly to Murchison's historical analysis is surely connected with the frustrated attempts made by Fitton two decades earlier to do justice to William Smith (1769–1839), who was to play such a major role in Murchison's development as a stratigrapher. Fitton's first publication on this topic had been a review of Smith's main publications up to 1817 (Fitton 1818). But his attempts then to develop the theme that Smith was a major figure in the development of English stratigraphy and palaeontology were soon frustrated. Fitton's effort to reprint this paper in the *Quarterly Journal of Science* with significant additions resulting from new investigations, was abandoned early in 1822 (Anon 1822) even after it had been printed in 1821. Smith, we should note, was then in exile in the north of England after a period of six months in a London prison in 1819 for debt, once again reminding us of the importance of Murchison's financial security.

Thomas Webster, the then Secretary of the Geological Society, reported in March 1822 on the problems with Fitton's new paper: 'whether it will now be published or at least so *fairly* [italics original], I will not take it on me to say ... What do you think of [Fitton's] declared intention of proposing Smith as an Honorary Member of the Geological Society on account of the services he has rendered to geology, and that Greenough [then the President] shall be the first to sign his certificate? Do you think Greenough will find this pill as difficult to swallow as any of his uncle's?!

This is at present *entre nous*' (Challinor 1962, pp. 153–154). But Greenough could not swallow this pill and Fitton's paper remained unpublished. As Smith's friend John Farey confirmed to James Sowerby in May 1822; 'poor Smith, he *is sunk,* as the Dandys say by all the *Anti-Smithian Association* [the Geological Society] in Bedford Street' (MSS in the Dibner library, Smithsonian Institution library, Washington DC).

As a result, Fitton's revised *Notes on the History of English Geology* were not finally published for another 11 years, in 1833, after Greenough's highly political grip on the Geological Society had been loosened. In a short preamble Fitton (1833, p. 1) noted that these were now largely reprinted from one of the original printed, but suppressed, copies of 1821, whose 'publication was at that time prevented by accidental circumstances'. This explains some of the confused datings in the earlier part of this paper, but which also now contained a number of additions to the 1821 printing. The polarization of the Geological Society in the early 1820s over the merits of Smith's case also explains the extra folding sheet inserted in copies of Conybeare & Phillips' highly influential book issued in June 1822 and headed 'Organic remains of the beds above the Chalk'. This too carried a strange note reading: 'This list is inserted on a separate sheet instead of being incorporated in the text, because at the time this part of the work passed through the press it was not intended to enter so much into detail upon this branch of the subject as was afterwards judged expedient; by this *addition* [italics here added] the work will now be found to contain full catalogues of the Organic Remains contained in the various formations' (Conybeare & Phillips 1822, before p. 3). Greenough (1819, pp. 284–295) had just gone on record about how little the 'history of strata' might be 'deduced from their Fossil Contents', in a highly sceptical book which drew comment from one reviewer after struggling through it, that he felt like 'John Bunyan's Pilgrim after he had escaped from *Doubting Castle*' ([Bakewell] 1819, p. 392).

Such polarization of the Society during the early 1820s much better explains the 'facts' that have guided recent extraordinary attempts to invoke a Smith 'cult' as in 'operation' later at the Geological Society in 1831, when the first Wollaston Medal was conferred on Smith (Rupke 1983). This should instead be seen as the simple redress of past metropolitan vindictiveness against Smith (Rudwick 1985) on the part of the previous 'ruling' fraction of the membership (Miller 1983). By 1831 Murchison was an important member of the new coterie now ruling the Society; as its Secretary and President-elect. The provincial attitude to Smith before 1831 had been different, with Honorary Membership of the Bristol Institution being conferred on him in March 1824, through its Secretary the same William Conybeare (Conybeare to Smith 27 March 1824; Smith archive, Oxford University Museum; and Anon 1830, p. 53). Similar assessments of his merits in York at the same date are demonstrated by Morrell (1989). Murchison's own assessment of Smith's work was the same and led him to become an avid disciple of Smithian stratigraphical methods.

Murchison as a historian

Murchison's Silurian achievement was enormous in scale and execution, and this paper is not designed to diminish it. It was literally 'epoch making' and one which had important economic consequences, as had so much of the early stratigraphy carried out in England and Wales. It was such work by Murchison and Sedgwick that allowed the new geological arrogance so well displayed by Andrew Ramsay in 1849: '6 July: Took horse and rode to Caernarvon . . . As I rode home I found them busy on the side of Caernarvon sinking for coal . . . They asked my opinion. I told them to let me know when they came to the coal and I would come down and eat it' (Geikie 1895, p. 148). Their Palaeozoic work now allowed such opinions to be held on the basis of science. *The Silurian System* was a massive and marvellous work of synthesis but the preface set the scene which the historical analysis simply supported; Murchison (1839, p. v.) 'having discovered that the region formerly inhabited by the Silures . . . contained a vast and regular succession of undescribed deposits of a remote age [had] named them'.

The historical survey could then claim that 'no one was aware of the existence below the Old Red Sandstone of a regular series of deposits containing peculiar organic remains' and that Murchison had been led to explore the borders of England and Wales in search of the key to the succession in these lower beds.

At least such claims help to explain the paradoxical gap in chronology noted in the introduction to this paper. There was clearly a lot of geological activity, at least in Shropshire, before Murchison started work, even to the extent of the publication of a short book by a Ludlow farmer called *Thoughts on the Formation of the Earth* (Anon 1802), which discussed the fossils and rocks of the Whitcliffe at Ludlow. No copy of this has been located and we know of it only from a review (Anon 1804). The supposed 130 years gap is an artefact, in part helped into existence by Murchison's historiography.

The main problem is that Murchison became his own historian, even to the extent of writing his own massive autobiography. Archibald Geikie, his biographer (1875), followed this received account, which extends to 26 manuscript volumes for those wanting to know what Murchison's view of 'reality' was (Secord 1986). Morrell (1989) has shown that Murchison had earlier failed to acknowledge another debt to John Phillips in 1826 which had greatly helped his work on the Jurassic rocks at Brora in Scotland. Sedgwick reacted with astonishment when he read the first draft of Murchison's intended Introduction to *The Silurian System* (Sedgwick to Murchison [25 Jan. 1836]; Geological Society archives M/S11/96b); 'I must honestly say I don't like the tone of your Introduction'. Sedgwick particularly complained that the claim that these rocks had been previously 'treated with comparative neglect' was too strong a statement. In particular, Sedgwick angrily disagreed that Murchison had ever set off to the Welsh Borderland in the summer of 1831 with any intention of specifically examining these ancient rocks. 'Buckland you told me, gave you your line of march. It was rich in organics [fossils] and abounded in igneous rocks; and you told me, by letter, that your main object was to see the pranks the igneous rocks were playing. Starting there without any anticipation of

X

12

what has turned up, you stumbled upon a rich field and have since gathered an ample harvest after enormous labours'. Secord (1981) has examined the motives behind Murchison's 1831 tour and shown that history is certainly on Sedgwick's side, and that the received view, as given by Murchison and his biographer, is 'almost entirely a myth' created with much hindsight.

Such problems of historical analysis, whether of Smith's or Murchison's work, were clearly a major reason for the power and detail of Fitton's review (1841) of Murchison's book. Fitton in particular pointed out that Murchison had been economical with the truth of his relationships with a number of those who had preceded him in Shropshire and the Welsh Borderland; notably Arthur Aikin 'whose notes and drawings of certain tracts around the Wrekin and Caradoc' Murchison (1839, p. 4) had acknowledged using. Fitton (1841, p. 10), however, added that these notes which he had seen, were both more extensive geographically than Murchison had admitted and 'appear to us [Fitton] to coincide with Mr Murchison's descriptions in so many points of detail that they must have been of great assistance'. It is noteworthy that Murchison's first stratigraphical standard of 1833, which confused the Wenlock and Aymestry limestones (see Fig. 2), simply repeated a mistake that Aikin had made before 1812.

---

[1] The subdivisions may be quoted here :—
  " I. *Upper Ludlow Rock*—Equivalent, Grauwacke Sandstone of Tortworth, etc.
  II. *Wenlock Limestone*—Equivalents, Dudley Limestone, Transition Limestone, etc.
  III. *Lower Ludlow Rock*—Equivalent, ' Die earth.'
  IV. *Shelly Sandstones*—Equivalent, ———?
  V. *Black Trilobite Flagstone, etc.*—Equivalent, ———?
  VI. Red Conglomerate, Sandstone, and Slaty Schist."
                                            Proc. Geol. Soc., vol. i. p. 475.
  In this table the Aymestry and Wenlock Limestones are confounded, and hence the Lower Ludlow Rock is placed under instead of above the Wenlock Limestone.

Fig. 2. Murchison's first stratigraphical standard of 1833 for the Silurian System. Reproduced from Geikie 1875, vol. 1, p. 217.

Fitton also noted that T. T. Lewis (whom he had been to visit at Aymestrey to go over the ground with him) had not been accorded the credit to which he was entitled, just as Thackray (1979) has documented. The only acknowledgement that Murchison (1842) seems to have made to Fitton's review, which had appeared in April 1841, was with regard to Lewis; this acknowledgement was in the form of a separate 'errata slip' issued with his 1842 address to the Dudley and Midland Geological Society. Such a provincial audience was hardly the place to make full metropolitan amends in a work which, in any case, again carried hardly any historical analysis. Furthermore, why did Murchison issue only a slip to be later inserted (and which only rarely has been) into this *Address,* when the latter was given in January 1842, many months after Fitton's review? The errata slip is reproduced here as Fig. 3 (from a copy preserved in a copy of *The Silurian System* at the National Museum of Wales). It refers only to the main text of *The Silurian System.* It does not refer to, and clearly now denies, the remarkable statement in the earlier historical analysis (1839, p. 4) which had read 'although it was supposed that the limestone of Dudley was of greater antiquity than the Old Red Sandstone, no one had observed that those deposits were connected by an intermediate formation . . . the "Ludlow rocks"'.

Conclusions

We should have learned from history the danger of allowing the protagonists in any scientific advance to prejudge the history of that advance. Just as we *should* be unhappy with police investigations of complaints against themselves, so we should resist, or at least very carefully examine, claims by 'great' scientists as to how 'great' their science was or how it advanced. The danger signals are clear in Murchison's particular case. We find Gideon Mantell, who seems to have had a balanced view of Murchison at least, if of few others, writing in June 1834 to his American friend Benjamin Silliman just before the establishment of the Silurian System: '*Roderick Impey* Murchison is too *omnivorous* of fame, grasping at what does not belong to him, and a little

Note omitted, p. 9, l. 21.

BEFORE I made sections of the different deposits around Dudley, my friend the Rev. Mr. Lewis, of Aymestry, had pointed out to me the true relations of the Sedgley and Dudley limestones; having recognised in the black limestone of Sedgley the equivalent of his Aymestry rock, from its containing the same *Pentamerus.* I very much regret having omitted to state this fact in my chapter on the Silurian rocks of this tract (*Sil. Syst.* p. 480 *et seq.*), the more so, as no person was of such essential service in my inquiries as Mr. Lewis, from the very accurate knowledge of the upper members of the Silurian strata which he had acquired in the typical districts around Aymestry and Ludlow before my first visit to that country.

R. I. M.

Fig. 3. Murchison's 'errata slip' for his 1842 *Address.*

too captious and decided, the latter generally belong to the military character: but he is a good fellow altogether and Mrs Murchison an excellent and highly intellectual lady but rather a la Madame de Stael' [1766–1817; the famous French authoress with close connections with all the most brilliant members of French Society] (Silliman MSS, Yale University Library).

I believe that Sedgwick was right to complain to Murchison of the tone of the early draft to the introductory chapter to *The Silurian System* in 1836; 'you set down as a pack of asses every one who had preceded you'. Exactly the same sentiment has been expressed by an anonymous hand in the copy of Geikie's *Life of Murchison* (1875) now at Ludlow Museum. 'The great blot on Murchison's fame [was] that he never acknowledged the services of others—upon which he built his work—taking all credit to himself ignoring every body else'. Perhaps Murchison's arrogance as an assessor of his ancestors should just remind us how history repeats itself, even if his attitude to his own contemporaries was only partly the same. Of some of the latter, Charles Darwin recorded that, on the publication of *The Silurian System,* Murchison 'announced [it] to the Council . . . and said, "You will every one of you find your name in the Index," as if this was the height of glory' (Barlow 1958, p. 103).

Thanks are due to T. Carr and the staffs of the Shrewsbury Library and Record Office, and to M. Rowlands, J. Secord and J. Thackray for many years of willing help. C. H. Holland provided encouragement at a crucial moment, and P. Lane, D. Bassett and M. Bassett kindly read and much improved earlier drafts of this paper.

References

AIKIN, A. 1797. *Journal of a Tour through North Wales and part of Shropshire with observations in Mineralogy* [etc]. Johnson: London.

ANON, 1802. *Thoughts on the Formation of the Earth.* Publisher unknown: Shrewsbury.

—— 1804. Review of *Thoughts on the Formation of the Earth* [Anon 1802 qv]. *British Critic,* **23,** 447–448.

—— 1822. Notice to Correspondents. *Quarterly Journal of Science,* **12,** no. 24, January 1822, unpaginated inserted slip.

—— 1830. List of the Honorary Members [of the Bristol Institution] elected from the establishment of the Society. *Proceedings of the Annual Meetings of the Bristol Institution,* **8,** 51–53.

—— 1903. Woolhope Naturalists' Field Club. Second Field Meeting Thursday June 27 1901. *Transactions of the Woolhope Naturalists Field Club,* 1900–1902, 157–170.

[BAKEWELL, R.]. 1819. Review of G. B. Greenough's *A Critical Examination* (qv). *Monthly Review,* December, 376–393.

—— 1830. A Visit to the Mantellian Museum at Lewes. *Magazine of Natural History,* **3,** 9–17.

16

BARLOW, N. 1958. *The Autobiography of Charles Darwin 1809–1882.* Collins, London.

CARSWELL, J. 1950. *The Prospector; being the Life and Times of Rudolf Erich Raspe (1737–1794).* Cresset Press, London.

CHALLINOR, J. 1962. Some correspondence of Thomas Webster, Geologist (1773–1844)-part II. *Annals of Science,* **18,** 147–75.

COCKERELL, J. D. A. 1922. Dru Drury, an Eighteenth century Entomologist. *Scientific Monthly,* January, 67–82.

CONYBEARE, W. D. & PHILLIPS, W. 1822. *Outlines of the Geology of England and Wales,* part I. Phillips, London.

DA COSTA, E. M. 1755. Description of a curious Fossile Animal. *Gentleman's Magazine,* **25,** 24–5.

EYLES, J. M. 1985. William Smith, Sir Joseph Banks and the French Geologists. *In:* WHEELER, A. & PRICE, J. H. (eds) *From Linnaeus to Darwin: Commentaries on the History of Biology and Geology.* Society for the History of Natural History, London, 37–50.

[FITTON, W. H.]. 1818. [Review of six publications by William Smith, 1815–1817]. *Edinburgh Review,* **29,** 311–37.

—— 1833. *Notes on the Progress of Geology in England.* Taylor: London.

[——] 1841. Review of Murchison's *The Silurian System* 1839. *Edinburgh Review,* **73,** 1–41.

GEIKIE, A. 1876. *Life of Sir Roderick I. Murchison.* Two volumes. Murray, London.

—— 1895. *Memoir of Sir Andrew Crombie Ramsay.* Macmillan, London.

GREENOUGH, G. B. 1819. *A Critical Examination of the First Principles of Geology.* Longman etc, London.

LEWIS, T. T. 1866. Address as retiring President January 24 1854. *Transactions of the Woolhope Field Club,* for 1852 to 1865, 94–100.

LLOYD, D. 1983. *The History of Ludlow Museum 1833–1983.* [Museum: Ludlow].

MILLER, D. P. 1983. Method and the 'Micropolitics' of Science: The early years of the Geological and Astronomical Societies of London. *In:* SCHUSTER, J. A. & YEO, R. R. (eds) *The Politics and Rhetoric of Scientific Method.* Reidel, Dordrecht, 227–57.

MORRELL, J. 1989. The Legacy of William Smith: the case of John Phillips in the 1820's. *Archives of Natural History,* **16,** 319–335.

MURCHISON, R. I. 1839. *The Silurian System* etc. Two volumes. Murray, London.

—— 1842. *The Inaugural Address delivered by . . . at the first General Meeting of the Dudley and Midland Geological Society.* Taylor, London.

OSPOVAT, A. M. 1979. Werner's concept of the Basement Complex. *In:* Kupsch, W. O. & Sarjeant, W. A. S. (eds) *History of Concepts in Precambrian Geology.* Geological Association of Canada Special Paper, **19,** 161–70.

RUDWICK, M. J. S. 1985. *The Great Devonian Controversy.* Chicago University Press, London & Chicago.

RUPKE, N. A. 1983. *The Great Chain of History: William Buckland and the English School of Geology 1814–1849.* Clarendon Press, Oxford.

SECORD, J. A. 1981. *A Romance of the Field: Roderick Murchison's Geological 'Discovery' of 1831.* Paper circulated in 1981 but not published [see Secord 1986, p. 342].

—— 1982. King of Siluria; Roderick Murchison and the Imperial Theme in nineteenth century British Geology. *Victorian Studies*, **25**, 413–42.

—— 1986. *Controversy in Victorian Geology: The Cambrian–Silurian Dispute*. Princeton University Press.

SMITH, J. E. 1821. *A Selection of the correspondence of Linnaeus and other naturalists*. Two volumes. Longman etc, London.

THACKRAY, J. C. 1979. T. T. Lewis and Murchison's *Silurian System*. *Transactions of the Woolhope Naturalists' Field Club*, **42**, 186–93.

TOMKEIEFF, S. I. 1950. James Hutton and the Philosophy of Geology. *Proceedings of the Royal Society of Edinburgh B*, **63**, 387–400.

TORRENS, H. S. 1982. The Reynolds–Anstice Shropshire geological collection. *Archives of Natural History*, **10**, 429–41.

—— 1983. Arthur Aikin's Mineralogical Survey of Shropshire 1796–1816 and the contemporary audience for geological publications. *British Journal for the History of Science*, **16**, 111–53.

—— 1987. John Gilbert (1812–1845) the Australian naturalist and explorer. New light on his work in England. *Archives of Natural History*, **14**, 211–9.

TOWNSON, R. 1799. A sketch of the Mineralogy of Shropshire. *In: Tracts and Observations in Natural History and Physiology*. White (for the author), London, 158–203.

TRINDER, B. 1981. *The Industrial Revolution in Shropshire*, second edition. Phillimore, Chichester.

—— 1988. *'The Most Extraordinary District in the World' Ironbridge and Coalbrookdale*, second edition. Phillimore, Chichester.

VALLANCE, T. G. & TORRENS, H. S. 1984. The Anglo–Australian traveller Robert Townson and his map of Hungarian 'Petrography'. *In: DUDICH, E. (ed.) Contributions to the History of Geological mapping*. Akademiai Kiado, Budapest, 391–8.

Joseph Harrison Fryer (1777-1855): geologist and mining engineer, in England 1803-1825 and South America 1826-1828.
A Study in 'Failure'

Abstract

Fryer trained as a land surveyor and was first based at Newcastle-on-Tyne, north-east England. From at least 1808 he spent part of each year in the Lake District, north-west England. Here he carried out pioneer geological investigations but was only able to publish one anonymous "Geological Sketch" in 1816. But he assisted many others, including Ami Boué with his work on the Geology of Scotland and surrounding areas. Boué wrote in 1820 that Fryer was "one of the best informed geologists I found in England".

During 1824 and 1825 a mania for mining concerns raged in London, after Mexico and other parts of Spanish colonial America opened to British trade. *The Potosi, La Paz and Peruvian Mining Association* was floated with a capital of £1,000,000 in 1825 to work silver mines then in Peru. John Buddle, the Newcastle mining engineer recruited Fryer by July 1825. Fryer set off for Peru early in 1826 as the Company's chief engineer and mining superintendent at the princely salary of £1,500 a year. But by the time he arrived in July 1826, the British banking system was in chaos and the Spanish-American mining boom was on the verge of collapse. Fryer spent about two years in what was by now also Bolivia; *not* superintending mines but instead, with time on his hands, studying South American archaeology and conchology!

When his South American nightmare ended, Fryer returned to the north-east of England and settled near Tynemouth. Here he was again active, but now as an *amateur* geologist and conchologist, becoming an active member of both the Natural History Society of Northumberland and Durham and of the Tyneside Naturalists Field Club. His large and once famous collection of South American shells survives at the Dorman Museum in Middlesborough.

XI

Scientific Relations and Exchanges

Introduction

Fryer represents an important group of people. Such "Mineral Surveyors", as they termed themselves in their country of origin Britain, were a direct result of, and an important element of, that country's "Industrial Revolution". They located its mineral resources. They mostly trained as land surveyors but often failed to publish their geological researches. This was either through the pressure of 'normal' work or from the financial problems that such 'new' careers created. Their failure to publish has helped them slip through the net of history, since history is heavily biassed towards those who published, rather than those who established, in other ways, some of the working practices of European geology[1].

Such considerations are particularly true of Fryer who notably failed to publish before he went to South America in 1826. His second 'failure' there compounded his problems, for his South America mining company was spectacularly unsuccessful. Fryer's three - all equally forgotten - careers, in South America as well as before and after, provide a case study of failure and demonstrate the difficulties that historians face. 'Failure' is one of the most notoriously difficult areas of historical analysis[2].

Fryer's first career in England: 1803-1825

Fryer was the second son of a schoolmaster, land surveyor and mathematician called John Fryer (1746-1825) of Newcastle-on-Tyne. Coal mining was long the staple industry here. The lead mines of the Pennines were also nearby, and John Fryer was involved in surveying such properties and a Commissioner for some of the mineral bearing estates. Such men were also involved in the new technologies of steam pumping, the winding and transport of coal and the smelting of ores.

John Fryer married first in 1770 and a son William was born in 1777[3]. Fryer married again in 1779, Elisabeth (c1750-1792), daughter of another remarkable man; Robert Harrison (1715-1802), lecturer, mathematician and schoolmaster[4]. He had been Master of Newcastle's Trinity House School from 1756 until replaced by John Fryer in 1771[5].

---

1   H.S. Torrens 1988, Hawking History - a vital future for Geology's past. *Modern Geology*, **13**, 83-93 (see 87).

2   H.S. Torrens 1992, A Study of 'Failure' with a 'Successful Innovation'. *Social Studies of Science*, **22**, 245-262 (see 259).

3   baptism at St John's, Newcastle.

4   for Harrison see *DNB*. The marriage was on 15 July 1779 at Warden, west of Newcastle.

5   E. Mackenzie 1827, *A Descriptive and Historical Account.... of Newcastle upon Tyne*. Newcastle: Mackenzie and Dent. vol. 1, 443-4.

Harrison was also an entomologist and a fine linguist. All sources agree that John and Elizabeth's eldest son Joseph Harrison Fryer (JHF) was born on Christmas Day in 1777 (or perhaps 1778)[6]. In either case it was before his parents married in 1779....

JHF was trained as a land surveyor, presumably by his father but nothing seems to be known of him until 1803 when "Mr J.H. Fryer" was elected a new member of the Newcastle Literary and Philosophical Society (LPSN[7]) which had been founded in 1793[8]. Equally little is known of his surveying, although three of his maps made in 1805, two of parts of the Lake District and one of Lincolnshire, survive[9]. He was a Commissioner for the enclosure of Bolton (north-west of Appleby) in Westmorland between 1808-1813[10]. But he was temporarily of Shield Field near Newcastle when, on 14 August 1809, he married Louisa Jane, daughter of Thomas James of Hensingham House, at Whitehaven[11] *in Cumberland. This was a coal mining area on the north-west coast of England, particularly important for the Irish market.*

Tragically, within months, his new wife had died, on 10 January 1810 aged only 23. She was buried at St Andrews, Newcastle[12]. Perhaps as an antidote, Fryer now took up the study of geology. Fryer was able to become well informed on this partly because of his other address, at which he was based for parts of the year from at least 1808 onwards; Lyzzick Hall, north-west of Keswick, in the Lake District. This is a house just below the mountain of Skiddaw (931 m) and ideally situated for an occupant with geological interests.

The contribution to the development of British geology made by such people as Fryer, has not yet been adequately recognised by historians of geology. They have paid too much attention to the much better recorded history of 'gentlemen'. This group of 'practical geologists', land surveyors, mining engineers and 'mineral surveyors' was certainly not "always small", neither was it in evidence just "in the first third of the century", as claimed[13]. The highly papyrophobic nature of their work has obscured their contribution.

---

6   His birth date was either Xmas Day 1777 or 1778, depending on which of the two ages recorded at his death, 77 or 78, is correct (see note 104). His late baptism, on 22 August 1782 at Saint John's, Newcastle, fails to solve the problem.

7   1803, *Tenth Year's Report of the LPSN*, 21.

8   R.S. Watson 1897, *The History of the LPSN*. London: Scott.

9   R.V. Tooley 1979, *Dictionary of Map Makers*. Tring: Map Collector Publications, 229 and P. Eden (ed.) 1979, *Dictionary of Land Surveyors... 1550-1850, Supplement*. Folkestone: Dawson, 107.

10   ex inf. C. Roy Hudleston.

11   ex inf. C. Roy Hudleston.

12   E. Mackenzie op. cit. 5, vol. 1, 332.

Scientific Relations and Exchanges

Fryer's first recorded scientific contact was with one of the best known naturalists of the north-east of England, Nathaniel John Winch (1768-1838) of Newcastle. Fryer's first letter to Winch was dated 5 January 1813 and dealt with botany[14]. The two men had probably come into contact through the LPSN. Winch was an iron merchant and anchor-smith there who was recovering from bankruptcy in 1808[15]. It has been claimed this was due to his neglect of business, because of his devotion to science! Winch had also turned to geology and been elected an early member of the Geological Society in 1808. He acted as local geological correspondent for the 'gentlemen' of this London-based Society.

In August 1813 Robert Bakewell (1767-1843) had lectured in Newcastle and inspired a new interest in geology here. This is reflected in Fryer's first letter on geology, addressed from Newcastle to G.B. Greenough (1778-1855), President of the Geological Society of London. It is dated 9 February 1814[16]. Fryer writes that "for his own amusement [he has] marked upon Maps of the Counties of Durham, Northumberland and Cumberland the boundaries of the principal Rock formations and made a section of their relative situation from Sunderland [on the east coast] to Whitehaven [on the west coast]". He now sends these to Greenough (who used them in his own 1820 Geological Map[17]), with details of the sometimes confusing stratigraphic sequence found in these counties. Winch soon sent the new President, Hon. Henry Grey Bennet (1777-1836), corrections and additions to Fryer's maps which were duly passed on to Greenough[18]. A copy of Fryer's "first sketch of the Geology of Cumberland" of this date survives[19].

It is clear that Fryer was already well informed about the geology of these areas which had previously been much ignored by the 'gentlemen' geologists. A second long letter to G.B. Greenough[20] dated 13 March 1814 and written from Lyzzick Hall, discusses the anomalous Coal Measures of Alston in Cumberland and the age of the debated Red Sandstone of Carlisle. On the same day Fryer's help was acknowledged by Winch when he read his important paper on the "Geology of Northumberland and Durham", later published by the Geological Society of London[21]. A letter to Winch of April 1814 shows

13   R.S. Porter 1978, Gentlemen and Geology. *Historical Journal*, **21**, 809-836 (see 817).
14   Winch MSS 3:017, LSL.
15   R. Welford 1895, *Men of Mark 'twixt Tyne and Tweed*. London: Scott, vol. 3, 653-657.
16   G.B. Greenough MSS Letter 663, UCL.
17   G.B. Greenough 1820, *Memoir of a Geological Map*, London: Geological Society, 5.
18   Greenough MSS Letter 1774, dated 19.2.1814, UCL.
19   Winch MSS 3:226, LSL.
20   Greenough MSS Letter 664, UCL.
21   N. J. Winch 1817, Observations on the Geology of Northumberland and Durham. *Transactions of the Geological Society of London*, **4**, 1-101.

Fryer was already taking an interest in identifying fossils, which had become such a vital method of advancing British stratigraphy in the previous decade[22]. In September 1814 Fryer guided G.B. Greenough and William Buckland (1784-1856), newly elected Reader in Mineralogy at Oxford University, round Cumberland to study its geology[23].

In January 1815 Robert Bakewell, author of the first (1813) 'modern' geology text book in English, published his "Observations on the Geology of Northumberland and Durham"[24] after his 1813 visit. This included a section across the north of England (see **Figure 1**) which showed six rock units A to G. The publication of this aroused the anger of the north-east's resident geologists who accused Bakewell of having plagiarised the section which Fryer had made earlier, in 1813 and sent to G.B. Greenough - as well as to Winch and William Turner (1761-1859) - early in 1814[25]. Clearly feeling in the north-east was on Fryer's side and a second letter of complaint against Bakewell's action, written by Winch, was published early in April 1815[26], complaining of the "selfish conduct (to give it no harsher a name) of travelling lecturers and writers" like Bakewell. Winch assured his readers that the original of Bakewell's section "was planned and executed by Mr Jos Frear [sic], a gentleman well known in the North for his professional talents as a land-surveyor and draftsman, and scientific knowledge as a mineralogist and geologist, and who, from residing a great part of the year at Keswick, has daily opportunities of forming a correct idea of the Cumberland Mountains".

Bakewell replied to both charges on 15 April 1815, now calling Fryer, "J.H. Frere", denying his charges and urging Fryer to publish his version[27]. The original of Fryer's section has not survived and the surviving correspondence[28] does not allow the dispute to be settled. Probably the sections were that common phenomenon in history, 'simulta-neous inventions', with Fryer's having slight priority of date. 1815 saw Fryer still busy as a land surveyor and his map of the Penshaw estate of Lady Frances Anne Vane-Tem-pest[29] survives. But he was spurred into geological action, by the predations of Bakewell and the metropolitan visitors to 'his' mountains from the Geological Society of London (which he named "the soi-disant junta of London Geologists" in 1816[30]). He read a

22 Winch MSS 3:059, LSL.
23 W. Buckland 1817, Description of an Insulated Group of Rocks... between Melmerby and Murton. *Transactions of the Geological Society of London*, 4, 105-116.
24 *Philosophical magazine*, 45, 81-96.
25 J.H. Fryer 1815, On Mr Bakewell's Geological Section of the Northern counties of England. *Philosophical magazine*, 45, 219.
26 Anon 1815, Plagiarisms of Tourists and Journalists. *Monthly Magazine*, 39, 223-4.
27 R. Bakewell 1815, In Reply to Mr Frere. *Philosophical magazine*, 45, 297-300.
28 Winch MSS 3:074-076, LSL.
29 D/LO/P/4, DRO.

Scientific Relations and Exchanges

Figure 1 - "Sketch of the arrangement of the Rocks and Strata in the Northern Counties of England" by Robert Bakewell 1815. This was claimed by Fryer to have been stolen from his earlier (and now lost) version.

paper on 26 December 1815 and 2 January 1816, "On certain Primitive and Transition Rocks from near Brough in Westmorland to Melmerby, Cumberland" to the LPSN[30]. But this was then only partly published and anonymously, although the MSS and a transcript survive[31]. The paper is one of the first descriptions of the Cross Fell inlier. It notes the need for the "united efforts of a number of individuals". Among those named in it is another forgotten 'practical geologist': William Evetts Sheffield (1752-1821), metallurgist, surveyor and patentee. He provides the first evidence that Fryer was in contact with any of the circle of 'practical men' which included William Smith. Sheffield and the Smith circle were in contact from at least 1808[32]. One 'Nicol' had also been involved with Fryer[33]. This may be the itinerant lecturer William Nicol (c1771-1851) of 'Nicol prism' fame[34] and thus give a lead to his movements at this period. In May 1816 Fryer records he was now in contact with Ami Bou (1794-1881) the Franco-German pioneer of the geology of Scotland[35]. Bou was then studying medicine in Edinburgh and put Fryer in contact with Robert Jameson (1774-1854), the 'Wernerian' professor at Edinburgh University. In 1817 Bou (not Fryer himself) published a short note on Fryer's work on the Caldbeck Fells[36]. 1816 also saw Fryer in touch with the pioneer of Irish Geology, Richard John Griffith (1784-1878) when he visited Whitehaven[37]. In the Lysons' brothers volume on Cumberland of 1816, Fryer's help with "the strata and mineralogy of Cumberland" is again acknowledged[38].

In 1817 "Joseph H. Frere" was included in the circle of John Farey's geological queryists in the North East of England[39]. Fryer was now busy preparing a topographic map of Westmorland[40] but which again was never published. His six sheet corrected "Map of Cumberland" was however published in 1818 and added to the LPSN library

30   E. Hughes 1962, The Diaries and Correspondence of James Losh, vol. 1. *Publications of the Surtess Society*, **171**, 57 and 1816 *23rd Years Report of the LPSN*, 3.
31   Anon [J.H. Fryer] 1816, A geological Sketch of a Part of Cumberland and Westmoreland. *Philosophical magazine*, **47**, 41-5. MSS in LPSN archives, transcript in Winch MSS 3:097, LSL. The latter adds two unpublished stratigraphic sections.
32   Letter, 12 March 1808 from Wilson Lowry to David Mushet, D 2646/9, Glos Rec. Office.
33   Winch MSS 3:101, LSL.
34   A.D. Morrison-Low 1992, William Nicol FRSE (c1771-1851) Lecturer, Scientist and Collector. *Book of the Old Edinburgh Club*, NS **2**, 123-131.
35   Winch MSS 3:120, LSL.
36   1817, Caldbeck Fells. *Annals of Philosophy*, **9**, 161.
37   Winch MSS 3:144, LSL.
38   D & S Lysons 1816, *Magna Britannia, vol. 4, Cumberland*. London: Cadell & Davies, c-cxi.
39   *Philosophical magazine*, **49**, 124.
40   Winch MSS 3:184, LSL.

Scientific Relations and Exchanges

in 1819[41]. In 1820 the well known "Map of Northumberland by J[ohn] Fryer and Sons" was published[42], again with JHF's involvement.

In 1819 JHF "of Lyzzick Hall" was elected a non-resident member of the Wernerian Natural History Society of Edinburgh[43]. Early the following year he sent Greenough further comments[44] on the geology of Cumberland. These may have arrived in time to be used in Greenough's *Geological Map* published in May 1820. In the same year Boué's *Essai Géologique sur l'Écosse* was published. It contains a number of references to Fryer and his discoveries in the Cheviots, Roxburghshire and Northumberland. He called Fryer "géoloque très intelligent' and 'très judicieux". Boué's most crucial comment on Fryer also relates to many of the often forgotten 'mineral surveyors' who were now active in Britain. Boué called Fryer "l'un des géologues les plus instruits que j'aie rencontrés en Angleterre, loin de la capitale". He concluded "*il serait bien à désirer qu'un homme tel que lui trouvât assez de loisir pour pouvoir décrire un jour ces montagnes si intéressantes du Cumberland*" (italics here added)[45]. In Boué's later *Autobiography* he noted "Fryer of Newcastle" among his geological contacts and his visits to Fryer in Keswick in 1816 & 1817[46].

January 1821 sees Fryer's first recorded contact with the man who was responsible for his going to South America, the colliery viewer John Buddle (1773-1843). Fryer's first surviving letter to Buddle merely notes that he would be unable to met Buddle on one of the latter's regular visits to the Whitehaven coal mines[47]. A new geological contact for Fryer is revealed in a letter of 20 March 1821 from Jonathan Stokes (1754-1831) to Winch. Stokes had earlier been one of the younger members of the famous Lunar Society[48]. His letter asks Winch "is your friend Mr Fryer a mineral surveyor" and significantly notes of him, "it is only underground men such as [Friedrich W.H. von] Trebra [1740-1819], [Johann F.W.T. von] Charpentier [1728-1805 both of the Bergakademie, Freiberg] and [William] Smith [1769-1839] and the mountaineers, the Saussures [H. B. de S. 1740-1799 and his son N. T. de S. 1765-1845] and [Friedrich W. H. A. von] Humboldt [1769-1859] that are to be depended upon. I used to go underground till I married"[49]!

41   1819, *26th years Report of the LPSN*, 16.
42   see E.M. Rodger 1972, *The Large Scale County Maps of the British Isles 1596-1850*. Oxford: Bodleian Library, 4 & 18.
43   1821, *Memoirs of the Wernerian Natural History Society*, 3, 540.
44   Greenough MSS 16/30, UCL.
45   1820, 484 (also 71 & 145).
46   1879, *Autobiographie du Docteur médécin Ami Boué)*. Vienne: Ullrich et fils, 66, 83 & 85.
47   NCB I/JB/534, DRO.
48   R.E. Schofield 1963, *The Lunar Society of Birmingham*. Oxford: Clarendon Press.

In August 1821 Buckland and Fryer were again in the field in the Newcastle Coal Field[50]. On 20 June 1822 Fryer - by now of Ormathwaite House to the south east of Lyzzick Hall - married Mary Lititia Wilbraham (born 1799) of Rode Hall in Cheshire as his second wife[51]. Her family was well-to-do and Roger Wilbraham, a cousin, had subscribed to Smith's Geological Map of 1815[52]. By October 1822 Stokes had met Fryer and wrote to Winch that "your friend the enlightened geologist and mineralogist of Ormathwaite merits everything M. Bou can say of him". Stokes had also met William Smith, while the latter was based at Kirkby Lonsdale in 1822-4, and "hoped they [Fryer and Smith] will soon find each other out" [i.e. meet] as "I venture to predict that in ten minutes he [Fryer] will feel that with [Smith's] nephew Phillips [John Phillips (1800-1874)] he is holding conversation with a congenial mind"[53]. It is not known if Smith and Fryer ever met. In 1823 Stokes and Fryer explored the coast of Allonby on the Cumberland coast, for conchological treasure[54].

Fryer's South American nightmare: 1825-1828

There was a deep post-Napoleonic War recession in Britain after 1815. When it ended, British capital and technology avidly sought new opportunities. In 1824 English speculators fell in love with the idea of investing English money, mining skills and technology[55] in the mines of the New World, newly liberated from colonial Spain. Mines in Mexico were their first target[56]. This was largely inspired by the lobbying of the Treasurer of the Geological Society of London, the mining engineer John Taylor (1779-1863). His 1824 *Selections from the works of the Baron de Humboldt relating to ... Mexico*[57] were very influential. Mining openings were soon sought all over South America. Such mining was only one of many manias then pursued by English investors[58].

49 Winch MSS 4:112, LSL. Stokes married in 1784.
50 Greenough MSS Buckland to Greenough 25 August 1821, UCL.
51 *Cumberland Pacquet*, 24 June and *Staffordshire Advertiser*, 13 July 1822.
52 J. Burke 1836, *History of the Commoners of Great Britain*. London: Colburn, vol. 1, 635-6.
53 Winch MSS 4:198, LSL.
54 Winch MSS 5:062, LSL.
55 The success of the Trevithick high-pressure steam engine in colonial Peru is a case in point demonstrated by J.R. Fisher 1977, *Silver Mines and Silver Miners in Colonial Peru, 1776-1824*. Centre for Latin-American Studies: University of Liverpool, Monograph Series 7, 114-6 & figure 2.
56 *GM*, March 1824, 260.
57 London: Longmans; see also A.C. Todd 1977, *The Search for Silver: Cornish Miners in Mexico 1824-1947*. Padstow: Lodenek Press.

Scientific Relations and Exchanges

The *Potosi, La Paz and Peruvian Mining Association* was registered late in April 1825[59]. Its capital was to be an impressive £1,000,000 of £50 shares. Its Prospectus (see **Figure 2**) noted that the "Spaniards [had had] the disadvantages of a heavy duty, a defective system of smelting and a want of knowledge of the correct principles of the art of Mining... Mines... with British capital, science and machinery, may afford a fair expectation of profit to those engaged in them"! The Prospectus quoted Humboldt, who encouraged the boom and the *Potosi Association*, without ever having visited the Potosi area, and Antonio Helms who had, but in 1789-1793. The latter then noted that "Peru might alone furnish annually four times a greater quantity of Gold and Silver than Mexico".

Backed with such advice, an advance agent was despatched in May with a credit of £5,000 to take possession of the Potosi mines. In the same month John Buddle was invited to a meeting in London by Charles Tennyson later D'Eyncourt (1784-1861) M.P., one of the Directors[60]. He would then "meet Mr [John] Taylor the Engineer", so involved with stimulating the whole American mining mania of the 1820's[61]. Buddle was given the task of finding skilled people prepared to work for the new *Association* in Peru. In June 1825 John Bateman Longmire (1785-1858), another forgotten 'practical geologist' who had worked as a coal mine engineer and prospector at Tula in Russia 1817-1822[62], declined Buddle's invitation[63]. By July, JHF had accepted in his place, writing from Ann's Hill near Cockermouth to Buddle on his way to Alston in Cumberland to recruit miners. By August, Fryer had found nearly all the miners needed for Peru and was now ordering mining equipment in Newcastle[64]. Meanwhile in South America, Peru and Chile had been "freed" from Spanish control in December 1824 and Bolivia had come

58 J. Farey 1825, Joint Stock Companies. *Monthly magazine*, **59**, 145-152.
59 The best descriptions of the *Potosi Association* disaster are 1) Edmond Temple 1829, *A Brief Account of the... Potosi .. Association*. London: Ridgway; 2) his 1830, *Travels in Various Parts of Peru, including a Year's Residence in Potosi*. London: Colborn and Bentley, two volumes and 3) R.A. Humphreys 1952, *Liberation in South America 1806-1827*. London: Athlone Press. The last is the best.
60 NCB 1/JB/1445, DRO.
61 J. Taylor 1824, *Selections from the works of the Baron de Humboldt relating to... Mexico*. London: Longman etc and see J. F. Rippy 1947, Latin America and the British Investment "Boom" of the 1820's. *Journal of Modern History*, **19**, 122-9.
62 H.S. Torrens 1991, J.B. Longmire (1785-1858), a Lakeland Geologist and his work as a coal prospector in Russia 1817-1822. *Proceedings of the Westmorland Geological Society*, **5**, 12-14.
63 NCB 1/JB/906, DRO.
64 NCB 1/JB/535-6, DRO

POTOSI, LA PAZ, AND PERUVIAN

MINING ASSOCIATION.

THE CAPITAL

TO BE

ONE MILLION POUNDS STERLING.

President.
DON JUAN GARCIA DEL RIO,
Late Minister Plenipotentiary from Peru to the Courts of Europe.

Vice President.
GENERAL JAMES PAROISSIEN,
Also late Minister Plenipotentiary from Peru to the Courts of Europe.

Directors.

Sir W. A. INGILBY, Bart. M. P.	WILLIAM RUSSELL, Esq. M. P.
CHARLES TENNYSON, Esq. M. P.	Hon. JOHN WALPOLE, M. P.
Sir FRANCIS DESANGES.	WILLIAM HOLMES, Esq. M. P.
LYNDON EVELYN, Esq. M. P.	C. A. THISELTON, Esq.
J. B. LOUSADA, Esq.	J. D. CARVALHO, Esq.
JAMES HUNTER, Jun. Esq.	EMANUEL LOUSADA, Esq.

Auditors.
Sir R. ARBUTHNOT, K. C. B.   J. R. WARD, Esq.
LEWIS HENRY DESANGES, Esq.

Bankers.
Sir WILLIAM CURTIS, Bart. ROBARTS, & CURTIS.
Sir RICHARD CARR GLYN, Bart. MILLS, & CO.

Agents in South America.

At Potosi	DON JOAQUIN DE LA QUINTANA.
At La Paz	DON N. MARIACA.
At Lima	DON FRANCISCO ALVAREZ CALDERON.
At Truxillo	DON MODESTO DE LA VEGA.
At Tucuman	DON JOSE IGNACIO GARMENDIA.
At Buenos Ayres	DON FELIX CASTRO.

Standing Counsel.
L. SHADWELL, Esq.

Solicitor.
JOHN CROSLAND, Esq.

Secretary.
JOHN CHANNON, Esq.

The object of this Association is to employ its capital, in working Mines of Gold, Silver, Platina, Quicksilver, Copper, and other Minerals, in the Provinces of Potosi and La Paz, and generally in upper and lower Perú, in South America; in the purchase and reduction of Ores, Minerals, and Metals; and in other matters connected with Mines.

The Association has already secured, by contract, for ninety-nine years, three-fourth parts of the four celebrated Silver Mines, of the Marquis de Casa Palacio,

Figure 2 - The Title page of the Prospectus for the *Potosi Association* of 1825.

Scientific Relations and Exchanges

into existence in August 1825 and now the Potosi Association faced two sets of unknown customs duties on their imports!

By 20 September 1825 the *Potosi Association* had "nearly completed its establishment for Potosi", Fryer was expected soon in London and General Pariossien was to leave London for Falmouth next day on route for South America[65]. General James Pariossien (1784-1827) was Vice-President and First Commissioner of the Association. It is his surviving correspondence which provides many details of Fryer's South American 'interlude'[66]. Fryer provides direct links with Alexander Humboldt (1769-1859) and J.B. Pentland, who both form subjects of papers in this volume. Pariossien was of Huguenot extraction, the son of an Essex schoolmaster. His introduction to South America had come in 1806 when he embarked for Montevideo as a commission agent[67]. His years in South America made him ideally qualified to lead this new venture, at a salary of £2500/year! Fryer was to be "Second Commissioner and Chief Engineer" (salary £1500/year) and Edmond Temple, the secretary at Potosi (salary £500/year). Hermann, Baron de Czettritz from Dresden was chief of the mining department and, according to a letter from Pariossien to Fryer, was "a young man of extensive mineralogical knowledge and extremely amiable. You will like him much". Czettritz had been one of Werner's last students at the Bergakademie, Freiberg from 1817[68]. John Scrivenor, who was to be his assistant, "appears to have made the situation he holds entirely subservient to his wish to travel in America". Pariossien's party left Falmouth on 28 September in the well-named H.M. Packet Brig *FROLIC!*[69] and arrived at the River Plate on 29 November 1825. Little did they know!

Fryer remained in London. To complicate matters his father died in Newcastle on 5 October 1825 and a major financial crisis in London followed when the wave of investment, which was to carry Fryer to Peru, crashed in December 1825 and all dealings in Spanish American mining shares halted[70]. Fryer's letter to Pariossien of 21 December 1825, complaining about the Association's mismanagement and the inadequacy of its

65   John Channon to Buddle NCB 1/JB/281, DRO.
66   Pariossien papers, D/DOb boxes A-C, uncatalogued, ERO.
67   R.A. Humphreys op. cit. 60.
68   K.G. Gottschalk 1867, Verzeichniss derer, welche seit Eröffung der Bergakademie... auf ihr studirt haben. In *Festschrift zum hundertjährigen Jubiläum der Königl. sächs. Bergakademie zu Freiberg*. Dresden: Meinhold, vol. 1, 249.
69   Humphreys op. cit. 60, 144 and see Pariossien to Fryer 1 March 1826, ERO.
70   P. Mathias 1986, *The First Industrial Nation*. London: Methuen, 294-5. The same crisis affected Mary Anning (1799-1847)'s provincial fossil dealing business; see M.A. Taylor & H.S. Torrens 1987, Saleswomen to a New Science. *Proceedings of the Dorset Natural history and Archaeological Society*, 108, 145.

Directors, shows the first signs of trouble brewing[71]! Capt. Henry Templer, the owner of the ship, now rechristened POTOSI, which was to carry Fryer and *his* party to Potosi, was "without exception the most unprincipled Scoudrel [Fryer] ever met with or ever heard of, and who will not do anything but what the Law obliges him to do. Although we are perfectly ready" to leave, Fryer still "had no hopes of our getting away for some time. Four Cornish miners had now been engaged but no smelter or refiner yet". Fryer's only praise was reserved for John Channon, the London Secretary.

Fryer first left England in January 1826 but his ship was forced to put back to Plymouth where the crew promptly deserted! The ship only left on March 10th and apart from Fryer, carried 44 other passengers including his wife Mary Lititia (with her piano) and Fryer's sister Mary (born 1799) with other Association staff. The cargo was valued at £20,000 and included quicksilver, gunpowder and mining equipment. Just as Fryer was leaving England, J.B. Pentland, who visited Potosi and later reported on the *Association*'s troubles in his "Report on Bolivia 1827"[72], was arriving in Lima.

The POTOSI finally arrived at Arica, Peru on 21 July 1826. William Templer, the brother of its owner, had been on board which did not help matters[73]. The ship arrived to find disaster had struck, working of the Potosi mines had been stopped and lawsuits and ships' manifests soon started to fly, back and forth between lawyers. The next relevant document, dated 19 September 1826, was from William Templer to Fryer. It gave notice that until all outward freight charges, of over £5,000, were paid, the ship was detained at Arica. Templer had seized the cargo to auction it off to pay these charges[74]. By 9 October the lawyers were busy trying to stop Templer's embargo[75]. 17 October 1826 saw a joint "protest and declaration" by Fryer and Pariossien, supported by the British merchants in Arica, protesting against Templer's action and countercharging him with all "loss, damage and injury to the *Association* which had arisen from his actions"[76]. Fryer next poured his heart out to Buddle in a long latter home, dated Arica 13 November 1826[77], of the ' overwhelming miseries which awaited us here". The first problem had been the immense customs charges levied on some of the cargo. The second was the fact that Bills drawn on London to supply Fryer with money to pay miners etc could not now

71   Letter dated 21 December 1825, ERO.
72   J.B. Pentland 1974, *Report on Bolivia 1827*, London: Royal Historical Society (Camden Miscellany XXV) (189-194, 208-11).
73   Fryer to Paroissien 28 July 1826 and see Hunphreys op. cit. 60, 152-7.
74   Fryer to Paroissien 22 September 1826 & English Letter Book Pariossien to Fryer 3 October 1826, ERO.
75   Fryer to Paroissien 9 October 1826.
76   ERO.
77   NCB 1/JB/537, DRO.

Scientific Relations and Exchanges

be discounted, because of the financial crisis in London and so Fryer was "left without a shilling". The third was that Fryer had just got the cargo landed, and sold a small part of it to liberate funds and was repacking the majority for transport to Potosi, when Templer embargoed the whole cargo on 14 September 1826 to pay the freight charges, including all passengers' private luggage!

Three of the London Directors; James Hunter junior, C.A. Thiselton and J[ohn B[aruh] Lousada had been responsible for paying these freight charges in London but finding their shares would not sell as the market collapsed, they refused to pay future instalments on their shares. They instead made the freight charges payable on delivery of goods in South America.

Fryer had no money to pay these or any other charges, so the *Association's* "people are many of them literally starving and we are only existing on the bounty of the British merchants here". Fryer asks Buddle to "use your influence to persuade [the Directors] to send us some money to extricate us from the horrid misery in which the cold-blooded villainy of three of the Directors has placed us". Similar letters dated 6 & 7 December 1826 to Pariossien show that some of the men were now applying to return to England. The lawyers were still fighting the case but Fryer still "had not a single Real to get bread with for tomorrow's breakfast". A letter of response from Buddle to Charles Tennyson dated 14 March 1827 shows both how long letters then took to reach Europe and that Buddle did his best to persuade Tennyson of the scale of crisis the *Association* now faced at Arica[78]. By 12 December 1826 Fryer noted also that "Bell (the Ore Dresser) has returned and gives a dreadful account of Potosi"[79]. By 18 December Fryer's sister was "very ill". By 26 December it had at last been possible to get the Association's goods out of the Custom House, "and in very good condition", but the *Association*'s 20,000 shares, which had reached a price of £13 each, were now only worth 2s/6d each back in London, a loss of £257,500! 23 mining companies of the 1825 mania had collectively lost £9,775,750[80]!

1827 started no better. Fryer's letter of 2 January 1827 from Arica shows that, although some items from the cargo were being sold, he had still not received any of the proceeds! But he notes that he "will be very glad to see Johnson's letter about the mines of Huantacoya" [Huancayo, Peru]. This was John Frederick Johnson (1798-1879), brother of the *Potosi Association*'s assay master in London (and founder of today's London precious metal dealers Johnson and Matthey). Johnson had gone out with the *Potosi Association* team, married a Potosi woman and then set up a hardware business in

78   NCB 1/JB/1448, DRO.
79   ERO.
80   *GM*, **96**, Dec 1826, 637.

Arequipa (probably by selling the cheaply bought cargo of the *Potosi*[81]!). Johnson remained in South America until the late 1870's. Fryer's letter of 2 January 1827 also notes that he has just "read some very interesting reports from Mr [Joseph Barclay] Pentland about the mines of Puno and Illimani - which if I could send copies to England would be a complete answer to [John] Channon [their London Secretary]'s nonsense - nothing he says is wanting but capital to make them extremely productive". Fryer was clearly sure these mines could still be worked profitably. Pentland had been in direct contact with Edmond Temple at Potosi but had rude things to say of Czettritz, "the fool appears to stand on etiquette and to think that this mark of respect is due to his German Barony". He ends "I have seen enough of your *Association* to judge that... success is very problematical"[82]. Fryer however remained "very much pleased" with Czettritz[83].

Letters of March & April 1827 to Pariossien are from the two Marys, Fryer's wife and sister, since Fryer had now been attacked by Tertian fever and dysentery! A letter of 27 April 1827 from John Channon to Charles Ralph Fryer (born 1799), Fryer's New-castle-based brother, shows that the Directors of the *Association* had decided to recall both Pariossien and Fryer[84]. By June Fryer was writing to Pariossien of the possibility of his return to England. Pariossien, worn out with the trials and tribulations of the affair, died at sea on his way home in September 1827 aged 43[85], and Fryer left "Arica some little time after Pariossien"[86], probably arriving back in England early in 1828.

The lawyers, busy already in Peru when the *Potosi*'s cargo had arrived, were now again busy in London with the aftermath of the *Potosi Association* disaster. The *Morning Chronicle* of 15 April 1829 carried news of the first trials in Chancery started on the Potosi Mining Company fiasco and Edmond Temple soon wrote a powerful and fascinating *Brief account*[87] of the affair to enlighten shareholders, and later historians. McCulloch was right to report in 1839 that the Spanish American mining mania had been a "disgraceful era in [British] commercial history"[88].

81   see D. McDonald 1964, *The Johnsons of Maiden Lane*. London: Martins, 93-5.
82   Pentland to Paroissien 4 January 1826 [recte 1827], ERO.
83·   Letter of 1 February 1827 to Paroissien, ERO.
84   NCB 1/JB/533, DRO.
85   Humphreys op. cit 60, 161.
86   James Beuzeville (Pariossien's nephew) to Fryer 1 July 1840, ERO.
87   E. Temple op. cit. 60.
88   J. R. McCulloch 1839, *A Dictionary... of Commerce and Commercial navigation*. London: Longman etc, new edition, 801-4.

Scientific Relations and Exchanges

Fryer back in England: 1828-1855.

Fryer left no apparent record of any geological or mineralogical activity in Peru, since he had been unable to do any. After his return, exhausted by the whole affair, he published only one relevant article, dated Newcastle 5 January 1829. This was "an account of certain Articles taken from the Graves of the Ancient Peruvians in the neighbourhood of Arica". This, with one plate, was published in 1829[89]. Fryer's South American interlude had been a terrible waste of time for a clearly talented man. 'Failure' had struck a second time.

Fryer now threw himself into the work of the *Natural History Society of Northumberland and Durham*, founded in Newcastle-on-Tyne in February 1829. Fryer is one of the four Honorary Curators for Mineralogy and Geology listed in the first volume of the Society's *Transactions*, published in 1831[90] and was also its Honorary Curator of Conchology. By 1831 JHF had moved to a fine stone house, variously called Whitley Hall or House[91] at Whitley Bay, the sea-side resort to the east of Newcastle. Here he subscribed to John Lindley and William Hutton's *Fossil Flora of Great Britain*[92].

Fryer's involvement with Newcastle continued when he was appointed a magistrate for Northumberland in 1838[93]. His involvement with *the Potosi Association* also continued. In 1838 both John Crosland, the Association's Solicitor and John Channon, its Secretary, died[94]. Their deaths seem to have inspired a new attempt by Pariossien's nephew to open legal proceedings against the *Association*. Fryer wrote to him on 21 January 1839[95] apologising that he had been unable to find any documents in his brother's offices in Newcastle; "he having been my attorney in the various law proceedings I had with the Directors of the *Potosi Association*". Fryer noted that "all the papers I had relating to the Potosi concerns [were] impounded in Chancery and as I got a settlement with the Directors without any decision from that Court, it was not thought worth the trouble and expense of applying for their restoration".

Fryer, "an annuitant" in the 1851 Census, seems now to have been comfortably off, probably as a result of the above out-of-court settlement. In March 1840, John Edward Gray (1800-1875) was appointed Keeper of Zoology at the British Museum, becoming

89   *Archaeologia Aeliana*, (1) **2**, 248-51 with plate 8, figs 1-12.
90   op. cit. liv.
91   W.W. Tomlinson 1893, *Historical Notes on Cullercoats, Whitley Bay and Monkseaton*. London: Scott, 124-5.
92   1831 vol. 1, List of Subscribers, p. v.
93   *Newcastle Journal*. 10 February 1838.
94   *GM*, March 1838, 329 and October 1838, 454.
95   21 January 1839, ERO.

the greatest of the holders of this office. One of Gray's bonds, for £750, had been provided by Fryer[96]. In 1846 Fryer became one of the founders of the new *Tyneside Field Club*[97]. Their field trip to Tynemouth on 29 October 1846 inspected the "very extensive and valuable collection of shells" which Fryer had accumulated, many from South America[98]. Fryer was its Vice-President in 1847 and helped with *their Catalogue of the Mollusca of Northumberland and Durham* published in 1848[99]. By 1848 Fryer had been elected to the new *Palaeontographical Society*, showing he had retained his old interest in fossils[100]. In 1849 he offered Whitley House for let[101], apparently without success since his will dated 2 December 1850 was made from the same address. It left all his property to his wife[102]. Fryer died on his birth day, Christmas Day, 1855[103] leaving an estate valued at below £800 and was buried in Christ Church, Tynemouth on 29 December[104]. None of the notices of his death and burial could decide whether his age was 77 or 78. They provide a nicely confused end to an unfulfilled life.

The contents of Whitley Hall were advertised for sale on 23 Feb. 1856[105] but the sale was held on March 10-13 & 18-19 according to the Sale Catalogue[106]. It included many geological books and several on South America, as well as his surveying and other instruments. Among these were "gold scales", perhaps an earlier enthusiastic purchase for South America? The sale also included his "splendid collection of shells, comprising 12,000 specimens" in a 140 drawer cabinet. This was sold to Sir Joseph Whitwell Pease (1828-1903) of Hutton Hall, Yorkshire. After *his* death it passed to the Dorman Museum in Middleborough where it remains, with at least one of Fryer's conchological books. The collection contains a good deal of South American material and now provides the

96   A.E. Gunther 1978, John George Children FRS (1777-1852). *Bulletin of the British Museum (Natural History)*, Historical Series, **6** (4), 103.
97   T.R. Goddard 1929, *History of the Natural History Society of Northumberland and Durham*. Newcastle: Reid, 57.
98   1848, *Transactions Tyneside Naturalists Field Club*, **1**, 18-21.
99   by Joshua Alder in their *Transactions*, **1**, 97-207.
100   1848. *List of the... Palaeontographical Society*, viii.
101   *Newcastle Journal*, 5 May 1849.
102   Durham Probate Records, University of Durham.
103   see obits of 1855 in *Newcastle Journal* 29 December 1855 and of 1858 in *Transactions of the Tyneside Naturalists Field Club*, **3**, 56 and the 1913 notice in *Archaeologia Aeliana* (3), **10**, 172.
104   Burial register at NRO.
105   *Newcastle Journal*.
106   *Catalogue of the... Household Furniture,... Books etc of the late J.H. Fryer Esq FSA... to be sold....* North Shields: Orange.

only tangible reminder of Fryer's ill-fated venture there[107]. A little more survives at the Hancock Museum, Newcastle-on-Tyne. Fryer had left no children who might have helped ensure his life and papers were better recorded.

Conclusion

Fryer's first English career was plagued by claims of plagiarism, amid the rivalries between provincial and metropolitan geology. But the critical problem was that identified in 1820 by Bou, his inability to find adequate time to devote to his geological research. Fryer's time in what was by now also Bolivia proved a greater disaster, although not of his making. As Veliz has noted, in relation to the four Chilean joint stock mining companies of 1825, it was not any failure in South American mining which precipitated the 1825 financial crash in London; as claimed in some of the silliest paragraphs in Latin American histories, but the reverse. *The Potosi and Chilean Associations* all failed simply because "they were established [too] late in the day"[108], *Potosi* last but one.

Acknowledgments

I gladly thank Sarah Bendall, J. Allan Charlton, John Cooper, Peter Davis, Gina Douglas, C. Roy Hudleston, Brian Newman and the late Peter Wallis for their kind help. This paper is gratefully dedicated to Peter's memory. The staffs of ERO, DRO and NRO and of the North East Institute of Mining Engineers all gave every possible assistance. This paper was helped by a grant from the Royal Society for Work on English Mineral Surveyors 1800-1820".

Abbreviations

DNB *Dictionary of National Biography*
DRO Durham Record Office
ERO Essex Record Office
GM *Gentlemans Magazine*
JHF Joseph Harrison Fryer
LPSN Literary and Philosophical Society, Newcastle
LSL Linnean Society, London
NRO Northumberland Record Office
UCL University College, London

107   J.D. Dean 1936, Conchological Cabinets of the Last Century. *Journal of Conchology,* **20,** 238.
108   C. Veliz 1975, Egaña, Lambert, and the Chilean Mining Associations of 1825. *Hispanic American History Review,* **55,** 638-63.

William Edmond Logan's Geological Apprenticeship in Britain 1831-1842[1]

He seems to have been mostly self-taught, though no doubt he learned much from the practical mining engineers with whom he came in daily contact (Flett, 1937, p. 40).

INTRODUCTION

William E. Logan (1798-1875), the first director of Canada's Geological Survey (1843-1869), has long, and rightly, been a man of great appeal to all interested in geology and in particular, Canadian geology. This is best demonstrated by the recent poll by *Maclean's Magazine* of the "Most important Canadians in History" which placed him as the most important scientist in Canada's history, "a man whose imprint remains on the land and whose surveys made it possible to tap Canada's treasury of minerals" (Anonymous, 1998, p. 39). Logan has the highest mountain in Canada named after him; rather appropriately, this has proved to be the fastest rising mountain in North America (*Episodes*, June 1992, v. 15, n. 2, cover).

But Logan is symptomatic of a major problem in history, and not just that of geology. He travelled and trained out-

side the country of his birth (he was born of Scottish parents in Montreal on 20 April 1798) and he also died "abroad," having returned from Canada to be near his geological training grounds in south Wales, where he died on 22 June 1875 at Castle Malgwyn, in Pembrokeshire (Winder, 1965). Such travel-filled lives complicate the historian's task, as records of them get split, separating across, in this case, the drifting continents of Europe and North America. Separate expertises, and considerable finance, are needed to deal with such records now preserved in widely separate archives.

Conscious of this difficulty I determined to seek out what I could of records in the United Kingdom to shed light on the thorny problem of when, where, and how Logan first learned the geology, at which he proved so proficient, on his permanent return to Canada in 1843. But, if only to illustrate the extent of the problem outlined above, I have not been able to use Canadian archival sources. I hope some future Canadian scholar may be able to build on these foundations.

[1] This paper sheds new light on the question of how William Logan acquired his initial skills in geology, while immersed in the commercial world of accounting and managing a large copper-smelting operation, yet following his interests in geology to the point of obtaining the recognition of the British academic and scientific community of the day Hugh Torrens gave the paper orally at the symposium "Hutton, Lyell, Logan and their influence in North America", held at the 1998 Geological Society of America Annual Meeting in Toronto (Conference Report, *Geoscience Canada*, 1998, v. 25, p. 185–188). Although Logan lacked formal training in geology, study of a hitherto almost unknown 1850 report by Logan on his work in Canada in the 1840s (Smith, *Geoscience Canada*, v. 26, p. 111–120, this issue) shows just how skilled Logan had become by 1850, and what major contributions he was making in Canada. R.W. Macqueen, editor.

AT EDINBURGH UNIVERSITY

Logan entered Edinburgh University for the academic year 1816-1817 intending to study medicine. In the event, he only spent this 1 year at the university. Professors here had to earn their livings by the numbers of students they attracted (Smith, 1976, v. 2, p. 760; Shapin, 1976, p. 17). University records show that Logan took classes in logic from Professor David Ritchie (died *ca* 1842), in chemistry from Professor Thomas Charles Hope M.D. (1766-1844), (whose class that year had 522 students; such numbers thus prove not to be a new phenomenon!), and in mathematics from a Mr. Nichol. But Logan left the university in 1817 to work at the counting house of his uncle Robert Hart Logan (1772-1838, hereafter Hart) in London. Hart was elected an MP for Suffolk in 1837 just before he died (Stenton, 1976, p. 242).

Gordon Winder has claimed that an earlier statement that Logan was not exposed to geology at Edinburgh University is probably not now correct, since Logan's mentor in chemistry was Hope "...an ardent supporter of the Neptunists" (geologists who believed that rocks formed by the action of water alone), so that "Logan probably was exposed to some geological concepts in his university course" (Winder 1965, 123-4). But Hope, whatever he may have taught Logan — and this certainly included some geology — was always a devoted Plutonist (or Huttonian), never a Neptunist. Winder was misled by a confusing letter from Louis Albert Necker (1786-1861), the Swiss Neptunist, who was expressing the wish that Hope might change his mind, when he wrote about him in 1807 (Eyles, 1948, p. 100-102). Hope instead believed, with his Edinburgh associate James Hutton (1726-1797), that the role of fire and heat in the production of some rocks, like granite and basalt, and in the consolidation of others, had been both crucial and central. It was in that cause that Hope was "not less zealous," to quote Necker.

Hope's true allegiances are proved by many sources, from G.B. Greenough's (the soon-to-be first president of the Geological Society of London in 1807) 1805 *Scottish Journal* (Rudwick, 1962, p. 124-125) to David Brewster (1781-1868) who insisted, some years later, that Hope was "a Huttonian philosopher" ([Brewster], 1837, p. 10). Hope's own lecture notes survive (Anderson, 1978, p. 37), as do others taken by an attending German student in October 1798 (Oxford, Bodleian Library, MS Eng. Miscellaneous d. 197). These were made by the later distinguished diplomat, linguist and historian Barthold Georg Niebuhr (1776-1831), (Bunsen *et al.,* 1852, v. 1, p. 106-107, 124, 128). Final confirmation comes from surviving lecture notes and other sources quoted in Jim Secord's analysis of Charles Darwin (1809-1882)'s attendance at Hope's lectures in 1825-1826. These further prove that "Dr. Hope thinks the Huttonian better accounts for the appearance of Nature than the Wernerian" (Secord, 1991, p. 139-142).

I believe we should continue to take seriously the claim by Logan's biographer, Bernard Harrington (1883, p. 9) that "teaching [at Edinburgh] probably had nothing to do with Logan's future devotion to geology." All available evidence still points to this being the correct view. But there is now evidence that Logan was soon busy as a collector of fossils. Several labelled specimens of fossil bivalves that he collected in Suffolk, where his uncle's estate was situated, probably in the 1820s, still survive in the Royal Institution of South Wales (RISW) collections, now at Swansea Museum. They deserve further research. Logan was soon busy extending such investigations. This is shown by his excursion to examine the London Clay formation (Eocene) on the Isle of Sheppey during an enforced stay in London in 1833 (Harrington, 1883, p. 55-58). Such rocks were close in geological age to the rocks from which he had already collected in Suffolk.

It might be tempting to see parallels between the geological apprenticeships of Darwin and Logan, since both took up the serious study of geology at much the same time. But I believe this would be misleading. Darwin was much influenced by his university careers, at both Edinburgh and Cambridge, while Logan was not. Darwin left us a mass of manuscript material on which the "Darwin industry" is now based, while Logan's have been hopelessly scattered or lost. Darwin was influenced all along by "gentlemanly" attitudes to geology, and those aspiring to these, at the Geological Society of London. Logan was instead in business, and could never be the leisured amateur (in its original sense) that Darwin remained. Logan's profession depended on his acquisition of geological knowledge. Gordon Winder asked the crucial question, "did [Logan] acquire geological knowledge through the business transactions of his uncle's company?" (Winder, 1965, p. 108). The answer is yes.

IN SOUTH WALES
Logan was first based in London after his studies in Edinburgh, and from 1827

took charge of his uncle's business affairs at his counting house there, leaving Hart to enjoy his Suffolk estates. Harrington noted that Logan's "study of geology [as opposed to fossil collecting] was apparently not begun until after he went to live in South Wales." This was early in 1831 (Harrington, 1883, p. 49), not 1829 (Christie, 1994, p. 169). It was Logan's first cousin William Logan Edmond (1808-1877) who had arrived here in 1829 as metallurgist to the Forest Copper Works, near Swansea (Dahne, 1971, p. 131). Logan certainly had earlier south Wales connections, such as those revealed by his visits to the Gower family at Castle Malgwyn between 1822 and1829. These must have helped lead to the marriage of his youngest sister Elizabeth (1799-1866) to Abel Lewes Gower (1796-1849) on 2 September 1828 (not 1837 as Winder, 1965, p. 10-5). Such connections in turn explain why Logan was to die there (Crisp, 1917, p. 51; Phillips, 1867, p. 142). Gower had been elected a Fellow of the Geological Society of London (FGS), well before Logan, on 12 June 1833 (Anonymous, 1833, p. 486). Gower was thus in a good position to advise Logan on the best geological reading available.

By the spring of 1833, Logan was using Conybeare and Phillips's fine 1822 textbook, which concentrated on uncovering the "regular succession and order in the arrangements of the mineral masses constituting the Earth's surface" (Eagan, 1992, p. 327). He was also quoting the third volume (1833) of Lyell's new *Principles of Geology* (Harrington, 1883, p. 56; Winder, 1965, p. 109). Logan's new Gower brother-in-law had been based at 31 Finsbury Square, London while Logan shared a house at nearby 47 Finsbury Square with Dr. Robert Dickson (1804-1875) MD Edinburgh 1826, (see Dictionary of National Biography). Both Gower and Dickson would have been able to help Logan discover "which are the best works in geology and mineralogy" (Harrington, 1883, p. 50) before Logan departed for south Wales.

At Swansea, or "Copperopolis," between 1800-1890, 90% of British copper was smelted using coal, and by 1845, 55% of the world's copper was being smelted here (Newell, 1990, 1997). A good description of the processes involved there was given by the Freiberg Bergakademie-trained metallurgist and geologist John Henry Vivian (1779-1855) in 1823 (Vivian, 1823).

Vivian had been a honorary Member of the Geological Society from its foundation in 1807. One of the many smelting firms involved at Swansea was the Forest Copper Works at Morriston, 3 miles upstream from the port of Swansea (Fig. 1).

These works had been purchased on 11 May 1827 by the firm of Usborne and Benson, whose partners were Henry Usborne and Thomas Starling Benson (1775-1858). By the end of that decade Benson had enlisted the financial support of Logan's uncle Hart, who soon joined the partnership. Members of the Benson and Usborne families also intermarried on 18 October 1831 (Anonymous, 1831a, p. 464). New records give useful data on the timing of Logan's

Figure 1 Swansea and the Harbour in 1848 (from the *Illustrated London News,* 19 August 1848, v. 13, p. 109).

business activities in south Wales. The articles of a new partnership, now between Starling Benson, Jr. (1808-1879) and Logan, dated 2 February 1839 (West Glamorgan Archives, D/D SB 12/13), show how Usborne and Benson next leased another copper premises and copper slag near Melyncriddan, Neath from 28 February 1829, while the firm was newly named Benson, Logan and Company from 20 April 1833 (Bayliffe and Harding, 1996).

Logan first joined these Forest Copper Works in 1831, as manager in charge of accounts, but he soon became concerned with all aspects of copper smelting, which of course involved locating and purchasing supplies of both the many types of copper ores, which had formerly come largely from Cornwall but which could now be imported from Ireland (Knockmahon), South America and Europe, and of coal, which was available in great abundance locally, again in various types, but of

which 2 tons were needed to smelt every ton of ore. On 1 February 1833 the first of seven patents assigned to Nicholas Troughton R.N. (died 1844; see *Cambrian,* 21 December 1844, the local newspaper published in Swansea) for "preparing materials for, and producing, a.... Metallic Cement" (British Patent number 6303, dated 8 September 1832) was assigned to Benson, Logan and Company This the firm also started to manufacture, under new articles of partnership signed on 20 April 1833. In these, Benson, Sr. transferred some of his shares to his son, and Hart Logan, part of his shares to his nephews William E. and Henry Logan. In 1834 the old Forest Works were demolished and rebuilt as part of Benson and Logan's major improvement scheme (Grant-Francis, 1881, p. 111). It is likely that while at Swansea, Logan lived at Cambrian Place (Fig. 2), sharing the residence of his friend and colleague, Starling Benson, both partners in the

Figure 2 Cambrian Place in the 1830s with the Benson, Logan house on the left (from Bayliffe and Harding, 1996, p. 49) by kind permission of Dorothy Bayliffe.

firm from 1833 (Bayliffe and Harding, 1996).

Logan started to take fuller managerial responsibility in these south Wales operations from April 1833. Exactly how the two partners separated their responsibilities remains unclear but Logan, clearly with an already extant interest in geology, was undoubtedly the more involved with supplies of coal and copper while Benson was more interested in their transport by rail, and in shipping improvements through the crucial development of Swansea Harbour, in which, however, Logan was also a Trustee (*Cambrian,* 19 August 1843). We should moreover recall that, long after Logan had left Swansea, Benson was also competent enough as a geologist to report to the British Association for the Advancement of Science (BAAS) in 1848 both "on a Boulder of Cannel Coal found in a vein of common bituminous coal" (Benson, 1849a) and to deliver a very significant paper on the relative positions of the various types of coals found in south Wales (Benson, 1849b).

As one immediate result of this new partnership, we find Logan writing to another brother James, in June 1833, of how "the study of the ores of copper had gradually led me to that of mineralogy and geology, and of specimens in both I have become a bit of a collector... I attend to nothing else but the making of copper and [the] digging of coal from morning to night" (Harrington, 1883, p. 50). This was the reason Logan was absent for several months in 1834 in France and Spain (see Logan to De la Beche, 14 April 1838, National Museum of Wales, Cardiff, Geology Dept. archives, letter 868; see Sharpe and McCartney, 1998, p. 67; Harrington, 1883, p. 58-59). He was seeking new supplies of copper ore in Spain. A large amount of documentation, and some specimens, from this search survive in the collections, publications and archives of the RISW, Swansea.

WELSH INFLUENCES ON LOGAN'S GEOLOGICAL KNOWLEDGE

The major influences that facilitated Logan's now professional interest in geology were first formed at Morriston, site of the Forest Works. This had been earlier the home of the first geological pioneer of the soon-to-be enormous South Wales Coalfield, the forgotten but important mineral engineer and land surveyor Edward Martin (1763-1818) (Torrens, in press). In 1806 he first published his ground-breaking, and much reprinted, *Description of the Mineral Basin of South Wales,* which contained a detailed stratigraphic log, listing all known coal seams within the Swansea part of this coal basin (Fig. 3).

We know that Logan was directly influenced by Martin's work in at least two ways. First, in 1838-1839, Logan donated a now apparently unique copy of a 1809 Swansea reprint of this paper, printed by T. Jenkins, to the library of the RISW (Anonymous, 1839, p. 57), where it survives. Second, Logan's Welsh geological MSS, as now preserved in the archives of the British Geological Survey (BGS) at Keyworth, Nottingham, quote several of "Old Martin's" notes and sections. These include
1. "Old Martin used to say that the Lansamlet [coal] Veins are to be found over at Aberavon" (in Notebook 1 (1837), p. 11, Logan's unnumbered field notebooks 1837-1842, numbered 1 to 13, BGS archives).
2. "Details of Pembray seams from Messrs Martin and Davies" (Logan's

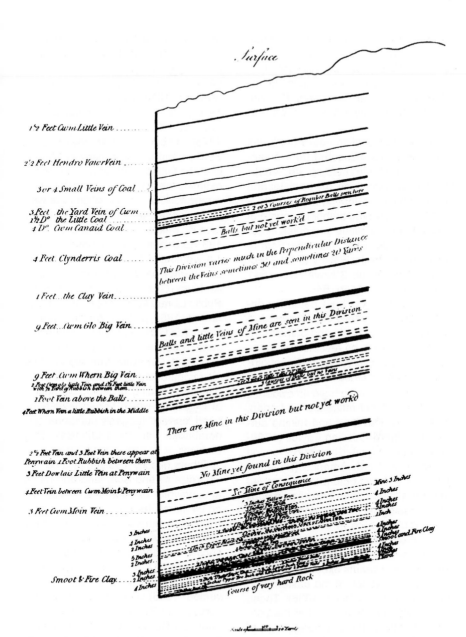

Figure 3 Edward Martin's detailed section of the Coal Measures as known in the South Wales Coalfield in 1806 (from Martin, 1806, plate 14, n. 2).

notes and sections relating to the South Wales Coalfield 1836-1842, BGS archives, 1/218, p. 27-28, 459). [Martin's son-in-law, the surveyor David Davies (1786-1819), see *Cambrian*, 12 June 1819, was Martin's business partner from 1807].

3. Geological section near Pont Yates with "distances measured from a section by Old Martin" (*ibid.*, p. 467-468). Martin's youngest son, the barrister and local land owner Joseph Martin (1807-1850), was also the author or source of several other sections and notes in Logan's manuscripts. This other Martin was also elected a Fellow of the Geological Society on 3 November 1841 (Anonymous, 1841, p. 545).

While Logan was busy gathering details of the occurrence of coal seams in the South Wales basin and of their correlation across it, as revealed by these notes, he came across a number of others who had preceded him in such work. One, but of whom we have no evidence yet of any direct influence on Logan, was the English land and mining surveyor Richard Cowling Taylor (1789-1851), who emigrated as a surveyor and engineer to North America (Philadelphia) in 1830 just before Logan arrived in south Wales. Taylor had been a pupil of the geological pioneer William Smith (1769-1839), also in south Wales in 1810. From 1825 Taylor made detailed and pioneering 3-D models of all the coal and iron seams exposed in the vicinity of Pontypool, at the eastern end of the coal field (Taylor, 1835). These won Taylor the Gold Medal of the London Society for the Encouragement of Arts, Manufactures and Commerce in 1830. Logan seems certain to have known of this work (Fig. 4).

Others known to have more directly helped and influenced Logan were members of the Kirkhouse family, who had long held important places in south Wales engineering and iron making (Wilkins, 1888, p. 236-239; Hughes, 1990, p. 127-131). William Kirkhouse, Sr. (*ca* 1785-1873; see *Cambrian*, 16 June 1873) had been employed by Usborne, Benson and Co. from early in 1830 to improve their copper works and then to examine the potential for, and then sink, a new colliery at Penclawdd (due west of Swansea), which they then leased (see W. Kirkhouse letters dated 15 July 1831 to Usborne, Benson and Co., and 1 November 1834 to Benson, Logan and Company, letter book, West Glamorgan Archives Office, SL 14/1 = Swansea Public Library MSS 466, p. 46, 68; Harrington, 1883, p. 388). William's brother Henry (*ca* 1781-1866; see *Cambrian*, 22 June 1866), who was manager at the important Cyfarthfa Iron works, later also contributed geological data to Logan by providing a geological section at Cyfarthfa, which Logan later annotated "correct" (Logan's numbered field notebooks 1 to 13, 1837-1842, BGS archives, v. 1, 1837, p. 103-106).

Others directly involved include "David Williams and Son, land and mineral surveyors" of Swansea. These two, on 24 March 1835, prepared a detailed "Report on minerals at Clyn Ithrim farm, Llangyfelach" with a map, which still survive in Logan's MSS papers (BGS archives, 1/67, v. 1). The senior Williams (died 1856; see *Cambrian*, 21 November 1856) was a land and mineral surveyor in Swansea by 1828 (*Cambrian*, 20 December 1828) as well as the engineer who had started the engine for Richard Trevithick's first experiment with a locomotive here in 1804 (Owen-Jones, 1981). He was soon joined by his land surveyor son David Hiram Williams (*ca* 1812-1848; see *Cambrian*, 2 January 1849).

LOGAN'S GEOLOGICAL MAPPING FROM 1835 AND HIS WORK FOR THE GEOLOGICAL SURVEY FROM 1838

Logan's systematic survey of the South Wales Coalfield is claimed to have started as early as 1831, by the metallurgist John Percy (1817-1889), an old friend of Logan's, writing in 1862. Exactly when this work first came to the attention of the Director of the Geological Survey, Henry De la Beche (1796-1855), seems uncertain. De la Beche himself only arrived at Swansea on 16 December 1837 (Sharpe, 1985, p. 6). Ramsay has pointed out how De la Beche

> ... well knew that the purely practical and possibly money-making part of the [Geological Survey] business would, at first, at all events, make most impression on the government and on the public, [if] he decided to commence this work in the important [metal] mining districts of Cornwall and Devonshire... Having finished [this], Sir Henry wisely saw, that the best thing to do was to begin on another [coal] mining region, and accordingly he transferred himself, for that was all the staff in those days to Glamorganshire (Ramsay, 1877, p. 365-366).

But Logan's unofficial work, later much used by the Geological Survey, had started well before this. 1836 is the first date in Logan's "Notes and sections relating to the South Wales Coalfield 1836-1842" (in BGS archives, 1/218) on paper also watermarked 1836. The first section in these is of a coal "section of the Bedwelty [Bedwellty] minerals adjoining Ebbw Vale property of the Monmouthshire Iron and Coal Company"

dated 1836 (BGS 1/218, p. 3-7). The Third Report of the RISW for 1837-1838 published in June 1838 specifically notes (Anonymous, 1838a, p. 17) "Logan has already exhausted three years in laying down on Ordnance Survey sheets... the coal basin between Kidwelly and the Vale of Neath." So Logan must have started his comprehensive geological mapping here in the summer of 1835. He was thus busy mapping in the area of his future Geological Survey work, well before he was elected to the Geological Society of London early in 1837, and his application to join the latter must have been inspired by the former.

It is thus impossible for this detailed mapping work to have already "directly contributed to scientific debates within the Geological Society of London," as Christie claims Logan's work did (1994, p. 162). In any case, its Fellows spent their time arguing "violently and at length, about coal seams and mineral veins... but their disputes concerned the nature of coal, the origin of mineral veins, *not where to find them*" (italics here added; Porter, 1973, p. 323). Logan's interest as a copper smelter was to find more coal. The availability of local coal was the single, simple reason that Swansea copper smelting then led the world. It was entirely based on the close proximity and great abundance of coal supplies. Logan's geological life in Wales thus far had been in search of better materials for his smelting works near Swansea, in which he was a partner from 1833.

It should not be thought, however, that the Geological Survey was entirely parasitic on Logan's growing knowledge of the South Wales Coalfield (Fig. 5). The Survey in turn duly improved Lo-

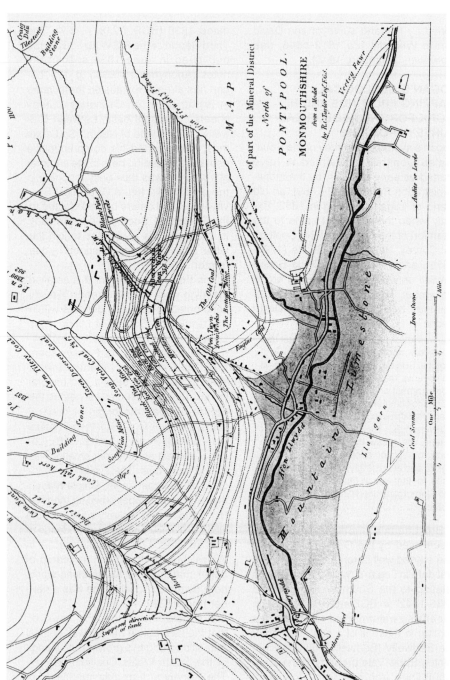

Figure 4 Richard Cowling Taylor's map (from his detailed and pioneering three dimensional model) of the coal (=solid) and iron (=dotted) seams, north of Pontypool, at the eastern end of the Welsh coal field (from Taylor 1835).

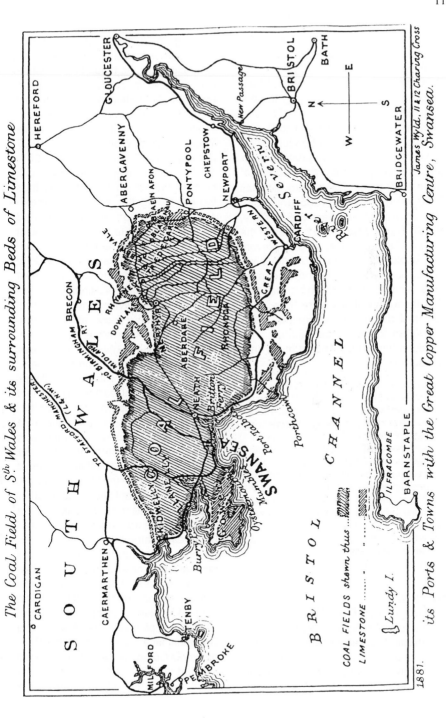

Figure 5 The South Wales Coalfield and Copper Works (from a sketch by Grant-Francis, 1881).

gan's operations. In December 1839 Benson, Logan and Company published an earlier July 1839 joint Report by the Survey's chemist, and curator of their Museum of Economic Geology in London Richard Phillips (1778-1851), and William Carpmael (1804-1867), the leading patent agent in London. Their Report was on improved processes for smelting copper ores, the subject of three other patents granted to Nicholas Troughton between 1835 and 1839 (British Patent numbers 6965, 7779, 8075). These, also in use by then at the Forest Copper Works, tried to prevent the wholesale escape of noxious vapours during the calcining of copper ores. This detailed Report concluded that these inventions were "new, useful, and decidedly successful" (see *Cambrian,* 28 December 1839).

Logan himself later noted of his time in south Wales:

... my whole connection with Geology is of a practical character. I am by profession a Miner and Metallurgist and for many years was one of the active managing partners in an establishment in Wales, where we annually melted 60,000 tons of copper ore, and excavated 60,000 tons of coal. It was my constant occupation to superintend and direct the minutest details of every branch of the business, A due regard to my own interest *forced me* [italics here added] into the practice of Geology, and it was more particularly to the economic bearings of the Science that my attention was devoted (Logan, 1855, p. 39).

MORE WELSH
MINING CONNECTIONS

Before and after his Geological Survey commission, Logan remained in touch with other mineral surveyors and the colliery overmen and viewers who were now such an important part of the burgeoning South Wales Coalfield. South Wales discovered a new market for its anthracite coal, as result of the technical advances made by George Crane (*ca* 1784-1846). He was the first, at least in Britain, to smelt iron with local anthracite fuel, using hot blast methods at his Yniscedwin Iron Works from early 1837 (Brough, 1836; Anonymous, 1837, 1846). Such men were papyrophobic, being doers not writers. They are thus too easily forgotten by today's historians, who rely too much on printed records. Lynn White, Jr. made the point best in 1962 when he noted how "history is a bag of tricks which the dead have played upon historians. The most remarkable of these illusions is the belief that the surviving written records provide us with a reasonably accurate facsimile of past human activity" (White, 1962, p. v). He might well have been thinking of such mining professionals.

Logan's survey of the South Wales Coalfield reveals at least one direct debt to such men. Logan naturally first became familiar with the Swansea area when he started his work, as this was where his works were sited and for which he needed coal. When he moved westward to survey the Llanelli coalfield, he was instead obliged to seek other sources, such as those revealed by the MSS "Extracts from the observations of B. Jones — gathered from the long experience of his father Rees Jones as a mineral surveyor, accompanying a Plan of the courses of the Seams in the Llanelly district made in 1835," which survive in Llanelli Public Library, but without the plan (Thomas Mainwaring Commonplace Book). The Llanelli Copperworks Company had commissioned a report in 1835 on the coal districts it then leased. Rees' son, Benjamin

Jones, was chosen to prepare this, and his Report also survives (National Library of Wales, Nevill MS XVIII, January 1836). These sources reveal the interplay between coal mining and geology which already formed part of the practice of the local coal viewers here (Symons, 1989, p. 70). They prove that Logan obtained much of his information on this coalfield (see his MSS notes BGS 1/218, 1836-1842) from these sources (Symons, 1979, p. 19, 24-25).

The Jones's were another typical dynasty of south Wales land and mineral surveyors. Rees Jones (*ca* 1769-1836; see *Cambrian,* 26 June 1836) was another land and mineral surveyor and engineer, who flourished from at least 1804 when he was active in Brecon and throughout Glamorgan. He had three sons, of whom the above Benjamin (1809-1891), third son, had "constructed the [railway] line between Wigan and Preston under [Isambard Kingdom] Brunel" and was "on the staff which completed the ordnance geological survey of South Wales," before becoming a solicitor in Llanelli in 1838 (Anonymous, 1891). Another son was Rhys William Jones (1804-1864), who was also active as a railway engineer after he too had been trained as a land surveyor (Bendall, 1997, v. 2, p. 283).

Logan's representations of this information were duly incorporated into the first 1 inch to 1 mile Geological Survey maps of that area. Logan's name appears as a joint author of Sheets 37, 41 and 42 SW. Parts of the different editions of Sheet 37 have been reproduced in black and white by Winder (1965, p. 114) and Bassett (1969, p. 22-23). Some 21 of Logan's original field slips have also been preserved (see Bassett, 1967, p. 45-46). These show in detail

the coal seams and faults which Logan had so carefully investigated. Bailey has pointed out how much Logan's methods, using theodolite and chain, influenced Geological Survey mapping practice from the early 1840s (Bailey, 1952, p. 32-33; Secord, 1986, p. 207-208). A.C. Ramsay, who was on the Geological Survey staff from 1841, recorded his own impressions of these maps. They were

... in a style of such beautiful detail, that no map of any coal-field that had been done before, approached it in excellence". Logan's mapping was done "with such excessive detail, that it enabled all interested in such subjects, not only to judge of the lie of the beds of coal with great accuracy, but to judge of the precise nature of the strata that they would have to sink through, in their attempts to seek for coal in regions where coal pits had not previously existed (Ramsay, 1877, p. 367).

We can see here the day-to-day routine of land and mining surveyors being transmitted into the normal practice of geologists. Ramsay gave further confirmation of the economic rationale behind Logan's mapping, and proves that his work was not "merely" to advance "scholarly" enquiry. Christie is completely wrong to claim that "Logan's interest in the coal bearing strata [here] bore no relation to their economic value" (Christie, 1994, p. 171).

Further confirmation of the respect that Logan was held in by the mining community here comes from the 1837 law suit at the King's Bench, London, which was referred to Logan alone for arbitration. The owner of the Penybailey estate in Loughor claimed that the Broadoak Colliery owed him royalties. Evidence was presented to Logan between April 1837 and November 1837. The owner of the Penybailey Colliery

XII

was the aforementioned Rhys William Jones, with whom Logan was already involved. The conclusion to be drawn from this is that Logan must have been regarded as well informed on such mining matters. He cannot have been seen as just a "scholarly gentleman geologist." He must also have been sufficiently trustworthy for the owner of the Broadoak Colliery to have accepted his arbitration, when it was known he was already in contact with Jones (Llanelly Public Library, Local Collection, MSS 46). Unfortunately, the outcome of this case remains unknown.

Another practical man who tried to help Logan was Thomas Richards, whose quaintly worded letter dated 2 March 1837 to "William Logan Esq, one of the company with Benson Esq at Graigola Colliery" survives (BGS 1/67 ii). This colliery was in the parish of Cadoxton, 4 miles from their smelting works, where in March 1831 Usborne, Benson and Logan had leased coal and other seams of culm and fireclay (Bayliffe and Harding, 1996, p. 22). This became Graigola Colliery (a useful map for naming and locating collieries in this coalfield is given by Brown, 1874) and was another pioneering venture of Logan and Benson's. Here William Kirkhouse had again earlier examined and reported on the facilities, the tramway, trams, and wharf that would be needed to transport this coal to their Forest Works. It was one of the first collieries at which the dry steam coals of the semi-anthracite series in this coal field were worked for the new steamship market. By 1840 experiments had been made to ascertain the calorific value of this coal, against Welsh anthracite and bituminous coal from Scotland (*Mining Journal*, v. 10, n. 274, 21 November

1840, p. 371) when Graigola coal was reported to be "decidedly the most powerful steam coal in the world" (see also John, 1950, p. 120).

Richards tried in 1837 to offer advice on how to improve the working of this coal on behalf of Logan's coal company. The reason for the survival of this letter may well only be its quaintness, but we should recall that when Richards wrote in English, this was in — for him, a Welsh collier — a foreign language. Logan had to check other such advice, like that of William Morgan of Penclawdd in 1837, more carefully. As Logan noted, "Mr. Morgan it must be remembered never hesitates to permit his invention to supply the deficiencies of his memory!" (BGS 1/218, p. 72). These were problems only to be expected in a mining culture that did not yet see any real need to commit such information to paper, and had great difficulty in doing so when it tried. To have been the first to put down this information on paper throughout the South Wales Coalfield so effectively was undoubtedly Logan's greatest achievement during his apprenticeship there.

Another who helped Logan with mineral surveying was William Price Struve (1809-1878; see *Cambrian,* 19 April 1878; Anonymous, 1878). Struve provides an interesting case study. On 8 July 1838 he and Logan measured a section at Penclawdd together (BGS 1/218, p. 92-93). Struve had been born on Jersey in 1809 and was articled in 1832 to his brother-in-law Henry Habberley Price (1794-1839), born a Quaker but forced from their Society when he married a non-Quaker, Struve's sister Julia in 1824 (*see Cambrian,* 11 December 1824). From 1818 Price had been a partner in the innovative Neath Abbey Iron Company, which had supplied a rotative stamping engine to Usborne, Benson and Co. in 1830 (Ince, 1984, p. 29, 105). Price was yet another local Member of the Geological Society of London, from 1825 (Woodward, 1907, p. 284).

Struve, after being managing partner of the local Millbrook Iron Works from 1834 until the partnership was dissolved in 1835 (*Cambrian*, 21 March 1835), had become consultant mining engineer to the Swansea collieries by 1838. His obituarist recorded that "his zeal for the interest of the Geological Survey was very great, and although he had plenty of other professional work, he nevertheless found time to render useful aid to Mr. Logan" (Anonymous, 1878). Logan employed Struve early in 1842, when Logan was trying hard to finish his geological mapping (see Logan to De la Beche, 3 February 1842, National Museum of Wales, Cardiff, Geology Department archives, letter 878; Sharpe and McCartney, 1998, p. 68). Logan was, however, unsuccessful in recommending Struve as Keeper of Mining Records in London to De la Beche in 1839 (see Logan to De la Beche, 27 November 1839, National Museum of Wales, Cardiff, Geology Department archives, letter 872; Sharpe and McCartney, 1998, p. 67). Struve is now best remembered for his important work in ventilating coal mines, patent 11,127, in March 1846 (Hinsley, 1972, p. 31, plate 1).

THE ROYAL INSTITUTION OF SOUTH WALES (RISW)
Before he joined the Geological Society, Logan had played an important role in the local Swansea Philosophical and Literary Institution founded in 1835 (Beanland, 1935). In 1839 it became the RISW, and it survives there in its magnificent restored building as the Swansea Museum (Fig. 6). Intriguingly, it had had a predecessor several years before, of which nothing has been recorded, the Cambrian Geological Society. This was founded in 1821 (*Cambrian*, 13 October, 20 October 1821) and was apparently only active until about 1823 (*Cambrian*, 11 November 1823). In 1835 its collections and library passed to this new Swansea Institution.

Logan was a founding member of this, and in June 1835 he was elected to its 10-man General Purpose Committee. At the first annual meeting in 1836 Logan was made its Honorary Secretary (Bayliffe and Harding, 1996, p. 50). He was also the Honorary Curator of its Geology Section. Its surviving donation books are full of Logan's donations of minerals, fossils, birds, reptiles, entomological and archeological specimens, as well as of books and surveying instruments. The specimens had came first from Wales and England, then from Spain, and Germany, and latterly Mexico and Canada (see Donations Books, 1835-1842 in RISW archives, and RISW Annual Reports 1836-1842). Logan also read a number of papers to the RISW (Logan, 1838a, 1840).

THE GEOLOGICAL SOCIETY OF LONDON (GSL)
Christie has wrongly claimed that "throughout his career Logan pursued fieldwork in geological strata that directly contributed to scientific debates within the Geological Society of London" (Christie, 1994, p. 162). Such a claim completely fails to acknowledge that his earlier work — of at least 5 years' dura-

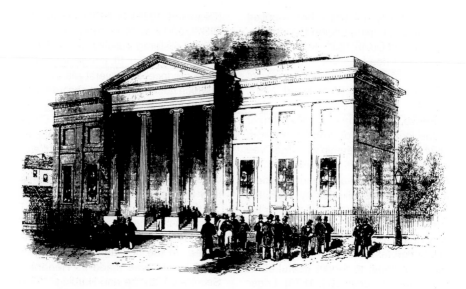

Figure 6 The Royal Institution of South Wales in 1848 (from the *Illustrated London News*, 19 August 1848, v. 13, p. 109).

tion — had been instead a direct contribution to the success of his own Swansea copper smelting firm before this. It was not until 13 December 1836 that Logan was proposed as a Fellow of the GSL (elected 18 January 1837). It is instructive to discover (especially in view of Christie's equally extraordinary claim that "Logan's interest in the coal-bearing strata bore no relation to their economic value" (Christie, 1994, p. 171), that all three of his sponsors were entirely "economic" in their geological interests.

The first, who had to recommend Logan from personal knowledge, was Richard Janion Nevill (1785-1856), builder of another major copper-smelting works at Llanelli in 1805 (Symons, 1979, p. 148-156; Torrens, 1984, p. 56). Nevill had been elected as a Member in 1817 (Woodward, 1907, p. 279). The

second was John Taylor FRS (1779-1863), who was the Treasurer of GSL from 1823-1843, as befits such a truly "economic geologist." Taylor had been elected a founding honorary member as far back as 1807 (Woodward, 1907, p. 43, 269, 298). He was the leading light in British and foreign mining geology throughout his distinguished career (Burt, 1977).

Logan's third sponsor was the hitherto misidentified W. Loughtrey (Winder, 1965, p. 118). He was in reality William Long Wrey (1792-1883), a member of a landed family from Devon (Townend, 1970, p. 2881). Wrey, after only matriculating at Cambridge University in 1811, had gone into the Army, but had retired by 1824 when he is again mis-recorded as "Mr. Ling Urey." He had now taken "a lease of extensive mineral tracts from Lord Cawdor, [John

Frederick Campbell (1790-1860) of Castlemartin] upon which he established collieries" along the Gwendreath valley (Wilkins, 1888, p. 40), but with whom he was involved in lawsuits by 1830 (*Cambrian*, 3 April 1830). By 1831, Wrey was living at Thornhill Farm, Great Mountain [Mynydd Mawr], west of Ammanford, Carmarthenshire when he was elected FGS (Anonymous, 1831b, p. 351). His publication record in geology may extend only to a local newspaper article (Wrey, 1840), but this demonstrates both his acquaintance with south Wales geology and his considerable investment in anthracite mining. This article was issued as a branch line railway to his collieries off the Llanelly Railway was being completed (Price, 1992, p. 28). His son and heir was born at Thornhill in 1826 (*Cambrian, 25 May 1826*). Wrey had a riding accident in 1840 (*Cambrian, 14 October 1840*). In 1843 Thornhill was sold, and in 1867 he or his son published a pamphlet on New Zealand and its investment potential, in London, and so one or other may have emigrated there. Records at GSL merely record his decease in 1883 (Anonymous, 1884, p. 14).

Logan's only GSL paper from his Welsh period was read to the GSL on 26 February 1840 (Logan, 1842). It concerned the beds of clay below coal seams, there commonly called underclays, with which "the miners of the district are so well acquainted [that] scarcely any would fail to recognise this material." Furthermore they "would as soon expect to live in a house without a foundation as work a coal seam that did not rest upon underclay." These are powerful testimonies to the unwritten knowledge already held in these mining communities. Logan had certainly come across the phenomenon of the underclay by the time, late in 1837, the Geological Survey arrived here (De la Beche, 1846, p. 145). Logan's paper analysed the wide occurrence of these underclays and pointed out they proved that coals must have originated in peaty swamps and not, as some supposed, as driftwood. This was a matter of real economic significance, as it meant that coal seams should prove more widespread and laterally extensive. It also established that coal had been formed *in situ* and was seen by Logan's GSL colleagues as a matter of real theoretical, and thus "gentlemanly," significance, although it soon emerged that another, equally practical, coal viewer and owner in Leicestershire, Edward Mammatt (1766-1835), had earlier made and published many of these same observations (Mammatt, 1834, p. 73-74). The second part of Logan's GSL paper discussed the occurrence of boulders or pebbles of coal in clay, which Logan had first noticed in 1833. Such coal pebbles gave Logan further insight into how such coal seams had formed (De la Beche, 1846, p. 193).

Logan's third coal discovery was of specimens of erect-standing fossil trees (*Sigillaria*) preserved in growth position. Lewis Weston Dillwyn FRS (1778-1855) noted Logan's discovery of these on 3 April 1838, thus:

Four large Sigillariae, rising vertically through strata of shale and sand stone, as if they had grown on the spot, were this day discovered by my friend, W. E. Logan Esq., in Cwm Lech, near the head of the Swansea valley, and a short account of the discovery, accompanied by an illustration, is given in the Third Report of our Philosophical and Literary Institution (Dillwyn, 1840, p. 54).

Figure 7 Logan's specimens of Carboniferous fossil trees (*Sigillaria*), preserved in life position at Cwm Llech, Vale of Swansea, as he discovered them on 3 April 1838 (from Logan 1838a).

Figure 8 "Logan's Trees" as they stand today outside Swansea Museum. These two fossil trees (*Sigillaria*) were discovered in 1838. The taller is 13.5 feet high and the shorter, 4 feet (photos by H.S. Torrens).

These were illustrated in an 1838 lithograph ([Logan], 1838a, p. 33) (Fig. 7) and again in 1846 (De la Beche, 1846, p. 183-184) and 1851 engravings (De la Beche, 1851, p. 577-578; the latter two from a sketch by Logan).

Two of these specimens, excavated under the superintendence of De la Beche, were taken to the RISW where they still stand in the grounds of Swansea Museum (Fig. 8).

Another such tree was later deposited in the Museum of the Cornish Geological Society by John Vigurs of Rosehill, Penzance who owned another local copper smelt works at Cwm Avon. These are not the earliest such trees to be discovered even in the British Coal Measures, as others had been found in 1837, during railway excavations in Lancashire (Torrens and Cooper, 1986, p. 258-259).

THE BRITISH ASSOCIATION FOR THE ADVANCEMENT OF SCIENCE (BAAS)

The BAAS meeting in 1837 was held in September at Liverpool, and at this meeting Logan both exhibited his geological map of the South Wales Coalfield between Neath and Kidwelly and read a paper in explanation (Logan, 1838b). This was his only paper read to the BAAS in this period, contrary to Christie (1994, p. 173) who wrongly reports earlier "timely papers" to both the GSL and BAAS, and that "Logan exhibited his first maps of the coal region of Swansea before the Liverpool meeting of the British Association for the Advancement of Science (BAAS)" in 1831! Logan's 1838 paper discussed the pattern of faulting which controlled the distribution of coal here in a very precise way. He also accurately outlined the

geographical distribution of bituminous and non bituminous coals in south Wales. This paper was also published in the *Welshman* and *Cambrian* newspapers.

FINANCIAL PROBLEMS

Benson, Logan and Company underwent a series of crises in 1837 and 1838. First Abel Anthony Gower (1748-1837), founder of the large trading firm of Gower, Nephews and Co., died in August 1837 (Montgomery-Massingberd, 1972, p. 389) leaving £400,000, at least on paper, to two relatives, one of whom, Abel Lewes Gower (1796-1849) was Logan's brother-in-law (Roberts, 1969, p. 224). Then both Logan's uncle Hart (Anonymous, 1838b) and his brother and partner Henry Logan (Anonymous, 1838c) died in April 1838. This brought about a change in Benson, Logan and Company, with Logan now holding all the Logan shares, amounting to 21/48, while Starling Benson held the remaining 27/48. Hart Logan left £5,000 and Henry left £10,000 (Public Record Office, London, PROB 6/214, folios 197 on). These deaths were the reason Logan could resign his salaried position at Swansea in 1838 (Evans, 1876, p. 76), but he did not sever his connection with the company, remaining a partner until at least 1850-1851 (Bayliffe and Harding, 1996, p. 83-85). His Forest Works at Morriston had passed, under a new lease, to the new English Copper Company in March 1845 (Grant-Francis, 1881, p. 112), but were only finally sold in 1851. They were converted to the manufacture of zinc in 1867 (Grant-Francis, 1881, p. 111).

By 1835 this company had become indebted to the Gowers for £50,000, and by the end of 1838 the Gowers were recalling the payment of this enormous debt, so that the "financial affairs of the Logans were [already] far from healthy... [Benson and Logan's] financial problems were, however, far from over; in 10 years' time they were to face even greater trials" (Bayliffe and Harding, 1996, p. 80). These financial problems, which were so soon to hit the whole Swansea copper industry, involved the creation of a new controlling English Copper Company, formed in 1841, but which soon had to be bailed out by the Bank of England when it was hit in turn by the financial crisis of 1847 (Roberts, 1969). These several crises had begun well before Logan finally left Britain in 1843 on being appointed, the previous year, to conduct a geological survey in Canada. Logan cryptically referred to these in 1843 when, feeling seasick on his way back to Canada, he wrote "the fact is that Coleman Street [the investment and financial centre of London] has made me bilious. What I gave [then] to the fishes was as yellow as gold" (in Logan notebook titled "Chaleur Bay-Bay of Fundy", National Archives of Canada, R.G. 45, Geological Survey of Canada, v. 158: Field Notebook 2606; a reference I owe to Charles Smith). Under such impossibly complex financial situations, it is by no means clear that Logan was already as "independently wealthy" when he left Wales for Canada, as Christie implies (1994, p. 168-169). One might instead see good reasons why Logan was now so actively looking to new, and helpfully distant, horizons in Canada!

In the autumn of 1841 Logan had gone to visit the coal fields of Pennsylvania and Nova Scotia, a visit which also helped to stimulate his aspiration to geologically survey his native country. For it was then he learned that a geological survey of Canada was to be funded by the newly united legislature of the colony in September 1841, and decided to apply for the position. While in the Americas, he also met Henry Darwin Rogers (1808-1866) of Virginia. At this time Logan "even talked of settling in the United States as a coal-viewer" (Harrington, 1883, p. 110), a position for which his expertise with Welsh coal would certainly have qualified him highly.

LOGAN AND THE GEOLOGICAL SURVEY OF INDIA

A further tribute to Logan's coal field work in south Wales is given in letters between him and De la Beche written in 1844 and 1845. Logan's first letter (see Logan to De la Beche, 11 November 1844, National Museum of Wales, Cardiff, Geology Department archives, letter 884; Sharpe and McCartney 1998, p. 68) gives a wonderfully vivid description of the horrors he had met with on geological field work in Canada

I have received one letter from you... on my return from the depths of the Forest, where for three months & a half I had no other bed than the moss which covered the ground, where my food in the way of flesh has been partridges, bears, porcupines, & otters, and when to protect myself from those little entomological devils, worse than all the other devils of hell, the black flies, I was under the necessity of constantly keeping my head in a bag with a gauze window in front; to be removed however whenever it become necessary to take a sight with my prismatic compass or measure an angle with my pocket sextant... it was necessary every now and then to climb the highest tree in the vicinity & there to submit to the martyrdom these virulent insects inflict, grinning & bearing it, restraining my breadth & leaving some hundreds of them to bite at once & at will, each drawing blood while I steadied my body... The little devils too like to bite under cover, so where ever they can find an opening they creep under your clothes, up your sleeves, down your neck, and up your trousers & when a man comes to look at his body - which in the woods is not very often - he finds it is spotted from head to foot with the effects of their operations.

De la Beche's response asks if Logan would go to India to form a Geological Survey there to examine the country for coal, at the princely salary of £1200 per year for at least 3 years (see De la Beche to Logan, 29 March 1845; Harrington, 1883, p. 228-229), perhaps hoping that Logan would find less excitement there. Logan replied:

I have your dispatch on India affairs, which renders it necessary that I should inform you of the position on my campaign in Canada. ...in the matter connected with the East India Coal, I fancy you will see that the Chances are I am tied to Canada...[but this will] shew my Canadian friends that geological investigations are something thought of in other parts and that if I do not accept pecuniary terms more advantageous than they give, they must not think the less of me (Logan to De la Beche, 12 May 1845, Harrington, 1883, p. 229-236; National Museum of Wales, Cardiff, Geology Department archives, letters 885, Sharpe and McCartney 1998, p. 68).

The Indian Geological Survey was duly founded in 1846 (Fox, 1947). This followed the search for a geologist to make a "survey of those districts in which coal fields are situated," with the new urgency of fuelling Britain's new steam-driven navy. After Logan's refusal, the choice, in December 1845, fell on the equally practically qualified David Hiram Williams (ca 1812-1848), (Grout, 1995, chapter 5), the Swansea-born son of the land surveyor David Williams, Sr.,

both of whom had helped Logan there in 1835. This son was the first of De la Beche's official geological assistants in England from April 1839, and who was described by De la Beche as "a very clever hand and a regular good one" (North, 1939, p. 255; North, 1936, p. 65-71). Williams soon returned home to work on the South Wales Survey.

After Williams' later tragic death from "jungle fever" (malaria?) in India in 1848 (see Cambrian, 12 January 1849), Charles Lyell called Williams the "best of [De la Beche's] practical men" (Lyell, 1881, v. 2, p. 153). Williams' case again demonstrated that it was men with actual knowledge of the practice of coal mining who were appointed by the British Government to direct the Geological Surveys in both Canada and India. Williams, Jr. also worked in Borneo for Rajah James Brooke (1803-1868) while based in India (Cambrian, 17 March 1848).

FINALE

It was a copy of a letter from Williams Jr., dated 1 November 1841, concerning the scientifically uninformed and doomed attempt to find impossible Welsh coal at Shirenewton, near Chepstow (Williams to De la Beche, 1 November 1841, National Museum of Wales, Cardiff, Geology Department archives, letter 2116; Sharpe and McCartney, 1998, p. 141), which the Professor of Geology at Oxford University, William Buckland (1784-1856), chose to send to the new Prime Minister, Sir Robert Peel (1788-1850), on 10 November 1841. This was in an attempt to get Peel's further support for the new Geological Survey of Great Britain (British Library Add MSS, 40494 folios 16-17). Williams's letter demonstrated, said

Buckland, "the practical value of the work [De la Beche's team] is doing. It is one of the endless cases of searching for coal where it is impossible to be found. I am sure that from 5 to10 thousand pounds a year are wasted in England in similar fruitless attempts which the Geological Survey will put an end to." Logan's work in south Wales had been in exactly this same practical, improving tradition.

The technical value of Logan's other work as a copper smelter in Wales was also demonstrated as late as 1864 when the *Mining and Smelting Magazine* suggested the adoption of his better formula for calculating the "returning charge" on copper ore, to cover the costs of transporting the ore from mine to smelting works. This vital figure was used to determine miners' wages and to regulate ore purchases (Newell, 1986). It should have pleased, at least, the mining and metallurgical communities in which Logan had learned his practical skills that these skills were proving useful over 20 years after he had left south Wales for Canada.

CONCLUSIONS

I hope this study has illuminated another historiographic problem, involving the treatment of Logan's Welsh work by historians. This concerns the slight attention they have given to the history of "applied, practical and/or economic" geology. As Paul Lucier has noted,

...the neglect of applied geology speaks to how historians have studied [this] science... To maintain a strict division between the science of [the well studied] gentleman-specialists and the random searching of [unstudied &] untrained prospectors amounts to simple stereotyping of social groups as well as to reinforcing a dichotomy between ornamental and economic geology

that might not have existed. Historians of science thus should attend to the relations of geology and industry. In future studies, it can only be hoped that applied geology will receive the careful attention that it surely deserves (Lucier, 1999).

Logan would surely have been the first to agree with such sentiments.

ACKNOWLEDGMENTS

I thank Dorothy Bayliffe (Swansea), who kindly read and much improved a first version and sent me so much new information, including details of the Forest Copper works illustration used here, Richard Brighton (Swansea), Norman Butcher (Edinburgh), Bernice Cardy (Swansea), Wendy Cawthorne (London), John Collins (London), Rosalyn Gee (Swansea), Andrew Grout (Edinburgh), Jean Jones (Edinburgh), Marilyn Jones (Swansea), Graham Mckenna (Keyworth), Gerry Middleton (Hamilton), Edmund Newell (Oxford), David Oldroyd (Sydney), Tom Sharpe (Cardiff), Gordon Winder (London, Ontario), Suzanne Zeller (Waterloo), and the staffs of the Swansea Museum, the National Museum of Wales (Cardiff), the Llanelli and Swansea public libraries, and the West Glamorgan Archives Service. Without their help this attempt to understand Logan's work in Wales would have been impossible. Bill Sarjeant (Saskatoon) and Charles H. Smith (Ottawa) carefully commented on, and improved, a final version. This work started with a invitation from Gerry Middleton to give a paper to the Geological Society of America's Annual Meeting in Toronto in October 1998, which is gratefully acknowledged, as are travel funds from the Canadian Geological Foundation to enable my attendance at the meeting. Completion of this work has been made possible only thanks to sabbatical leave funded by the Leverhulme Trust.

REFERENCES

Anderson, R.G.W., 1978, The Playfair Collection: Royal Scottish Museum, Edinburgh, UK.

Anonymous, 1831a, Marriages: Gentleman's Magazine, v. 101, n. 2, November 1831, p. 464.

Anonymous, 1831b, [Election of William Long Wrey as Fellow]: Geological Society of London, Proceedings, v. 1, n. 25, p. 351.

Anonymous, 1833, [Election of Abel Lewis Gower as Fellow]: Geological Society of London, Proceedings, v. 1, n. 32, p. 486.

Anonymous, 1837, Successful Application of Anthracite to Smelting: Mining Journal, v. 4, 22 April 1837, p. 142.

Anonymous, 1838a, [Note on Logan's Mapping]: [Third] Swansea Philosophical and Literary Institution, Proceedings for 1837-1838, E. Griffiths, Swansea, p. 17.

Anonymous, 1838b, [Death of Robert Hart Logan]: Annual Register, 1838, p. 210.

Anonymous, 1838c, [Death of Henry Logan]: Gentleman's Magazine, NS 9, June 1838, p. 665.

Anonymous, 1839, Donations of works on Wales: [Fourth] Annual report of the RISW for 1838-1839, p. 57.

Anonymous, 1841, [Election of Joseph Martin as Fellow]: Geological Society of London, Proceedings, v. 3, n. 82, p. 545.

Anonymous, 1846, Obituary of the late George Crane: Mining Journal, v. 16, 30 May 1846, p. 230.

Anonymous, 1878, Memoir of W. P. Struve: Institution of Civil Engineers, Minutes of Proceedings, v. 52, p. 278-80.

Anonymous, 1884, Deceased Fellows 1883: Geological Society of London, Quarterly Journal, v. 40, p. 14.

Anonymous, 1891, Obituary – Mr Benjamin Jones: Llanelly and County Guardian, 19 November 1891.

Anonymous, 1998, The 100 Most Important

Canadians in History: Scientists – Sir William Logan: Maclean's Magazine, 1 July 1998, p. 39.

Bailey, E.B., 1952, Geological Survey of Great Britain: Murby, London, UK.

Bassett, D. A., 1967, A Source -Book of Geological... Maps for Wales (1800-1966): National Museum, Cardiff, UK.

Bassett, D.A., 1969, Wales and the geological map: Amgueddfa, v. 3, p. 10-25.

Bayliffe, D.M. and Harding, J.N., 1996, Starling Benson of Swansea: D. Brown and Sons, Cowbridge.

Beanland, W.A., 1935, History of the Royal Institution of South Wales: Royal Institution, Swansea, UK.

Bendall, S., 1997, Dictionary of Land Surveyors and Local map makers of Great Britain and Ireland 1530-1850: British Library, London, UK, [two volumes].

Benson, S., 1849a, On a Boulder of Cannel Coal found in a vein of common bituminous coal: British Association for the Advancement of Science, Reports, 1848, pt. 2, p. 64-65.

Benson, S., 1849b, On the relative position of the various qualities of Coals in the South Wales Coal-Measures: British Association for the Advancement of Science, Reports, 1848, pt. 2, p. 65-66.

[Brewster, D.], 1837, Review of Buckland's Geology and Mineralogy considered: Edinburgh Review, v. 65, p. 1-39.

Brough, W., 1836, [Potential use of Anthracite in Smelting]: Mining Journal, v. 3, 1 October 1836, p. 107.

Brown, T.F., 1874, On the South Wales Coalfield: North of England Institute of Mining and Mechanical Engineers, Transactions, v. 23, p. 197-256, map.

Bunsen, C.K.J. von, Brandis, J. and Loebell, J.W., 1852, The life and letters of Barthold George Niebuhr: Chapman and Hall, London, UK, [three volumes].

Burt, R., 1977, John Taylor Mining Entrepreneur and Engineer 1779-1863: Moorland, Hartington.

Christie, N., 1994, Sir William Logan's Geological Empire and the 'Humbug' of Economic Utility: Canadian Historical Review, v. 75, n. 2, p. 161-204.

Crisp, F.A., 1917, Visitation of England and Wales, volume 19: privately printed, London, UK.

Dahne, S.F.L., 1971, Sir William Edmond Logan (1798-1875): Honourable Society of Cymmrodorion, Transactions for 1970, p. 130-137.

De la Beche, H.T., 1846, On the Formation of the Rocks of South Wales and South Western England: Geological Survey of Great Britain, Memoirs, v. 1, p. 1-296.

De la Beche, H.T., 1851, The Geological Observer: Longman, Brown, Green & Longmans, London, UK.

Dillwyn, L.W., 1840, Contributions Towards a History of Swansea: Murray and Rees, Swansea, UK.

Eagan, W.E., 1992, Reading Conybeare and Phillips: Reflections on the Geology of History: The Compass, v. 69, n. 4, p. 326-333.

Evans, J., 1876, Obituary notice of Sir William Edmond Logan: Geological Society of London, Quarterly Journal, v. 32, p. 75-80.

Eyles, V.A., 1948, Louis Albert Necker, of Geneva, and his Geological Map of Scotland: Edinburgh Geological Society, Transactions, v. 14, p. 93-127.

Flett, J.S., 1937, The First Hundred Years of the Geological Survey of Great Britain: His Majesty's Stationary Office, London, UK.

Fox, C., 1947, The Geological Survey of India, 1846-1947: Nature, v. 160, p. 889-891.

Grant-Francis, G., 1881, The Smelting of Copper in the Swansea District, 2nd edition: Sotheran, London, UK.

Grout, A., 1995, Geology and India 1770-1851. A study in the methods and motivations of a colonial science: Ph. D. thesis, School of African and Oriental Studies, London University, London, UK.

Harrington, B.J., 1883, Life of Sir William E. Logan Kt.: Sampson Low, London, UK.

Hinsley, F.B., 1972, The Development of Coal mine Ventilation in Great Britain: Newcomen Society, Transactions, v. 42, p. 25-39.

Hughes, S., 1990, The Brecon Forest Tramroads: Royal Commission on Ancient Monuments in Wales, Aberystwyth.

Ince, L., 1984, The Neath Abbey Iron Company: De Archaeologische Pers, Eindhoven.

John, A.H., 1950, The Industrial Development of South Wales: University of Wales Press, Cardiff, UK.

[Logan, W.E.], 1838a, [Fossil trees], [Third] Proceedings of. ....Swansea Philosophical and Literary Institution 1837-1838: E. Griffiths, Swansea, p. 33 and frontispiece.

Logan, W.E., 1838b, On that part of the South Welsh Coal Basin which lies between the Vale of Neath and Carmarthen Bay: British Association for the Advancement of Science, Reports for 1837, p. 83-85.

Logan, W.E., 1840, On the Characters of the Beds of Clay immediately below the Coal-Seams of South Wales: Royal Institution of South Wales, 5th annual report, p. 47-51.

Logan, W.E., 1842, On the Characters of the Beds of Clay immediately below the Coal-Seams of South Wales, and on the occurrence of Boulders of Coal in the Pennant Grit of that district: Geological Society of London, Transactions, v. 2, n. 6, p. 491-497.

Logan, W.E., 1855, in Report of the Select Committee on the Geological Survey: Lovell and Lamoureux, Quebec.

Lucier, P., 1999, A Plea for some history of applied geology: History of Science, v. 37, in press.

Lyell, K.M., 1881, Life, Letters and Journals of Sir Charles Lyell, Bart.: Murray, London, UK, [two volumes].

Mammatt, E., 1834, A Collection of Geological Facts and Practical Observations... of the Ashby Coal Field, Ashby de la Zouch: Hextall.

Martin, E., 1806, Description of the Mineral Basin of South Wales: Royal Society of London, Philosophical Transactions for 1806, p. 342-347.

Montgomery-Massingberd, H., ed., 1972, Burke's ... Landed Gentry, 18th edition, volume 3: Burke's Peerage, London, UK.

Newell, E., 1986, Interpreting the Cornish copper standard: Journal of the Trevithick Society, v. 13, p. 36-45.

Newell, E., 1990, Copperopolis: the Rise and Fall of the Copper Industry in the Swansea District, 1826-1921, in Harvey, C. and Press, J., eds., International Competition and Industrial Change: Essays in the History of Mining and Metallurgy: Frank Cass, London, UK, p. 75-97.

Newell, E., 1997, Atmospheric pollution and the British Copper Industry 1690-1920: Technology and Culture, v. 38, p. 655-689.

North, F.J., 1936, Further Chapters in the History of Geology in South Wales: Cardiff Naturalists' Society, Transactions, v. 67, p. 31-103.

North, F.J., 1939, H.T. de la Beche: Geologist and Business Man: Nature, v. 143, p. 254-255.

Owen-Jones, S., 1981, The Penydarren Locomotive: National Museum of Wales, Cardiff, UK.

[Percy J.], 1862, Notes on Logan in Report on Minerals exhibited in Class 1 at the 1862 International Exhibition, London: The Times, 24 July 1862, p. 12.

Phillips, J.R., 1867, History of Cilgerran: J. R. Smith, London, UK.

Porter, R., 1973, The Industrial Revolution and the Rise of the Science of Geology, in Teich M. and Young R., eds., Changing Perspectives in the History of Science: Heinemann, London, UK, p. 320-343

Price, M.R.C., 1992, The Llanelly and Mynydd Mawr Railway: Oakwood Press, Headington.

Ramsay, A.C., 1877, The Origin and Progress of the Geological Survey of the British Isles, in Conferences held in connection with the Special Loan Collection of Scientific Apparatus 1876, Chemistry, Biology, Physical Geography, Geology, Mineralogy and Meteorology: Chapman and Hall, London, UK.

Roberts, R.O., 1969, The Bank of England, the Company of Copper Miners and the Cwmavon Works 1847-1852: Welsh History Review, v. 4, p. 219-234.

Rudwick, M.J.S., 1962, Hutton and Werner compared: British Journal for the History of Science, v. 1, p. 117-135.

Secord, J., 1986, Controversy in Victorian geology: Princeton University Press, Princeton, NJ.

Secord, J., 1991, The discovery of a vocation: Darwin's early geology: British Journal for the History of Science, v. 24, p. 133-157.

Shapin, S., 1976, Brewster and the Edinburgh Career in Science, p. 17-23, in Morrison-Low A.D. and Christie J.R. R., eds., Martyr of Science: Sir David Brewster 1781-1868: Royal Scottish Museum Studies, Edinburgh, UK.

Sharpe, T., 1985, Henry De la Beche and the Geological Survey in Swansea: Gower Journal, v. 36, p. 5-12.

Sharpe, T. and McCartney P.J., 1998, The papers of H. T. De la Beche: National Museums and Galleries of Wales, Geological Series 17, Cardiff, UK.

Smith, A., 1976, An Inquiry into the... Wealth of Nations, in Campbell, R.H. and Skinner, A.S., eds.: Clarendon Press, Oxford, [two volumes].

Stenton, M., 1976, Who's Who of British Members of Parliament, volume 1, 1832-1885: Harvester Press, Hassocks.

Symons, M.V., 1979, Coal Mining in the Llanelli Area, volume 1, 16th Century to 1829: Borough Council, Llanelli, UK.

Symons, M.V., 1989, Growth of geological knowledge of the Llanelli Coalfield: Archives of Natural History, v. 16, p. 59-80.

Taylor, R.C., 1835, Notice of two models and sections of... a part of the Mineral Basin of South Wales: Geological Society of London, Transactions, v. 2, n. 3, p. 433-436, pl. 42.

Torrens, H.S., 1984, Men of Iron: The History of the McArthur Group: privately, Bristol, UK.

Torrens, H.S., 1999, New Dictionary of National Biography entry for Edward Martin: University Press, Oxford, UK, in press.

Torrens, H.S. and Cooper J.A., 1986, George Fleming Richardson (1796-1848) – Man of letters, Lecturer and Geological Curator: Geological Curator, v. 4, n. 5, p. 249-272.

Townend, P., ed., 1970, Burke's... Peerage, Baronetage and Knightage, 105th edition: Burke's Peerage, London, UK.

Vivian, J.H., 1823, An account of the Process of Smelting Copper... at the Hafod Copper Works, *in* Proceedings of the Subscribers to the Fund for obviating... the smoke produced by Smelting Copper Ores: Murray, Swansea, p. 69-87.

White, L., Jr., 1962, Medieval Technology and Social Change: Oxford University Press, London, UK.

Wilkins, C., 1888, The South Wales Coal Trade: Daniel Owen, Cardiff, UK.

Winder, C.G., 1965, Logan and South Wales: Geological Association of Canada, Proceedings, v. 16, p. 103-124.

Woodward, H.B., 1907, The History of the Geological Society of London: Geological Society, London, UK.

Wrey, W.L., 1840, Crane's Patent [and the Anthracite question], Cambrian (19 September 1840), v. 3.

JAMES BUCKMAN (1814-1884) ENGLISH CONSULTING GEOLOGIST AND HIS VISIT TO THE GUYANDOTTE COAL-FIELDS IN 1854

HUGH S. TORRENS

WILLIAM R. BRICE

ABSTRACT

This paper reveals the background behind the visits paid by the English consulting geologists James Buckman and David T. Ansted to coalfields along the Guyandotte River in Virginia (now West Virginia) in 1853 and 1854. These were operations hoping to raise English capital to advance the opening of mines here. It was thought vital that existing American geological reports by John Locke should be checked by English experts. Buckman visited the sites with Locke and was able to confirm most of Locke's expectations. These visits shed light on both how such operations were then being planned and funded and how international geological consultancy was then developing. Sadly the financial panic of 1857 and then the American Civil War put an end to these expectations.

INTRODUCTION

The conjunction of events which drew this English professor of geology to survey coal deposits in West Virginia in 1854 can be traced back to a letter written by the radical English politician Joseph Hume (1777-1855) in June 1845, seeking information on the quality of coals being used by the British Navy (De la Beche and Playfair, 1848, p. 539). Hume pointed out that the United States had already made such experiments, in 1842-43, and that there was now a public laboratory in Craig's Court, London perfectly qualified to direct and test such British coals for the British Admiralty

without delay. Hume's letter caused the Lords of the Admiralty to ask the establishment that Hume had named, the Museum of Practical Geology - founded in 1835 - to undertake such an investigation.

JOHN WILSON AND COAL

The "superintendence of the economical part of the experiments" was immediately confided in 1845 to John Wilson (1812-1888), who had trained at University College, London and then in medicine, chemistry and general science in Paris, (Clarke, 1909). Wilson was still busy on this investigation in August 1846, having then just visited all South Wales coal mines, by when he had clearly come to be regarded as something of an expert on coal.

But, following financial crises at the recently founded Royal Agricultural College, at Cirencester in Gloucestershire, Wilson was instead appointed Professor of Agriculture there in the autumn of 1846, and in 1847 was made Principal of the College (Sayce, 1992). His letter sending the Director of the Museum of Practical Geology, Henry de la Beche (1796-1855), the first installment of his Coal Report, which was on the evaporative power of coals, was embossed with the Museum of Practical Geology's stamp, although written from the College on 18 May [1847] (Geology Dept., National Museum of Wales, De la Beche archive). His College's survival now depended on reaching student admission targets and when these failed to be met, more money still had to be saved, by 'remodelling' the professorships. Early in 1848, James

Buckman was appointed to an amalgamated chair of Geology, Natural History and Botany under Wilson (Torrens, 1988).

Buckman and Wilson were some of the first professional scientists trying to make livings from science in England, in Buckman's case from 1844. Buckman's career, as one of these early professional scientists, is thus of particular interest. He had previously been the paid Curator and Secretary of the Birmingham Philosophical Institution until financial problems there had forced his departure in September 1847. All these events should remind us of the precarious financial situations facing those who professed science without independent means in 1840's Britain.

At Cirencester, Buckman started his botanical experiments to solve the problem of the identity of species, which Charles Darwin applauded in the first edition of his *Origin of Species*, where he noted "Mr. Buckman's recent experiments on plants seem extremely valuable" (Darwin, 1859, p. 10). Buckman also here continued to publish widely, right across the fields of his professorship and proved an inspirational teacher. Wilson and Buckman worked happily together at Cirencester until 1851 when, following further financial crises at the College, Wilson resigned to be appointed Deputy Juror for raw materials to the "Great Exhibition of the Works of Industry of all Nations", which opened on 1 May 1851 at Hyde Park, London. The raw material then, both in America and Britain, was of course coal. The annotator of the raw materials entries in the Official Catalogue of this Exhibition (Anonymous, 1851a, volume 1, p. 88) was another English consulting geologist, D.T. Ansted, who also became an American coal prospector in Virginia in 1853 and who will re-emerge in this paper. Ansted wrote the "Account of the nature and extent of the various Deposits of Mineral Fuel in various parts of the World" for this Catalogue (Anonymous, 1851a, volume 1, p. 178-183).

THE GREAT EXHIBITIONS AND THE CRYSTAL PALACE COMPANY

The 1851 Exhibition caused a sensation in both Britain and America, partly on account of the quality of many American exhibits. The magazine *Punch* coined the name Crystal Palace, which was used by the new Company which later purchased the original structure and permanently re-erected it with some modifications at Sydenham, South London where it re-opened in 1854. *Punch* also joked (Anonymous, 1851b) how

"Yankee Doodle sent to town
His goods for exhibition;
Every body ran him down,
And laughed at his position."
But soon we
"must now be viewed all
As having been completely licked
By glorious Yankee Doodle."

This sudden and unexpected revelation of the prowess of American manufacturing methods has been rightly called the "High Noon in Hyde Park" of British Victorian engineering (Rolt, 1970, p. 148). American reaction to the Exhibition was gratitude that its remarkable industrial exploits had been so publicly and quickly recognized and, in view of the great profitability of the 1851 Exhibition to its English organizers, a rival 1853 New York Industrial Exhibition, modelled on that held in London, was soon organized (Rosenberg, 1969).

The British, worried about the quality of American exhibits in 1851, now proved the extent of their concern in 1853 by sending a team of special Royal Commissioners to report on this American Exhibition, and the whole state of American industry under the leadership of Francis Egerton (1800-1857), first Lord Ellesmere (Anonymous, 1853a, p. 6), who was 1842 President of the British Association for the Advancement of Science - hereafter BAAS (Boase, 1908). Wilson was one of those chosen to report, on U.S. minerals, as far as their economic and metallurgical operations were concerned, among many other fields which also included agriculture and tanneries. The famous English geologist Charles Lyell (1797-1875) was anoth-

BUCKMAN AND THE GUYANDOTTE COAL FIELDS

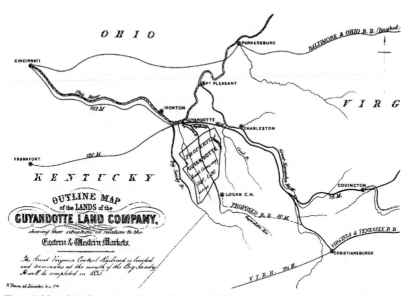

Figure 1. Map of the Guyandotte lands published in 1853 to show the location of the Company's property.

er, asked to report on U.S. mining, quarrying and mineral productions. Lyell and Wilson's reports were finally presented to the British Parliament on 6 February 1854 (Lyell, 1854; Wilson, 1854). There were great delays with the New York Exhibition which was not opened until 14 July 1853, with some of the Commissioners, like Lyell, having to return home early in August. So the American geologist James Hall (1811-1898) was asked to help write Lyell's report (Lucier, 1995, p. 262-3). Wilson was instead given the additional task of reporting on American raw materials outside those exhibited at New York and, during his extended stay, he was able to "visit various parts of the United States in which raw materials were likely to be most abundant" (Anonymous, 1854a, p. 390), and gave lectures to local American agricultural societies, before his departure for home on 19 October 1853.

Amidst much mutual goodwill, there was then considerable political animosity between the British and the Americans, largely on account of the vexed question of slavery. This had

been abolished by the British who were now trying to encourage Americans to do the same. Both Buckman and Ansted (Ansted, 1854, p. 294-311) were to refer to this, from their own experiences in America. With such different and highly political attitudes current, it was vital that some Anglo-Americans came forward to 'build bridges'. Two of those who did are of particular importance in this story: the philanthropist George Peabody (1795-1869) and General James Watson Webb (1802-1884). Peabody, an American banker permanently based in England since 1837, had been the chief source of funds for the American Pavilion at the 1851 Great Exhibition, after "Congress failed to appropriate money for a display at the Crystal Palace exhibition, his gift of $15,000 made it possible to show American products and inventions [there] beside those of other nations" (Albion, 1934). Webb, after army service between 1819 to 1827, instead became a highly successful American journalist and proprietor of the Whig newspaper, the *New York Courier and Enquirer* between 1827 and 1861 (Crouthamel,

1969), with a short spell as a rejected diplomat in Vienna.

GENERAL WEBB AND HIS GUYANDOTTE COMPANY

Webb sent a special giant edition of his newspaper to the Crystal Palace Exhibition in 1851 which was nearly twice the size of the London *Times* (Crouthamel, 1969, p. 94). Webb was to visit London three times during 1853-54, the first as soon as the 1853 New York Exhibition closed. He was now deeply involved in journalism on the "Eastern Question", which exercised people both in Britain and America and which was to lead to the Crimean War of 1854, when Webb became involved in a bitter controversy with the editor of the London *Times*. Earlier, in October 1853, Webb had recorded in that same English newspaper, his "thanks [for] our kindly feeling for the land of our fathers - our recollections of the past and our hopes for the future - to our common origin, language, literature and laws - and, above all over all, to our natural love of liberty and constitutional freedom." He further commented on how "the pecuniary interests of England and America have become so interwoven and so inseparable, that this consideration alone, aside from their common origin, should bind them together as one people" (Webb, 1853, p. 9).

Webb was then particularly seeking English investment in his Guyandotte Company in West Virginia (Figure 1). This company had been established in 1849 as the Guyandotte Land Company (Anonymous, 1853b, p. 1), but its considerable mineral wealth was soon pointed out in 1850, by the geologists, Charles Upham Shepherd (1804-1886) and William Barton Rogers (1804-1882) and an American engineer, who had been much based in Britain, named Joseph Gill. Rogers had been the Virginia State Geologist from 1835 until 1848, despite funds not being renewed after 1841 (Aldrich and Leviton, 1982).

By 1852 the directors of the Guyandotte Company were five New York-based businessmen who now sought to raise a capital of $1 million, at $30 to $40 a share on their over 330,000 acres there. By mid 1853 Webb had obtained control of the entire stock of this Company and started to advertise this property in London. His first letter extolling the potential of the Company was written in London on 15 September 1853 at the request of one Gerard Ralston (Anonymous, 1853b, p. 16) a London agent who had been earlier involved (in 1835 and 1836) in the supply of British wrought iron rails for the Baltimore and Susquehanna railroad (Elsas, 1960, p. 190-1).

Webb had commissioned a "hasty" Geological Report in August 1853 on the Company's lands from John Locke (1792-1856) who had just resigned from the chair of chemistry and pharmacy at the Medical College of Ohio, having been appointed professor of chemistry there in 1835 (Winchell, 1894). This contained detailed coal sections and sketch plans showing their accurate locations on the Company's lands. Locke, between 1837 and 1848, had been involved in the State Geological Surveys of Ohio and Michigan and in the Surveys of the Mineral Lands of the United States (Merrill, 1906, p. 704). Rogers, who might instead have been involved in reporting, had resigned his position at the University of Virginia in 1853 (Aldrich and Leviton, 1982, p. 100). These are names to add to the significant number of consulting geologists then active in eastern America (Lucier, 1995).

Webb, in London in September 1853, now "felt the necessity of having this coal field examined - and the explorations of an American geologist verified - by an English geologist of high character" with Peabody paying for the survey (Anonymous, 1853b, p. 18-9), although this survey was to be much delayed. Webb wanted Locke's "Report" checked and validated by an English geologist to encourage English investment in his Company. On 10 February 1854 Webb was one of the four promoters (the other three were all based in Britain) who provisionally registered the newly renamed Guyandotte Land, Coal and Iron Company in London, with registered offices at 22 Moorgate. Registration was granted on 13 February 1854 (Public Record Office, London, BT 41/280/ 1610) and this was the origin of the new 1854

"Prospectus" which the Company published, again in London (Anonymous, 1854b). The only notices Webb's biographer takes of this company were a letter to Webb dated 14 March 1854 and a New York newspaper notice of the following month, but he did record how Webb enjoyed the hospitality of his titled English friends, and used them to combine business with pleasure in marketing stock in this Company to them (Crouthamel, 1969, p. 131-2). The only one of those friends named by Crouthamel known to have been involved with this Guyandotte Company was Lord Ellesmere, the leader of the British Commissioners sent to the New York Industrial Exhibition.

BUCKMAN IS APPOINTED

Webb and Peabody clearly became involved with Wilson through these Anglo-American Exhibitions of 1851 and 1853 (although no documentation of exactly how seems now to survive). It was certainly through Wilson that Buckman was invited by Webb's Guyandotte Company to be the English geologist who would go to the States to give this second opinion. Buckman had equally clearly been chosen because he had been actively involved before this in industrial consulting work on coal mining (he was also then active as industrial consultant in botany - both of which activities were to cause his career at Cirencester to come to a sudden, and sad, end in 1863 - Torrens, 1988).

In 1848 Buckman had read a paper to the BAAS meeting in the South Wales coal field at Swansea, on two earlier attempts made in the 1840's to find coal in England, both of which proved completely abortive, and on both of which Buckman was professionally consulted. The first was near Droitwich, in Worcestershire in Jurassic, Lower Liassic rocks, where workmen found a black mineral they took to be coal. This encouraged a local capitalist to purchase the estate to exploit this "coal." This unknown capitalist had first bored down through 300 feet of Triassic Keuper Marls without success, and only then sought Buckman's advice, who immediately urged this search be abandoned. The second attempt was near Malmesbury, Wilt-

shire where several trials had been previously made (from 1784 to 1789 and in 1816) before those of the mid 1840's, in lignite-bearing Upper Jurassic Oxford Clays, which were here, as so often in England, once more confused by the scientifically uninformed with true coal. Again Buckman urged the already 300 feet deep shaft here be immediately abandoned.

Buckman argued that both attempts were misguided and doomed to failure on correct stratigraphic grounds (Buckman, 1849, see also Buckman, 1855a and 1858a). The BAAS President for Geology, Henry De la Beche, noted after Buckman's paper was read, how it provided "another instance of persons fooling with large sums of money in boring for coal in places, as must be known by persons having the slightest geological information, coal could not have been in existence" (Anonymous, 1848, p. 3).

Wilson's first recorded contact with Buckman regarding his visit to America was in person in London on 27 May 1854 by which time Buckman already possessed a copy of the first Guyandotte Company Prospectus (Anonymous, 1853b). On 31 May Wilson sent Buckman his written instructions, on Museum of Practical Geology notepaper, in an envelope embossed with the Crystal Palace Company logo (to confirm Wilson's continuing involvement with both these organizations). The Museum of Practical Geology had opened its fine new premises in May 1851, which a later president of the Geological Society of London, Roderick Murchison (1792-1871), called "the first palace ever raised from the ground in Britain... entirely devoted to the advancement of Science!" (Geikie, 1895, p. 184). Wilson's instructions were that the Guyandotte Company wanted Buckman to re-examine Locke's Geological Survey Report, already submitted to them by the present proprietor Webb. The property was now of 360,000 acres and contained both coal and iron.

Wilson thought Locke's previous geological examination had been by "a Geologist of some standing." It had been published in 1853 (Anonymous, 1853b, p. 33-51) and was summarized again in 1854 (Anonymous, 1854b). "It had been produced to the projectors of the proposed

Guyandotte Company as evidence of the value of the estate" and Wilson and Webb wanted Buckman to check its accuracy, to examine the extent of the mineral deposits there, and collect and bring back carefully identified samples and finally to report on the availability of labour to work any future mines. From the great extent of the property, it would be also turned eventually to agricultural or township purposes, so Buckman was also asked to report on the general physical character of the surface and on its timber growth. Webb alone had to disprove its reported occupation by "squatters." Buckman was asked to return to England by the end of July, giving him a clear month in the United States (Wilson to Buckman letter, 31 May 1854, British Geological Survey - hereafter BGS - archives, 1/1565/1, Keyworth, UK).

BUCKMAN AND LOCKE IN AMERICA

The small brass-locked (6.5 by 4 inches) field notebook that Buckman took to, and used in, the United States has also survived (BGS archives, 1/1565/2). It records that he departed from Liverpool on the British and North American Royal Mail Steamship's (later Cunard) new paddleship *Arabia* on 3 June 1854 (Anonymous, 1854c, p. 1). It was the last wooden vessel to be built for the Cunard Co., launched in 1852. On his way across the Atlantic, Buckman noted icebergs and on 12 June a "fresh breeze said to be the air of freedom - at 400 miles [distance] not tainted by the smell of slavery." He arrived in New York late on 13 June and on the 15th met Webb at Tarrytown up the Hudson River. On 19 June Buckman set off again from New York by train, via Philadelphia and Pittsburgh. On 21 June he boarded the *Challenger* paddle steamer (of which a sketch survives in his notebook) to travel down the Ohio River. After being stuck on a sandbar the whole day of 23 June, Buckman arrived at the settlement of Guyandotte on the morning of the 25th. On 26 June he met Locke and from 27 to 30 June inclusive they went together on their "Coal Expedition", checking the several sections that Locke had illustrated (Anonymous, 1853b, plates 1 - 8), of which an original uncut version

again survives in the Buckman papers (BGS archives, 1/1565/3). Locke had correctly reported that coal could be directly loaded here from the veins exposed along the local rivers into boats trading on the Guyandotte River (Anonymous, 1853b, p. 44).

Over 1 and 2 July, Buckman stayed at Guyandotte, whose "inhabitants betray a free country where everyone may say what he pleases if he dare." On 2 July he now sent Webb a short note saying that he had completed his Survey, accompanied by Locke, whose "Report" Buckman found was "in its main features substantially correct." That same day Buckman also sent Wilson a letter to the same effect, noting that the Coal Measures on the estate were "fully prepared for work, that there is a rich mine... of about 28 feet of coal... in such a position as to be easily worked." And that his journey from the mineral districts to the Guyandotte Township, "... had been accomplished in a Steam Boat worked with this Coal." Buckman was less convinced of the availability of iron here. Locke's "Report", Buckman thought, "had been prepared with great care and as you would expect from his reputation for skill and ability is generally accurate." Buckman would be sending Wilson his full Report later (copies of his two letters from Guyandotte survive only in this notebook), but his full Report now seems lost, and no details have survived of how much Buckman was paid.

Buckman started his long journey home via Cincinnati to Cleveland by train where, now clearly in more relaxed mood, he moved by boat on to Buffalo, then to Niagara to see the Falls, and via Saratoga Springs to Pokahoe. This was Webb's estate at Tarrytown which he had bought in 1838 and sold by 1862 (Crouthamel, 1969, p. 80 and 197). Today this is recorded only in the former Pokahoe Drive - recently renamed Sleepy Hollow - of North Tarrytown. Here Buckman again met Webb before moving to New York City, where he started his Atlantic return on the *Europa* (another Cunard liner launched in 1848) on 12 July 1854, arriving back at Liverpool on 24 July after an absence of over 7 weeks.

BUCKMAN AND THE GUYANDOTTE COAL FIELDS

FALLOUT IN LONDON

On 14 July, soon after Buckman left, Webb wrote a long letter from Poke-a-hoe to James Edward Coleman (c1789-1868) of London about the future of the Guyandotte Company. Coleman was a major London accountant, then much involved in investigations of the solvency of suspect firms (Jones, 1986) and in trying to properly register the Company in Britain and in finding investors there. This copy letter is the last document to survive in the Buckman papers to relate to his work in America (BGS archives, 1/1565/4). In it Webb took a highly euphoric view of his company's prospects, "we have the most valuable coal Property in the World, with greater facilities for reaching a market than any other we can possess. He [Buckman] will report at least, 24 feet of coal, the seams of which are from 5 to 10 feet in width [*sic - i.e.* thickness] and all of which may be opened at hundreds of different places and the coal slided from the openings, into boats lying in from 7 to 18 feet water." Webb then discussed the costs of, and profits from, mining such coal, where "without a shadow of a doubt the demand very greatly exceeds the supply and will continue to increase much more rapidly than the supply." Webb also forwarded to Coleman a report from the Cumberland Coal and Iron Co., which had been incorporated in 1841 and which was then working 12,000 acres on the eastern slopes of the Allegheny mountains by railroad. Webb also cited the Kanawha Saline Company working similar coals much nearer to the Guyandotte property but which lay at twice the distance from markets. Despite this problem, Webb reported that the Kanawha Co. had divided in that year (1853-1854) $600,000 profit on a capital of $184,000!

Webb's letter names a number of others involved with the Guyandotte Company in England, of whom Sir Henry Bulwer (1801-1872) is the most significant. He had been British Ambassador in Washington from 1849 to 1852 and had there enjoyed an immense popularity (Kent, 1908). Bulwer's brother Edward (1803-1873) was also Webb's favorite author (Crouthamel, 1969, p. 80). It seems likely however that their collective attempts to raise sufficient investors in England failed, as the last date in the relevant British company file is dated 9 March 1854. The Company was never registered in Britain, under new legislation which came into force in 1856.

THE KANAWHA COMPANY AND D.T. ANSTED

The above Kanawha Saline Company was one of those primarily involved in that most important industry of the Kanawha valley. In 1854 salt made there had amounted to 3 million bushels and was valued at $1 million. There were by 1855 at least 20 coal companies doing business in Charleston (Dunaway, 1922, p. 180). The Great Kanawha Company must have been another of these, organized in 1855 according to their "Statement", apparently published in that same year (copy in University of Kentucky library, Lexington). Certainly in either 1859 or 1860 they too had also published separate English and American editions of their "Evidence of value and title" (Anonymous, 1860a and b). These contained an 1854 Geological Survey and Report on their property, again by John Locke and his son Joseph, as well as an 1857 Survey and Mining Report by Joseph Gill, exactly the same people as had been earlier involved with surveys for Webb's Guyandotte Company.

Perhaps most intriguing of all, these Kanawha coal fields had also been the subject of a survey by another English geologist early in 1853, in this case Professor David Thomas Ansted (1814-1880), a Fellow of the Royal Society (elected 1844). He was soon after this, in March 1853, forced to resign his chair at King's College, London from the "pressure of business engagements"(Hearnshaw, 1929, p. 246). Ansted had arrived in New York on 31 December 1852 to survey the Coal Basin of the Kanawha and published his Report in New York later in 1853 (Ansted, 1853). The township of Ansted, 30 miles ESE of Charleston is now named after him, in response to his work here.

SECTION 4.

1. Millstone Grit. 2. Coal. 3. Lower New Red.

Figure 2. Buckman's section of the Coal Measures across the Guyandotte River Valley published in 1858.

BUCKMAN REPORTS BACK IN ENGLAND

Buckman soon sent a report on his America work to be read to the BAAS at its Liverpool meeting in September 1854, of which only an 8 line summary was published (Buckman, 1855b). He also published observations on the grass *Poa pratense* in America, which were again used by Darwin (Burkhardt and Smith, 1991, p. 242-3). In these Buckman noted "in the United States and Canada, hundreds of acres may be seen occupied with the cultivated form - timothy grass; and on the alluvial flats of the Ohio, and the broad alluvial lands left by the contraction of the American lakes, this grass yields enormous crops with spikes of flowers sometimes as much as six inches in length." These are comments clearly based on his personal observations here in 1854 (Buckman, 1856, p. 515 and Buckman, 1858b, p. 36).

Buckman published a more general paper on "The Practical Application of Geology in Coal-Seeking" in 1858 which gave fuller details of his activities in Virginia (Buckman, 1858a). In this Buckman again noted the English attempts, at Droitwich and Malmesbury, with which he had been earlier involved, and how they showed the importance of a basic knowledge of geology to the practical coal seeker. From which it was "often easier to decide where coal is not than where it is." Finally Buckman reported on his American experience, "which showed that correct stratigraphic principles are universally practical, being a sure guide in a coal investigation 3,000 miles distant." Buckman confirmed that it had been a group of English gentlemen

which had asked him to ascertain whether the large estates at Guyandotte really did posses the coal they were claimed to have. At Guyandotte, Buckman noted that he had made a good start by discovering that a sandstone exposed there was the equivalent of the coal-grits in the roof of coal seams in English (Staffordshire) mines. From the dip of this bed, it became clear to Buckman that, as he ascended the Guyandotte river to its mountain source, he would meet with progressively older beds, so, having started from the roof beds of the coal, it was clear that he should soon expect to find Coal Measures below these.

Buckman traced the limits of these coal veins from north to south as one after another were exposed in creeks opening onto the Guyandotte river "until ultimately all sign of coal was lost and a hard rock presented itself, which I could readily identify as the floor of the coal. This peculiar rock was a rough, hard, gritty sandstone, with occasional impressions of such plants as mark our own coal measures - *Stigmaria, Sigillaria, Lepidodendron, Calamites,* Ferns and other relics of an ancient flora, which differed much less from our own of that period than the American and European floras do from each other at the present day." Buckman concluded that "no better preparation can be made for studying the[se] great western [American] coal deposits than by obtaining a knowledge of our own Welsh coal-field." He demonstrated the stratigraphic relationships here by a diagram - his section 4 - reproduced here in figure 2.

Later in that same year, we have news of Buckman's final involvement in American mining. In at least the English edition of the booklet promoting the Great Kanawha Estate (Anonymous, 1860b) is a short letter from Buckman, dated 5 August 1858 giving his testimonial for Professor John Locke. It reads "I know Dr Locke very well and have the highest respect for his character as a gentleman and his ability and judgement as a professional man" (Anonymous, 1860b, p. 23). This shows only that Buckman was quite unaware that Locke had died, on 10 July 1856 in Cincinnati, since their last meeting.

THE GUYANDOTTE COMPANY FAILS

Sadly we know little further of the Guyandotte Company's activities. The fact that their only other known surviving Prospectus is a 12 page American edition signed by the then President, Henry M'Farlan, and dated April 1857 (in the Library of Congress, Washington, DC) must indicate that their 1853-54 attempts to raise English capital had failed. The Company had by 1857 only opened three adits 100 to 250 yards long into a hill in the north of its estates and was now planning to lease collieries here, instead of working them itself. It also planned to move its offices to Philadelphia. The financial panic of 1857 must have made all these plans redundant.

The start of the horrendous American Civil War in 1861 prevented any further exploration of either the Guyandotte or Kanawha estates. In final irony the Great Kanawha Company was registered in London on 25 January 1861, less than three months before the start of the Civil War. It is little wonder that the surviving Company file here notes that "no returns were sent in 1862-1877." This Company was dissolved in March 1882 (Public Record Office, London, BT 31/530/2131).

When interest in these coal fields was again re-kindled after the Civil War, this was led by an English-trained mining engineer, called Matthew Fontaine Maury junior (died 1886), Fellow of the Geological Society of London (elected 1870), and son of the famous American hydrographer of the same name (1806-1873) (Schlee, 1975). The son had trained at the London Royal College of Chemistry and the nearby Royal School of Mines between 1866 and 1869 (Reeks, 1920, p. 130). In 1873 he issued his book "The Resources of the Coalfield of the Upper Kanawha... setting forth some of their markets and means of development" (Maury, 1873). But it is clear from a later book (Edwards, 1892) how little development of these Kanawha and Guyandotte fields had taken place even by that date. The wilderness condition of the country and the problems of transportation there (whether of coal or men) were cited as the main reasons for this. Edwards further noted that it had been the wild condition of the rivers and the frequent losses of whole boatloads of coal on them which had brought an end to the 1850's explorations which brought Buckman to the United States. The frontier spirit of America was not able to unlock these coal fields until the twentieth century.

GEOLOGICAL CONSULTING

One final comment concerns the too-often hidden careers of these geological consultants. Buckman was unusual in having published a little on his private coal-prospecting work, both in England and America. Although the printed reports on Ansted's consulting activity are excessively rare, at least he wrote a fascinating account of his career as a mining geologist. The publication of such a book is however highly unusual, while the standard account of his life gives the usual short shrift to his consulting work (Anonymous, 1908). The normal historical silence towards the mining and industrial activities of such academic geologists has been similarly accorded to the American John Locke, whose American biographers seem in equal ignorance of any such activity by him. One is forced to agree with Geoffrey Tweedale (1991) that applied geological work has so far proved of little interest to historians, in part because of the particular difficulty in locating source materials and also because of the long bias towards academic and theoretic geology by historians. Paul Lucier's recent work (1995) has started to give us a much needed corrective.

ACKNOWLEDGMENTS

Libraries from Cleveland, Ohio to Cambridge, England and many in between have been quarried to uncover this story. Our grateful thanks to all who keep our library and archive resources so available on both sides of the Atlantic and in particular to John Thackray (London), to whom we dedicate this paper in tribute. Bob Dott (Wisconsin), Tom Sharpe (Cardiff) and Earle Spamer (Philadelphia) gave vital specific assistance. Hugh Torrens owes grateful thanks to Bill and Heather Brice for library investigations and their wonderful hospitality and transportation on a rapid exploration of the area that Buckman had visited 145 years earlier.

REFERENCES CITED

Albion, R.G., 1934, George Peabody (1795-1869): Dictionary of American Biography, v. 14, p. 336-8, H. Milford, London.

Aldrich, M.L. and Leviton, A.E., 1982, William Barton Rogers and the Virginia Geological Survey, 1835-1842, in Corgan, J.X., editor, The Geological Sciences in the Antebellum South: University of Alabama Press, Birmingham, p. 83-104.

Anonymous, 1848, Comment by Henry De la Beche: The Cambrian, 11 August 1848, p. 3.

Anonymous, 1851a, Official Descriptive and Illustrated Catalogue of the Great Exhibition of the Works of Industry of all Nations: Spicer Bros, London, volume 1, cxcii + 478 p.

Anonymous, 1851b, The Last Appendix to Yankee Doodle: Punch, v. 21, 13 September 1851, p. 117.

Anonymous, 1853a, Exhibition in New York: The Times, 26 April 1853, p. 6.

Anonymous, 1853b, Reports and Letters relating to the Guyandotte Land Company 1853: William Penny, London, 53 p, (copy in Library of Congress).

Anonymous, 1854a, Report: Gentleman's Magazine, April 1854, p. 390.

Anonymous, 1854b, Guyandotte Land, Coal, & Iron Company. Synopsis of Reports, Geological Surveys, and other facts in relation to this property: William Penny, London, 32 p, (copy in Library of Western Reserve Historical Society, Cleveland, Ohio).

Anonymous, 1854c, Advertisements: The Times, 15 May and 22 May 1854, p. 1.

Anonymous, [1860a], Great Kanawha estate. Evidence of value and title: Philadelphia, H.G. Leisenring, 84 p. (copy in New York Public Library).

Anonymous, [1860b], Great Kanawha estate. Evidence of value and title: London, no publisher named, 75 p. (copy in the British Library, London).

Anonymous, 1908, David Thomas Ansted (1814-1880): Dictionary of National Biography, v. 1, p. 509.

Ansted, D.T., 1853, Report on the "Wilson Survey" near the Great Kanawha River, Virginia: Wm.C. Bryant, New York, 16 p. (copy at University of Wisconsin).

Ansted, D.T., 1854, Scenery, Science and Art; being Extracts from the Note-Book of a geologist and mining engineer: J. Van Voorst, London, 323 p.

Boase, G.C., 1908, Francis Egerton (1800-1857): Dictionary of National Biography, v. 6, p. 571-2.

Buckman, J., 1849, On some Experimental Borings in search of Coal: Report of the meeting of the British Association for the Advancement of Science, Swansea 1848, p. 67.

Buckman, J., 1855a, On some Coal mining Operations at Malmesbury: Wiltshire Archaeological Magazine, v. 2, p. 159-161.

Buckman, J., 1855b, An account of coal deposits in West Virginia: Report of the meeting of the British Association for the Advancement of Science, Liverpool 1854, p. 78.

Buckman, J., 1856, On the natural history of British meadow and pasture grasses: Journal of the Royal Agricultural Society of England, v. 17, p. 513-542.

Buckman, J., 1858a, The practical application of Geology in Coal-Seeking: Geologist, v. 1, p. 129-134 & 184-189.

Buckman, J., 1858b, The Natural History of British Meadow and Pasture Grasses: Hamilton, Adams & Co., London, 73 p.

Burkhardt, F. and Smith, S., 1991, The Correspondence of Charles Darwin, v. 7, 1858-9: University Press, Cambridge, 671 p.

Clarke, E., 1909, John Wilson (1812-1888): Dictionary of National Biography, v. 21, p. 586-7.

Crouthamel, J.L., 1969, James Watson Webb, A biography: Wesleyan Univ. Press, Middletown, Conn., 262 p.

Darwin, C., 1859, The Origin of Species: Murray, London, 502 p.

De la Beche, H. and Playfair, L., 1848, First Report on the Coals suited to the Steam navy: Memoirs of the Geological Survey of Great Britain, v. 2, part 2, p. 539-630.

Dunaway, W.F., 1922, History of the James River and Kanawha Company: Columbia University, New York, 251 p.

Edwards, W.S., 1892, Coals and Cokes in West Virginia: R. Clarke and Co., Cincinnati, 162 p.

Elsas, M., 1960, Iron in the making. Dowlais Iron Company Letters 1782-1860: Cardiff, Glamorgan County Council, 247 p.

Geikie, A., 1895, Memoir of Sir Andrew Crombie Ramsay: Macmillan and Co., London, 397 p.

Hearnshaw, F.J.C., 1929, The Centenary History of King's College London, 1828-1928: G. Harrap, London, 543 p.

Jones, E., 1986, William Turquand (1818/9-1894): Dictionary of Business Biography, v. 5, p. 582-4, Butterworths, London.

Kent, C., 1908, William Henry Lytton Earle Bulwer (1801-1872): Dictionary of National Biography, v. 3, p. 263-5.

BUCKMAN AND THE GUYANDOTTE COAL FIELDS

Lucier, P., 1995, Commercial Interests and Scientific Disinterestedness: Consulting Geologists in Antebellum America: Isis, v. 86, p. 245-267.

Lyell, C., 1854, New York Industrial Exhibition. Special report of Sir Charles Lyell: Harrison and sons, London, 50 p.

Maury, M.F., 1873, The Resources of the Coalfield of the Upper Kanawha... setting forth some of their markets and means of development: Sherwood and Co., Baltimore, 44 p.

Merrill, G.P., 1906, Contributions to the History of American Geology: Report of the U.S. National Museum in Annual Report of the Smithsonian Institution, 1904, p. 189-733.

Reeks, M., 1920, Register... of the Royal School of Mines, London: School of Mines, London, 233 + 212 p.

Rolt, L.T.C., 1970, Victorian Engineering: Penguin Press, London, 300 p.

Rosenberg, N., editor, 1969, The American System of Manufactures: University Press, Edinburgh, 440 p.

Sayce, R., 1992, The History of the Royal Agricultural College, Cirencester: Alan Sutton, Stroud, 370 p.

Schlee, S., 1975, A History of Oceanography: Robert Hale, London, 398 p.

Torrens, H.S., 1988, What Price the Advancement of Science: unpublished paper presented to the 150th annual meeting of the British Association for the Advancement of Science, Oxford 1988 (copy in Royal Agricultural College library, Cirencester).

Tweedale, G., 1991, Geology and industrial consultancy: British Journal for the History of Science, v. 24, p. 435-51.

Webb, J.W., 1853, Letter: The Times, 3 October 1853, p. 9.

Wilson, J., 1854, New York Industrial Exhibition. Special report of Professor Wilson: Harrison and sons, London, 133 p.

Winchell, N., 1894, Sketch of Dr. John Locke: The American Geologist, v. 14, p. 341-356.

INDEX

Moggridge, John Hodder: III 242
Monthly Magazine: VI 7; VII 183
Morand J.-F.-C.: IV 106
Mostyn, Sir Thomas: VIII 68
Mount Logan, Canada: XII 1
Mountain Limestone (=Carboniferous
    Limestone): IV 112
Mulgrave, Lord: VI 17
Murchison, Roderick: 1 19; IX 111, 127,
    139–43; X; XIII 195
Murray, Dr. John: II 12; VIII 78
Museum of Practical Geology (London):
    XII 12; XIII 191, 195
Mushet, David: VI 15
Music: VI 2, 15, 18

Napoleonic Wars: V 68; VII 177; XI 37
Natural History of the Mineral Kingdom
    (Williams): II 168–72
Natural History Society of Northumberland
    and Durham: XI 44
Neale (or Neill), Thomas: VII 178
Neill, Patrick: II 153
Neath Abbey Iron Works: XII 14
Necker, Louis Albert: XII 2
Nevill, Richard Janion: XII 16
Newcastle (Australia): I 11
Newcastle-on-Tyne: VI 17; VIII 76; XI 30,
    38, 46
Newcastle Literary and Philosophical
    Society: IX 113; XI 31–2
Newcomen engine: VIII 68
Newent Coalfield: III 242
New York Industrial Exhibition (1853):
    XIII 192
Newick, Sussex: VII 184
Nicol, William: XI 35
Norfolk: III 228
Notes on the History of English Geology
    (Fitton): X 9
Nova Scotia: XII 21
Nuttall, John: V 54

Oaktree Clay: I 15 (*see also* Kimmeridge
    Clay)
Ogden, Edmund: III 238–9
Olivi, Guiseppe: II 187
Order of Superposition of Strata
    (Buckland): V 68
Origin of Species (Darwin): XIII 192
Otley, Jonathan: VI 19
Outliers: VI 21
Overton, Derbyshire: V 53
Oxford Clay: I 13, 15; IV 106 (*see also*
    Clunch Clay)

Pacifism: VI 22
Palaeontographical Society: XI 45
Panton, Paul: IX 150
Papyrophobia: II 152; VIII 68; XI 30–31;
    XII 12; XIII 199
Parallel Roads (*see* Glenroy)
Pariossien, General James: XI 40, 43
Paris, France: IV 105
Parker, Thomas Netherton: IX 148
Parkinson, James: VI 23
Palmer, Sambourn: III 242
Parry, Caleb Hillier: III 225, 227, 240
Parry, Charles Henry: III 225, 240
Parsons, Robert: III 227
Parsons, Thomas: III 227–8
Payne, David Beaumont: IV 110, 115
Payton (or Peyton) Mr: VII 181
Peabody, George: XIII 193
Peale, Rembrandt: V 58
Pease, Sir Joseph Whitwell: XI 45
Peel, Sir Robert: XII 22
Pelham, Thomas: VI 6; VII 182
Pembrokeshire: XII 1
Pennant, Thomas: II 159–60; III 222
Pennsylvania: XII 21
Pentamerus knightii: X 6
Pentland, Joseph Barclay: XI 40–41, 43
Pepys, William Hasledine: IX 144
Perceval, Theophilus: IV 105, 108–10, 115
Percy, John: XII 9
Perkins, Richard junior: III 242
Perkins, Richard senior: III 242
Perry, Samuel: VIII 70
Perthshire: II 156
Peru: XI 38, 45
Pew, Dr. Richard: III 238, 244; IV 112
Philanthropy: I 11
Philosophical Magazine: V 59, 68–9
Phillips, Prof. John: I 20; IV 113; IX 111; X
    11; XI 37
Phillips, Richard: V 62; VI 8; XII 12
Phillips, William (of London): VIII 73
Phillips, William (of Shropshire): IX 148
Philosophical Society (of Edinburgh): I 11
Pinkerton, John: II 190; IX 116–17, 139
Plaitford, Hampshire: I 14; III 235
Playfair, Prof. John: VI 7; IX 130
Plymley, Katherine: IX 128 (*see also*
    Corbett)
Poa pratense: XIII 198
Pococke, Rev. Richard: V 52; X 2
Pokahoe, Tarrytown, USA: XIII 196
Polymathy: VI 2
Pontypool, Monmouthshire: XII 8–10